Improving your C# Skil

Solve modern challenges with functional programming and test-driven techniques of C#

Ovais Mehboob Ahmed Khan
John Callaway
Clayton Hunt
Rod Stephens

BIRMINGHAM - MUMBAI

Improving your C# Skills

First published: February 2019

Production reference: 1220219

Published by Packt Publishing Ltd.
Livery Place
35 Livery Street
Birmingham
B3 2PB, UK.

ISBN 978-1-83855-838-3

www.packtpub.com

mapt.io

Mapt is an online digital library that gives you full access to over 5,000 books and videos, as well as industry-leading tools to help you plan your personal development and advance your career. For more information, please visit our website.

Why subscribe?

- Spend less time learning and more time coding with practical eBooks and Videos from over 4,000 industry professionals

- Improve your learning with Skill Plans built especially for you

- Get a free eBook or video every month

- Mapt is fully searchable

- Copy and paste, print, and bookmark content

Packt.com

Did you know that Packt offers eBook versions of every book published, with PDF and ePub files available? You can upgrade to the eBook version at www.packt.com and as a print book customer, you are entitled to a discount on the eBook copy. Get in touch with us at customercare@packtpub.com for more details.

At www.packt.com, you can also read a collection of free technical articles, sign up for a range of free newsletters, and receive exclusive discounts and offers on Packt books and eBooks.

Contributors

About the authors

Ovais Mehboob Ahmed Khan is a seasoned programmer and solution architect with an experience of over 14 years in software development. He has worked in organizations across Pakistan, USA, and the Middle East. Currently, he is working for a government entity based in Dubai. A Microsoft MVP, he specializes mainly in Microsoft .NET, the cloud, and web development. He writes blogs, has published technical articles on MSDN, TechNet, and has authored two other books published by Packt Publications: JavaScript for .NET Developers and Enterprise Application Architecture with .NET Core.

John Callaway, a Microsoft MVP, has been a professional developer since 1999. He has focused primarily on web technologies and has experience with everything from PHP, C#, ReactJS, to SignalR. Clean code and professionalism are particularly important to him, along with mentoring and teaching others what he has learned along the way.

Clayton Hunt has been programming professionally since 2005, doing mostly web development with an emphasis on JavaScript and C#. He focuses on Software Craftsmanship and is a signatory of both the Agile Manifesto and the Software Craftsmanship manifesto. He believes that through short iterations and the careful gathering of requirements, we can deliver the highest quality and most value in the shortest time. He enjoys learning and encouraging others to continuously improve themselves.

Rod Stephens has been a software developer, consultant, instructor, and author. He has written more than 30 books and 250 magazine articles covering such topics as three-dimensional graphics, algorithms, database design, software engineering, interview puzzles, C#, and Visual Basic. Rod's popular C# Helper and VB Helper websites receive millions of hits per year and contain thousands of tips, tricks, and example programs for C# and Visual Basic developers.

Packt is searching for authors like you

If you're interested in becoming an author for Packt, please visit `authors.packtpub.com` and apply today. We have worked with thousands of developers and tech professionals, just like you, to help them share their insight with the global tech community. You can make a general application, apply for a specific hot topic that we are recruiting an author for, or submit your own idea.

Table of Contents

Preface

This Learning Path shows you how to create high performing applications and solve programming challenges using a wide range of C# features. You'll begin by learning how to identify the bottlenecks in writing programs, highlight common performance pitfalls, and apply strategies to detect and resolve these issues early. You'll also study the importance of micro-services architecture for building fast applications and implementing resiliency and security in .NET Core. Then, you'll study the importance of defining and testing boundaries, abstracting away third-party code, and working with different types of test double, such as spies, mocks, and fakes. In addition to describing programming trade-offs, this Learning Path will also help you build a useful toolkit of techniques, including value caching, statistical analysis, and geometric algorithms. This Learning Path includes content from the following Packt products:

- C# 7 and .NET Core 2.0 High Performance by Ovais Mehboob Ahmed Khan
- Practical Test-Driven Development using C# 7 by John Callaway, Clayton Hunt
- The Modern C# Challenge by Rod Stephens

Who this book is for

If you want to improve the speed of your code and optimize the performance of your applications or you are looking for a practical resource on test driven development, this is just the Learning Path for you. Some familiarity with C# and .NET will be beneficial for you.

What this book covers

Chapter 1, What's New in .NET Core 2 and C# 7?, discusses the .NET Core Framework and covers some improvements that were introduced with .NET Core 2.0. We will also look into the new features of C# 7 and see how we can write cleaner code and simplify syntactic expressions. Lastly, we cover the topic of writing quality code. We'll see how we can leverage the Code Analysis feature of Visual Studio 2017 to add analyzers to our project and improve code quality.

Chapter 2, Understanding .NET Core Internals and Measuring Performance, discusses the core concepts of .NET Core, including the compilation process, garbage collection, building highly-performant .NET Core applications utilizing multiple cores of the CPU, and publishing an application using a release build. We will also explore the benchmarking tool that is highly used for code optimization and provides results specific to in-memory objects.

Chapter 3, Multithreading and Asynchronous Programming in .NET Core, explores the core fundamentals of multithreaded and asynchronous programming. The chapter starts with the basic differences between multithreaded and asynchronous programming and walks you through the core concepts. It explores APIs and how to use them when writing a multithreaded application. We will learn how the Task Programming Library can be used to serve asynchronous operations, and how to implement the Task Asynchronous pattern. Lastly, we will explore parallel programming techniques and some of the best design patterns being used.

Chapter 4, Securing and Implementing Resilience in .NET Core Applications, takes you through resiliency, which is a very important factor when developing highly-performant applications in .NET Core. We will learn different policies and use the Polly framework to use those policies in .NET Core. We will also learn about safe storage mechanisms and how to use them in the development environment in order to keep sensitive information separate from the project repository. At the end of this chapter, we will learn some security fundamentals, which include SSL, CSRF, CORS, security headers, and the ASP.NET Core Identity framework, in order to protect ASP.NET Core applications.

Chapter 5, Why TDD is Important, asks what is TDD and why should you care? In this chapter, you will learn what TDD is and why it matters. A compelling argument for TDD will be made and the benefits, and more importantly, the execution will be shown.

Chapter 6, Setting Up the .NET Test Environment, explains how to set up your IDE and configure the testing framework so that you can easily run your tests in C# and .NET, with more detail and many more examples of growing complexity in the Speaker Meet API.

Chapter 7, Setting Up a JavaScript Environment, configures the JavaScript testing framework so that you can easily run your tests in your IDE. It provides more detail and many more examples of growing complexity in the Speaker Meet React application.

Chapter 8, What to Know Before Getting Started, dives deeper into the why and how of TDD. You will learn the importance of defining and testing boundaries and abstracting away third-party code (including the .NET Framework), and you'll discover more advanced concepts such as spies, mocks, and fakes, and how to avoid pitfalls along the way.

Chapter 9, Tabula Rasa - Approaching an Application with TDD in Mind, explains how to get started with a new application. You'll apply what you've learned in the previous chapters and take the same approach with a full-sized application using Speaker Meet as an example.

Chapter 10, Testing JavaScript Applications, focuses on creating a Single Page Application in JavaScript using React. It focuses on test-driven actions and reducers and any functionality within the application.

Chapter 11, Exploring Integrations, explains how to write integration tests to ensure that your application is functioning properly.

Chapter 12, Changes in Requirements, focuses on what happens when the requirements change. What happens if a bug is discovered? No problem, change a test or write a new one to cover the new requirement or to defend against the discovered bug. Now, write some new code or change some existing code to make all of the new/modified tests pass. If you do everything correctly, you should feel safe to make these changes as your existing test suite will prevent you from introducing new bugs.

Chapter 13, The Legacy Problem, explains that there are a lot of applications out there without sufficient (any?) test coverage, and even fewer were written test-first. You'll discover some of the major problems with legacy applications that weren't written with testability in mind; they will be identified, and also how best to recover will be covered.

Chapter 14, Unraveling a Mess, dives into how to go about safely modifying a legacy application that wasn't written with testing in mind. How can you add tests to minimize the potential for introducing new bugs when modifying the existing code? An extreme example will be used to explore these topics and more.

Chapter 15, Geometry, presents problems that perform geometric calculations. These ask you to find values such as the roots of equations, the points where lines and circles intersect, and the areas of polygons. Many of these problems ask you to draw shapes such as lines, circles, arrowheads, polygons, and stars.

Chapter 16, Randomization, poses problems that use randomization to produce various kinds of randomized data. For example, they ask you to generate random floating point numbers within a range, pick random items from a list or array, and generate random passwords.

Chapter 17, Files and Directories, covers problems that deal with the filesystem. Its problems ask you to remove blank lines from a file, calculate a directory's total size, detect duplicate files, and generate thumbnails for image files in a directory.

Chapter 18, Advanced C# and .NET Features, includes problems that deal with more advanced features such as Language Integrated Query (LINQ), Parallel LINQ (PLINQ), Transact Parallel Library (TPL), and the yield statement.

Chapter19, Cryptography, describes cryptographic problems. Some, such as the problems that deal with Caesar and Vigenère ciphers, are interesting mostly for fun and historical perspective. Others, such as those that deal with prime numbers, hashing, and string encryption, demonstrate strong, modern cryptographic methods.

To get the most out of this book

To start using this book, you will need the following software installed on your local desktop:

- Visual Studio 2017 or Visual Studio Code
- Linux distro
- InfluxDB
- Grafana
- .NET Core 2.0

Download the example code files

You can download the example code files for this book from your account at www.packt.com. If you purchased this book elsewhere, you can visit www.packt.com/support and register to have the files emailed directly to you.

You can download the code files by following these steps:

1. Log in or register at www.packt.com.
2. Select the **SUPPORT** tab.
3. Click on **Code Downloads & Errata**.
4. Enter the name of the book in the **Search** box and follow the onscreen instructions.

Once the file is downloaded, please make sure that you unzip or extract the folder using the latest version of:

- WinRAR/7-Zip for Windows
- Zipeg/iZip/UnRarX for Mac
- 7-Zip/PeaZip for Linux

The code bundle for the book is also hosted on GitHub at `https://github.com/PacktPublishing/Improving-your-C-Sharp-Skills`. In case there's an update to the code, it will be updated on the existing GitHub repository.

We also have other code bundles from our rich catalog of books and videos available at `https://github.com/PacktPublishing/`. Check them out!

Conventions used

There are a number of text conventions used throughout this book.

`CodeInText`: Indicates code words in the text, database table names, folder names, filenames, file extensions, pathnames, dummy URLs, user input, and Twitter handles. Here is an example: "The `input()` method is used to get an input from the user."

A block of code is set as follows:

```
private int FindError(string string1, string string2)
{
int error = 0;
for (int i = 0; i < string1.Length; i++)
error += Math.Abs((int)string1[i] - (int)string2[i]);
return error;
}
```

Any command-line input or output is written as follows:

```
Install-Package App.Metrics
Install-Pacakge App.Metrics.AspnetCore.Mvc
```

Bold: Indicates a new term, an important word, or words that you see onscreen. For example, words in menus or dialog boxes appear in the text like this. Here is an example: "If you need something different, click on the **DOWNLOADS** link in the header for all possible downloads: "

Warnings or important notes appear like this.

 Tips and tricks appear like this.

Get in touch

Feedback from our readers is always welcome.

General feedback: If you have questions about any aspect of this book, mention the book title in the subject of your message and email us at customercare@packtpub.com.

Errata: Although we have taken every care to ensure the accuracy of our content, mistakes do happen. If you have found a mistake in this book, we would be grateful if you would report this to us. Please visit www.packt.com/submit-errata, selecting your book, clicking on the Errata Submission Form link, and entering the details.

Piracy: If you come across any illegal copies of our works in any form on the Internet, we would be grateful if you would provide us with the location address or website name. Please contact us at copyright@packt.com with a link to the material.

If you are interested in becoming an author: If there is a topic that you have expertise in and you are interested in either writing or contributing to a book, please visit authors.packtpub.com.

Reviews

Please leave a review. Once you have read and used this book, why not leave a review on the site that you purchased it from? Potential readers can then see and use your unbiased opinion to make purchase decisions, we at Packt can understand what you think about our products, and our authors can see your feedback on their book. Thank you!

For more information about Packt, please visit packt.com.

What's New in .NET Core 2 and C# 7?

.NET Core is a development platform by Microsoft that runs cross-platform and is maintained by Microsoft and the community at GitHub. It is the most emergent and popular framework in development communities due to its performance and platform portability. It targets every developer that can develop any application for any platform that includes web, cloud, mobile, embedded, and IoT scenarios.

With .NET Core, we can develop applications using C#, F#, and now VB.NET as well. However, C# is the most widely used language among developers.

In this chapter, you will learn the following topics:

- Performance improvements in .NET Core 2.0
- Upgrading the path from .NET Core 1.x to 2.0
- .NET Standard 2.0
- What comes with ASP.NET Core 2.0
- New features in C# 7.0

Evolution of .NET

In early 2002, when Microsoft first introduced the .NET Framework, it targeted developers who were working on classic ASP or VB 6 platforms since they didn't have any compelling framework for developing enterprise-level applications. With the release of the .NET Framework, developers had a platform to develop applications and could choose any of the languages from VB.NET, C#, and F#. Irrespective of the language chosen, the code is interoperable, and developers can create a project with VB.NET and reference it in their C# or F# project and vice versa.

The core component of .NET Framework includes **Common Language Runtime (CLR)**, **Framework Class Libraries (FCL)**, **Base Class Libraries (BCL)**, and a set of application models. New features and patches have been introduced with the newer version of the .NET Framework, which comes with the new release of Windows, and developers have had to wait for a year or so to get those improvements. Every team at Microsoft worked on a different application model, and each team had to wait for the date when the new framework was released to port their fixes and improvements. Windows Forms and Web Forms were the primary application models at that time that were widely used by .NET developers.

When Web Forms was first introduced, it was a breakthrough which attracted both web developers who worked on Classic ASP and desktop application developers who worked on Visual Basic 6.0. The developer experience was appealing and provided a decent set of controls that could easily be dragged and dropped to the screen, followed to their events and properties that could be set either through the view file (`.aspx`) or code-behind files. Later on, Microsoft introduced the **Model View Controller (MVC)** application model that implemented the separation of concerns design principle, so that View, Model, and Controller are separate entities. The View is the user interface that renders the Model, where the Model represents the business entity and holds the data, and the Controller that handles the request and updates the model and injects it into the View. MVC was a breakthrough that let developers write cleaner code and bind their model with the HTML controls using model binding. With the passage of time, more features were added and the core .NET web assembly `System.Web` became quite big and bloated, and contained lots of packages and APIs that were not always useful in every type of application. However, with .NET, several groundbreaking changes were introduced and `System.Web` got split into NuGet packages that can be referenced and added individually based on requirements.

.NET Core (codename .NET vNext) was first introduced in 2014, and the following are the core benefits of using .NET Core:

Benefit	Description
Cross Platform	.NET Core can run on Windows, Linux, and macOS
Host Agnostic	.NET Core on the server side is not dependent on IIS and, with two lightweight servers, *Kestrel* and *WebListener*, it can be self-hosted as a Console application and can be also gelled with mature servers such as IIS, Apache, and others through a reverse proxy option
Modular	Ships as NuGet packages
Open Source	The entire source code is released as open source via the .NET Foundation
CLI tooling	Command line tools to create, build, and run projects from the command line

.NET Core is a cross-platform, open-source framework that implements .NET Standard. It provides a runtime known as .NET Core CLR, framework class libraries, which are primitive libraries known as *CoreFX*, and APIs that are similar to what .NET Framework has, but have a smaller footprint (lesser dependencies on other assemblies):

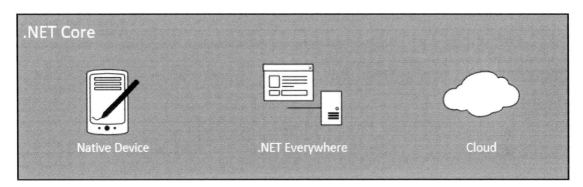

.NET Core provides flexible deployment options as follows:

- **Framework-Dependent Deployment (FDD)**: needs .NET Core SDK to be installed on the machine
- **Self-Contained Deployment (SCD)**: No machine-wide installation of .NET Core SDK is needed on the machine and .NET Core CLR and framework class libraries are part of the application package

To install .NET Core 2.0, you can navigate to the following link `https://www.microsoft.com/net/core` and go through the options for installing it on Windows, Linux, MAC, and Docker.

New improvements in .NET Core 2.0

The most recent version of .NET Core, 2.0, comes with a number of improvements. .NET Core 2.0 is the fastest version of all times and can run on multiple platforms including various Linux distros, macOS (operating system), and Windows.

 Distros stands for Linux distribution (often abbreviated as distro), and it is an operating system made from a software collection, which is based upon the Linux kernel and, often, a package management system.

Performance improvements

.NET Core is more robust and performance efficient and, since it's open source, the Microsoft team with other community members are bringing more improvements.

The following are the improvements that are part of .NET Core 2.0.

RyuJIT compiler in .NET Core

RyuJIT is a next-generation JIT compiler that is a complete rewrite of the **Just In Time (JIT)** compiler and generates a lot more efficient native machine code. It is twice as fast as the previous 64-bit compiler and provides 30% faster compilation. Initially, it runs on only X64 architectures, but now it supports X86 as well and developers can use the RyuJIT compiler for both X64 and X86. .NET Core 2.0 uses RyuJIT for both X86 and X64 platforms.

Profile guided optimization

Profile-guided optimization (PGO) is a compilation technology used by C++ compiler to generate optimized code. It applies to the internal native compiled components of the runtime and JIT. It performs compilation in two steps, which are as follows:

1. It records the information about code execution.
2. From this information, it generates better code.

The following diagram depicts the life cycle of how the code is compiled:

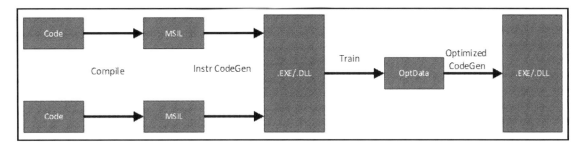

In .NET Core 1.1, Microsoft already released the PGO for Windows X64 architecture, but in .NET Core 2.0, this has been added for both Windows X64 and X86 architectures. Also, as per observatory results, it was noted that the actual startup time is mostly taken by `coreclr.dll` and `clrjit.dll` for Windows. Alternatively, on Linux, there are `libcoreclr.so` and `libclrjit.so`, respectively.

Comparing RyuJIT with the old JIT compiler known as JIT32, RyuJIT is more efficient in code generation. The startup time of the JIT32 was faster than the RyuJIT; however, the code is not efficient. To overcome the initial startup time taken by the RyuJIT compiler, Microsoft used PGO, which brought the performance closer to JIT32 performance and achieved both efficient code and performance on startup.

For Linux, the compiler toolchain is different for each distro, and Microsoft is working on a separate Linux version of .NET that uses the PGO optimizations applicable to all distros.

Simplified packaging

With .NET Core, we can add libraries to our project from NuGet. All framework and third-party libraries can be added as NuGet packages. With a large sized application that refers many libraries, adding each library one by one is a cumbersome process. .NET Core 2.0 has simplified the packaging mechanism and introduced meta-packages that can be added as one single package that contains all the assemblies that are linked to it.

For example, if you wanted to work on ASP.NET Core in .NET Core 2.0, you just have to add one single package, `Microsoft.AspNetCore.All`, using NuGet.

The following is the command that will install this package into your project:

```
Install-Package Microsoft.AspNetCore.All -Version 2.0.0
```

Upgrading path from .NET Core 1.x to 2.0

.NET Core 2.0 comes with lots of improvements, and this is the primary reason people wanted to migrate their existing .NET Core applications from 1.x to 2.0. However, there is a checklist which we will go through in this topic to ensure smooth migration.

1. Install .NET Core 2.0

First of all, install the .NET Core 2.0 SDK on your machine. It will install the latest assemblies to your machine, which will help you to execute further steps.

2. Upgrade TargetFramework

This is the most important step, and this is where the different versions need to be upgraded in the .NET Core project file. Since we know that, with the `.csproj` type, we don't have `project.json`, to modify the framework and other dependencies, we can edit the existing project using any Visual Studio editor and modify the XML.

The XML Node that needs to be changed is the `TargetFramework`. For .NET Core 2.0, we have to change the `TargetFramework` moniker to `netcoreapp2.0`, which is shown as follows:

```
<TargetFramework>netcoreapp2.0</TargetFramework>
```

Next, you can start building the project which will upgrade the .NET Core dependencies to 2.0. However, there is a chance of a few of them still referencing the older version, and upgrading those dependencies needs to be done explicitly using NuGet package manager.

3. Update .NET Core SDK version

If you have `global.json` added to your project, you have to update the SDK version to `2.0.0`, which is shown as follows:

```
{
  "sdk": {
    "version": "2.0.0"
  }
}
```

4. Update .NET Core CLI

.NET Core CLI is also an important section in your .NET Core project file. When migrating, you have to upgrade the version of `DotNetCliToolReference` to `2.0.0`, which is shown as follows:

```
<ItemGroup>
  <DotNetCliToolReference Include=
  "Microsoft.VisualStudio.Web.CodeGeneration.Tools" Version="2.0.0" />
</ItemGroup>
```

There might be more tools added depending on whether you are using Entity Framework Core, User Secrets, and others. You have to update their versions.

Changes in ASP.NET Core Identity

There have been some more improvements and changes to the ASP.NET Core Identity model. Some of the classes are renamed and you can find them at:

`http://docs.microsoft.com/en-us/aspnet/core/migration.`

Exploring .NET Core CLI and New Project Templates

Command Line Interface (CLI) is a very popular tool is almost all popular frameworks like Yeoman Generator, Angular, and others. It lends developers access to execute commands to create, build, and run projects, restore packages, and so on.

.NET CLI provides a toolset with a handful commands that can be executed from the command line interface to create .NET Core projects, restore dependencies, and build and run projects. Under the wire, Visual Studio 2015/2017 and Visual Studio Code even uses this tool to perform different options taken by the developers from their IDE; for example, to create a new project using .NET CLI, we can run the following command:

```
dotnet new
```

It will list down the available templates and the short name that can be used while creating the project.

Here is the screenshot containing the list of project templates that can be used to create/scaffold projects using .NET Core CLI:

```
c:\>dotnet new
Usage: new [options]

Options:
  -h, --help            Displays help for this command.
  -l, --list            Lists templates containing the specified name. If no name is specified, lists all templates.
  -n, --name            The name for the output being created. If no name is specified, the name of the current directory is used.
  -o, --output          Location to place the generated output.
  -i, --install         Installs a source or a template pack.
  -u, --uninstall       Uninstalls a source or a template pack.
  --type                Filters templates based on available types. Predefined values are "project", "item" or "other".
  --force               Forces content to be generated even if it would change existing files.
  -lang, --language     Specifies the language of the template to create.


Templates                                     Short Name         Language          Tags
----------------------------------------------------------------------------------------------------------
Console Application                           console            [C#], F#, VB      Common/Console
Class library                                 classlib           [C#], F#, VB      Common/Library
Unit Test Project                             mstest             [C#], F#, VB      Test/MSTest
xUnit Test Project                            xunit              [C#], F#, VB      Test/xUnit
ASP.NET Core Empty                            web                [C#], F#          Web/Empty
ASP.NET Core Web App (Model-View-Controller)  mvc                [C#], F#          Web/MVC
ASP.NET Core Web App                          razor              [C#]              Web/MVC/Razor Pages
ASP.NET Core with Angular                     angular            [C#]              Web/MVC/SPA
ASP.NET Core with React.js                    react              [C#]              Web/MVC/SPA
ASP.NET Core with React.js and Redux          reactredux         [C#]              Web/MVC/SPA
ASP.NET Core Web API                          webapi             [C#], F#          Web/WebAPI
global.json file                              globaljson                           Config
Nuget Config                                  nugetconfig                          Config
Web Config                                    webconfig                            Config
Solution File                                 sln                                  Solution
Razor Page                                    page                                 Web/ASP.NET
MVC ViewImports                               viewimports                          Web/ASP.NET
MVC ViewStart                                 viewstart                            Web/ASP.NET


Examples:
    dotnet new mvc --auth Individual
    dotnet new console
    dotnet new --help
```

And by running the following command, a new ASP.NET Core MVC application will be created:

```
dotnet new mvc
```

The following screenshot shows the provisioning of the new MVC project after running the preceding command. It creates the project in the same directory where the command is running and restores all the dependencies:

```
c:\testproject>dotnet new mvc
The template "ASP.NET Core Web App (Model-View-Controller)" was created successfully.
This template contains technologies from parties other than Microsoft, see https://aka.ms/template-3pn for details.

Processing post-creation actions...
Running 'dotnet restore' on c:\testproject\testproject.csproj...
  Restoring packages for c:\testproject\testproject.csproj...
  Restore completed in 143.61 ms for c:\testproject\testproject.csproj.
  Generating MSBuild file c:\testproject\obj\testproject.csproj.nuget.g.props.
  Generating MSBuild file c:\testproject\obj\testproject.csproj.nuget.g.targets.
  Restore completed in 7.09 sec for c:\testproject\testproject.csproj.

Restore succeeded.
```

To install the .NET Core CLI toolset, there are some native installers available for Windows, Linux, and macOS. These installers can install and set up the .NET CLI tooling on your machine and developers can run the commands from the CLI.

Here is the list of commands with their descriptions that are provided in the .NET Core CLI:

Command	Description	Example
new	Creates a new project based on the template selected	dotnet new razor
restore	Restores all the dependencies defined in the project	dotnet restore
build	Builds the project	dotnet build
run	Runs the source code without any additional compile	dotnet run
publish	Packages the application files into a folder for deployment	dotnet publish
test	Used to execute unit tests	dotnet test
vstest	Executes unit tests from specified files	dotnet vstest [<TEST_FILE_NAMES>]
pack	Packs the code into a NuGet package	dotnet pack

`migrate`	Migrates .NET Core preview 2 to .NET Core 1.0	`dotnet migrate`
`clean`	Cleans the output of the project	`dotnet clean`
`sln`	Modifies a .NET Core solution	`dotnet sln`
`help`	Displays the list of commands available to execute through .NET CLI	`dotnet help`
`store`	Stores the specified assemblies in the runtime package store	`dotnet store`

Here are some of the project level commands that can be used to add a new NuGet package, remove an existing one, list references, and others:

Command	Description	Example
`add package`	Adds a package reference to the project	`dotnet add package Newtonsoft.Json`
`remove package`	Removes a package reference from the project	`dotnet remove package Newtonsoft.Json`
`add reference`	Adds a project reference to the project	`dotnet add reference chapter1/proj1.csproj`
`remove reference`	Removes the project reference from the project	`dotnet remove reference chapter1/proj1.csproj`
`list reference`	List down all the project references in the project	`dotnet list reference`

The following are some common Entity Framework Core commands that can be used to add migration, remove migration, update the database, and so on.

Command	Description	Example
`dotnet ef migrations add`	Adds a new migration	`dotnet ef migrations add Initial` - `Initial` is the name of migration
`dotnet ef migrations list`	List available migrations	`dotnet ef migrations list`
`dotnet ef migrations remove`	Remove specific migration	`dotnet ef migrations remove Initial` - `Initial` is the name of migration

dotnet ef database update	To update the database to a specified migration	dotnet ef database update Initial - Initial is the name of migration
dotnet ef database drop	Drops the database	dotnet ef database drop

Here are some of the server level commands that can be used to delete the NuGet package from its actual source repository from the machine, add NuGet package into its actual source repository on the machine, and so on:

Command	Description	Example
nuget delete	Deletes the package from the server	dotnet nuget delete Microsoft.AspNetCore.App 2.0
nuget push	Pushes a package to the server and publishes it	dotnet nuget push foo.nupkg
nuget locals	Lists the local NuGet resources	dotnet nuget locals -l all
msbuild	Builds a project and all of its dependencies	dotnet msbuild
dotnet install script	The script to install the .NET CLI tools and the shared runtime	./dotnet-install.ps1 -Channel LTS

To run the preceding commands, we can use the tool known as dotnet from the command line and specify the actual command followed by that. When the .NET Core CLI is installed, it is set into the PATH variable in Windows OS and can be accessed from any folder. So, for example, if you are at your project root folder and wanted to restore the dependencies, you can just call the following command and it will restore all the dependencies that have been defined in your project file:

```
dotnet restore
```

The preceding command will start restoring the dependencies or project-specific tools, as defined in the project file. The restoration of tools and dependencies are done in parallel:

```
c:\Users\ovais\Source\Repos\Chapter1\Chapter1>dotnet restore
  Restoring packages for c:\Users\ovais\Source\Repos\Chapter1\Chapter1\Chapter1WebApp.csproj...
  Restoring packages for c:\Users\ovais\Source\Repos\Chapter1\Chapter1\Chapter1WebApp.csproj...
  Restore completed in 801.88 ms for c:\Users\ovais\Source\Repos\Chapter1\Chapter1\Chapter1WebApp.csproj.
  Generating MSBuild file c:\Users\ovais\Source\Repos\Chapter1\Chapter1\obj\Chapter1WebApp.csproj.nuget.g.props.
  Restore completed in 1.72 sec for c:\Users\ovais\Source\Repos\Chapter1\Chapter1\Chapter1WebApp.csproj.
```

We can also set the path where packages can be restored by using the `--packages` argument. However, if this is not specified, it uses the `.nuget/packages` folder under the system's user folder. For example, the default NuGet folder for Windows OS is `{systemdrive}:\Users\{user}\.nuget\packages` and `/home/{user}` for Linux OS, respectively.

Understanding .NET Standard

In the .NET ecosystem, there are many runtimes. We have the .NET Framework, which is a full machine-wide framework installed on the Windows operating system and provides app models for **Windows Presentation Foundation (WPF)**, Windows Forms, and ASP.NET. Then, we have .NET Core, which is targeted at cross-platform operating systems and devices and provides ASP.NET Core, **Universal Windows Platform (UWP)**, and a Mono runtime that is targeted at Xamarin applications and developers who can use Mono runtime to develop applications on Xamarin and run on iOS, Android, and Windows OS.

The following diagram depicts how the .NET Standard Library provides an abstraction of .NET Framework, .NET Core, and Xamarin with the common building blocks:

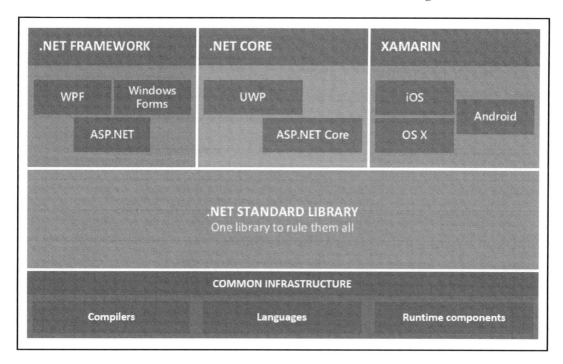

All of these runtimes implement an interface known as .NET Standard, where .NET Standard is the specification of .NET APIs that have the implementation for each runtime. This makes your code portable across different platforms. This means the code created for one runtime can also be executed by another runtime. .NET Standard is the next generation of **Portable Class Libraries** (PCL) we used earlier. Just to recap, PCL is a class library that targets one or more frameworks of .NET. When creating a PCL, we can select the target frameworks where this library needs to be used, and it minimizes the assemblies and uses only those that are common to all frameworks.

The .NET Standard is not an API or executable that can be downloaded or installed. It is a specification that defines the API that each platform implements. Each runtime version implements a specific .NET Standard version. The following table shows the versions of .NET Standard each platform implements:

.NET Standard	.NET Core	.NET Framework (with .NET Core 1.x SDK)	.NET Framework (with .NET Core 2.0 SDK)	Mono	Universal Windows Platform	Windows	Windows Phone	Windows Phone Silverlight	Xamarin.Mac	Xamarin.Android	Xamarin.iOS
1.0		4.5	4.5			8.0		8.0			
1.1							8.1				
1.2		4.5.1	4.5.1		10.0	8.1					
1.3	1.0	4.6	4.6	4.6					3.0	7.0	10.0
1.4		4.6.1									
1.5		4.6.2	4.6.1								
1.6					10.0.16299						
2.0	2.0			5.4					3.8	8.0	10.14

We can see that .NET Core 2.0 implements .NET Standard 2.0 and that .NET Framework 4.5 implements .NET Standard 1.1., so for example, if we have a class library developed on .NET Framework 4.5, this can easily be added into the .NET Core project because it implements a greater version of .NET Standard. On the other hand, if we wanted to reference the .NET Core assembly into .NET Framework 4.5, we can do so by changing the .NET Standard version to 1.1 without recompiling and building our project.

As we learned, the basic idea of .NET Standard is to share code between different runtimes, but how it differs from PCL is shown as follows:

Portable Class Library (PCL)	.NET Standard
Represents the Microsoft platform and targets a limited set of platforms	Agnostic to platform
APIs are defined by the platforms you target	Curated set of APIs
They are not linearly versioned	Linearly versioned

.NET Standard is also mapped to PCL, so if you have an existing PCL library that you wanted to convert to .NET Standard, you can reference the following table:

PCL Profile	.NET Standard	PCL Plaforms
7	1.1	.NET Framework 4.5, Windows 8
31	1.0	Windows 8.1, Windows Phone Silverlight 8.1
32	1.2	Windows 8.1, Windows Phone 8.1
44	1.2	.NET Framework 4.5.1, Windows 8.1
49	1.0	.NET Framework 4.5, Windows Phone Silverlight 8
78	1.0	.NET Framework 4.5, Windows 8, Windows Phone Silverlight 8
84	1.0	Windows Phone 8.1, Windows Phone Silverlight 8.1
111	1.1	.NET Framework 4.5, Windows 8, Windows Phone 8.1
151	1.2	.NET Framework 4.5.1, Windows 8.1, Windows Phone 8.1
157	1.0	Windows 8.1, Windows Phone 8.1, Windows Phone Silverlight 8.1
259	1.0	.NET Framework 4.5, Windows 8, Windows Phone 8.1, Windows Phone Silverlight 8

Considering the preceding table, if we have a PCL that targets .NET Framework 4.5.1, Windows 8.1, and Windows Phone 8.1 with the PCL profile set to 151, it can be converted to the .NET Standard library with version 1.2.

Versioning of .NET Standard

Unlike PCL, each version of .NET Standard is linearly versioned and contains the APIs for the previous versions and so on. Once the version is shipped, it is frozen and cannot be changed, and the application can easily target that version.

The following diagram is a representation of how .NET Standard is versioned. The higher the version is, the more APIs will be available, whereas the lower the version is, the more platforms will be available:

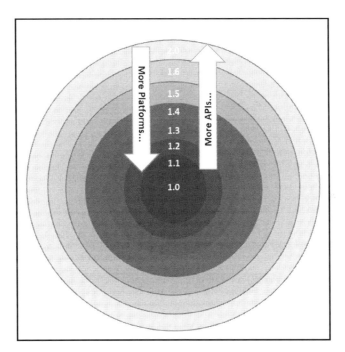

New improvements in .NET Standard 2.0

.NET Core 2.0 is targeted at .NET Standard 2.0 and provides two major benefits. This includes the increase in the number of APIs provided from the previous version and its compatibility mode, as we will discuss further in this chapter.

More APIs in .NET Standard 2.0

More APIs have been added into .NET Standard 2.0 and the number is almost double that of the previous .NET Standard, 1.0. Additionally APIs like DataSet, collections, binary serialization, XML schema, and others are now part of .NET Standard 2.0 specification. This has increased the portability of code from .NET Framework to .NET Core.

The following diagram depicts the categorical view of APIs added in each area:

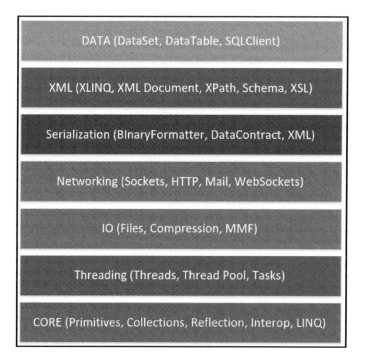

Compatibility mode

Although more than 33K APIs have been added into .NET Standard 2.0, many of the NuGet packages still target .NET Framework, and moving them to .NET Standard is not possible, since their dependencies are still not targeted at .NET Standard. However, with .NET Standard 2.0, we can still add packages which show a warning but don't block adding those packages into our .NET Standard library.

Under the hood, .NET Standard 2.0 uses compatibility shim, which solves the third party library compatibility issue and makes it easy in referencing those libraries. In the CLR world, the identity of the assembly is part of the type identity. This means that when we say `System.Object` in .NET Framework, we are referencing `[mscorlib]System.Object` and with .NET Standard, we are referencing `[netstandard]System.Object`, so if we are referencing any assembly which is part of .NET Framework, it cannot be easily run on .NET Standard and so compatibility issues arise. To solve this problem, they have used type forwarding which provides a fake `mscorlib` assembly that type forwards all the types to the .NET Standard implementation.

Here is a representation of how the .NET Framework libraries can run in any of the .NET Standard implementations using the type forwarding approach:

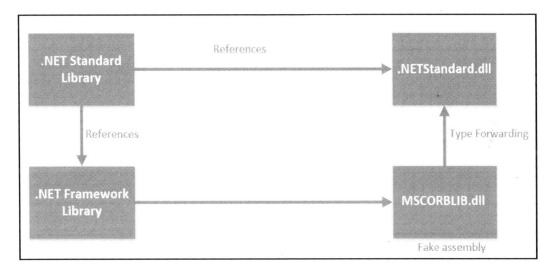

On the other hand, if we have a .NET Framework library and we wanted to reference a .NET Standard library, it will add the `netstandard` fake assembly and perform type forwarding of all the types by using the .NET Framework implementation:

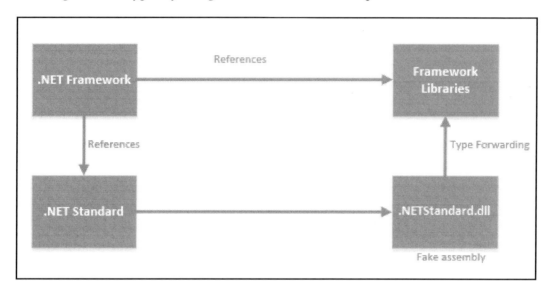

 To suppress warnings, we can add NU1701 for particular NuGet packages whose dependencies are not targeting .NET Standard.

Creating a .NET Standard library

To create a .NET Standard library, you can either use Visual Studio or the .NET Core CLI toolset. From Visual Studio, we can just click on the .NET Standard option as shown in the following screenshot, and select **Class Library** (.NET Standard).

Once the .NET Standard library is created, we can reference it to any project and change the version if needed, depending on which platform we want to reference. The version can be changed from the properties panel, as shown in the following screenshot:

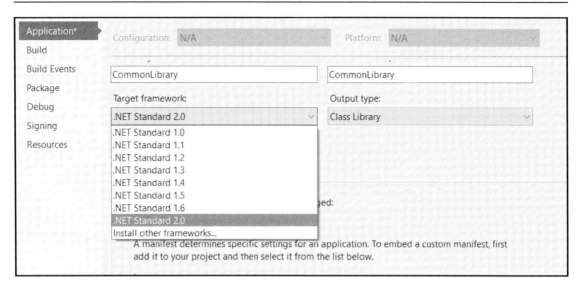

What comes with ASP.NET Core 2.0

ASP.NET Core is one of the most powerful platforms for developing cloud-ready and enterprise web applications that run cross-platform. Microsoft has added many features with ASP.NET Core 2.0, and that includes new project templates, Razor Pages, simplified provisioning of Application Insights, connection pooling, and so on.

The following are some new improvements for ASP.NET Core 2.0.

ASP.NET Core Razor Pages

Razor syntax-based pages have been introduced in ASP.NET Core. Now, developers can develop applications and write syntax on the HTML with no controller in place. Instead, there is a code behind file where other events and logic can be handled. The backend page class is inherited from the `PageModel` class and its member variables and methods can be accessed using the `Model` object in Razor syntax. The following is a simple example that contains the `GetTitle` method defined in the `code-behind` class and used in the view page:

```
public class IndexModel : PageModel
{
    public string GetTitle() => "Home Page";
}
```

Here is the `Index.cshtml` file that displays the date by calling the `GetCurrentDate` method:

```
@page
@model IndexModel
@{
  ViewData["Title"] = Model.GetTitle();
}
```

Automatic Page and View compilation on publishing

On publishing the ASP.NET Core Razor pages project, all the views are compiled into one single assembly and the published folder size is comparatively small. In case we want view and all the `.cshtml` files to be generated when the publishing process takes place, we have to add an entry, which is shown as follows:

```
<Project Sdk="Microsoft.NET.Sdk.Web">
  <PropertyGroup>
    <TargetFramework>netcoreapp2.0</TargetFramework>
    <MvcRazorCompileOnPublish>false</MvcRazorCompileOnPublish>
  </PropertyGroup>
```

Razor support for C# 7.1

Now, we can use C# 7.1 features such as inferred tuple names, pattern matching with generics, and expressions. In order to add this support, we have to add one XML tag as follows in our project file:

```
<LangVersion>latest</LangVersion>
```

Simplified configuration for Application Insights

With ASP.NET Core 2.0, you can enable Application Insights with a single click. A user can enable Application Insights by just right clicking **Project** and hitting **Add | Application Insights Telemetry** before going through a simple wizard. This allows you to monitor the application and provides complete diagnostics information from Azure Application Insights.

We can also view the complete telemetry from the Visual Studio 2017 IDE from the Application Insights Search window and monitor trends from Application Insights Trends. Both of these windows can be opened from the **View | Other Windows menu**.

Pooling connections in Entity Framework Core 2.0

With the recent release of Entity Framework Core 2.0, we can pool connections by using the `AddDbContextPool` method in the `Startup` class. As we already know, in ASP.NET Core, we have to add the `DbContext` object using **Dependency Injection (DI)** in the `ConfigureServices` method in the `Startup` class, and when it is used in the controller, a new instance of the `DbContext` object is injected. To optimize performance, Microsoft has provided this `AddDbContextPool` method, which first checks for the available database context instance and injects it wherever it is needed. On the other hand, if the database context instance is not available, a new instance is created and injected.

The following code shows how `AddDbContext` can be added in the `ConfigureServices` method in the `Startup` class:

```
services.AddDbContextPool<SampleDbContext>(
    options => options.UseSqlServer(connectionString));
```

 There are some more features added to **Owned Types**, **Table splitting**, **Database Scalar Function** mapping, and string interpolation that you can refer to from the following link:
https://docs.microsoft.com/en-us/ef/core/what-is-new/.

New features in C# 7.0

C# is the most popular language in the .NET ecosystem and was first introduced with the .NET Framework in 2002. The current stable version of C# is 7. The following chart shows how C# 7.0 has progressed and what versions were introduced in different years:

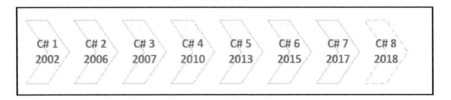

Here are some of the new features that were introduced with C# 7.0:

- Tuples
- Pattern matching
- Reference returns
- Exceptions as expressions
- Local functions
- Out variables Literals
- Async Main

Tuples

Tuples solve the problem of returning more than one value from a method. Traditionally, we can use out variables that are reference variables, and the value is changed if they are modified from the calling method. However, without parameters, there are some limitations, such as that it cannot be used with `async` methods and is not recommended to be used with external services.

Tuples have the following characteristics:

- They are value types.
- They can be converted to other Tuples.
- Tuple elements are public and mutable.

A Tuple is represented as `System.Tuple<T>`, where `T` could be any type. The following example shows how a Tuple can be used with the method and how the values can be invoked:

```
static void Main(string[] args)
{
  var person = GetPerson();
  Console.WriteLine($"ID : {person.Item1},
  Name : {person.Item2}, DOB : {person.Item3}");
}
static (int, string, DateTime) GetPerson()
{
  return (1, "Mark Thompson", new DateTime(1970, 8, 11));
}
```

As you may have noticed, items are dynamically named and the first item is named `Item1`, the second `Item2`, and so on. On the other hand, we can also name the items so that the calling party should know about the value, and this can be done by adding the parameter name for each parameter in the Tuple, which is shown as follows:

```
static void Main(string[] args)
{
  var person = GetPerson();
  Console.WriteLine($"ID : {person.id}, Name : {person.name},
  DOB : {person.dob}");
}
static (int id, string name, DateTime dob) GetPerson()
{
  return (1, "Mark Thompson", new DateTime(1970, 8, 11));
}
```

 To learn more about Tuples, please check the following link: https://docs.microsoft.com/en-us/dotnet/csharp/tuples.

Patterns

Patterns matching is the process of performing syntactical testing of the value to verify whether it matches the certain model. There are three types of patterns:

- Constant patterns.
- Type patterns.
- Var patterns.

Constant pattern

A constant pattern is a simple pattern that checks for the constant value. Consider the following example: if the `Person` object is null, it will return and exit the `body` method.

The `Person` class is as follows:

```
class Person
{
  public int ID { set; get; }
  public string Name { get; set; }
```

```
    public DateTime DOB { get; set; }
}
```

In the preceding code snippet, we have a `Person` class that contains three properties, namely `ID`, `Name`, and `DOB` (Date of Birth).

The following statement checks for the `person` object with a null constant value and returns it if the object is null:

```
if (person is null) return;
```

Type pattern

The type pattern can be used with an object to verify whether it matches the type or suffices the expression based on the conditions specified. Suppose we need to check whether the `PersonID` is `int`; assign that `ID` to another variable, `i`, and use it in the program, otherwise return:

```
if (!(person.ID is int i)) return;

Console.WriteLine($"Person ID is {i}");
```

We can also use multiple logical operators to evaluate more conditions, as follows:

```
if (!(person.ID is int i) && !(person.DOB>DateTime.Now.AddYears(-20)))
return;
```

The preceding statement checks whether the `Person.ID` is null or not and whether the person is older than 20.

Var pattern

The var pattern checks if the `var` is equal to some type. The following example shows how the `var` pattern can be used to check for the type and print the `Type` name:

```
if (person is var Person) Console.WriteLine($"It is a person object and
type is {person.GetType()}");
```

To learn more about patterns, you can refer to the following link: `https:/` `/docs.microsoft.com/en-us/dotnet/csharp/whats-new/csharp-` `7#pattern-matching`.

Reference returns

Reference returns allow a method to return an object as a reference instead of its value. We can define the reference return value by adding a `ref` keyword before the type in the method signature and when returning the object from the method itself.

Here is the signature of the method that allows reference returns:

```
public ref Person GetPersonInformation(int ID);

Following is the implementation of the GetPersonInformation method that
uses the ref keyword while returning the person's object.

Person _person;
public ref Person GetPersonInformation(int ID)
{
  _person = CallPersonHttpService();
  return ref _person;
}
```

Expression bodied member extended

Expression bodied members were introduced in C# 6.0 where the syntactical expression of the method can be written in a simpler way. In C# 7.0, we can use this feature with a constructor, a destructor, an exception, and so on.

The following example shows how the constructor and destructor syntactic expressions can be simplified using expression bodied members:

```
public class PersonManager
{
  //Member Variable
  Person _person;

  //Constructor
  PersonManager(Person person) => _person = person;

  //Destructor
  ~PersonManager() => _person = null;
}
```

With properties, we can also simplify the syntactic expression, and the following is a basic example of how this can be written:

```
private String _name;
public String Name
{
  get => _name;
  set => _name = value;
}
```

We can also use an expression bodied syntactic expression with exceptions and simplify the expression, which is shown as follows:

```
private String _name;
public String Name
{
  get => _name;
  set => _name = value ?? throw new ArgumentNullException();
}
```

In the preceding example, if the value is null, a new `ArgumentNullException` will be thrown.

Creating Local Functions

Functions that are created within a function are known as Local Functions. These are mainly used when defining helper functions that have to be in the scope of the function itself. The following example shows how the factorial of the number can be obtained by writing a Local Function and calling it recursively:

```
static void Main(string[] args)
{
  Console.WriteLine(ExecuteFactorial(4));
}

static long ExecuteFactorial(int n)
{
  if (n < 0) throw new ArgumentException("Must be non negative",
  nameof(n));
  else return CheckFactorial(n);

  long CheckFactorial(int x)
  {
```

```
        if (x == 0) return 1;
        return x * CheckFactorial(x - 1);
    }
}
```

Out variables

With C# 7.0, we can write cleaner code when using out variables. As we know, to use out variables, we have to first declare them. With the new language enhancement, we can now just write out as a prefix and specify the name of the variable that we need that value to be assigned to.

To clarify this concept, we will first see the traditional approach, which is shown as follows:

```
public void GetPerson()
{
    int year;
    int month;
    int day;
    GetPersonDOB(out year, out month, out day);
}

public void GetPersonDOB(out int year, out int month, out int day )
{
    year = 1980;
    month = 11;
    day = 3;
}
```

And here with C# 7.0, we can simplify the preceding GetPerson method, which is shown as follows:

```
public void GetPerson()
{
    GetPersonDOB(out int year, out int month, out int day);
}
```

Async Main

As we already know, in .NET Framework, the Main method is the main entry point from where the application/program is executed by the OS. For example, in ASP.NET Core, Program.cs is the main class where the Main method is defined, which creates a WebHost object, runs the Kestrel server, and loads up the HTTP pipeline as configured in the Startup class.

In the previous version of C#, the Main method had the following signatures:

```
public static void Main();
public static void Main(string[] args);
public static int Main();
public static int Main(string[] args);
```

In C# 7.0, we can use Async Main to perform asynchronous operations. The Async/Await feature was initially released in .NET Framework 4.5 in order to execute methods asynchronously. Today, many APIs provides Async/Await methods to perform asynchronous operations.

Here are some additional signatures of the Main method that have been added with C# 7.1:

```
public static Task Main();
public static Task Main(string[] args);
public static Task<int> Main();
public static Task<int> Main(string[] args);
```

Because of the preceding async signatures, we can now call async methods from the Main entry point itself and use await to perform an asynchronous operation. Here is a simple example of ASP.NET Core that calls the RunAsync method instead of Run:

```
public class Program
{
  public static async Task Main(string[] args)
  {
    await BuildWebHost(args).RunAsync();
  }
  public static IWebHost BuildWebHost(string[] args) =>
    WebHost.CreateDefaultBuilder(args)
    .UseStartup<Startup>()
    .Build();
}
```

Async Main is a feature of C# 7.1, and to enable this feature in Visual Studio 2017, you can go to the project properties, click on the **Advance** button and set the **Language version** as C# **latest minor version (latest)**, which is shown as follows:

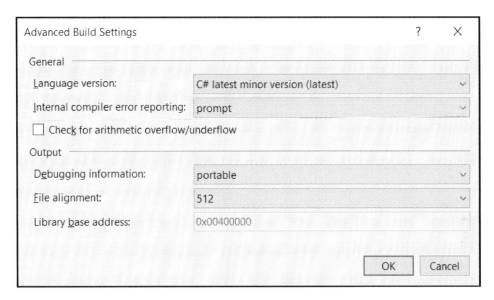

Writing quality code

For every performance-efficient application, code quality plays an important role. As we already know, Visual Studio is the most popular **Integrated Development Environment (IDE)** for developing .NET applications, and since Roslyn (.NET Compiler SDK) exposes compiler platforms as APIs, many features have been introduced that do not only extend the capabilities of Visual Studio, but enhance the development experience.

Live Static Code analysis is one of the core features that can be used in Visual Studio in developing .NET applications which provides code analysis during development while writing code. As this feature uses the Roslyn APIs, many other third-party companies have also introduced sets of analyzers that can be used. We can also develop our own analyzer for a particular requirement, and it's not a very complicated procedure. Let's look at a quick introduction on how we can use Live Static Code analysis in our .NET Core project and how it benefits the development experience by analyzing code and giving warnings, errors, and potential fixes for them.

We can add analyzer as a NuGet package. In NuGet.org, there are many analyzers available, and once we add any analyzer into our project, it adds a new *Analyzer* node into the *Dependencies* section of the project. We can then customize rules, suppress warnings or errors, and so on.

Let's add a new analyzer from Visual Studio in our .NET Core project. If you don't know which analyzer you want to add, you can just type *analyzers* in the NuGet Package manager window and it will list all the analyzers for you. We will just add the `Microsoft.CodeQuality.Analyzers` analyzer, which contains some decent rules:

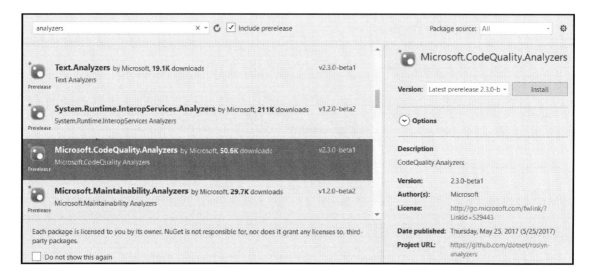

Once the selected Analyzer is added, a new `Analyzers` node is added into our project:

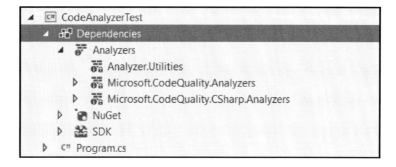

In the preceding picture, we can see that three nodes have been added to the `Analyzers` node, and to see/manage the rules, we can expand the subnodes `Microsoft.CodeQuality.Analyzers` and `Microsoft.CodeQuality.CSharp.Analyzers`, which is shown as follows:

Moreover, we can also change the rule severity by right-clicking on the rule and selecting the severity, which is shown as follows:

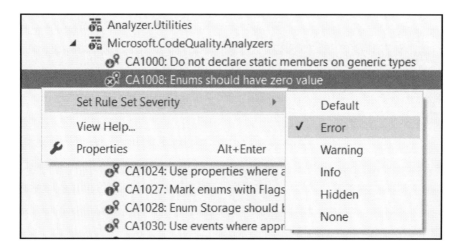

In the preceding picture, rule **CA1008** states that Enums should have a value of zero. Let's test this out and see how it works.

Create a simple Enum and specify the values, which are shown as follows:

```
public enum Status
{
  Create =1,
  Update =2,
  Delete =3,
}
```

You will notice as soon as you write this code, it will show the following error and it will provide potential fixes:

```
public enum Status
{
    Create =1,
    Update =2,
    Delete =3,
}
}
```

enum CodeAnalyzerTest.Program.Status

Add a member to Status that has a value of zero with a suggested name of 'None'.

Show potential fixes (Alt+Enter or Ctrl+.)

Finally, here is the fix we can apply, and the error will disappear:

You can also use one of the popular Visual Studio extensions known as Roslynator, which can be downloaded from the following link. It contains more than 190 analyzers and refactorings for C# based projects: `https://marketplace.visualstudio.com/items?itemName=josefpihrt.Roslynator`.

Live Static Code analysis is a great feature that helps developers to write quality code that conforms to the best guidelines and practices.

Summary

In this chapter, we learned about the .NET Core Framework and some new improvements that are introduced with .NET Core 2.0. We also looked into the new features of C# 7 and how we can write cleaner code and simplify syntactic expressions. Finally, we covered the topic of writing quality code and how we can leverage with the Code analysis feature provided in Visual Studio 2017 to add analyzers into our project which serve our needs. The next chapter will be an in-depth chapter about .NET Core that will cover topics around .NET Core internals and performance improvements.

2
Understanding .NET Core Internals and Measuring Performance

When developing application architecture, knowing the internals of how the .NET framework works plays a vital role in ensuring the quality of the application's performance. In this chapter, we will focus on the internals of .NET Core that can help us write quality code and architecture for any application. This chapter will cover some of the core concepts of .NET Core internals, including the compilation process, garbage collection, and **Framework Class Library (FCL)**. We will complete this chapter by going through the *BenchmarkDotNet* tool, which is mostly used in measuring code performance, and is highly recommended for benchmarking code snippets within an application.

In this chapter, you will learn the following topics:

- .NET Core internals
- Utilizing multiple cores of the CPU for high performance
- How releasing builds increases performance
- Benchmarking .NET Core 2.0 applications

.NET Core internals

.NET Core contains two core components—the runtime CoreCLR and the base-class libraries CoreFX. In this section, we will cover the following topics:

- CoreFX
- CoreCLR
- Understanding MSIL, CLI, CTS, and CLS

- How CLR works
- From compilation to execution—under the hood
- Garbage collection
- .NET Native and JIT compilation

CoreFX

CoreFX is the code name of .NET Core's set of libraries. It contains all the libraries that start with Microsoft.* or System.*and contains collections, I/O, string manipulation, reflection, security, and many more features.

The CoreFX is runtime agnostic, and it can run on any platform regardless of what APIs it supports.

 To learn more about each assembly, you can refer to the .NET Core source browser at `https://source.dot.net`.

CoreCLR

CoreCLR provides the common language runtime environment for .NET Core applications, and manages the execution of the complete application life cycle. It performs various operations when the program is running. Operations such as memory allocation, garbage collection, exception handling, type safety, thread management, and security are part of CoreCLR.

.NET Core's runtime provides the same **Garbage Collection (GC)** as .NET Framework and a new **Just In Time (JIT)** compiler that is more optimized, codenamed *RyuJIT*. When .NET Core was first released, it was only supported for 64-bit platforms, but with the release of .NET Core 2.0, it is now available for 32-bit platforms as well. However, the 32-bit version is only supported by Windows operating systems.

Understanding MSIL, CLI, CTS, and CLS

When we build our project, the code is compiled into the **Intermediate Language** (**IL**), also known as **Microsoft Intermediate Language** (**MSIL**). MSIL is compliant with the **Common Language Infrastructure** (**CLI**), where CLI is the standard that provides a common type system and a language specification, respectively known as the **Common Type System** (**CTS**) and **Common Language Specification** (**CLS**).

The CTS provides a common type system and compiles the language-specific types into the compliant data types. It standardizes all the .NET languages' data types to a common data type for language interoperability. For example, if the code is written in C#, it will be converted to the specific CTS.

Suppose we have two variables, defined in the following code fragment using C#:

```
class Program
{
  static void Main(string[] args)
  {
    int minNo = 1;
    long maxThroughput = 99999;
  }
}
```

On compilation, the compiler generates the MSIL into an assembly that will be available through the CoreCLR to perform the JIT and convert it into the native machine code. Note that the int and long types are converted to the int32 and int64 respectively:

```
.method private hidebysig static void  Main(string[] args) cil managed
{
  .entrypoint
  // Code size       11 (0xb)
  .maxstack  1
  .locals init (int32 V_0,
           int64 V_1)
  IL_0000:  nop
  IL_0001:  ldc.i4.1
  IL_0002:  stloc.0
  IL_0003:  ldc.i4      0x1869f
  IL_0008:  conv.i8
  IL_0009:  stloc.1
  IL_000a:  ret
} // end of method Program::Main
```

It is not necessary for every language to comply completely with the CTS, and it can support the smaller footprint of the CTS, too. For example, when VB.NET was first released in .NET Framework, it only supported the signed integer data types, and there was no provision to use unsigned integers. With later versions of .NET Framework, and now with .NET Core 2.0, we can use all managed languages, such as C#, F#, and VB.NET, to develop applications and easily reference any project's assembly.

How the CLR works

The CLR is implemented as a set of in-process libraries that are loaded with the application, and runs inside the context of the application process. In the following diagram, we have two .NET Core applications running, named **App1.exe** and **App2.exe**. Each black box represents the application process address space, where the applications **App1.exe** and **App2.exe** are running their own CLR version side by side:

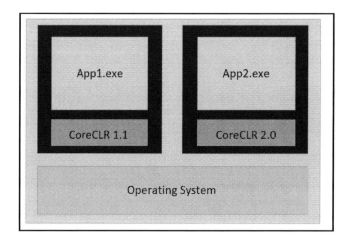

When packaging the .NET Core applications, we can either publish them as **framework-dependent deployments (FDDs)** or **self-contained deployments (SCDs)**. In FDDs, the published package does not contain the .NET Core runtime, and expects that the .NET Core is present on the target/hosting system. With SCDs, all the components, such as the .NET Core runtime and .NET Core libraries, are included in the published package, and the .NET Core installation on the target system is not required.

To learn more about FDDs or SCDs, please refer to `https://docs.`
`microsoft.com/en-us/dotnet/core/deploying/`.

From compilation to execution – Under the hood

The .NET Core compilation process is like the one used with the .NET Framework. When the project is built, the internal .NET CLI command is invoked by the MSBuild system, which builds the project and generates the assembly (`.dll`) or executable (`.exe`) file. This assembly contains the manifest that contains the assembly's metadata, and includes the version number, culture, type-reference information, information about the referenced assemblies, and a list of other files in the assembly and their association. This assembly manifest is stored either in the MSIL code or in a standalone **portable executable** (**PE**) file:

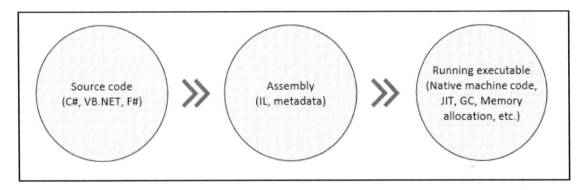

Now, when the executable is run, a new process is started and bootstraps the .NET Core runtime, which then initializes the execution environment, sets up the heap and thread pool, and loads the assembly into the process address space. Based on the program, it then executes the main entry point method (`Main`) and performs a JIT compilation. From here, the code starts executing and the objects start allocating memory on heap, where primitive types store on stack. For each method, the JIT compilation is done and the native machine code gets generated.

When JIT compilation is done, and before generating a native machine code, however, it also performs a few validations. These validations include the following:

- Verifying, that the MSIL was generated during the build process
- Verifying, whether any code was modified or new types added during the JIT compilation process
- Verifying, that the optimized code for the target machine has been generated

Garbage collection

One of the most important features of CLR is the garbage collector. Since the .NET Core applications are managed applications, most of the garbage collection is done automatically by the CLR. The allocation of objects in the memory is efficiently done by the CLR. The CLR not only tunes the virtual memory resources from time to time, but it also reduces the fragmentation of underlying virtual memory to make it more efficient in terms of space.

When the program is run, the objects start allocating memory on the heap and each object's address is stored on the stack. This process continues until the memory reaches its maximum limit. Then the GC comes into play and starts reclaiming memory by removing the unused managed objects and allocating new objects. This is all done automatically by the GC, but there is also a way to invoke the GC to perform garbage collection by calling the GC.Collect method

Let's take an example where we have a Car object called c in the Main method. When the function is executed, the Car object will be allocated by the CLR into the heap memory and the reference to that c object will be stored in the stack address pointing to the Car object on the heap. When the garbage collector runs, it reclaims the memory from the heap and removes the reference from the stack:

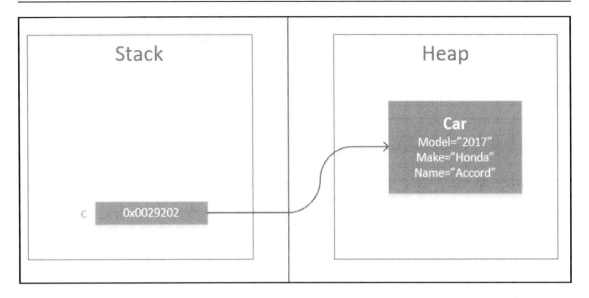

Some important points to note are that the garbage collection is done automatically by the GC on managed objects, and that if there are any unmanaged objects, such as database connections, I/O operations, and so on, they need to be garbage collected explicitly. Otherwise, GC works efficiently on managed objects and ensures that the application will not experience any decrease in performance when the GC is performed.

Generations in GC

There are three kinds of generation in garbage collection known as **Generation** 0, **Generation 1**, and **Generation 2**. In this section, we will look at the concept of generations and how it affects the performance of the garbage collector.

Let's suppose we run an application that creates three objects named **Object1**, **Object2**, and **Object3**. These objects will allocate the memory in **Generation 0**:

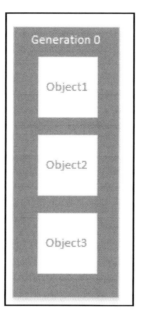

Now, when the garbage collector runs (this is an automatic process, unless you explicitly call the garbage collector from the code), it checks for the objects that are not needed by the application and have no reference in the program. It will simply remove those objects. For example, if the scope of **Object1** is not referenced anywhere, the memory for this object will be reclaimed. However, the other two objects, **Object1** and **Object2**, are still referenced in the program, and will be moved to **Generation 1**.

Now, let's suppose two more objects, called **Object4** and **Object5**, are created. We will store them in the **Generation 0** slot, as shown in the following diagram:

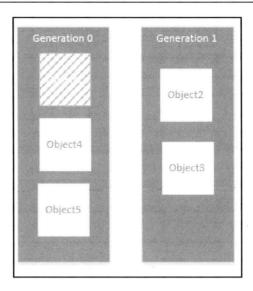

When garbage collection runs the second time, it will find two objects called **Object4** and **Object5** in **Generation 0** and two objects called **Object2** and **Object3** in **Generation 1**. Garbage collector will first check the reference of those objects in **Generation 0** and, if they are not used by the application, they will be removed. The same goes for the **Generation 1** objects. For example, if **Object3** is still referenced, it will be moved to **Generation 2** and **Object2** will be removed from **Generation 1**, as shown in the following diagram:

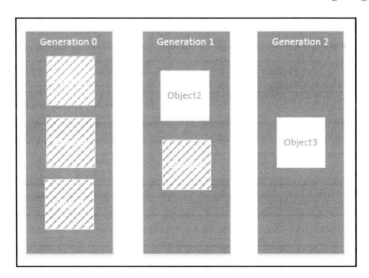

This concept of generations actually optimizes the performance of GC, and the objects stored in **Generation 2** are more likely to be stored for a longer period. GC performs fewer visits and gains time instead of checking each object again and again. The same goes for **Generation 1**, which is also less likely to reclaim the space than **Generation 0**.

.NET Native and JIT compilation

JIT compilation is done mostly at runtime, and it converts the MSIL code to the native machine code. This is when the code is run the first time, and it takes a little bit more time than its successive runs. In .NET Core today, we are developing applications for mobile and handheld devices that have limited resources in terms of CPU power and memory. Currently, the **Universal Windows Platform (UWP)** and the Xamarin platform run on .NET Core. With these platforms, .NET Core automatically generates that native assembly at compilation time or while generating the platform-specific packages. Though it does not require the JIT compilation process to be done at runtime, this eventually increases the performance of the application's boot-up time. This native compilation is done through a component known as .NET Native.

.NET Native begins the compilation process after the language-specific compiler finishes up the compilation process that is done at build time. The .NET Native toolchain reads the MSIL generated from the language compiler and performs the following operations:

- It eliminates the metadata from the MSIL.
- It replaces the code that relies on reflection and metadata with the static native code when comparing field values.
- It checks the code that is invoked by the application and includes only that in the final assembly.
- It replaces the full CLR with a refactored runtime that contains the garbage collector and no JIT compiler. The refactored runtime goes with the app and is contained in the assembly named `mrt100_app.dll`.

Utilizing multiple cores of the CPU for high performance

These days, the nature of applications focuses more on connectivity, and there are cases where their operations take more time to execute. We also know that nowadays, all computers come with a multi-core processor, and using these cores effectively increases the performance of the application. Operations such as network/IO have latency issues, and the synchronous execution of the application program may often lead to a long waiting time. If the long-running tasks are executed in a separate thread or in an asynchronous manner, the resulting operation will take less time and increase responsiveness. Another benefit is performance that actually utilizes multiple cores of the processor and executes the task simultaneously. In the .NET world, we can achieve responsiveness and performance by splitting the tasks into multiple threads and using classic multithreading programming APIs, or a more simplified and advanced model known as the **task programming library** (**TPL**). The TPL is now supported in .NET Core 2.0, and we will soon explore how it can be used to execute tasks on multiple cores.

The TPL programming model is based on the task. A task is a unit of work—an object's representation of an ongoing operation.

A simple task can be created by writing the following lines of code:

```
static void Main(string[] args)
{
    Task t = new Task(execute);
    t.Start();
    t.Wait();
}

private static void Execute() {
    for (int i = 0; i < 100; i++)
    {
        Console.WriteLine(i);
    }
}
```

In the preceding code, the task can be initialized using a `Task` object, where `Execute` is the computational method that is executed when the `Start` method is called. The `Start` method tells the .NET Core that the task can start and returns immediately. It forks the program execution into two threads that run concurrently. The first thread is the actual application thread and the second one is the one that executes the `execute` method. We have used the `t.Wait` method to wait for the worker task to show the result on the console. Otherwise, once the program exits the block of code under the `Main` method, the application ends.

The goal of parallel programming is to effectively use multiple cores. For example, we are running the preceding code in a single-core processor. These two threads will run and share the same processor. However, if the same program can run on a multi-core processor, it can run on multiple cores by utilizing each core separately, increasing the performance and achieving true parallelism:

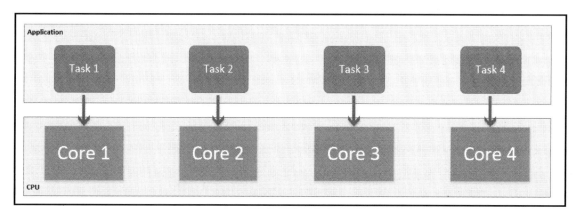

Unlike TPL, the classic `Thread` object doesn't guarantee that your thread will be running on distinct cores of the CPU. With TPL, however, it guarantees that each thread will run on the distinct thread unless it reaches the number of tasks as per the CPU and shares the cores.

To learn more about what TPL provides, please refer to https://docs.microsoft.com/en-us/dotnet/standard/parallel-programming/task-parallel-library-tpl.

How releasing builds increases performance

Release and debug builds are two build modes provided in .NET applications. Debug mode is mostly used when we are in the process of writing code or troubleshooting errors, whereas release build mode is often used while packaging the application to deploy on production servers. When developing the deployment package, developers often miss updating the build mode to the release build, and then they face performance issues when the application is deployed:

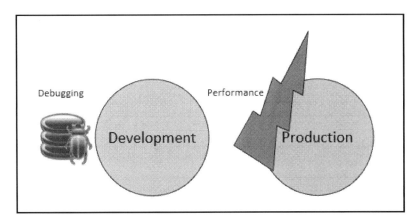

The following table shows some differences between the debug and release modes:

Debug	Release
No optimization of code is done by the compiler	Code is optimized and minified in size when built using release mode
Stack trace is captured and thrown at the time of exception	No stack trace is captured
The debug symbols are stored	All code and debug symbols under #debug directives are removed
More memory is used by the source code at runtime	Less memory is used by the source code at runtime

Benchmarking .NET Core 2.0 applications

Benchmarking applications is the process of evaluating and comparing artifacts with the agreed upon standards. To benchmark .NET Core 2.0 application code, we can use the BenchmarkDotNet tool, which provides a very simple API to evaluate the performance of code in your application. Usually, benchmarking at the micro-level, such as with classes and methods, is not an easy task, and requires quite an effort to measure the performance, whereas BenchmarkDotNet does all the low-level plumbing and the complex work associated with benchmark solutions.

Exploring BenchmarkDotNet

In this section, we will explore BenchmarkDotNet and learn how effectively it can be used to measure application performance.

It can simply be installed using a NuGet package manager console window or through the Project References section of your project. To install BenchmarkDotNet, execute the following command:

```
Install-Package BenchmarkDotNet
```

The preceding command adds a BenchmarkDotNet package from NuGet.org.

To test the BenchmarkDotNet tool, we will create a simple class that contains two methods to generate a Fibonacci series for a sequence of 10 numbers. The Fibonacci series can be implemented in multiple ways, which is why we are using it to measure which code snippet is faster and more performance efficient.

Here is the first method that generates the Fibonacci sequence iteratively:

```
public class TestBenchmark
{
  int len= 10;
  [Benchmark]
  public  void Fibonacci()
  {
    int a = 0, b = 1, c = 0;
    Console.Write("{0} {1}", a, b);

    for (int i = 2; i < len; i++)
    {
      c = a + b;
      Console.Write(" {0}", c);
      a = b;
```

```
        b = c;
      }
   }
}
```

Here is another method that uses the recursive approach to generate the Fibonacci series:

```
[Benchmark]
public   void FibonacciRecursive()
{
   int len= 10;
   Fibonacci_Recursive(0, 1, 1, len);
}

private void Fibonacci_Recursive(int a, int b, int counter, int len)
{
   if (counter <= len)
   {
      Console.Write("{0} ", a);
      Fibonacci_Recursive(b, a + b, counter + 1, len);
   }
}
```

Note that both of the main methods of the Fibonacci series contain a `Benchmark` attribute. This actually tells the `BenchmarkRunner` to measure methods that contain this attribute. Finally, we can call the `BenchmarkRunner` from the main entry point of the application that measures the performance and generates a report, as shown in the following code:

```
static void Main(string[] args)
{
   BenchmarkRunner.Run<TestBenchmark>();
   Console.Read();
}
```

Once the benchmark is run, we will get the report as follows:

```
C:\Program Files\dotnet\dotnet.exe                                              —  □  ×
// * Summary *

BenchmarkDotNet=v0.10.9, OS=Windows 10 Redstone 2 (10.0.15063)
Processor=Intel Core i7-4900MQ CPU 2.80GHz (Haswell), ProcessorCount=8
Frequency=2728057 Hz, Resolution=366.5613 ns, Timer=TSC
.NET Core SDK=2.0.0
  [Host]     : .NET Core 2.0.0 (Framework 4.6.00001.0), 64bit RyuJIT DEBUG  [AttachedDebugger]
  DefaultJob : .NET Core 2.0.0 (Framework 4.6.00001.0), 64bit RyuJIT


            Method |     Mean |    Error |   StdDev |
------------------ |---------:|---------:|---------:|
          Fibonacci | 22.62 us | 0.6201 us | 1.8087 us |
 FibonacciRecursive | 17.54 us | 0.2192 us | 0.1943 us |

// * Warnings *
Environment
  Summary                              -> Benchmark was executed with attached debugger
  TestBenchmark.Fibonacci: Default     -> Benchmark was built without optimization enabled (most probably a DEBUG c
onfiguration). Please, build it in RELEASE.
  TestBenchmark.FibonacciRecursive: Default -> Benchmark was built without optimization enabled (most probably a DEBUG c
onfiguration). Please, build it in RELEASE.

// * Legends *
  Mean   : Arithmetic mean of all measurements
  Error  : Half of 99.9% confidence interval
  StdDev : Standard deviation of all measurements
  1 us   : 1 Microsecond (0.000001 sec)

// ***** BenchmarkRunner: End *****
// * Artifacts cleanup *
```

As well as this, it also generates files in the root folder of an application that runs the `BenchmarkRunner`. Here is the .html file that contains the information about the version of `BenchmarkDotNet` and the OS, the processor, frequency, resolution, and timer details, the .NET version (in our case, .NET Core SDK 2.0.0), host, and so on:

```
BenchmarkDotNet=v0.10.9, OS=Windows 10 Redstone 2 (10.0.15063)
Processor=Intel Core i7-4900MQ CPU 2.80GHz (Haswell), ProcessorCount=8
Frequency=2728057 Hz, Resolution=366.5613 ns, Timer=TSC
.NET Core SDK=2.0.0
  [Host]     : .NET Core 2.0.0 (Framework 4.6.00001.0), 64bit RyuJIT DEBUG  [AttachedDebugger]
  DefaultJob : .NET Core 2.0.0 (Framework 4.6.00001.0), 64bit RyuJIT
```

Method	Mean	Error	StdDev
Fibonacci	22.62 us	0.6201 us	1.8087 us
FibonacciRecursive	17.54 us	0.2192 us	0.1943 us

The table contains four columns. However, we can add more columns, which are optional by default. We can also add custom columns as well. The **Method** is the name of the method that contains the benchmark attribute, the **Mean** is the average time it takes for all the measurements to be taken (where **us** is microseconds), **Error** is the time taken to process errors, and **StdDev** is the standard deviation of the measurements.

After comparing both the methods, the `FibonacciRecursive` method is more efficient as the **Mean**, **Error**, and **StdDev** values are smaller than the `Fibonacci` method.

Other than the HTML, two more files are created, a **Comma Separated Value (CSV)** file and a **Markdown Documentation (MD)** file which contains the same information.

How it works

Benchmark generates a project at runtime for each benchmark method and builds it in release mode. It tries multiple combinations to measure the method's performance by launching that method multiple times. Once the multiple cycles are run, the report is generated, containing files and information about Benchmark.

Setting parameters

In the previous example, we tested the method with only one value. Practically, when testing an enterprise application, we want to test it with different values to estimate the method's performance.

First of all, we can define a property for each parameter, set the `Params` attribute, and specify the value(s) for which we need that method to be tested. Then we can use that property in the code. `BenchmarkRun` automatically tests that method with all of the parameters and generates the report. Here is the complete code snippet of the `TestBenchmark` class:

```
public class TestBenchmark
{

  [Params(10,20,30)]
  public int Len { get; set; }
  [Benchmark]
  public  void Fibonacci()
  {
    int a = 0, b = 1, c = 0;
    Console.Write("{0} {1}", a, b);
```

```
    for (int i = 2; i < Len; i++)
    {
      c = a + b;
      Console.Write(" {0}", c);
      a = b;
      b = c;
    }
  }

  [Benchmark]
  public  void FibonacciRecursive()
  {
    Fibonacci_Recursive(0, 1, 1, Len);
  }

  private void Fibonacci_Recursive(int a, int b, int counter, int len)
  {
    if (counter <= len)
    {
      Console.Write("{0} ", a);
      Fibonacci_Recursive(b, a + b, counter + 1, len);
    }
  }
}
```

After running Benchmark, the following report is generated:

```
BenchmarkDotNet=v0.10.9, OS=Windows 10 Redstone 2 (10.0.15063)
Processor=Intel Core i7-4900MQ CPU 2.80GHz (Haswell), ProcessorCount=8
Frequency=2728057 Hz, Resolution=366.5613 ns, Timer=TSC
.NET Core SDK=2.0.0
  [Host]    : .NET Core 2.0.0 (Framework 4.6.00001.0), 64bit RyuJIT DEBUG
  DefaultJob : .NET Core 2.0.0 (Framework 4.6.00001.0), 64bit RyuJIT
```

Method	Len	Mean	Error	StdDev
Fibonacci	10	16.35 us	0.3267 us	0.3889 us
FibonacciRecursive	10	17.69 us	0.2207 us	0.2064 us
Fibonacci	20	36.52 us	0.6865 us	0.6742 us
FibonacciRecursive	20	38.50 us	0.7291 us	0.7488 us
Fibonacci	30	59.66 us	0.8321 us	0.7377 us
FibonacciRecursive	30	65.35 us	1.2867 us	1.1406 us

Memory diagnostics using BenchmarkDotnet

With `BenchmarkDotnet`, we can also diagnose any problems with the memory and measure the number of allocated bytes and garbage collection.

It can be implemented using a `MemoryDiagnoser` attribute at the class level. To start, let's just add the `MemoryDiagnoser` attribute to the `TestBenchmark` class that we created in the last example:

```
[MemoryDiagnoser]
public class TestBenchmark {}
```

Rerun the application. Now it will collect other memory allocation and garbage collection information and generate logs accordingly:

```
BenchmarkDotNet=v0.10.9, OS=Windows 10 Redstone 2 (10.0.15063)
Processor=Intel Core i7-4900MQ CPU 2.80GHz (Haswell), ProcessorCount=8
Frequency=2728057 Hz, Resolution=366.5613 ns, Timer=TSC
.NET Core SDK=2.0.0
  [Host]    : .NET Core 2.0.0 (Framework 4.6.00001.0), 64bit RyuJIT DEBUG
  DefaultJob : .NET Core 2.0.0 (Framework 4.6.00001.0), 64bit RyuJIT
```

Method	Len	Mean	Error	StdDev	Median	Gen 0	Gen 1	Allocated
Fibonacci	10	16.50 us	0.3281 us	0.7604 us	16.37 us	0.1984	-	848 B
FibonacciRecursive	10	25.46 us	3.2510 us	9.3799 us	20.97 us	0.1984	-	880 B
Fibonacci	20	62.13 us	3.8042 us	10.8537 us	62.22 us	0.4272	0.0012	1816 B
FibonacciRecursive	20	81.60 us	15.0942 us	44.5056 us	63.55 us	0.4272	-	1848 B
Fibonacci	30	99.37 us	9.4387 us	27.3834 us	97.40 us	0.6714	-	2856 B
FibonacciRecursive	30	103.11 us	7.1130 us	20.1784 us	103.42 us	0.6714	-	2888 B

In the preceding table, the **Gen 0** and **Gen 1** columns each contain the number of that particular generation per 1,000 operations. If the value is 1, then it means that the garbage collection was done after 1,000 operations. However, note that in the first row, the value is *0.1984*, which means that the garbage collection was done after *198.4* seconds, whereas for **Gen 1** of that row, no garbage collection took place. **Allocated** represents the size of the memory that is allocated while invoking that method. It does not include the Stackalloc/heap native allocations.

Adding configurations

Benchmark configuration can be defined by creating a custom class and inheriting it from the `ManualConfig` class. Here is an example of the `TestBenchmark` class that we created earlier containing some benchmark methods:

```
[Config(typeof(Config))]
public class TestBenchmark
{
  private class Config : ManualConfig
  {
    // We will benchmark ONLY method with names with names (which
    // contains "A" OR "1") AND (have length < 3)
    public Config()
    {
      Add(new DisjunctionFilter(
        new NameFilter(name => name.Contains("Recursive"))
      ));
    }
  }

  [Params(10,20,30)]
  public int Len { get; set; }
  [Benchmark]
  public  void Fibonacci()
  {
    int a = 0, b = 1, c = 0;
    Console.Write("{0} {1}", a, b);

    for (int i = 2; i < Len; i++)
    {
      c = a + b;
      Console.Write(" {0}", c);
      a = b;
      b = c;
    }
  }

  [Benchmark]
  public  void FibonacciRecursive()
  {
    Fibonacci_Recursive(0, 1, 1, Len);
  }

  private void Fibonacci_Recursive(int a, int b, int counter, int len)
  {
    if (counter <= len)
```

```
      {
        Console.Write("{0} ", a);
        Fibonacci_Recursive(b, a + b, counter + 1, len);
      }
    }
  }
```

In the preceding code, we defined the `Config` class that inherits the `ManualConfig` class provided in the benchmark framework. Rules can be defined inside the `Config` constructor. In the preceding example, there is a rule that stipulates that only those benchmark methods that contain `Recursive` should be executed. In our case, we have only one method, `FibonacciRecursive`, that will be executed and whose performance we will measure.

Another way of doing this is through the fluent API, where we can skip creating a `Config` class and implement the following:

```
static void Main(string[] args)
{
  var config = ManualConfig.Create(DefaultConfig.Instance);
  config.Add(new DisjunctionFilter(new NameFilter(
    name => name.Contains("Recursive"))));
  BenchmarkRunner.Run<TestBenchmark>(config);
}
```

To learn more about `BenchmarkDotNet`, refer to `http://benchmarkdotnet.org/Configs.htm`.

Summary

In this chapter, we have learned about the core concepts of .NET Core, including the compilation process, garbage collection, how to develop high-performant .NET Core applications by utilizing multiple cores of the CPU, and publishing an application using a release build. We have also explored the benchmarking tool, which is highly used for code optimization, and provides results specific to class objects.

3
Multithreading and Asynchronous Programming in .NET Core

Multithreading and asynchronous programming are two essential techniques that facilitate the development of highly scalable and performant applications. If the application is not responsive, it affects the user experience and increases the level of dissatisfaction. On the other hand, it also increases the resource usage on the server side, or where the application is running, and also increases the memory size and/or CPU usage. Nowadays, hardware is very cheap, and every machine comes with multiple CPU cores. Implementing multithreading and using asynchronous programming techniques not only increases the performance of the application, but also makes the application more responsive in nature.

This chapter examines the core concepts of multithreading and the asynchronous programming model to help you use them in your projects and increase the overall performance of your applications.

The following is a list of the topics that we will learn about in this chapter:

- Multithreading versus asynchronous programming
- Multithreading in .NET Core
- Threads in .NET Core
- Thread synchronization
- Task parallel library (TPL)
- Creating a task using TPL
- Task-based asynchronous pattern
- Design patterns for parallel programming

I/O bound operations are code that is dependent on external resources. Examples include accessing a filesystem, accessing a network, and so on.

Multithreading versus asynchronous programming

Multithreading and asynchronous programming, if properly implemented, improve the performance of an application. Multithreading refers to the practice of executing multiple threads at the same time to execute multiple operations or tasks in parallel. There could be one main thread and several background threads, usually known as worker threads, running in parallel at the same time, executing multiple tasks concurrently, whereas both synchronous and asynchronous operations can run on a single-threaded or a multithreaded environment.

In a single-threaded synchronous operation, there is only one thread that performs all the tasks in a defined sequence, and it executes them one after the other. In a single-threaded asynchronous operation, there is only one thread that executes the tasks, but it allocates a time slice in which to run each task. When the time slice is over, it saves the state of that task and starts executing the next one. Internally, the processor performs the context switching between each task and allocates a time slice in which to run them.

In a multithreaded synchronous operation, there are multiple threads that run the tasks in parallel. There is no context switching between the tasks, like we have in an asynchronous operation. One thread is responsible for executing the tasks assigned to it and then starting another task, whereas in a multithreaded asynchronous operation, multiple threads run multiple tasks and the task can be served and executed by single or multiple threads.

The following diagram depicts the differences between the single and multithreaded synchronous and asynchronous operations:

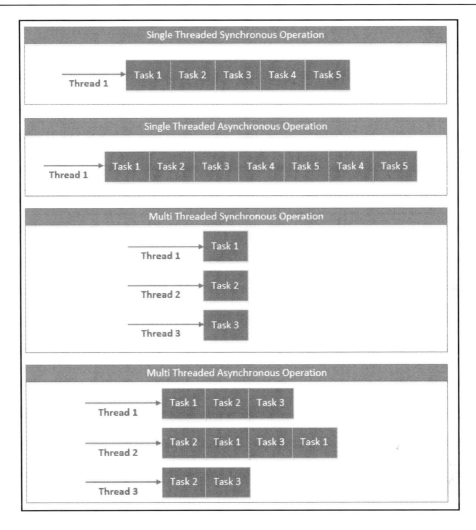

The preceding diagram shows four types of operations. In the single-threaded synchronous operation, we have one thread running five tasks sequentially. Once **Task 1** is completed, **Task 2** is executed, and so on. In the single-threaded asynchronous operation, we have a single thread, but each task will get a time slice to execute before the next task is executed and so on. Each task will be executed multiple times and resume from where it was paused. In the multi-threaded synchronous operation, we have three threads running three tasks **Task 1**, **Task 2**, and **Task 3** in parallel. Lastly, in the multithreaded asynchronous operation, we have three tasks—**Task 1**, **Task 2**, and **Task 3**—running by three threads, but each thread performs some context switching based on the time slice allocated to each task.

In asynchronous programming, it is not always the case that each asynchronous operation will be running on a new thread. Async/Await is a good example of a situation where there is no additional thread created. The *async* operation is executed in the current synchronization context of the main thread and queues the asynchronous operation executed in the allocated time slice.

Multithreading in .NET Core

There are many benefits in using multithreading in CPU and/or I/O-bound applications. It is often used for long-running processes that have a longer or infinite lifetime, working as background tasks, keeping the main thread available in order to manage or handle user requests. However, unnecessary use may completely degrade the application's performance. There are cases where creating too many threads is not a good architecture practice.

Here are some examples where multithreading is a good fit:

- I/O operations
- Running long-running background tasks
- Database operations
- Communicating over a network

Multithreading caveats

Although there are many benefits to multithreading, there are some caveats that need to be thoroughly addressed when writing multithreaded applications. If the machine is a single or two-core machine and the application is creating lots of threads, the context switching between these threads will slow the performance:

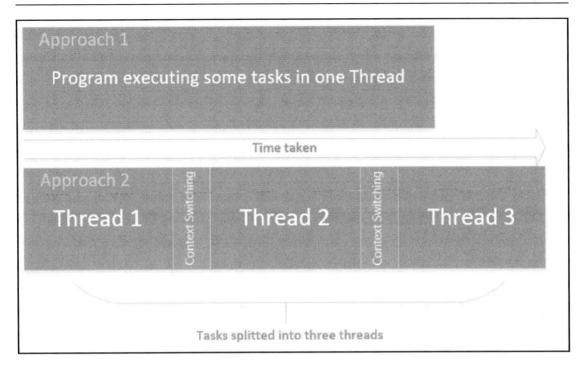

The preceding diagram depicts the program running on a single-processor machine. The first task executes synchronously, and runs comparatively faster than the three threads running on the single processor. The system executes the first thread, then waits for a while before moving on to execute the second thread, and so on. This adds an unnecessary overhead of switching between threads and, thus, delays the overall operation. In the field of threading, this is known as context switching. The boxes between each thread represent the delay occurring during each context switch between threads.

As far as the developer experience is concerned, debugging and testing are two other issues that are challenging for developers when creating a multithreaded application.

Threads in .NET Core

Every application in .NET starts with a single thread, which is the main thread. A thread is the basic unit that the operating system uses to allocate processor time. Each thread has a priority, exception handlers, and a data structure saved in its own thread context. If the exception is thrown, it is thrown inside the context of the thread and other threads are not affected by it. The thread context contains some low-level information about, for example, the CPU registers, the address space of the thread's host process, and so on.

If an application is running multiple threads on a single processor, each thread will be assigned a period of processor time and will be executed one after the other. The time slice is usually small, which makes it seem as if the threads are being executed at the same time. Once the allocated time is over, the processor moves to the other thread and the previous thread wait for the processor to become available again and execute it based on the time slice allocated. On the other hand, if the threads are running on multiple CPUs, then they may execute at the same time, but if there are other processes and threads running, the time slice will be allocated and executed accordingly.

Creating threads in .NET Core

In .NET Core, the threading API is the same as that used in the full .NET Framework version. A new thread can be created by creating a Thread class object and passing the ThreadStart or ParameterizedThreadStart delegate as a parameter. ThreadStart and ParameterizedThreadStart wrap a method that is invoked when the new thread is started. ParameterizedThreadStart is used for method containing parameters.

Here is a basic example that runs the ExecuteLongRunningOperation method on a separate thread:

```
static void Main(string[] args)
{
  new Thread(new ThreadStart(ExecuteLongRunningOperation)).Start();
}
static void ExecuteLongRunningOperation()
{
  Thread.Sleep(100000);
  Console.WriteLine("Operation completed successfully");
}
```

We can also pass parameters while starting the thread and use the ParameterizedThreadStart delegate:

```
static void Main(string[] args)
{
  new Thread(new ParameterizedThreadStart
  (ExecuteLongRunningOperation)).Start(100000);
}
static void ExecuteLongRunningOperation(object milliseconds)
{
  Thread.Sleep((int)milliseconds);
  Console.WriteLine("Operation completed successfully");
}
```

The `ParameterizedThreadStart` delegate takes an object as a parameter. So, if you want to pass multiple parameters, this can be done by creating a custom class and adding the following properties:

```
public interface IService
{
  string Name { get; set; }
  void Execute();
}

public class EmailService : IService
{
  public string Name { get; set; }
  public void Execute() => throw new NotImplementedException();

  public EmailService(string name)
  {
    this.Name = name;
  }
}

static void Main(string[] args)
{
  IService service = new EmailService("Email");
  new Thread(new ParameterizedThreadStart
  (RunBackgroundService)).Start(service);
}

static void RunBackgroundService(Object service)
{
  ((IService)service).Execute(); //Long running task
}
```

Every thread has a thread priority. When a thread is created, its priority is set to normal. The priority affects the execution of the thread. The higher the priority, the higher the precedence that will be given to the thread. The thread priority can be defined on the thread object, as follows:

```
static void RunBackgroundService(Object service)
{
  Thread.CurrentThread.Priority = ThreadPriority.Highest;
  ((IService)service).Execute(); //Long running task
}
```

`RunBackgroundService` is the method that executes in a separate thread, and the priority can be set by using the `ThreadPriority` enum and referencing the current thread object by calling `Thread.CurrentThread`, as shown in the preceding code snippet.

Thread lifetime

The lifetime of the thread depends on the method executing within that thread. Once the method is executed, CLR de-allocates the memory taken by the thread and disposes of. On the other hand, the thread can also be disposed of explicitly by calling the `Interrupt` or `Abort` methods.

Another very important factor to consider is exceptions. If the exceptions are not properly handled within a thread, they are propagated to the `calling` method and so on until they reach the `root` method in the call stack. When it reaches this point, CLR will shut down the thread if it is not handled.

For continuous or long-running threads, the shutdown process should be properly defined. One of the best approaches to smoothly shut down the thread is by using a `volatile bool` variable:

```
class Program
{

  static volatile bool isActive = true;
  static void Main(string[] args)
  {
    new Thread(new ParameterizedThreadStart
    (ExecuteLongRunningOperation)).Start(1000);
  }

  static void ExecuteLongRunningOperation(object milliseconds)
  {
    while (isActive)
    {
      //Do some other operation
      Console.WriteLine("Operation completed successfully");
    }
  }
}
```

In the preceding code, we have used the `volatile bool` variable `isActive`, that decides if the `while` loop execute or not.

The `volatile` keyword indicates that a field may be modified by multiple threads that are executing at the same time. Fields that are declared volatile are not subject to compiler optimizations that assume access by a single thread. This ensures that the most up-to-date value is present in the field at all times. To learn more about volatile, kindly refer the following URL:

https://docs.microsoft.com/en-us/dotnet/csharp/language-reference/keywords/volatile

The thread pool in .NET

CLR provides a separate thread pool that contains the list of threads to be used to execute tasks asynchronously. Each process has its own specific thread pool. CLR adds and removes threads in or from the thread pool.

To run a thread using `ThreadPool`, we can use `ThreadPool.QueueUserWorkItem`, as shown in the following code:

```
class Program
{
  static void Main(string[] args)
  {
    ThreadPool.QueueUserWorkItem(ExecuteLongRunningOperation, 1000);
    Console.Read();
  }
  static void ExecuteLongRunningOperation(object milliseconds)
  {

    Thread.Sleep((int)milliseconds);
    Console.WriteLine("Thread is executed");
  }
}
```

`QueueUserWorkItem` queues the task to be executed by the CLR in a thread that is available in the thread pool. The task queues are maintained in **First In, First Out (FIFO)** order. However, depending on the thread's availability and the task job itself, the task completion may be delayed.

Thread synchronization

In multithreaded applications, we have shared resources that are accessible by multiple threads executing simultaneously. The area where the resources are shared across multiple threads is known as the critical section. To protect these resources and provide thread-safe access, there are certain techniques that we will discuss in this section.

Let's take an example where we have a singleton class for logging a message into the filesystem. A singleton, by definition, denotes that there should only be one instance shared across multiple calls. Here is the basic implementation of a singleton pattern that is not thread-safe:

```
public class Logger
{
  static Logger _instance;

  private Logger() { }

  public Logger GetInstance()
  {
    _instance = (_instance == null ? new Logger() : _instance);
    return _instance;
  }

  public void LogMessage(string str)
  {
    //Log message into file system
  }

}
```

The preceding code is a lazy initialization singleton that creates an instance on the first call on the GetInstance method. GetInstance is the critical section and is not thread-safe. If multiple threads enter into the critical section, multiple instances will be created and the race condition will occur.

The race condition is a problem in multithreaded programming that occurs when the outcome depends on the timing of events. A race condition arises when two or more parallel tasks access a shared object.

To implement the thread-safe singleton, we can use a locking pattern. Locking ensures that only one thread can enter into the critical section, and if another thread attempts to enter, it will wait until the thread is released. Here is a modified version that enables a singleton to be thread-safe:

```
public class Logger
```

```
{

  private static object syncRoot = new object();
  static Logger _instance;

  private Logger() { }

  public Logger GetInstance()
  {
    if (_instance == null)
    {
      lock (syncRoot)
      {
        if (_instance == null)
        _instance = new Logger();
      }
    }
    return _instance;
  }

  public void LogMessage(string str)
  {
    //Log message into file system
  }
}
```

Monitors

Monitors are used to provide thread-safe access to the resource. It is applicable to multithread programming, where there are multiple threads that need access to a resource simultaneously. When multiple threads attempt to enter monitor to access any resource, CLR allows only one thread at a time to enter and the other threads are blocked. When the thread exits the monitor, the next waiting thread enters, and so on.

If we look into the Monitor class, all the methods such as Monitor.Enter and Monitor.Exit operate on object references. Similarly to lock, Monitor also provides gated access to the resource; however, a developer will have greater control in terms of the API it provides.

Here is a basic example of using Monitor in .NET Core:

```
public class Job
{

  int _jobDone;
```

```
object _lock = new object();

public void IncrementJobCounter(int number)
{
  Monitor.Enter(_lock);
  // access to this field is synchronous
  _jobDone += number;
  Monitor.Exit(_lock);
}

}
```

The preceding code snippet represents a job process where multiple threads are working on certain tasks. When the task completes, they call the IncrementJobCounter method to increment the _jobDone counter.

There are certain cases where the critical section has to wait for the resources to be available. Once they are available, we want to pulse the waiting block to execute.

To help us understand, let's take an example of a running Job whose task is to run the jobs added by multiple threads. If no job is present, it should wait for the threads to push and start executing them immediately.

In this example, we will create a JobExecutor class that runs in a separate thread. Here is the code snippet of JobExecutor:

```
public class JobExecutor
{
  const int _waitTimeInMillis = 10 * 60 * 1000;
  private ArrayList _jobs = null;
  private static JobExecutor _instance = null;
  private static object _syncRoot = new object();
  //Singleton implementation of JobExecutor
  public static JobExecutor Instance
  {
    get{
    lock (_syncRoot)
    {
      if (_instance == null)
      _instance = new JobExecutor();
    }
    return _instance;
  }
}

private JobExecutor()
{
```

```
  IsIdle = true;
  IsAlive = true;
  _jobs = new ArrayList();
}
private Boolean IsIdle { get; set; }
public Boolean IsAlive { get; set; }

//Callers can use this method to add list of jobs
public void AddJobItems(List<Job> jobList)
{
  //Added lock to provide synchronous access.
  //Alternatively we can also use Monitor.Enter and Monitor.Exit
  lock (_jobs)
  {
    foreach (Job job in jobList)
    {
      _jobs.Add(job);
    }
    //Release the waiting thread to start executing the //jobs
    Monitor.PulseAll(_jobs);
  }
}
/*Check for jobs count and if the count is 0, then wait for 10 minutes by
calling Monitor.Wait. Meanwhile, if new jobs are added to the list,
Monitor.PulseAll will be called that releases the waiting thread. Once the
waiting is over it checks the count of jobs and if the jobs are there in
the list, start executing. Otherwise, wait for the new jobs */
public void CheckandExecuteJobBatch()
{
  lock (_jobs)
  {
    while (IsAlive)
    {
      if (_jobs == null || _jobs.Count <= 0)
      {
        IsIdle = true;
        Console.WriteLine("Now waiting for new jobs");
        //Waiting for 10 minutes
        Monitor.Wait(_jobs, _waitTimeInMillis);
      }
      else
      {
        IsIdle = false;
        ExecuteJob();
      }
    }
  }
}
```

```
//Execute the job
private void ExecuteJob()
{
  for(int i=0;i< _jobs.Count;i++)
  {
    Job job = (Job)_jobs[i];
    //Execute the job;
    job.DoSomething();
    //Remove the Job from the Jobs list
    _jobs.Remove(job);
    i--;
  }
}
}
```

It's a singleton class, and other threads can access the JobExecutor instance using the static Instance property and call the AddJobsItems method to add the list of jobs to be executed. The CheckandExecuteJobBatch method runs continuously and checks for new jobs in the list every 10 minutes. Or, if it is interrupted by the AddJobsItems method by calling the Monitor.PulseAll method, it will immediately move to the while statement and check for the items count. If the items are present, the CheckandExecuteJobBatch method calls the ExecuteJob method that runs that job.

Here is the code snippet of the Job class containing two properties, namely JobID and JobName, and the DoSomething method that will print the JobID on the console:

```
public class Job
{
  // Properties to set and get Job ID and Name
  public int JobID { get; set; }
  public string JobName { get; set; }
  //Do some task based on Job ID as set through the JobID
  //property
  public void DoSomething()
  {
    //Do some task based on Job ID
    Console.WriteLine("Executed job " + JobID);
  }
}
```

Finally, on the main Program class, we can invoke three worker threads and one thread for JobExecutor, as shown in the following code:

```
class Program
{
  static void Main(string[] args)
```

```
{
  Thread jobThread = new Thread(new ThreadStart(ExecuteJobExecutor));
  jobThread.Start();

  //Starting three Threads add jobs time to time;
  Thread thread1 = new Thread(new ThreadStart(ExecuteThread1));
  Thread thread2 = new Thread(new ThreadStart(ExecuteThread2));
  Thread thread3 = new Thread(new ThreadStart(ExecuteThread3));
  Thread1.Start();
  Thread2.Start();
  thread3.Start();

  Console.Read();
}
//Implementation of ExecuteThread 1 that is adding three
//jobs in the list and calling AddJobItems of a singleton
//JobExecutor instance
private static void ExecuteThread1()
{
  Thread.Sleep(5000);
  List<Job> jobs = new List<Job>();
  jobs.Add(new Job() { JobID = 11, JobName = "Thread 1 Job 1" });
  jobs.Add(new Job() { JobID = 12, JobName = "Thread 1 Job 2" });
  jobs.Add(new Job() { JobID = 13, JobName = "Thread 1 Job 3" });
  JobExecutor.Instance.AddJobItems(jobs);
}

//Implementation of ExecuteThread2 method that is also adding
//three jobs and calling AddJobItems method of singleton
//JobExecutor instance
private static void ExecuteThread2()
{
  Thread.Sleep(5000);
  List<Job> jobs = new List<Job>();
  jobs.Add(new Job() { JobID = 21, JobName = "Thread 2 Job 1" });
  jobs.Add(new Job() { JobID = 22, JobName = "Thread 2 Job 2" });
  jobs.Add(new Job() { JobID = 23, JobName = "Thread 2 Job 3" });
  JobExecutor.Instance.AddJobItems(jobs);
}

//Implementation of ExecuteThread3 method that is again
// adding 3 jobs instances into the list and
//calling AddJobItems to add those items into the list to execute
private static void ExecuteThread3()
{
  Thread.Sleep(5000);
  List<Job> jobs = new List<Job>();
  jobs.Add(new Job() { JobID = 31, JobName = "Thread 3 Job 1" });
```

```
    jobs.Add(new Job() { JobID = 32, JobName = "Thread 3 Job 2" });
    jobs.Add(new Job() { JobID = 33, JobName = "Thread 3 Job 3" });
    JobExecutor.Instance.AddJobItems(jobs);
}

//Implementation of ExecuteJobExecutor that calls the
//CheckAndExecuteJobBatch to run the jobs
public static void ExecuteJobExecutor()
{
    JobExecutor.Instance.IsAlive = true;
    JobExecutor.Instance.CheckandExecuteJobBatch();
}
}
```

The following is the output of running this code:

```
C:\WINDOWS\system32\cmd.exe
Now waiting for new jobs
Executed job 21
Executed job 22
Executed job 23
Executed job 11
Executed job 12
Executed job 13
Now waiting for new jobs
Executed job 31
Executed job 32
Executed job 33
Now waiting for new jobs
```

Task parallel library (TPL)

So far, we have learned some core concepts about multithreading, and have used threads to perform multiple tasks. Compared to the classic threading model in .NET, TPL minimizes the complexity of using threads and provides an abstraction through a set of APIs that helps developers to focus more on the application program instead of focusing on how the threads will be provisioned, as well as other things.

There are several benefits of using TPL over threads:

- It autoscales the concurrency to a multicore level
- It autoscales LINQ queries to a multicore level
- It handles the partitioning of the work and uses `ThreadPool` where required
- It is easy to use and reduces the complexity of working with threads directly

Creating a task using TPL

TPL APIs are available in the `System.Threading` and `System.Threading.Tasks` namespaces. They work around the task, which is a program or a block of code that runs asynchronously. An asynchronous task can be run by calling either the `Task.Run` or `TaskFactory.StartNew` methods. When we create a task, we provide a named delegate, anonymous method, or a lambda expression that the task executes.

Here is a code snippet that uses a lambda expression to execute the `ExecuteLongRunningTasks`method using `Task.Run`:

```
class Program
{
  static void Main(string[] args)
  {
    Task t = Task.Run(()=>ExecuteLongRunningTask(5000));
    t.Wait();
  }

  public static void ExecuteLongRunningTask(int millis)
  {
    Thread.Sleep(millis);
    Console.WriteLine("Hello World");
  }
}
```

In the preceding code snippet, we have executed the `ExecuteLongRunningTask` method asynchronously using the `Task.Run` method. The `Task.Run` method returns the `Task` object that can be used to further wait for the asynchronous piece of code to be executed completely before the program ends. To wait for the task, we have used the `Wait` method.

Alternatively, we can also use the `Task.Factory.StartNew` method, which is more advanced and provides more options. While calling the `Task.Factory.StartNew` method, we can specify `CancellationToken`, `TaskCreationOptions`, and `TaskScheduler` to set the state, specify other options, and schedule tasks.

TPL uses multiple cores of the CPU out of the box. When the task is executed using the TPL API, it automatically splits the task into one or more threads and utilizes multiple processors, if they are available. The decision as to how many threads will be created is calculated at runtime by CLR. Whereas a thread only has an affinity to a single processor, running any task on multiple processors needs a proper manual implementation.

Task-based asynchronous pattern (TAP)

When developing any software, it is always good to implement the best practices while designing its architecture. The task-based asynchronous pattern is one of the recommended patterns that can be used when working with TPL. There are, however, a few things to bear in mind while implementing TAP.

Naming convention

The method executing asynchronously should have the naming suffix `Async`. For example, if the method name starts with `ExecuteLongRunningOperation`, it should have the suffix `Async`, with the resulting name of `ExecuteLongRunningOperationAsync`.

Return type

The method signature should return either a `System.Threading.Tasks.Task` or `System.Threading.Tasks.Task<TResult>`. The task's return type is equivalent to the method that returns `void`, whereas `TResult` is the data type.

Parameters

The `out` and `ref` parameters are not allowed as parameters in the method signature. If multiple values need to be returned, tuples or a custom data structure can be used. The method should always return `Task` or `Task<TResult>`, as discussed previously.

Here are a few signatures for both synchronous and asynchronous methods:

Synchronous method	Asynchronous method
`Void Execute();`	`Task ExecuteAsync();`
`List<string> GetCountries();`	`Task<List<string>> GetCountriesAsync();`
`Tuple<int, string> GetState(int stateID);`	`Task<Tuple<int, string>> GetStateAsync(int stateID);`
`Person GetPerson(int personID);`	`Task<Person> GetPersonAsync(int personID);`

Exceptions

The asynchronous method should always throw exceptions that are assigned to the returning task. However, the usage errors, such as passing null parameters to the asynchronous method, should be properly handled.

Let's suppose we want to generate several documents dynamically based on a predefined templates list, where each template populates the placeholders with dynamic values and writes it on the filesystem. We assume that this operation will take a sufficient amount of time to generate a document for each template. Here is a code snippet showing how the exceptions can be handled:

```
static void Main(string[] args)
{
  List<Template> templates = GetTemplates();
  IEnumerable<Task> asyncDocs = from template in templates select
  GenerateDocumentAsync(template);
  try
  {
    Task.WaitAll(asyncDocs.ToArray());

  }catch(Exception ex)
  {
    Console.WriteLine(ex);
  }
  Console.Read();
}

private static async Task<int> GenerateDocumentAsync(Template template)
{
  //To automate long running operation
  Thread.Sleep(3000);
  //Throwing exception intentionally
  throw new Exception();
}
```

In the preceding code, we have a `GenerateDocumentAsync` method that performs a long running operation, such as reading the template from the database, populating placeholders, and writing a document to the filesystem. To automate this process, we used `Thread.Sleep` to sleep the thread for three seconds and then throw an exception that will be propagated to the calling method. The `Main` method loops the templates list and calls the `GenerateDocumentAsync` method for each template. Each `GenerateDocumentAsync` method returns a task. When calling an asynchronous method, the exception is actually hidden until the `Wait`, `WaitAll`, `WhenAll`, and other methods are called. In the preceding example, the exception will be thrown once the `Task.WaitAll` method is called, and will log the exception on the console.

Task status

The task object provides a `TaskStatus` that is used to know whether the task is executing the method running, has completed the method, has encountered a fault, or whether some other occurrence has taken place. The task initialized using `Task.Run` initially has the status of `Created`, but when the `Start` method is called, its status is changed to `Running`. When applying the TAP pattern, all the methods return the `Task` object, and whether they are using the `Task.Run` inside, the method body should be activated. That means that the status should be anything other than `Created`. The TAP pattern ensures the consumer that the task is activated and the starting task is not required.

Task cancellation

Cancellation is an optional thing for TAP-based asynchronous methods. If the method accepts the `CancellationToken` as the parameter, it can be used by the caller party to cancel a task. However, for a TAP, the cancellation should be properly handled. Here is a basic example showing how cancellation can be implemented:

```
static void Main(string[] args)
{
  CancellationTokenSource tokenSource = new CancellationTokenSource();
  CancellationToken token = tokenSource.Token;
  Task.Factory.StartNew(() => SaveFileAsync(path, bytes, token));
}

static Task<int> SaveFileAsync(string path, byte[] fileBytes,
CancellationToken cancellationToken)
{
  if (cancellationToken.IsCancellationRequested)
  {
    Console.WriteLine("Cancellation is requested...");
    cancellationToken.ThrowIfCancellationRequested
```

```
    }
    //Do some file save operation
    File.WriteAllBytes(path, fileBytes);
    return Task.FromResult<int>(0);
}
```

In the preceding code, we have a `SaveFileAsync` method that takes the `byte` array and the `CancellationToken` as parameters. In the `Main` method, we initialize the `CancellationTokenSource` that can be used to cancel the asynchronous operation later in the program. To test the cancellation scenario, we will just call the `Cancel` method of the `tokenSource` after the `Task.Factory.StartNew` method and the operation will be canceled. Moreover, when the task is canceled, its status is set to `Cancelled` and the `IsCompleted` property is set to `true`.

Task progress reporting

With TPL, we can use the `IProgress<T>` interface to get real-time progress notifications from the asynchronous operations. This can be used in scenarios where we need to update the user interface or the console app of asynchronous operations. When defining the TAP-based asynchronous methods, defining `IProgress<T>` in a parameter is optional. We can have overloaded methods that can help consumers to use in the case of specific needs. However, they should only be used if the asynchronous method supports them. Here is the modified version of `SaveFileAsync` that updates the user about the real progress:

```
static void Main(string[] args)
{
  var progressHandler = new Progress<string>(value =>
  {
    Console.WriteLine(value);
  });

  var progress = progressHandler as IProgress<string>;

  CancellationTokenSource tokenSource = new CancellationTokenSource();
  CancellationToken token = tokenSource.Token;

  Task.Factory.StartNew(() => SaveFileAsync(path, bytes,
  token, progress));
  Console.Read();

}
static Task<int> SaveFileAsync(string path, byte[] fileBytes,
CancellationToken cancellationToken, IProgress<string> progress)
{
  if (cancellationToken.IsCancellationRequested)
```

```
  {
    progress.Report("Cancellation is called");
    Console.WriteLine("Cancellation is requested...");
  }

  progress.Report("Saving File");
  File.WriteAllBytes(path, fileBytes);
  progress.Report("File Saved");
  return Task.FromResult<int>(0);


}
```

Implementing TAP using compilers

Any method that is attributed with the `async` keyword (for C#) or `Async` for (Visual Basic) is called an asynchronous method. The `async` keyword can be applied to a method, anonymous method, or a Lambda expression, and the language compiler can execute that task asynchronously.

Here is a simple implementation of the TAP method using the compiler approach:

```
static void Main(string[] args)
{
  var t = ExecuteLongRunningOperationAsync(100000);
  Console.WriteLine("Called ExecuteLongRunningOperationAsync method,
  now waiting for it to complete");
  t.Wait();
  Console.Read();
}

public static async Task<int> ExecuteLongRunningOperationAsync(int millis)
{
  Task t = Task.Factory.StartNew(() => RunLoopAsync(millis));
  await t;
  Console.WriteLine("Executed RunLoopAsync method");
  return 0;
}

public static void RunLoopAsync(int millis)
{
  Console.WriteLine("Inside RunLoopAsync method");
  for(int i=0;i< millis; i++)
  {
```

```
        Debug.WriteLine($"Counter = {i}");
    }
    Console.WriteLine("Exiting RunLoopAsync method");
}
```

In the preceding code, we have the `ExecuteLongRunningOperationAsync` method, which is implemented as per the compiler approach. It calls the `RunLoopAsync` that executes a loop for a certain number of milliseconds that is passed in the parameter. The `async` keyword on the `ExecuteLongRunningOperationAsync` method actually tells the compiler that this method has to be executed asynchronously, and, once the `await` statement is reached, the method returns to the `Main` method that writes the line on a console and waits for the task to be completed. Once the `RunLoopAsync` is executed, the control comes back to `await` and starts executing the next statements in the `ExecuteLongRunningOperationAsync` method.

Implementing TAP with greater control over Task

As we know, that the TPL is centered on the `Task` and `Task<TResult>` objects. We can execute an asynchronous task by calling the `Task.Run` method and execute a `delegate` method or a block of code asynchronously and use `Wait` or other methods on that task. However, this approach is not always adequate, and there are scenarios where we may have different approaches to executing asynchronous operations, and we may use an **Event-based Asynchronous Pattern (EAP)** or an **Asynchronous Programming Model (APM)**. To implement TAP principles here, and to get the same control over asynchronous operations executing with different models, we can use the `TaskCompletionSource<TResult>` object.

The `TaskCompletionSource<TResult>` object is used to create a task that executes an asynchronous operation. When the asynchronous operation completes, we can use the `TaskCompletionSource<TResult>` object to set the result, exception, or state of the task.

Here is a basic example that executes the `ExecuteTask` method that returns `Task`, where the `ExecuteTask` method uses the `TaskCompletionSource<TResult>` object to wrap the response as a `Task` and executes the `ExecuteLongRunningTask` through the `Task.StartNew` method:

```
static void Main(string[] args)
{
    var t = ExecuteTask();
    t.Wait();
    Console.Read();
```

```
  }

public static Task<int> ExecuteTask()
{
  var tcs = new TaskCompletionSource<int>();
  Task<int> t1 = tcs.Task;
  Task.Factory.StartNew(() =>
  {
    try
    {
      ExecuteLongRunningTask(10000);
      tcs.SetResult(1);
    }catch(Exception ex)
    {
      tcs.SetException(ex);
    }
  });
  return tcs.Task;

}

public static void ExecuteLongRunningTask(int millis)
{
  Thread.Sleep(millis);
  Console.WriteLine("Executed");
}
```

Design patterns for parallel programming

There are various ways in which the tasks can be designed to run in parallel. In this section, we will learn some top design patterns used in TPL:

- Pipeline pattern
- Dataflow pattern
- Producer-consumer pattern
- Parallel.ForEach
- Parallel LINQ (PLINQ)

Pipeline pattern

The pipeline pattern is commonly used in scenarios where we need to execute the asynchronous tasks in sequence:

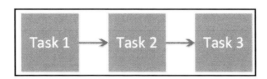

Consider a task where we need to create a user record first, then initiate a workflow and send an email. To implement this scenario, we can use the `ContinueWith` method of TPL. Here is a complete example:

```
static void Main(string[] args)
{

  Task<int> t1 = Task.Factory.StartNew(() =>
  { return CreateUser(); });

  var t2=t1.ContinueWith((antecedent) =>
  { return InitiateWorkflow(antecedent.Result); });
  var t3 = t2.ContinueWith((antecedant) =>
  { return SendEmail(antecedant.Result); });

  Console.Read();


}

public static int CreateUser()
{
  //Create user, passing hardcoded user ID as 1
  Thread.Sleep(1000);
  Console.WriteLine("User created");
  return 1;
}

public static int InitiateWorkflow(int userId)
{
  //Initiate Workflow
  Thread.Sleep(1000);
  Console.WriteLine("Workflow initiates");

  return userId;
}
```

```
public static int SendEmail(int userId)
{
  //Send email
  Thread.Sleep(1000);
  Console.WriteLine("Email sent");

  return userId;
}
```

Dataflow pattern

The dataflow pattern is a generalized pattern with a one-to-many and a many-to-one relationship. For example, the following diagram represents two tasks, **Task 1** and **Task 2**, that execute in parallel, and a third task, **Task 3**, that will only start when both of the first two tasks are completed. Once **Task 3** is completed, **Task 4** and **Task 5** will be executed in parallel:

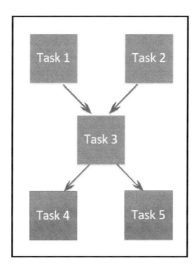

We can implement the preceding example using the following code:

```
static void Main(string[] args)
{
  //Creating two tasks t1 and t2 and starting them at the same //time
  Task<int> t1 = Task.Factory.StartNew(() => { return Task1(); });
  Task<int> t2 = Task.Factory.StartNew(() => { return Task2(); });

  //Creating task 3 and used ContinueWhenAll that runs when both the
  //tasks T1 and T2 will be completed
  Task<int> t3 = Task.Factory.ContinueWhenAll(
  new[] { t1, t2 }, (tasks) => { return Task3(); });

  //Task 4 and Task 5 will be started when Task 3 will be completed.
  //ContinueWith actually creates a continuation of executing tasks
  //T4 and T5 asynchronously when the task T3 is completed
  Task<int> t4 = t3.ContinueWith((antecendent) => { return Task4(); });
  Task<int> t5 = t3.ContinueWith((antecendent) => { return Task5(); });
  Console.Read();
}
//Implementation of Task1
public static int Task1()
{
  Thread.Sleep(1000);
  Console.WriteLine("Task 1 is executed");
  return 1;
}

//Implementation of Task2
public static int Task2()
{
  Thread.Sleep(1000);
  Console.WriteLine("Task 2 is executed");
  return 1;
}
//Implementation of Task3
public static int Task3()
{
  Thread.Sleep(1000);
  Console.WriteLine("Task 3 is executed");
  return 1;
}
Implementation of Task4
public static int Task4()
{
  Thread.Sleep(1000);
  Console.WriteLine("Task 4 is executed");
  return 1;
```

```
    }

    //Implementation of Task5
    public static int Task5()
    {
        Thread.Sleep(1000);
        Console.WriteLine("Task 5 is executed");
        return 1;
    }
```

Producer/consumer pattern

One of the best patterns to execute long-running operations is the producer/consumer pattern. In this pattern, there are producers and consumers, and one or more producers are connected to one or more consumers through a shared data structure known as BlockingCollection. BlockingCollection is a fixed-sized collection used in parallel programming. If the collection is full, the producers are blocked, and if the collection is empty, no more consumers should be added:

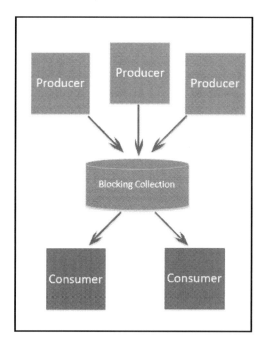

In a real-world example, the producer could be a component reading images from a database and the consumer could be a component that processes that image and saves it into a filesystem:

```
static void Main(string[] args)
{
    int maxColl = 10;
    var blockingCollection = new BlockingCollection<int>(maxColl);
    var taskFactory = new TaskFactory(TaskCreationOptions.LongRunning,
    TaskContinuationOptions.None);

    Task producer = taskFactory.StartNew(() =>
    {
        if (blockingCollection.Count <= maxColl)
        {
            int imageID = ReadImageFromDB();
            blockingCollection.Add(imageID);
            blockingCollection.CompleteAdding();
        }
    });


    Task consumer = taskFactory.StartNew(() =>
    {
        while (!blockingCollection.IsCompleted)
        {
            try
            {
                int imageID = blockingCollection.Take();
                ProcessImage(imageID);
            }
            catch (Exception ex)
            {
                //Log exception
            }
        }
    });

    Console.Read();

}

public static int ReadImageFromDB()
{
    Thread.Sleep(1000);
    Console.WriteLine("Image is read");
    return 1;
}
```

```
public static void ProcessImage(int imageID)
{
  Thread.Sleep(1000);
  Console.WriteLine("Image is processed");
}
```

In the preceding example, we initialized the generic `BlockingCollection<int>` to store the `imageID` that will be added by the producer and processed through the consumer. We set the maximum size of the collection to 10. Then, we added a `Producer` item that reads the image from a database and calls the `Add` method to add the `imageID` in the blocking collection, which can be further picked up and processed by the consumer. The consumer task just checks any available item in the collection and processes it.

 To learn more about the data structures available for parallel programming, please refer to `https://docs.microsoft.com/en-us/dotnet/standard/parallel-programming/data-structures-for-parallel-programming`.

Parallel.ForEach

The `Parallel.ForEach` is a multithreaded version of the classic `foreach` loop. The `foreach` loop runs on a single thread, whereas the `Parallel.ForEach` runs on multiple threads and utilizes multiple cores of the CPU, if available.

Here is a basic example using `Parallel.ForEach` on a list of documents that needs to be processed, and which contains an I/O-bound operation:

```
static void Main(string[] args)
{
  List<Document> docs = GetUserDocuments();
  Parallel.ForEach(docs, (doc) =>
  {
    ManageDocument(doc);
  });
}
private static void ManageDocument(Document doc) => Thread.Sleep(1000);
```

To replicate the I/O-bound operation, we just added a delay of 1 second to the `ManageDocument` method. If you execute the same method using the `foreach` loop, the difference will be obvious.

Parallel LINQ (PLINQ)

Parallel LINQ is a version of LINQ that executes queries in parallel on multi-core CPUs. It contains the full set of standard LINQ query operators plus some additional operators for parallel operations. It is highly advisable that you use this for long-running tasks, although incorrect use may slow down the performance of your app. Parallel LINQ operates on collections such as `List`, `List<T>`, `IEnumerable`, `IEnumerable<T>` and so on. Under the hood, it splits the list into segments and runs each segment on a different processor of the CPU.

Here is a modified version of the previous example, with `Parallel.ForEach` instead of the PLINQ operation:

```
static void Main(string[] args)
{
    List<Document> docs = GetUserDocuments();

    var query = from doc in docs.AsParallel()
    select ManageDocument(doc);
}

private static Document ManageDocument(Document doc)
{
    Thread.Sleep(1000);
    return doc;
}
```

Summary

In this chapter, we have learned about the core fundamentals of multithreaded and asynchronous programming. The chapter starts with the basic differences between both and walks you through some core concepts about multithreading, what APIs there are available, and how to write multithreading applications. We also looked at how the task-programming library can be used to serve asynchronous operations and how to implement the task asynchronous pattern. Finally, we explored parallel programming techniques and some of the best design patterns that are used for these techniques.

4
Securing and Implementing Resilience in .NET Core Applications

Security and resilience are two important aspects that should be considered when developing applications of any scale. Security protects an application's secrets, performs authentication, and provides authorized access to secure content, whereas resiliency embraces the application if it fails so that it can degrade gracefully. Resiliency makes an application highly available and allows the application to function properly at the time when an error occurs or when it is in a faulty state. It is widely used with the microservices architecture, where an application is decomposed into multiple services and each service communicates with other services to perform an operation.

There are various techniques and libraries available in .NET Core that we can use to implement security and resiliency. In ASP.NET Core applications, we can use Identity to implement user authentication/authorization, a popular Polly framework to implement patterns such as circuit breaker, the retry pattern, and others.

In this chapter, we will look at the following topics:

- Introduction to resilient applications
- Implementing health checks to monitor application performance
- Implementing the retry pattern in ASP.NET Core applications to retry operations on transient faults
- Implementing circuit breaker patterns to prevent calls that are likely to fail
- Protecting ASP.NET Core applications and enabling authentication and authorization using the Identity framework
- Using safe storage to store application secrets

Introduction to resilient applications

Developing applications with resiliency as an important factor always makes your customers happy. Today, applications are distributed by nature and involve lots of communication over the wire. Problems arise when the service is down or not responding on time due to network failure, which eventually leads to a delay before the client operation is terminated. The purpose of resiliency is to make your application recover from a failure and make it responsive again.

Complexity increases when you call one service and that service calls another service, and so on. In a long chain of operations, considering resiliency is important. This is the reason it is one of the most widely adopted principles in microservice architecture.

Resilient policies

Resilient policies are classified into two categories:

- Reactive policies
- Proactive policies

In this chapter, we will implement both reactive and proactive policies using the Polly framework, which can be used with .NET Core applications.

Reactive policies

According to the reactive policy, we should instantly retry the service request if the request fails on its first attempt. To implement the reactive policy, we can use the following patterns:

- **Retry**: Retries immediately when the request fails
- **Circuit breaker**: Stops all requests to a service in a faulted state
- **Fallback**: Returns a default response if the service is in a faulted state

Implementing the retry pattern

The retry pattern is used to retry the faulted service a number of times in order to get a response. It is widely used in scenarios involving intercommunication between services, where one service is dependent on another service to perform a particular operation. Transient faults occur when services are hosted separately and communicate over the wire, most likely over a HTTP protocol.

The following diagram represents two services: a user registration service that registers and save the user's record in a database, and email service to send a confirmation email to the user so that they can activate their account. Suppose an email service does not respond. This will return some sort of error, and if a retry pattern is implemented, it will retry the request the number of times it has been implemented to do so and will call the email service if it fails:

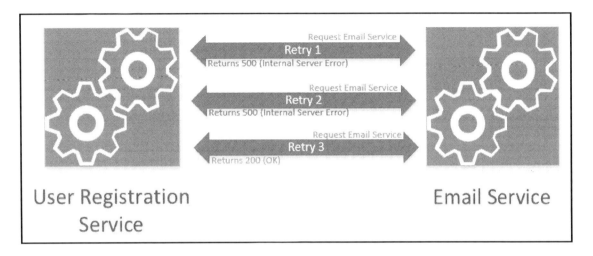

The **User Registration Service** and the **Email Service** are ASP.NET Core Web API projects where user registration implements the retry pattern. We will use the Polly framework by adding it as a NuGet package in the user registration service. To add Polly, we can execute the following command from the NuGet package manager console window in Visual Studio:

```
Install-Package Polly
```

The Polly framework is based on policies. You can define policies that contain specific configurations related to the pattern you are implementing and then invoke that policy by calling its ExecuteAsync method.

Here is the `UserController` which contains a POST method that implements a retry pattern to invoke the email service:

```
[Route("api/[controller]")]
public class UserController : Controller
{

  HttpClient _client;
  public UserController(HttpClient client)
  {
    _client = client;
  }
  // POST api/values
  [HttpPost]
  public void Post([FromBody]User user)
  {
    //Email service URL
    string emailService = "http://localhost:80/api/Email";

    //Serialize user object into JSON string
    HttpContent content = new
StringContent(JsonConvert.SerializeObject(user));

    //Setting Content-Type to application/json
    _client.DefaultRequestHeaders
    .Accept
    .Add(new MediaTypeWithQualityHeaderValue("application/json"));


    int maxRetries = 3;

    //Define Retry policy and set max retries limit and duration between
each retry to 3 seconds
    var retryPolicy =
Policy.Handle<HttpRequestException>().WaitAndRetryAsync(
    maxRetries, sleepDuration=> TimeSpan.FromSeconds(3));


    //Call service and wrap HttpClient PostAsync into retry policy
    retryPolicy.ExecuteAsync(async () => {
      var response = _client.PostAsync(emailService, content).Result;
      response.EnsureSuccessStatusCode();
    });
  }
}
```

In the preceding code, we have used the `HttpClient` class to make a RESTful request to the email service API. The `HTTP POST` method receives a user object that contains the following five properties:

```
public class User
{
  public string FirstName { get; set; }
  public string LastName { get; set; }
  public string EmailAddress { get; set; }
  public string UserName { get; set; }
  public string Password { get; set; }
}
```

Since the request will be sent in JSON format, we have to set the `Content-Type` header value to `application/json`. Then, we have to define the retry policy to wait and retry the operation every three seconds, with the maximum amount of retries being three. Finally, we call the `ExecuteAsync` method to invoke the `client.PostAsync` method so that it calls the email service.

After running the preceding example, if the email service is down or throws an exception, it will be retried three times to try and get the required response.

Implementing circuit breaker

Implementing the retry pattern is a good practice when calling services that are communicating over a network. However, the calling mechanism itself takes resources and bandwidth to execute the operation and delay the response. If the services are already in a faulted state, it is not always a good practice to retry it multiple times for every request. This is where circuit breaker plays its role.

Circuit breaker works in three states, as shown in the following diagram:

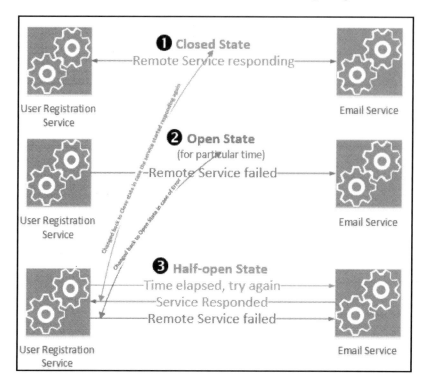

Initially, the circuit breaker is in a **Closed State**, which means the communication between services are working and the target remote service is responding. If the target remote service fails, the circuit breaker changes to **Open State**. When the state becomes open, then all subsequent requests cannot invoke the target remote service for a particular, specified time, and directly returns the response to the caller. Once the time elapses, the circuit turns to **Half-open State** and tries to invoke the target remote service to get the response. If the response is received successfully, the circuit breaker changes back to **Closed State**, or if it fails, the state changes back to closed and remains closed for the time specified in the configuration.

To implement the circuit breaker pattern, we will use the same Polly framework, which you can add from the NuGet package. We can add the circuit breaker policy as follows:

```
var circuitBreakerPolicy = Policy.HandleResult<HttpResponseMessage>(result
=> !result.IsSuccessStatusCode)
   .CircuitBreakerAsync(3, TimeSpan.FromSeconds(10), OnBreak, OnReset,
OnHalfOpen);
```

Add the preceding circuit breaker policy inside the `ConfigureServices` method in the `Startup` class. The reason for defining it in the `Startup` class is to inject the circuit breaker object as a singleton object through **Dependency Injection (DI)**. Therefore, all requests will share the same instance and the state will be maintained properly.

While defining the circuit breaker policy, we set the number of events allowed before breaking the circuit as three, which checks how many times the request has failed and breaks the circuit once it reaches the threshold value of three. It will keep the circuit break *Open* for 10 seconds and then change the state to *Half-Open* when the first request comes in after the time has elapsed.

Finally, if the remote service is still failing ,the circuit state changes to the *Open* state again; otherwise, it is set as *Close*. We have also defined `OnBreak`, `OnReset`, and `OnHalfOpen` delegates that are invoked when the circuit state changes. We can log this information somewhere in the database or file system if required. Add these delegate methods in the `Startup` class:

```
private void OnBreak(DelegateResult<HttpResponseMessage> responseMessage,
TimeSpan timeSpan)
{
  //Log to file system
}
private void OnReset()
{
  //log to file system
}
private void OnHalfOpen()
{
  // log to file system
}
```

Now, we will add the `circuitBreakerPolicy` and `HttpClient` objects using DI in the `ConfigureServices` method in the `Startup` class:

```
services.AddSingleton<HttpClient>();
services.AddSingleton<CircuitBreakerPolicy<HttpResponseMessage>>(circuitBre
akerPolgicy);
```

Here is our `UserController` that takes the `HttpClient` and `CircuitBreakerPolicy` object in the parameterized constructor:

```
public class UserController : Controller
{
  HttpClient _client;
  CircuitBreakerPolicy<HttpResponseMessage> _circuitBreakerPolicy;
  public UserController(HttpClient client,
  CircuitBreakerPolicy<HttpResponseMessage> circuitBreakerPolicy)
  {
    _client = client;
    _circuitBreakerPolicy = circuitBreakerPolicy;
  }
}
```

And this is the `HTTP POST` method that uses the circuit breaker policy and invokes the email service:

```
// POST api/values
[HttpPost]
public async Task<IActionResult> Post([FromBody]User user)
{

  //Email service URL
  string emailService = "http://localhost:80/api/Email";

  //Serialize user object into JSON string
  HttpContent content = new
StringContent(JsonConvert.SerializeObject(user));

  //Setting Content-Type to application/json
  _client.DefaultRequestHeaders
  .Accept
  .Add(new MediaTypeWithQualityHeaderValue("application/json"));

  //Execute operation using circuit breaker
  HttpResponseMessage response = await
_circuitBreakerPolicy.ExecuteAsync(() =>
  _client.PostAsync(emailService, content));

  //Check if response status code is success
  if (response.IsSuccessStatusCode)
  {
    var result = response.Content.ReadAsStringAsync();
    return Ok(result);
  }

  //If the response status is not success, it returns the actual state
```

```
    //followed with the response content
    return StatusCode((int)response.StatusCode,
response.Content.ReadAsStringAsync());
    }
```

This is the classic circuit breaker example. Polly also comes with an advanced circuit breaker, which is more useful in cases where you have to break the circuit based on the percentage of failed requests in a particular amount of time. When working with big applications or applications that involve lots of transactions within a minute, there's a chance that 2% to 5% of transactions will fail due to other non-transient failure issues, so we don't want the circuit to break. In this case, we can implement the advanced circuit breaker pattern and define the policy in our `ConfigureServices` method, which is shown as follows:

```
public void ConfigureServices(IServiceCollection services)
{
    var circuitBreakerPolicy = Policy.HandleResult<HttpResponseMessage>(
    result => !result.IsSuccessStatusCode)
    .AdvancedCircuitBreaker(0.1, TimeSpan.FromSeconds(60),5,
TimeSpan.FromSeconds(10),
    OnBreak, OnReset, OnHalfOpen);
    services.AddSingleton<HttpClient>();
services.AddSingleton<CircuitBreakerPolicy<HttpResponseMessage>>(circuitBre
akerPolicy);
    }
```

The first parameter in the `AdvancedCircuitBreakerAsync` method contains a value of 0.1, which is the percentage of requests that have failed in the time frame, which is 60 seconds, as specified in the second parameter. The third parameter which, defines the value of 5, is the minimum throughput of requests being served in that particular time, as specified in the second parameter which is 60 seconds. Finally, the fourth parameter defines the amount of time the circuit remains open if any request fails and tries to serve the request again once the time has elapsed. The Other parameters are just delegate methods that are called when each state is changed, which is the same as in the previous classic circuit breaker example.

Wrapping the circuit breaker with retry

So far, we have learned how circuit breaker and retry patterns can be used and implemented using the Polly framework. The retry pattern is used to retry the request if it fails for a specified amount of time, where the circuit breaker keeps the state of the circuit and, based on the threshold of the requests being failed, makes the circuit open and stops calling the remote service for some time, as specified in the configuration to save network bandwidth.

With the Polly framework, we can use the retry and circuit breaker patterns in conjunction and wrap the circuit breaker with the retry pattern to open the circuit if the retry pattern reaches the count of the failed request threshold limit.

In this section, we will develop a custom HttpClient class that provides methods such as GET, POST, PUT, and DELETE, and use retry and circuit breaker policies to make it resilient.

Create a new IResilientHttpClient interface and add four methods for HTTP GET, POST, PUT, and DELETE:

```
public interface IResilientHttpClient
{
  HttpResponseMessage Get(string uri);

  HttpResponseMessage Post<T>(string uri, T item);

  HttpResponseMessage Delete(string uri);

  HttpResponseMessage Put<T>(string uri, T item);
}
```

Now, create a new class called ResilientHttpClient, which implements the IResilientHttpClient interface. We will add a parameterized constructor to inject the circuit breaker policy and a HttpClient object, which will be used to make HTTP GET, POST, PUT, and DELETE requests. Here is the constructor implementation of the ResilientHttpClient class:

```
public class ResilientHttpClient : IResilientHttpClient
{
  static CircuitBreakerPolicy<HttpResponseMessage> _circuitBreakerPolicy;
  static Policy<HttpResponseMessage> _retryPolicy;
  HttpClient _client;
  public ResilientHttpClient(HttpClient client,
  CircuitBreakerPolicy<HttpResponseMessage> circuitBreakerPolicy)
  {
    _client = client;
    _client.DefaultRequestHeaders.Accept.Clear();
```

```
    _client.DefaultRequestHeaders.Accept.Add(
    new MediaTypeWithQualityHeaderValue("application/json"));

    //circuit breaker policy injected as defined in the Startup class
    _circuitBreakerPolicy = circuitBreakerPolicy;

    //Defining retry policy
    _retryPolicy = Policy.HandleResult<HttpResponseMessage>(x =>
    {
      var result = !x.IsSuccessStatusCode;
      return result;
    })
    //Retry 3 times and for each retry wait for 3 seconds
    .WaitAndRetry(3, sleepDuration => TimeSpan.FromSeconds(3));

  }
}
```

In the preceding code, we have defined the
`CircuitBreakerPolicy<HttpResponseMessage>` and `HttpClient` objects, which are
injected through DI. We have defined the retry policy and set the retry threshold to three
times, where each retry will wait for three seconds before making a call to the service.

Next, we will create the `ExecuteWithRetryandCircuitBreaker` method, which takes a
URI and a delegate function that will be executed within the retry and circuit breaker
policies. Here is the code snippet of the `ExecuteWithRetryandCircuitBreaker` method:

```
//Wrap function body in Retry and Circuit breaker policies
public HttpResponseMessage ExecuteWithRetryandCircuitBreaker(string uri,
Func<HttpResponseMessage> func)
{

  var res = _retryPolicy.Wrap(_circuitBreakerPolicy).Execute(() => func());
  return res;
}
```

We will call this method from our GET, POST, PUT, and DELETE implementation and
define the code that will be executed within the retry and circuit breaker policies.

Here is the implementation for the GET, POST, PUT, and DELETE methods, respectively:

```
public HttpResponseMessage Get(string uri)
{
  //Invoke ExecuteWithRetryandCircuitBreaker method that wraps the code
  //with retry and circuit breaker policies
  return ExecuteWithRetryandCircuitBreaker(uri, () =>
  {
```

```
    try
    {
      var requestMessage = new HttpRequestMessage(HttpMethod.Get, uri);
      var response = _client.SendAsync(requestMessage).Result;
      return response;
    }
    catch(Exception ex)
    {
      //Handle exception and return InternalServerError as response code
      HttpResponseMessage res = new HttpResponseMessage();
      res.StatusCode = HttpStatusCode.InternalServerError;
      return res;
    }
  });
}


//To do HTTP POST request
public HttpResponseMessage Post<T>(string uri, T item)
{
  //Invoke ExecuteWithRetryandCircuitBreaker method that wraps the code
  //with retry and circuit breaker policies
  return ExecuteWithRetryandCircuitBreaker(uri, () =>
  {
    try
    {
      var requestMessage = new HttpRequestMessage(HttpMethod.Post, uri);

      requestMessage.Content = new
StringContent(JsonConvert.SerializeObject(item),
      System.Text.Encoding.UTF8, "application/json");

      var response = _client.SendAsync(requestMessage).Result;

      return response;
    }catch (Exception ex)
    {
      //Handle exception and return InternalServerError as response code
      HttpResponseMessage res = new HttpResponseMessage();
      res.StatusCode = HttpStatusCode.InternalServerError;
      return res;
    }
  });
}


//To do HTTP PUT request
public HttpResponseMessage Put<T>(string uri, T item)
{
  //Invoke ExecuteWithRetryandCircuitBreaker method that wraps
```

```
    //the code with retry and circuit breaker policies
    return ExecuteWithRetryandCircuitBreaker(uri, () =>
    {
      try
      {
        var requestMessage = new HttpRequestMessage(HttpMethod.Put, uri);

        requestMessage.Content = new
StringContent(JsonConvert.SerializeObject(item),
        System.Text.Encoding.UTF8, "application/json");

        var response = _client.SendAsync(requestMessage).Result;

        return response;
      }
      catch (Exception ex)
      {
      //Handle exception and return InternalServerError as response code
      HttpResponseMessage res = new HttpResponseMessage();
      res.StatusCode = HttpStatusCode.InternalServerError;
      return res;
      }

    });
}

//To do HTTP DELETE request
public HttpResponseMessage Delete(string uri)
{
  //Invoke ExecuteWithRetryandCircuitBreaker method that wraps the code
  //with retry and circuit breaker policies
  return ExecuteWithRetryandCircuitBreaker(uri, () =>
  {
    try
    {
      var requestMessage = new HttpRequestMessage(HttpMethod.Delete, uri);

      var response = _client.SendAsync(requestMessage).Result;

      return response;

    }
    catch (Exception ex)
    {
      //Handle exception and return InternalServerError as response code
      HttpResponseMessage res = new HttpResponseMessage();
      res.StatusCode = HttpStatusCode.InternalServerError;
      return res;
```

```
    }
  });

}
```

Finally, in our startup class, we will add the dependencies as follows:

```
public void ConfigureServices(IServiceCollection services)
{

  var circuitBreakerPolicy = Policy.HandleResult<HttpResponseMessage>(x=> {
    var result = !x.IsSuccessStatusCode;
    return result;
  })
  .CircuitBreaker(3, TimeSpan.FromSeconds(60), OnBreak, OnReset,
OnHalfOpen);

   services.AddSingleton<HttpClient>();
  services.AddSingleton<CircuitBreakerPolicy<HttpResponseMessage>>(circuitBre
akerPolicy);
   services.AddSingleton<IResilientHttpClient, ResilientHttpClient>();
   services.AddMvc();
   services.AddSwaggerGen(c =>
   {
     c.SwaggerDoc("v1", new Info { Title = "User Service", Version = "v1"
});
   });
 }
```

In our `UserController` class, we can inject our custom `ResilientHttpClient` object through DI and modify the POST method, which is shown as follows:

```
[Route("api/[controller]")]
public class UserController : Controller
{

  IResilientHttpClient _resilientClient;

  HttpClient _client;
  CircuitBreakerPolicy<HttpResponseMessage> _circuitBreakerPolicy;
  public UserController(HttpClient client, IResilientHttpClient
resilientClient)
  {
    _client = client;
    _resilientClient = resilientClient;
  }
```

```
// POST api/values
[HttpPost]
public async Task<IActionResult> Post([FromBody]User user)
{

  //Email service URL
  string emailService = "http://localhost:80/api/Email";

  var response = _resilientClient.Post(emailService, user);
  if (response.IsSuccessStatusCode)
  {
    var result = response.Content.ReadAsStringAsync();
    return Ok(result);
  }

  return StatusCode((int)response.StatusCode,
response.Content.ReadAsStringAsync());
  }
}
```

With this implementation, the circuit will be initially closed when the application starts. When the request is made to the `EmailService`, if the service does not respond, it will try to call the service three times, waiting for three seconds on each request. If the service doesn't respond, the circuit will become open and for all subsequent requests, will stop calling the email service and will return the exception to the user for 60 seconds, as specified in the circuit breaker policy. After 60 seconds, the next request will be made to the `EmailService` and the circuit breaker state will be changed to Half-open. If it responds, the circuit state becomes closed again; otherwise, it remains in an open state for the next 60 seconds.

Fallback policy with circuit breaker and retry

Polly also provides a fallback policy that returns some default responses if the service is failing. It can be used in conjunction with both the retry and circuit breaker policies. The basic idea behind fallback is to send a default response to the consumer rather than returning the actual error in the response. The response should give some meaningful information to the user that is specific to the application's nature. This is very beneficial when your services are used by external consumers of applications.

We can modify the preceding example and add fallback policies for both the retry and circuit breaker exceptions. In the ResilientHttpClient class, we will add these two variables:

```
static FallbackPolicy<HttpResponseMessage> _fallbackPolicy;
static FallbackPolicy<HttpResponseMessage> _fallbackCircuitBreakerPolicy;
```

Next, we add the circuit breaker policy to handle the circuit breaker exception and return the HttpResponseMessage with our custom content message. Add the following code in the parameterized constructor of the ResilientHttpClient class:

```
_fallbackCircuitBreakerPolicy = Policy<HttpResponseMessage>
.Handle<BrokenCircuitException>()
.Fallback(new HttpResponseMessage(HttpStatusCode.OK)
  {
     Content = new StringContent("Please try again later[Circuit breaker is
Open]")
  }
);
```

Then, we will add another fallback policy, which will wrap the circuit breaker to handle any other exceptions that are not circuit breaker exceptions:

```
_fallbackPolicy = Policy.HandleResult<HttpResponseMessage>(r =>
r.StatusCode == HttpStatusCode.InternalServerError)
.Fallback(new HttpResponseMessage(HttpStatusCode.OK) {
  Content = new StringContent("Some error occured")
});
```

Finally, we will modify the ExecuteWithRetryandCircuitBreaker method and wrap both the retry and circuit breaker policy inside the fallback policies, which returns the general message with the 200 status code to the user:

```
public HttpResponseMessage ExecuteWithRetryandCircuitBreaker(string uri,
Func<HttpResponseMessage> func)
{

  PolicyWrap<HttpResponseMessage> resiliencePolicyWrap =
  Policy.Wrap(_retryPolicy, _circuitBreakerPolicy);

  PolicyWrap<HttpResponseMessage> fallbackPolicyWrap =
_fallbackPolicy.Wrap(_fallbackCircuitBreakerPolicy.Wrap(resiliencePolicyWra
p));

  var res = fallbackPolicyWrap.Execute(() => func());
  return res;
}
```

With this implementation, the user will not get any errors in response. The content contains the actual error, which is shown in the following snapshot, taken from Fiddler:

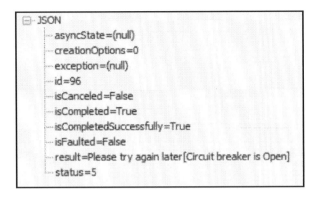

Proactive policies

According to the proactive policy, we should proactively respond to a request if it is leading towards a failure. We can use techniques such as timeout, caching, and health checks to proactively monitor application performance, and use them to proactively respond in the event of failure.

- **Timeout**: If a request takes more than the usual time, it ends the request
- **Caching**: Caches previous responses and uses them for future requests
- **Health checks**: Monitor the application's performance and invokes alerts in the event of failure

Implementing timeout

Timeout is a proactive policy, which is applicable in scenarios where the target service takes a long time to respond, and rather than letting the client wait for a response, we return a general message or response. We can use the same Polly framework to define the timeout policy, and it can also be used with the combination of retry and circuit breaker patterns we learned earlier:

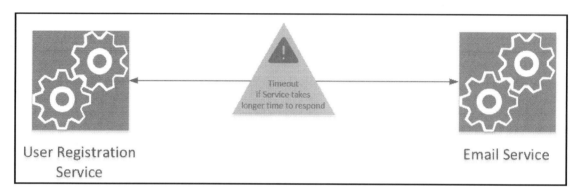

In the preceding diagram, the user registration service is calling the email service to send emails. Now, if the email service does not respond in a particular amount of time, as specified in the timeout policy, the timeout exception will be raised.

To add a timeout policy, declare a `_timeoutPolicy` variable in the `ResilientHttpClient` class:

```
static TimeoutPolicy<HttpResponseMessage> _timeoutPolicy;
```

Then, add the following code to initialize the timeout policy:

```
_timeoutPolicy = Policy.Timeout<HttpResponseMessage>(1);
```

Finally, we will wrap the timeout policy and add it in `resiliencyPolicyWrap`. Here is the modified code of the `ExecuteWithRetryandCircuitBreaker` method:

```
public HttpResponseMessage ExecuteWithRetryandCircuitBreaker(string uri,
Func<HttpResponseMessage> func)
{

  PolicyWrap<HttpResponseMessage> resiliencePolicyWrap =
  Policy.Wrap(_timeoutPolicy, _retryPolicy, _circuitBreakerPolicy);

  PolicyWrap<HttpResponseMessage> fallbackPolicyWrap =
  _fallbackPolicy.Wrap(_fallbackCircuitBreakerPolicy.Wrap(resiliencePolicyWra
  p));
```

```
    var res = fallbackPolicyWrap.Execute(() => func());
    return res;
}
```

Implementing caching

When making a web request or calling a remote service, Polly can be used to cache the response from the remote service and improve the performance of the application's response time. The Polly cache is classified into two caches, known as the in-memory cache and the distributed cache. We will configure the in-memory cache in this section.

First, we need to add another `Polly.Caching.MemoryCache` package from NuGet. Once this is added, we will modify our `Startup` class and add the `IPolicyRegistry` as a member variable:

```
private IPolicyRegistry<string> _registry;
```

In the `ConfigurationServices` method, we will initialize the registry and add it as a singleton object through DI:

```
_registry = new PolicyRegistry();
services.AddSingleton(_registry);
```

In the configure method, we will define the cache policy that takes the cache provider and the time to cache the responses. Since we are using in-memory cache, we will initialize the memory cache provider and specify it in the policy as follows:

```
Polly.Caching.MemoryCache.MemoryCacheProvider memoryCacheProvider = new
MemoryCacheProvider(memoryCache);

CachePolicy<HttpResponseMessage> cachePolicy =
Policy.Cache<HttpResponseMessage>(memoryCacheProvider,
TimeSpan.FromMinutes(10));
```

Finally, we will add the `cachepolicy` to our registry, which is initialized in the `ConfigurationServices` method. We named our registry `cache`:

```
_registry.Add("cache", cachePolicy);
```

Modify our `UserController` class and declare the generic `CachePolicy` as follows:

```
CachePolicy<HttpResponseMessage> _cachePolicy;
```

We will now modify our `UserController` constructor and add the registry, which will be injected through the DI. This registry object is used to get the cache defined in the `Configure` method.

Here is the modified constructor of the `UserController` class:

```
public UserController(HttpClient client, IResilientHttpClient
resilientClient, IPolicyRegistry<string> registry)
{
  _client = client;
  // _circuitBreakerPolicy = circuitBreakerPolicy;
  _resilientClient = resilientClient;

  _cachePolicy = registry.Get<CachePolicy<HttpResponseMessage>>("cache");
}
```

Finally, we will define a GET method that calls another service to get the list of users and cache it in the memory. To cache the responses, we will wrap our custom resilient client GET method with the `Execute` method of the cache policy as follows:

```
[HttpGet]
public async Task<IActionResult> Get()
{
  //Specify the name of the Response. If the method is taking
  //parameter, we can append the actual parameter to cache unique
  //responses separately
  Context policyExecutionContext = new Context($"GetUsers");

  var response = _cachePolicy.Execute(()=>
  _resilientClient.Get("http://localhost:7637/api/users"),
policyExecutionContext);
  if (response.IsSuccessStatusCode)
  {
    var result = response.Content.ReadAsStringAsync();
    return Ok(result);
  }

  return StatusCode((int)response.StatusCode,
response.Content.ReadAsStringAsync());
}
```

When the request is returned, it will check whether the cache context is empty or expired, and the request will be cached for 10 minutes. All subsequent requests during that time will read the response from the in-memory cache store. Once the cache has expired, based on the set time limit, it will invoke the remote service again and cache the response.

Implementing health checks

Health checks are part of the proactive strategy, where the services' health can be monitored in a timely fashion. They also allow you to take actions proactively if any service is not responding or is in a failure state.

In ASP.NET Core, we can easily implement health checks by using the `HealthChecks` library, which is available as a NuGet package. To use `HealthChecks`, we can just simply add the following NuGet package to our ASP.NET Core MVC or Web API project:

`Microsoft.AspNetCore.HealthChecks`

We have to add this package to the application that monitors the services and the services whose health needs to be monitored.

Add the following code in the `ConfigureServices` method of the `Startup` class of the application that is used to check the health of services:

```
services.AddHealthChecks(checks =>
{
  checks.AddUrlCheck(Configuration["UserServiceURL"]);
  checks.AddUrlCheck(Configuration["EmailServiceURL"]);
});
```

In the preceding code, we have added two service endpoints to check the health status. These endpoints are defined in the `appsettings.json` file.

The health check library checks the health of the services specified using the `AddUrlCheck` method. However, the services whose health needs to be monitored by external applications or services need some modification in the `Startup` class. We have to add the following code snippet to all of the services to return their health status:

```
services.AddHealthChecks(checks =>
{
  checks.AddValueTaskCheck("HTTP Endpoint", () => new
  ValueTask<IHealthCheckResult>(HealthCheckResult.Healthy("Ok")));
});
```

If their health is good and the service is responding, it will return `Ok`.

Finally, we can add the URI in the monitoring application, which will trigger the health check middleware to check the services' health and display the health status. We have to add `UseHealthChecks` and specify the endpoint used to trigger the services' health status:

```
public static IWebHost BuildWebHost(string[] args) =>
WebHost.CreateDefaultBuilder(args)
.UseHealthChecks("/hc")
.UseStartup<Startup>()
.Build();
```

When we run our monitoring application and access the URI, for example, `http://{base_address}/hc` to get the health status, if all the services are in working order, we should see the following response:

Storing sensitive information using Application Secrets

Every application has some configuration holding sensitive information, such as database connection strings, the secret keys of some third providers, and other sensitive information usually stored in the configuration files or the database. It is always a better option to secure all sensitive information to protect these resources from intruders. Web applications are usually hosted on servers, and this information can be read by just navigating to the server's path and accessing files, even though servers always have protected access and only authorized users are eligible to access the data. However, keeping information in plain text is not a good practice.

In .NET Core, we can use the Secret Manager tool to protect the sensitive information of an application. The Secret Manager tool allows you to store information in a `secrets.json` file, which is not stored within the application folder itself. Instead, that file is saved at the following path for different platforms:

```
Windows: %APPDATA%microsoftUserSecrets{userSecretsId}secrets.json
Linux: ~/.microsoft/usersecrets/{userSecretsId}/secrets.json
Mac: ~/.microsoft/usersecrets/{userSecretsId}/secrets.json
```

{userSecretId} is the unique ID (GUID) associated with your application. Since this is saved in the separate path, each developer has to define or create this file in their own directory under the UserSecrets directory. This restricts the developer from checking in the same file for the source control and keeps the information separate to each user. There are scenarios where a developer uses their own account credentials for database authentication and so this facilitates in keeping certain information isolated from other information.

From Visual Studio, we can simply add the secrets.json file by right-clicking on the project and selecting the **Manage User Secrets** option, which is shown as follows:

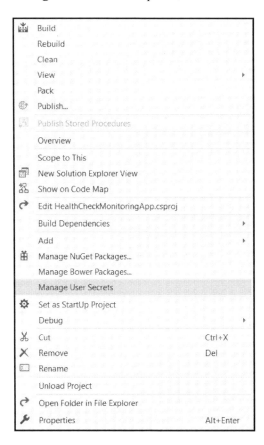

When you select **Manage User Secrets**, Visual Studio creates a `secrets.json` file and opens it in Visual Studio to add configuration settings in JSON format. If you open the project file, you see the entry of the `UserSecretsId` stored in your project file:

```
<Project Sdk="Microsoft.NET.Sdk.Web">

  <PropertyGroup>
    <TargetFramework>netcoreapp2.0</TargetFramework>
    <UserSecretsId>de247bd5-6f82-45ac-b8d4-645428545fff</UserSecretsId>
  </PropertyGroup>
```

So, if you accidently close the `secrets.json` file, you can open it from the path where `UserSecretsId` is the subfolder inside the user secrets path, which is shown in the preceding screenshot.

Here is the sample content of the `secrets.json` file that contains the logging information, remote services URL, and the connection string:

```
{
  "Logging": {
    "IncludeScopes": false,
    "Debug": {
      "LogLevel": {
        "Default": "Warning"
      }
    },
    "Console": {
      "LogLevel": {
        "Default": "Warning"
      }
    }
  },
  "EmailServiceURL": "http://localhost:6670/api/values",
  "UserServiceURL": "http://localhost:6546/api/user",
  "ConnectionString": "Server=OVAISPC\sqlexpress;Database=FraymsVendorDB;
  User Id=sa;Password=P@ssw0rd;"
}
```

To access this in the ASP.NET Core application, we can add the following namespace in our `Startup` class:

```
using Microsoft.Extensions.Configuration;
```

Then, inject the `IConfiguration` object and assign it to the `Configuration` property:

```
public Startup(IConfiguration configuration)
{
  Configuration = configuration;
}
public IConfiguration Configuration { get; }
```

Finally, we can access the variables using the `Configuration` object as follows:

```
var UserServicesURL = Configuration["UserServiceURL"]
services.AddEntityFrameworkSqlServer()
.AddDbContext<VendorDBContext>(options =>
{
  options.UseSqlServer(Configuration["ConnectionString"],
  sqlServerOptionsAction: sqlOptions =>
  {
    sqlOptions.MigrationsAssembly(typeof(Startup)
    .GetTypeInfo().Assembly.GetName().Name);
    sqlOptions.EnableRetryOnFailure(maxRetryCount: 10,
    maxRetryDelay: TimeSpan.FromSeconds(30), errorNumbersToAdd: null);
  });
}, ServiceLifetime.Scoped
);
}
```

Protecting ASP.NET Core APIs

Securing web applications is an important milestone for any enterprise-grade application to protect not only the data, but also to protect it from different attacks from malicious sites.

There are various scenarios where security is an important factor for any web application:

- The information sent over the wire contains sensitive information.
- APIs are exposed publicly and are used by users to perform bulk operations.
- APIs are hosted on a server where the user can use some tools to do packet sniffing and read sensitive data.

To address the preceding challenges and to secure our application, we should consider the following options:

SSL (Secure Socket Layer)

Add security at the transport or network level, where when, the data is sent from the client to the server, it should be encrypted. The **SSL (Secure Socket Layer)** is the recommended way of securing information sent over the wire. Use SSL in a web application to encrypt all of the data that is sent from the client's browser to the server over the wire where it is decrypted at the server level. Apparently, it seems like a performance overhead, but due to the specifications of the server resources we have in today's world, it seems quite negligible.

Enabling SSL in an ASP.NET Core application

To enable SSL in our ASP.NET Core project, we can add filters in the `AddMvc` method defined in the `ConfigureServices` method of our `Startup` class. Filters are used to filter the HTTP calls and take certain actions:

```
services.AddMvc(options =>
{
  options.Filters.Add(new RequireHttpsAttribute())
});
```

Filters added in the `AddMvc` method are global filters and interrupt all HTTP requests, irrespective of a specific controller or action. We added the `RequireHttpsAttribute` filter, which validates the incoming request and checks whether the request is on HTTP or HTTPS. If the request is on HTTP, it will auto redirect the request to HTTPS and use the default port, which is `443` in the case of HTTPS. Adding the preceding code snippet is not enough to run our application on SSL. We also need to tell the `launchSettings.json` file to use the HTTPS port and enable SSL for our project. One way to do this is to enable SSL from the **Debug** tab in the Visual Studio project properties window, which is shown as follows:

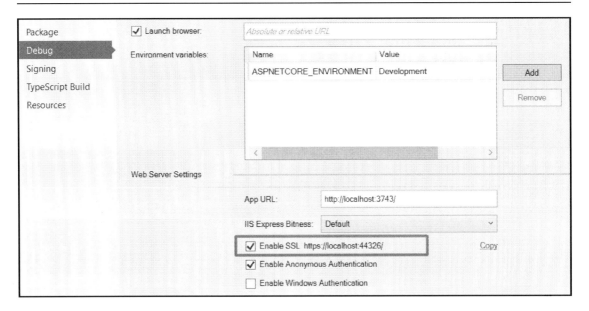

This also modifies the launchSettings.json file and adds the SSL. Another way is to directly modify the port number from the launchSetttings.json file itself. Here is the launchsettings.json file that uses port 44326 for SSL, which has been added under iisSettings:

```
{
  "iisSettings": {
    "windowsAuthentication": false,
    "anonymousAuthentication": true,
    "iisExpress": {
      "applicationUrl": "http://localhost:3743/",
      "sslPort": 44326
    }
  },
```

The default HTTP port, which is shown in the preceding code, is set to *3743*. As in the AddMvc middleware, we have specified a filter to use SSL for all incoming requests. It will automatically redirect to the HTTPS and use port 44326.

To host ASP.NET Core on IIS, please refer to the following link. Once the website is up and running, the HTTPS binding can be added through the Site bindings options in IIS: https://docs.microsoft.com/en-us/aspnet/core/host-and-deploy/iis/index?tabs=aspnetcore2x

Preventing CSRF (Cross-Site Request Forgery) attacks

CSRF is an attack that executes unsolicited operations on a web application on behalf of the authenticated user. Since the attacker is unable to forge the response of the request, it is implicated mostly on HTTP POST, PUT, and DELETE methods, which are used to modify the insert, update, or delete data on the server.

ASP.NET Core provides a built-in token to prevent CSRF attacks, and you can do this yourself by adding the ValidateAntiForgeryTokenAttribute filter while adding MVC in the ConfigureServices method of the Startup class. Here is the code to add an anti-forgery token globally to your ASP.NET Core application:

```
public void ConfigureServices(IServiceCollection services)
{
services.AddMvc(options => { options.Filters.Add(new
ValidateAntiForgeryTokenAttribute()); });
  }
```

Alternatively, we can also add ValidateAntyForgeryToken on specific controller action methods. In that case, we don't have to add the ValidateAntiForgeryTokenAttribute filter in the ConfigureServices method of the Startup class. Here is the code to protect the HTTP POST action method from CSRF attacks:

```
[HttpPost]

[ValidateAntiForgeryToken]
public async Task<IActionResult> Submit()
{
  return View();
}
CORS (Cross Origin Security)
```

The second option is to enable CORS (Cross-Origin Security) for authenticated origins, headers, and methods. Setting CORS allows your APIs to be only accessible from configured origins. In ASP.NET Core, CORS can be easily set by adding middleware and defining its policy.

The ValidateAntiForgery attribute tells ASP.NET Core to put the token in the form, and when it's submitted, it validates and ensures that the token is valid. This prevents your application from CSRF attacks by validating the token for every HTTP POST, PUT, and other HTTP requests, and protects the forms from being posted maliciously.

Reinforcing security headers

Many modern browsers provide additional security features. These security features are automatically enabled by the browser running your site if the response contains those headers. In this section, we will discuss how we can add those headers in our ASP.NET Core application and enable additional security in the browser.

To investigate which headers are missing in our application, we can use the `www.SecurityHeaders.io` site. However, to use this, we need our site to be publicly accessible on the internet.

Alternatively, we can use `ngrok` to make a HTTP tunnel to our local application, which makes our site accessible from the internet. The `ngrok` tool can be downloaded from the following link: `https://ngrok.com/download`.

You can select the version of OS you have and download a particular installer accordingly.

Once `ngrok` is installed, you can open it and the run following command. Please note that your site should be running locally before executing the following command:

```
ngrok http -host-header localhost 7204
```

You can replace `localhost` with your server IP and `7204` to the port your application is listening on.

Running the preceding command will generate the public URL, as specified in the `Forwarding` property, as follows:

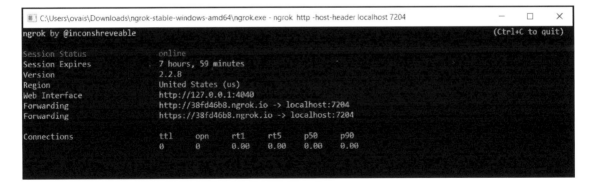

We can now use this public URL in `www.securityheaders.io`, which scans our site and gives us the result. It categorizes the site and provides an alphabet starting from A to F, where A is an excellent score that means the site contains all security headers, and F means that the site is not secure and does not contain security headers. Scanning the default ASP.NET Core site generated from the default template scored F, which is shown as follows. It also shows the missing headers, which are boxed in red:

First of all, we should enable HTTPS on our site. To enable HTTPS, please refer to the section related to SSL. Next, we will add the `NWebsec.AspNetCore.Middleware` package from NuGet as follows:

NWebsec comes with various **middleware** that can be added to our application from the `Configure` method of the `Startup` class.

Adding the HTTP strict transport security header

The strict transport security header is an excellent feature that strengthens the implementation of **TLS (Transport Level Security)** by getting the **User Agent** and forcing it to use HTTPS. We can add the strict transport security header by adding the following middleware to our `Configure` method of the `Startup` class:

```
app.UseHsts(options => options.MaxAge(days:365).IncludeSubdomains());
```

This middleware enforces your site so that it can only be accessed over HTTPS for a year. This applies to subdomains as well.

Adding the X-Content-Type-Options header

This header stops a browser from trying to `MIME-sniff` the content type and forces it to stick with the declared content-type. We can add this middleware as follows, in the `Configure` method of the `Startup` class:

```
app.UseXContentTypeOptions();
```

Adding the X-Frame-Options header

This header allows the browser to protect your site from being rendered inside a frame. By using the following middleware, we can prevent our site from framing so that we can defend it against different attacks, where the most famous one is clickjacking:

```
app.UseXfo(options => options.SameOrigin());
```

Adding the X-Xss-Protection header

This header allows the browser to stop pages from loading when they detect Cross Site scripting attacks. We can add this middleware in the `Configure` method of the `Startup` class, as follows:

```
app.UseXXssProtection(options => options.EnabledWithBlockMode());
```

Adding the Content-Security-Policy header

The *Content-Security-Policy* header protects your application by whitelisting the sources of approved content and preventing the browser from loading malicious resources. This can be added by adding the `NWebsec.Owin` package from NuGet and defining it in the `Configure` method of the `Startup` class as follows:

```
app.UseCsp(options => options
.DefaultSources(s => s.Self())
.ScriptSources(s => s.Self()));
```

In the preceding code, we have mentioned the `DefaultSources` and `ScriptSources` to load all the resources from the same origin. If there are any scripts or images that need to be loaded from external sources, we can define the custom sources as follows:

```
app.UseCsp(options => options
   .DefaultSources(s => s.Self()).ScriptSources(s =>
s.Self().CustomSources("https://ajax.googleapis.com")));
```

 For the complete documentation on this topic, please refer to the following URL: `https://docs.nwebsec.com/en/4.1/nwebsec/Configuring-csp.html`.

Adding the referrer-policy header

When a user navigates the site and click links to other sites, the destination site usually receives information about the origin site the user came from. The referrer header lets you control what information should be present in the header, which can be read by the destination site. We can add the referrer policy middleware in the `Configure` method of the `Startup` class as follows:

```
app.UseReferrerPolicy(opts => opts.NoReferrer());
```

The `NoReferrer` option means that no referrer information will be sent to the target site.

After enabling all of the preceding middleware in our ASP.NET Core application, when we scan through the `securityheaders.io` site, we will see that we have a security report summary with an **A+**, which means that the site is completely secured:

Enabling CORS in the ASP.NET Core application

CORS stands for Cross-Origin Resource Sharing, and it is restricted by browsers to prevent API requests across domains. For example, we have an SPA (Single-Page Application) running on a browser using a client-side framework like Angular or React to make calls to the Web APIs hosted on another domain, like my SPA site having a domain (*mychapter8webapp.com*) and accessing the APIs of another domain (`appservices.com`), which is restricted. Making calls to the services hosted on some other server and domain is restricted by browsers, and users will not be able to call those APIs. Enabling CORS on the server-side level addresses this problem.

To enable CORS in our ASP.NET Core project, we can add CORS support in the `ConfigureServices` method:

```
services.AddCors();
```

In the `Configure` method, we can use CORS by calling the `UseCors` method and defining the policies to allow cross-domain requests. The following code allows requests to be made from any header, origin, or method, and also allows us to pass credentials in the request header:

```
app.UseCors(config => {
  config.AllowAnyHeader();
  config.AllowAnyMethod();
  config.AllowAnyOrigin();
  config.AllowCredentials();
});
```

The preceding code will allow CORS globally in the application. Alternatively, we can also define CORS policies and enable them on specific controllers depending on different scenarios.

The following table defines the basic terminology used in defining CORS:

Terminology	Description	Sample
Header	Request header allowed to be passed within the request	Content-Type, Accept, and so on
Method	HTTP verb of the request	GET, POST, DELETE, PUT, and so on
Origin	Domain or request URL	http://techframeworx.com

To define the policies, we can add a policy when adding CORS support in the `ConfigureServices` method. The following code shows two policies that have been defined while adding CORS support:

```
services.AddCors(config =>
{
  //Allow only HTTP GET Requests
  config.AddPolicy("AllowOnlyGet", builder =>
  {
    builder.AllowAnyHeader();
    builder.WithMethods("GET");
    builder.AllowAnyOrigin();
  });

  //Allow only those requests coming from techframeworx.com
  config.AddPolicy("Techframeworx", builder => {
    builder.AllowAnyHeader();
    builder.AllowAnyMethod();
    builder.WithOrigins("http://techframeworx.com");
  });
});
```

The `AllowOnlyGet` policy will only allow requests that are making a `GET` request; the `Techframeworx` policy will only allow requests that are being made from `techframeworx.com`.

We can use these policies on Controllers and Actions by using the `EnableCors` attribute and specifying the name of the attribute:

```
[EnableCors("AllowOnlyGet")]
public class SampleController : Controller
{

}
```

Authentication and authorization

Secure APIs only allow access to authenticated users. In ASP.NET Core, we can use the ASP.NET Core Identity framework to authenticate users and provide authorized access to protected resources.

Using ASP.NET Core Identity for authentication and authorization

Security, in general, is divided into two mechanisms, which are as follows:

- Authentication
- Authorization

Authentication

Authentication is the process of authenticating the user's access by getting their username, password, or authentication token and then validating it from the backend database or service. Once the user is authenticated, certain actions are done, which involves setting up a cookie in the browser or returning a token to the user so that it can be passed in the request message to access protected resources.

Authorization

Authorization is the process that is done after user authentication. Authorization is used to learn the permissions of the user accessing the resource. Even though the user is authenticated, it does not mean that all the protected or secured resources are accessible. This is where authorization comes into play and only allows the user to access resources that they are permitted to access.

Implementing authentication and authorization using the ASP.NET Core Identity framework

ASP.NET Core Identity is the security framework developed by Microsoft and is now contributed to by the open source community. This allows a developer to enable user authentication and authorization in an ASP.NET Core application. It provides the complete system of storing user identities, roles, and claims in a database. It contains certain classes for user identity, roles, and so on, which can be extended further to support more properties, depending on the requirements. It uses Entity Framework Core code for the first model to create the backend database and can be easily integrated with existing data models or the application's specific tables.

In this section, we will create a simple application to add ASP.NET Core Identity from scratch and modify the `IdentityUser` class to define additional properties and use cookie-based authentication to validate requests and secure ASP.NET MVC controllers.

When creating an ASP.NET Core project, we can change the authentication option to **Individual User Account** authentication, which scaffolds all the security-specific classes and configures security in your application:

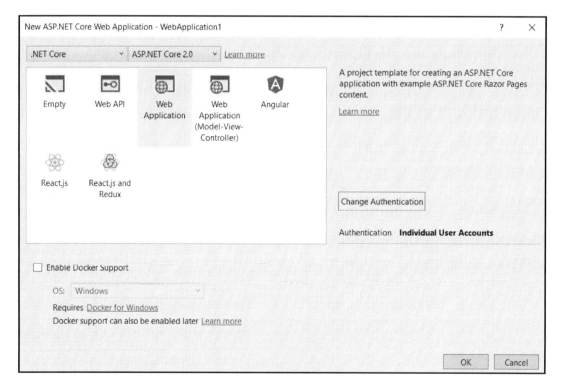

This creates an `AccountController` and `PageModels` to register, login, forgot password, and other user management-related pages.

The `Startup` class also contains some entries related to security. Here is the `ConfigureServices` method, which adds some code that is specific to security:

```
public void ConfigureServices(IServiceCollection services)
{
  services.AddDbContext<ApplicationDbContext>(options =>
options.UseSqlServer(Configuration.GetConnectionString("DefaultConnection")
));

  services.AddIdentity<ApplicationUser, IdentityRole>()
  .AddEntityFrameworkStores<ApplicationDbContext>()
  .AddDefaultTokenProviders();

  services.AddMvc()
  .AddRazorPagesOptions(options =>
  {
    options.Conventions.AuthorizeFolder("/Account/Manage");
    options.Conventions.AuthorizePage("/Account/Logout");
  });

  services.AddSingleton<IEmailSender, EmailSender>();
}
```

`AddDbContext` uses the SQL server to create Identity tables in the database, as specified in the `DefaultConnection` key as follows:

- `services.AddIdentity` is used to enable Identity in our application. It takes `ApplicationUser` and `IdentityRole` and defines `ApplicationDbContext` to use as the Entity framework, which is used to store the created entities.
- `AddDefaultTokenProviders` is defined to generate tokens for reset passwords, changing email, changing telephone number, and two-factor authentication.

In the `Configure` method, it adds the `UseAuthentication` middleware, which enables the authentication and protects the pages or controllers that are configured to authorize requests. Here is the `Configure` method that enables authentication in the pipeline. The middleware which is defined is executed in a sequence. Therefore, the `UseAuthentication` middleware is defined before the `UseMvc` middleware so that all of the requests that will be invoking the controllers will be authenticated first:

```
public void Configure(IApplicationBuilder app, IHostingEnvironment env)
{
  if (env.IsDevelopment())
```

```
    {
      app.UseBrowserLink();
      app.UseDeveloperExceptionPage();
      app.UseDatabaseErrorPage();
    }
    else
    {
      app.UseExceptionHandler("/Error");
    }

    app.UseStaticFiles();

    app.UseAuthentication();

    app.UseMvc();
}
```

Adding more properties in the user table

`IdentityUser` is the base class, which contains properties such as email, password, and phone number, which are related to the user. When we create the ASP.NET Core application, it creates an empty `ApplicationUser` class that inherits from the `IdentityUser` class. In the `ApplicationUser` class, we can add more properties that will be created once the entity framework migration is run. We will add `FirstName`, `LastName`, and `MobileNumber` properties in our `ApplicationUser` class, which will be considered when the table is created:

```
public class ApplicationUser : IdentityUser
{
  public string FirstName { get; set; }
  public string LastName { get; set; }
  public string MobileNumber { get; set; }
}
```

Before running the migration, make sure that the `DefaultConnection` string specified in the `ConfigureServices` method of the `Startup` class is valid.

We can run the migration from the **Package Manager Console** in Visual Studio or through the *dotnet CLI* toolset. From Visual Studio, select the specific project and run the `Add-Migration` command, specifying the migration name, which is Initial in our case:

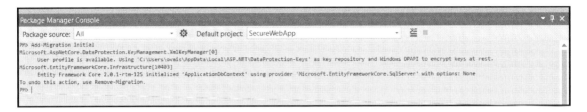

The preceding command creates the `{timestamp}_Initial` class file containing the `Up` and `Down` methods. The `Up` method is used to publish the changes in the backend database, whereas the `Down` method is used to revert the changes done in the database. To apply the changes to the backend database, we will run the `Update-Database` command, which creates a database that contains `AspNet`-related tables, which are part of the Identity framework. If you open the `AspNetUsers` table in design mode, you will see that the custom columns `FirstName`, `LastName`, and `MobileNumber` are there:

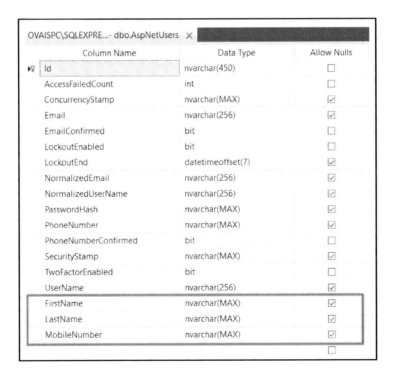

We can run the application and create users using the **Register** option. To protect our APIs, we have to add the `Authorize` attribute to the `Controller` or `Action` level. When the request comes and the user is authenticated, the method will be executed; otherwise, it redirects the request to the **Login** page.

Summary

In this chapter, we have learned about resiliency, which is a very important factor when developing highly performant applications in .NET Core. We learned about different policies and used the Polly framework to use those policies in .NET Core. We also learned about safe storage mechanisms and how to use them in a development environment in order to keep sensitive information separate from the project repository. At the end of this chapter, we learned about some core fundamentals, which included SSL, CSRF, CORS, enabling security headers, and the ASP.NET Core Identity framework to protect ASP.NET Core applications.

Why TDD is Important

5

In the next few chapters, we'll introduce you to the terms, the structure, and the ideology around TDD so that you'll have sufficient knowledge to re-enter the world as a Test-Driven Developer and feel confident about using your skills throughout your long and prosperous career.

So, why is TDD so important? As more businesses and industries rely on software solutions, it's increasingly important that those solutions be robust and error-free. The cheaper and more consistent, they are the better. Applications developed with TDD in mind are inherently more testable, easier to maintain, and demonstrate a certain level of correctness not easily achieved otherwise.

In this chapter, we will gain an understanding of:

- Defining TDD and exploring the basics
- Creating our first tests in C# and JavaScript
- Exploring the basic steps of Red, Green, Refactor
- Growing complexity through tests

First, a little background

It's possible that you've had some exposure to unit tests in your career. It's highly likely that you've written a test or two. Many developers, unfortunately, haven't had the opportunity to experience the joys of Test-Driven Development.

John's story on TDD

I was first introduced to TDD about five years ago. I was interviewing for a lead developer position for a small startup. During the interview process, the CTO mentioned that the development team was practicing TDD. I informed him that I didn't have any practical TDD experience, but that I was sure I could adapt.

In all honesty, I was a bit nervous. Up to that point, I had never even written a single unit test! What had I gotten myself into? An offer was extended and I accepted. Once I joined the small company I was told that, while TDD was the goal, they weren't quite there yet. Phew; crisis averted. However, I was still intrigued. It wasn't until a few months later that the team delved into the world of TDD, and the rest, as they say, is history.

Clayton's story on TDD

My introduction to TDD is a little different from John's. I have been writing code since I was in middle school in the early 1990s. From then until 2010, I always struggled with writing applications that didn't require serious architectural changes when new requirements were introduced. In 2010, I finally got fed up with the constant rewrites and began researching tools and techniques to help me with my problem. I quickly found TekPub, an e-learning site that was, at the time, owned and operated by Rob Conery. Through TekPub I began learning the SOLID principles and TDD. After banging my head against the wall for close to six months, I started to grasp what TDD was and how I could use those principles. Coupled with the SOLID principles, TDD helped me to write easy to understand code that was flexible enough to stand up to any requirements the business could throw at me. I eventually ended up at the same company where John was employed and worked with him and, as he said, the rest is history.

The SOLID principles, which will be explained in detail later, are guiding principles that help produce clean, maintainable, and flexible code. They help reduce rigidity, fragility, and complexity. Generally thought of as object-oriented principles, I have found them to be applicable in all coding paradigms.

So, what is TDD?

Searching online, you will certainly find that TDD is an acronym for Test-Driven Development. We, however, use a slightly more meaningful definition. So, what *is* TDD? In the simplest terms, TDD is an approach to software development that is intended to reduce errors and enable flexibility within the application. If done correctly, TDD is a building block for rapid, accurate, and fearless application development.

Test-Driven Development is a means of letting your tests drive the design of the system. What does that mean, exactly? It means that you mustn't start with a solution in mind, you must let your tests drive the code being written. This helps minimize needless complexity and avoid over-architected solutions. The rules of Test-Driven Development

Staunch proponents of TDD dictate that you may not write a single line of production code without writing a failing unit test, and failing to compile is a failure. This means that you write a simple test, watch it fail, then write some code to make it pass. The system slowly evolves as the tests and the production application grow in functionality.

 TDD is not about testing, it's about design.

Many would argue that TDD is about testing, and by extension, about test coverage of an application. While these are great side-effects of TDD, they are not the driving force behind the practice.

Additionally, if code coverage and metrics become the goal, then there is a risk that developers will introduce meaningless tests just to inflate the numbers. Perhaps it is less a risk and more a guarantee that this will happen. Let delivered functionality and happy customers be the metrics with which you measure success.

TDD is about design. Through TDD, an application will grow in functionality without introducing needless complexity. It's incredibly difficult to introduce complexity if you write small tests and only enough production code to make the test pass. Refactoring, modifying the structure of the code without adding or changing behavior, should not introduce complexity, either.

An approach to TDD

TDD is also referred to as Test First Development. In both names, the key aspect is that the test must be written before the application code. Robert C. Martin, affectionately called "Uncle Bob" by the developer community, has created *The Three Laws of TDD*. They are as follows:

1. You are not allowed to write any production code unless it is to make a failing unit test pass
2. You are not allowed to write any more of a unit test than is sufficient to fail, and compilation failures are failures
3. You are not allowed to write any more production code than is sufficient to pass the one failing unit test

You can learn more about these laws at `http://butunclebob.com/ArticleS.UncleBob.TheThreeRulesOfTdd`

By following these rules, you will ensure that you have a very tight feedback loop between your test code and your production code. One of the main components of Agile software development is working to reduce the feedback cycle. A small feedback cycle allows the project to make a course correction at the first sign of trouble. The same applies to the testing feedback cycle. The smaller you can make your tests, the better the end result will be.

 For a video on Agile, check out *Getting Started with Agile* by Martin Esposito and Massimo Fascinari (`https://www.packtpub.com/application-development/getting-started-agile-video`).

An alternative approach

The original approach to TDD has caused some confusion over the years. The problem is that the principles and approaches just weren't structured enough. In 2006, Dan North wrote an article in Better Software magazine (`https://www.stickyminds.com/better-software-magazine/behavior-modification`). The purpose of the article was to clear up some of this confusion and help to reduce the pitfalls that developers fell into while learning the TDD process. This new approach to TDD is called **Behavior Driven Development (BDD)**. BDD provides a structure for testing, and a means of communicating between business requirements and unit tests, that is almost seamless.

The process

It's difficult to start any journey without a goal in mind. There are a few tips and tricks that can be used to help get you started in TDD. The first is *red, green, refactor*.

Red, green, and refactor

We already discussed writing a failing test before writing production code. The goal is to build the system slowly through a series of tiny improvements. This is often referred to as *red, green, refactor*. We write a small test (red), then we make it pass by writing some production code (green), then we refactor our code (refactor) before we start the process again.

Many TDD practitioners advocate an *It Exists* test first. This will help determine that your environment is set up properly and you won't receive false positives. If you write an *It Exists* test and don't receive a failure right off the bat, you know something is wrong. Once you receive your first failure, you're safe to create the class, method, or function under test. This will also ensure that you don't dive in too deeply right off the bat with lines and lines of code before you're sure your system is working properly.

Once you have your first failure and the first working example, it's time to grow the application, slowly. Choose the next most interesting step and write a failing test to cover this step.

At each iteration, you should pause and evaluate whether there is any cleanup that can happen. Can you simplify a code block? Perhaps a more descriptive variable name is in order? Can any sins committed in the code be corrected, safely, at this time? It's important that you evaluate both the production code and the test suite. Both should be clean, accurate, and maintainable. After all, if it's such a mess that no one would be able to make head or tail of it, what good is the code?

Coder's block

TDD will also help you avoid what writers often call *writer's block* and what we're calling *coder's block*. Coder's block happens when you sit down at the keyboard in an attempt to solve a problem but don't know where to begin. We begin at the beginning. Write the easiest, simplest test you can imagine. Write *It Exists*.

Why should we care?

We're professionals. We want to do a good job. We feel bad if someone finds fault with our code. If QA finds a bug, it makes us sad. If a user of our system encounters an error, we may cry. We should strive to deliver quality, error-free code and a fully functional, feature-rich application.

We're also lazy, but it's the good kind of lazy. We don't want to have to run the entire application just to validate that a simple function returns the proper value.

Arguments against TDD

There are arguments against TDD, some valid and some not. It's quite possible that you've heard some of them before, and likely that you've repeated some of these yourself.

Testing takes time

Of course, testing takes time. Writing unit tests takes time. Adhering to the *red, green, refactor* cycle of TDD does take time. But, how else do you check your work if not through tests?

Do you validate that the code you wrote works? How do you do this without tests? Do you manually run the application? How long does that take? Are there conditional scenarios that you need to account for within the application? Do you have to set up those scenarios while manually testing the application? Do you skip some and just *trust that they work*?

What about regression testing? What if you make a change a day, a week, or a month later? Do you have to manually regression-test the entire application? What if someone else makes a change? Do you trust that they were also as thorough in their testing, *as I'm sure you are*?

How much time would you save if your code were covered by a test suite that you could run at the click of a button?

Testing is expensive

By writing tests, you're effectively doubling the amount of code you're writing, right? Well, yes and no. Okay, in an extreme case, you might approach double the code. Again, *in an extreme case*.

 Don't make tests a line item.

In some instances, consulting companies have written unit tests into a contract with a line item and dollar amount attached. Inevitably, this allows the customer the chance to argue to have this line item removed, thus saving them money. This is absolutely the wrong approach. Testing will be done, period, whether manually by the developer running the application to validate her work, by a QA tester, or by an automated suite of tests. Testing is not a line item that can be negotiated or removed (yikes!).

You would never buy an automobile that didn't pass quality control. Light bulbs must pass inspection. A client, customer, or company will never, ever, save money by foregoing testing. The question becomes, do you write the tests early, while the code is being authored, or manually, at a later date?

Testing is difficult

Testing can be difficult. This is especially true with an application that was not written with testability in mind. If you have static methods and implementations using concrete references scattered throughout your code, you will have difficulty adding tests at a later date.

We don't know how

I don't know how to test is really the only acceptable answer, assuming it is quickly followed by, *but I'm willing to learn*. We're developers. We're the experts in the room. We're paid to know the answers. It's scary to admit that we don't know something. It's even scarier to start something new. Rest assured, it will be OK. Once you get the hang of TDD, you'll wonder how you managed before. You'll refer to those times as *the dark ages, before the discovery of the wheel.*

Arguments in favor of TDD

What we would like to focus on here are the positives, the arguments in favor of TDD.

Reduces the effort of manual testing

We already mentioned that we, as professionals, will not ship anything without first determining that it works. Throwing something over the wall to QA, to our users, or to the general public and hoping that it all works as expected just isn't how we do business. We will verify that our code and our applications work as expected. In the beginning, while the application is small and has little functionality, we can manually test everything we can think of. But, as the application grows in size and complexity, it just isn't feasible for developers or anyone else to manually test an entire application. It's too time-consuming and costly to do this manually. We can save ourselves time and our clients and companies money by automating our testing. We can do so quite easily, from the beginning, through TDD.

Reduces bug count

As our application grows, so do our tests. Or shall we say, our test suite has grown, and by making our tests pass, our application has grown. As both have grown, we've covered the happy path (for example: 2 + 2 = 4) as well as potential failures (for example: 2 + banana = exception). If the method or function under test can accept an input parameter, there is a potential for failure. You can reduce the potential for unexpected behavior, bugs, and exceptions by writing code to guard against these scenarios. As you write tests to express potential failures, your production code will inherently become more robust and less prone to errors. If a bug does slip by and make it to QA, or even to a production environment, then it's easy enough to add a new test to cover the newly discovered defect.

The added benefit of approaching bugs in this fashion is that the same bug rarely crops up again at some later date, as the new tests guard against this. If the same bug does appear, you know that, while the same result has happened, the bug occurred in a new and different way. With the addition of another test to cover this new scenario, this will likely be the last time you see the same old bug.

Ensures some level of correctness

With a comprehensive suite of tests, you can demonstrate some level of correctness. At some point, someone somewhere will ask you whether you are done. How will you show that you have added the desired functionality to an application?

Removes the fear of refactoring

Let's face it, we've all worked on legacy applications that we were scared to touch. Imagine if the class you were tasked with modifying were covered by a comprehensive set of unit tests. Picture how easy it would be to make a change and know that all was right with the world because all of the unit tests still passed.

A better architecture

Writing unit tests tends to push your code towards a decoupled design. Tightly coupled code quickly becomes burdensome to test, and so, to make one's life easier, a Test-Driven Developer will begin to decouple the code. Decoupled code is easier to swap in and out, which means that, instead of modifying a tangled knot of production code, often all that a developer needs to do to make the necessary changes is swap out a subcomponent with a new module of code.

Faster development

It may not feel like it at first (in fact, it definitely will not feel like it at first), but writing unit tests is an excellent way to speed up development. Traditionally, a developer receives requirements from the business, sits down, and begins shooting lightning from her fingertips, allowing the code to pour out until an executable application has been written. Before TDD, a developer would write code for a few minutes and then launch the application so that she could see if the code worked or not. When a mistake was found, the developer would fix it and launch the application once again to check whether the fix worked. Often, a developer would find that her fix had broken something else and would then have to chase down what she had broken and write another fix. The process described is likely one that you and every other developer in the world are familiar with. Imagine how much time you have lost fixing bugs that you found while doing developer testing. This does not even include the bugs found by QA or in production by the customer.

Now, let's picture another scenario. After learning TDD, when we receive requirements from the business, we quickly convert those requirements directly into tests. As each test passes we know that, as per the requirements, our code does exactly what has been asked of it. We might discover some edge cases along the way and create tests to ensure the code has the correct behavior for each one. It would be rare to discover that a test is failing after having made it pass. But, when we do cause a test to fail, we can quickly fix it by using the undo command in our editor. This allows us to hardly even run the application until we are ready to submit our changes to QA and the business. Still, we try to verify that the application behaves as required before submitting, but now we don't do this manually, every few minutes. Instead, let your unit tests verify your code each time you save a file.

Different types of test

Over the course of the next few chapters, we will be leaning towards a particular style of testing, but it is important to understand the terminology that others will use so that you can relate when they speak about a certain type of test.

Unit tests

Let's jump right in with the most misused and least understood test type. In Kent Beck's book, *Test-Driven Development by Example*, he defines a unit test as simply a test that runs in isolation from the other tests. All that means is that for a test to be a unit test, all that has to happen is that the test must not be affected by the side-effects of the other tests. Some common misconceptions are that a unit test must not hit the database, or that it must not use code outside the method or function being tested. These simply aren't true. We tend to draw the line in our testing at third-party interactions. Any time that your tests will be accessing code that is outside the application you are writing, you should abstract that interaction. We do this for maximum flexibility in the design of the test, not because it wouldn't be a unit test. It is the opinion of some that unit tests are the only tests that should ever be written. This is based on the original definition, and not on the common usage of the term.

Acceptance tests

Tests that are directly affected by business requirements, such as those suggested in BDD, are generally referred to as acceptance tests. These tests are at the outermost limit of the application and exercise a large swathe of your code. To reduce the coupling of tests and production code, you could write this style of test almost exclusively. Our opinion is, if a result cannot be observed outside the application, then it is not valuable as a test.

Integration tests

Integration tests are those that integrate with an external system. For instance, a test that interacts with a database would be considered an integration test. The external system doesn't have to be a third-party product; however, sometimes, the external system is just an imported library that was developed independently from the application you are working on but is still considered in-house software. Another example that most don't consider is interactions with the system or language framework. You could consider any test that uses the functions of C#'s `DateTime` object to be an integration test.

End to end tests

These tests validate the entire configuration and usage of your application. Starting from the user interface, an end to end test will programmatically click a button or fill out a form. The UI will call into the business logic of the application, executing all the way down to the data source for the application. These tests serve the purpose of ensuring that all external systems are configured and operating correctly.

Quantity of each test type

Many developers ask the question: How many of each type of test should be used? Every test should be a unit test, as per Kent Beck's definition. We will cover variations on testing later that will have some impact on specific quantities of each type; but, generally, you might expect an application to have very few end to end tests, slightly more integration tests, and to consist mostly of acceptance tests.

Parts of a unit test

The simplest way to get started and ensure that you have the human-readable code is to structure your tests using *Arrange*, *Act*, and *Assert*.

Arrange

Also known as the context of a unit test, *Arrange* includes anything that exists as a prerequisite of the test. This includes everything from parameter values, stored in variables to improve readability, all the way to configuring values in a mock database to be injected into your application when the test is run.

 For more information on Mocking, see Chapter 7, *Setting Up the JavaScript Environment*, the *Abstract Third Party Software* and *Test Double Types* sections.

Act

An action, as part of a unit test, is simply the piece of production code that is being tested. Usually, this is a single method or function in your code. Each test should have only a single action. Having more than one action will lead to messier tests and less certainty about where the code should change to make the test pass.

Assert

The result, or *assertion* (the expected result), is exactly what it sounds like. If you expect that the method being tested will return a 3, then you write an assertion that validates that expectation. The Single Assert Rule states that there should be only one assertion made per test. This does not mean that you can only assert once; instead, it means that your assertions should only confirm one logical expectation. As a quick example, you might have a method that returns a list of items after applying a filter. After setting up the test context, calling the method will result in a list of only one item, and that item will match the filter that we have defined. In this case, you will have a programmatic assert for the count of items in the list and one programmatic assert for the filter criterion we are testing.

Requirements

While this book is not about business analysis or requirement generation, requirements will have a huge impact on your ability to effectively test-drive an application. We will be providing requirements for this book in a format that lends itself very well to high-quality tests. We will also cover some scenarios where the requirements are less than optimal, but for most of this book, the requirements have been labored over to ensure a high-quality definition of the systems we are testing.

Why are they important?

We firmly believe that quality requirements are essential to a well-developed solution. The requirements inform the tests and the tests shape the code. This axiom means that with poor requirements, the application will result in lower quality architecture and overall design. With haphazard requirements, the resulting tests and application will be chaotic and poorly factored. On the bright side, even poorly thought out or written requirements aren't the death knoll for your code. It is our responsibility, as professional software developers, to correct bad requirements. It is our task to ask questions that will lead to better requirements.

User stories

User stories are commonly used in Agile software development for requirement definitions. The format for a user story is fairly simple and consists of three parts: `Role`, `Request`, and `Reason`.

```
As a <Role>
 I want <Request>
 So that <Reason>
```

Role

The role of the user story can provide a lot of information. When specifying the role, we have the ability to imply the capabilities of the user. Can the user access certain functionalities, or are they physically impaired in such a way that requires an alternate form of interaction with the system? We can also communicate the user's mindset. Having a new user could have an impact on the design of the user interface, in contrast to what an experienced user might expect. The role can be a generic user, a specific role, a persona, or a specific user.

Generic users are probably the most used and, at the same time, the least useful. Having a story that provides no insight into the user limits our decision making for this story by not restricting our context. If possible, ask your business analyst or product owner for a more specific definition of who the requirement is for.

Defining a specific role, such as Admin, User, or Guest, can be very helpful. Specific roles provide user capability information. With a specific role, we can determine if a user should even be allowed into the section of the application we are defining functionality for. It is possible that a user story will cause the modification of a user's rights within the system, simply because we specified a role instead of a generic user.

Using a persona is the most telling of the wide-reaching role types. A persona is a full definition of an imaginary user. It includes a name, any important physical attributes, preferences, familiarity with the subject of the application, familiarity with computers, and anything else that might have an impact on the imaginary user's interactions with the software. By having all this information, we can start to roleplay the user's actions within the system. We can start to make assumptions or decisions about how that user would approach or feel about a suggested feature and we can design the user interface with that user in mind.

Request

The request portion of the user story is fairly simple. We should have a single feature or a small addition to functionality that is being requested. Generally, the request is too large if it includes any joining words, such as *and* or *or*.

Reason

The reason is where the business need is stated. This is the opportunity to explain how the feature will add value to the company. By connecting the reason to the role, we can enhance the impact of the feature's usefulness.

A complete user story might look like the following:

```
As a Conference Speaker
 I want to search for nearby conferences by open submission date
 So that I may plan the submission of my talks
```

Gherkin

Gherkin is a style of requirements definitions that is often used for acceptance criteria. We can turn these requirements directly into code, and QA can turn them directly into test cases. The Gherkin format is generally associated with BDD, and it is used in Dan North's original article on the subject.

The Gherkin format is just as simple as the user story format. It consists of three parts: Given, When, and Then.

```
Given <Context>
 And Given <More Context>
 When <Action>
 Then <Result>
 And Then <More Results>
```

Givens

Because the Gherkin format is fairly simple, givens are broken out to one per contextual criterion. As part of specifying the context, we want to see any and all preconditions of this scenario. Is the user logged in? Does the user have any special rights? Does this scenario require any settings to be put into force before execution? Has the user provided any input on this scenario? One more thing to consider is that there should only be a small number of givens.

The more givens that are present in a scenario, the more likely it is that the scenario is too big or that the givens can somehow be logically grouped to reduce the count.

When we start writing our tests, a Given is analogous to the Arrange section of a test.

When

The when is the action taken by the user. There should be one action and only one action. This action will depend on the context defined by the Given and output the result expected by the Then. In our applications, this is equivalent to a function or method call.

When we start writing our tests, a When is analogous to the Act section of a test.

Then

Thens equate to the output of the action. *Then's* describe what can be verified and tested from the output of a method or function, not only by developers but also by QA. Just like with the Givens, we want our *Thens* to be singular in their expectation. Also like Givens, if we find too many *Thens*, it is either a sign that this scenario is getting too big, or that we are over-specifying our expectations.

When we start writing our tests, a Then is analogous to the Assert section of a test.

Complete acceptance criteria based on the user story presented earlier might look like the following:

```
Given I am a conference speaker
And Given a search radius of 25 miles
And Given an open submission start date
And Given an open submission end date
When I search for conferences
Then I receive only conferences within 25 miles of my location
And Then I receive only conferences that are open for submission within
the specified date range
```

Just like in life, not everything in this book is going to be perfect. Do you see anything wrong with the preceding acceptance criteria? Go on and take a few minutes to examine it; we'll wait.

If you've given up, we'll tell you. The above acceptance criteria are just too long. There are too many Givens and too many Thens. How did this happen? How could we have created such a mistake? When we wrote the user story, we accidentally included too much information for the reason that we specified. If you go back and look at the user story, you will see that we threw `nearby` in the request. Adding `nearby` seemed harmless; it even seemed more correct. I, as the user, wasn't so interested in traveling too far for my speaking engagements.

When you start to see user stories or acceptance criteria getting out of hand like this, it is your responsibility to speak with the business analyst or product owner and work with them to reduce the scope of the requirements. In this case, we can extract two user stories and several acceptance criteria.

Here is a full example of the requirements we have been examining:

```
As a conference speaker
 I want to search for nearby conferences
 So that I may plan the submission of my talks
Given I am a conference speaker
 And Given search radius of five miles
 When I search for conferences
 Then I receive only conferences within five miles of my location
Given I am a conference speaker
 And Given search radius of 10 miles
 When I search for conferences
 Then I receive only conferences within 10 miles of my location
Given I am a conference speaker
 And Given search radius of 25 miles
 When I search for conferences
 Then I receive only conferences within 25 miles of my location

As a conference speaker
 I want to search for conferences by open submission date
 So that I may plan the submission of my talks
Given I am a conference speaker
 And Given open submission start and end dates
 When I search for conferences
 Then I receive only conferences that are open for submission within the
specified date range
Given I am a conference speaker
 And Given an open submission start date
 And Given an empty open submission end date
```

```
 When I search for conferences
 Then an INVALID_DATE_RANGE error occurs for open submission date
Given I am a conference speaker
 And Given an empty open submission start date
 And Given an open submission end date
 When I search for conferences
 Then an INVALID_DATE_RANGE error occurs for open submission date
```

One thing that we have not discussed is the approach to the content of the user stories and acceptance criteria. It is our belief that requirements should be as agnostic about the user interface and data storage mechanism as possible. For that reason, in the requirement examples, you'll notice that there is no reference to any kind of buttons, tables, modals/popups, clicking, or typing. For all we know, this application is running in a Virtual Reality Helmet with a Natural User Interface. Then again, it could be running as a RESTful web API, or maybe a phone application. The requirements should specify the system interactions, not the deployment environment.

In software development, it is everyone's responsibility to ensure high-quality requirements. If you find the requirements you have received to be too large, vague, user interface-dependent, or just unhelpful, it is your responsibility to work with your business analyst or product owner to make the requirements better and ready for development and QA.

Our first tests in C#

Have you ever created a new MVC project in Visual Studio? Have you noticed the checkbox towards the bottom of the dialog box? Have you ever selected, Create Unit Test Project? The tests created with this Unit Test Project are largely of little use. They do little more than validate that the default MVC controllers return the proper type. This is perhaps one step beyond, `ItExists`. Let's look at the first set of tests created for us:

```
using System.Web.Mvc;
using Microsoft.VisualStudio.TestTools.UnitTesting;
using SampleApplication.Controllers;

namespace SampleApplication.Tests.Controllers
{
  [TestClass]
  public class HomeControllerTest
  {
    [TestMethod]
    public void Index()
    {
      // Arrange
```

```
    HomeController controller = new HomeController();

    // Act
    ViewResult result = controller.Index() as ViewResult;
    // Assert
    Assert.IsNotNull(result);
}

[TestMethod]
public void About()
{
    // Arrange
    HomeController controller = new HomeController();

    // Act
    ViewResult result = controller.About() as ViewResult;

    // Assert
    Assert.AreEqual("Your application...", result.ViewBag.Message);
}

[TestMethod]
public void Contact()
{
    // Arrange
    HomeController controller = new HomeController();

    // Act
    ViewResult result = controller.Contact() as ViewResult;

    // Assert
    Assert.IsNotNull(result);
}
    }
}
```

Here, we can see the basics of a test class, and the test cases contained within. Out of the box, Visual Studio ships with MSTest, which is what we can see here. The test class must be decorated with the [TestClass] attribute. Individual tests must likewise also be decorated with the [TestMethod] attribute. This allows the test runner to determine which tests to execute.

For now, we can see that the `HomeController` is being tested. Each of the public methods has a single test, for which you may want to create additional tests and/or extract tests to separate files in the future. Later we'll be covering options and best practices to help you arrange your files in a much more manageable fashion. All of this should be part of your *refactor* step in your *red, green, refactor* cycle.

Growing the application with tests

Perhaps you want to accept a parameter for one of your endpoints. Maybe you will take a visitor's name to display a friendly greeting. Let's take a look at how we might make that happen:

```
[TestMethod]
public void ItTakesOptionalName()
{
  // Arrange
  HomeController controller = new HomeController();

  // Act
  ViewResult result = controller.About("") as ViewResult;

  // Assert
  Assert.AreEqual("Your application description page.",
result.ViewBag.Message);
}
```

We start by creating a test to allow for the `About` method to accept an optional string parameter. We're starting with the idea that the parameter is optional since we don't want to break any existing tests. Let's see the modified method:

```
public ActionResult About(string name = default(string))
{
  ViewBag.Message = "Your application description page.";
  return View();
}
```

Now, let's use the `name` parameter and just append it to our `ViewBag.Message`. Wait, not the controller. We need a new test first:

```
[TestMethod]
public void ItReturnsNameInMessage()
{
  // Arrange
  HomeController controller = new HomeController();
```

```
  // Act
  ViewResult result = controller.About("Fred") as ViewResult;

  // Assert
  Assert.AreEqual("Your application description page.Fred",
result.ViewBag.Message);
}
```

And now we'll make this test pass:

```
public ActionResult About(string name = default(string))
{
  ViewBag.Message = $"Your application description page.{name}";
  return View();
}
```

Our first tests in JavaScript

To get the ball rolling in JavaScript, we are going to write a Simple Calculator class. Our calculator only has the requirement to add or subtract a single set of numbers. Much of the code you write in TDD will start very simply, just like this example:

```
import { expect } from 'chai'

class SimpleCalc {
  add(a, b) {
    return a + b;
  }

  subtract(a, b) {
    return a - b;
  }
}

describe('Simple Calculator', () => {
  "use strict";

  it('exists', () => {
    // arrange
    // act
    // assert
    expect(SimpleCalc).to.exist;
  });

  describe('add function', () => {
    it('exists', () => {
```

```
        // arrange
        let calc;

        // act
        calc = new SimpleCalc();

        // assert
        expect(calc.add).to.exist;
    });

    it('adds two numbers', () => {
        // arrange
        let calc = new SimpleCalc();

        // act
        let result = calc.add(1, 2);

        // assert
        expect(result).to.equal(3);
    });
});

describe('subtract function', () => {
    it('exists', () => {
        // arrange
        let calc;

        // act
        calc = new SimpleCalc();

        // assert
        expect(calc.subtract).to.exist;
    });

    it('subtracts two numbers', () => {
        // arrange
        let calc = new SimpleCalc();

        // act
        let result = calc.subtract(3, 2);

        // assert
        expect(result).to.equal(1);
    });
  });
});
```

If the preceding code doesn't make sense right now, don't worry; this is only intended to be a quick example of some working test code. The testing framework used here is Mocha, and the assertion library used is `chai`. In the JavaScript community, most testing frameworks are built with BDD in mind. Each described in the code sample above represents a scenario or a higher-level requirements abstraction; whereas, each `it` represents a specific test. Within the tests, the only required element is the expect, without which the test will not deliver a valuable result.

Continuing this example, say that we receive a requirement that the add and subtract methods must be allowed to chain. How would we tackle that requirement? There are many ways, but in this case, I think I would like to do a quick redesign and then add some new tests. First, we will do the redesign, again driven by tests.

By placing `only` on a `describe` or a `test`, we can isolate that `describe/test`. In this case, we want to isolate our add tests and begin making our change here:

```
it.only('adds two numbers', () => {
  // arrange
  let calc = new SimpleCalc(1);

  // act
  let result = calc.add(2).result;

  // assert
  expect(result).to.equal(3);
});
```

Previously, we have changed the test to use a constructor that takes a number. We have also reduced the number of parameters of the add function to a single parameter. Lastly, we have added a result value that must be used to evaluate the result of adding.

The test will fail because it does not use the same interface as the class, so now we must make a change to the class:

```
class SimpleCalc {
  constructor(value) {
    this._startingPoint = value || 0;
  }

  add(value) {
    return new SimpleCalc(this._startingPoint + value);
  }
  ...
  get result() {
    return this._startingPoint;
  }
```

```
    }
```

This change should cause our test to pass. Now, it's time to make a similar change for the subtract method. First, remove the `only` that was placed in the previous example:

```
it('subtracts two numbers', () => {
  // arrange
  let calc = new SimpleCalc(3);

  // act
  let result = calc.subtract(2).result;

  // assert
  expect(result).to.equal(1);
});
```

Now for the appropriate change in the class:

```
subtract(value) {
   return new SimpleCalc(this._startingPoint - value);
}
```

Out tests now pass again. The next thing we should do is create a test that verifies everything works together. We will leave this test up to you as an exercise, should you want to attempt it.

Why does it matter?

So, why does all this matter? Why write more code than we have to? Because it's worth it. And to be honest, most of the time it isn't more code. As you take the time to grow your application with tests, simple solutions are produced. Simple solutions are almost always less code than the slick solution you might have come up with otherwise. And inevitably, slick solutions are error-prone, difficult to maintain, and often just plain wrong.

Summary

If you didn't before, you should now have a good idea of what TDD is and why it is important. You have been exposed to unit tests in C# and JavaScript and how writing tests first can help grow an application.

As we continue, we'll learn more about TDD. We'll explore what it means to write testable code.

In Chapter 6, *Setting Up the .NET Test Environment*, we'll set up your development environment and explore additional aspects of a unit test.

6
Setting Up the .NET Test Environment

In this chapter, we'll explore setting up your development environment. We'll be covering both C# and .NET. In the following chapter, we will focus on setting up a JavaScript and React environment. We'll delve into more examples, starting with the classic code kata entitled *FizzBuzz*, and then into more real-world samples from the *Speaker Meet* site.

In this chapter, you will gain an understanding of:

- Installing your IDE
- How to set up your testing framework
- Writing your first tests in C#

Installing the .NET Core SDK

Before you get started with the development environments, you will want to install the .NET Core SDK. You'll need to navigate to the .NET Core download page on the Microsoft website (https://www.microsoft.com/net/download/core). Select the proper installer for your system. For Windows machines, the .exe download is recommended.

Follow the onscreen instructions for the install wizard to install the .NET Core SDK.

Getting set up with VS Code

One benefit of choosing VS Code for your development is that it is an excellent IDE for both
.NET and JavaScript. To get started using VS Code, you must first download the IDE.

Downloading the IDE

Visit the VS Code website (`https://code.visualstudio.com/`) and choose the proper
version for your operating system:

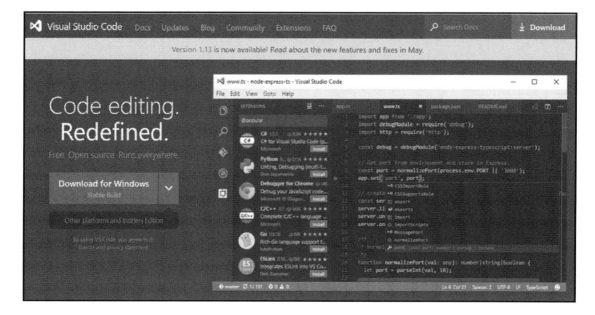

Installing the VS Code

Follow the instructions in the wizard to install the VS Code:

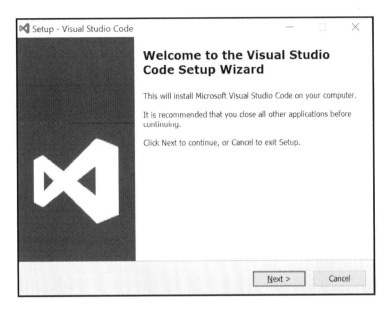

Be sure to read and accept the **License Agreement**:

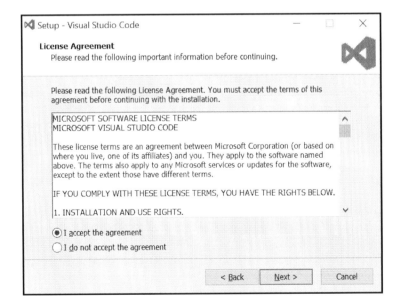

Choose a location on your hard drive to install VS Code. The default path is usually acceptable:

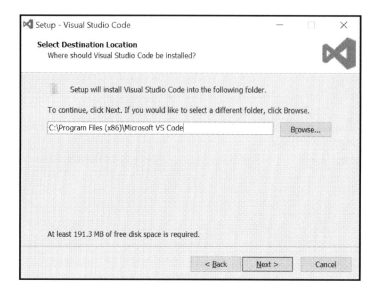

Choose to create a Start menu folder for the application, select a location, or choose to not create a Start menu folder:

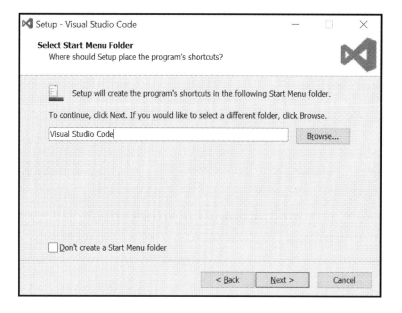

Select additional tasks. The default should be fine for our purposes, as shown in the following screenshot:

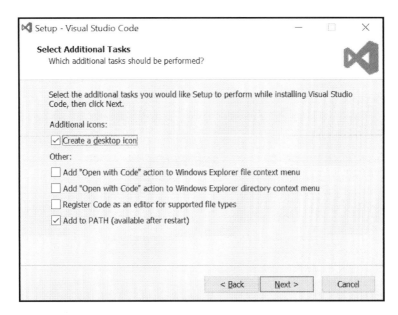

Review your installation settings and click on **Install**:

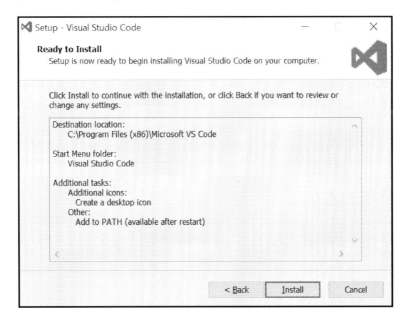

Once the install is finished, you're OK to launch the application:

Adding extensions

VS Code is a fairly lightweight and bare-bones IDE. You'll need to install C# to get started. When you launched VS Code for the first time, your browser should have opened to the **Getting Started** page on the VS Code website. If it didn't, go there now (`https://code.visualstudio.com/docs`).

There are a variety of useful extensions that you can install from the marketplace. For now, all you will need is C#. At the time of writing, C# was listed near the top of the **Top Extensions** list. Click on the C# tile (or find it by searching in the marketplace) to learn more about this extension.

You should see that the installation instructions direct you to launch VS Code Quick Open (*Ctrl-P*) and paste the following command:

```
ext install csharp
```

From within VS Code, paste the command into the **Quick Open** section and press *Enter*. Find the C# version powered by OmniSharp and choose **Install**. Once the C# extension is installed, you will need to reload VS Code to activate the C# extension (choose **reload**).

Creating a project in VS Code

Now that your VS Code IDE is properly installed with the C# extension enabled, you are ready to create your first project.

With VS Code open, choose **Open Folder** from the **File** menu. Choose a location that is easily accessible. Many developers will create a Development folder on the root of their drive. Whatever convention you're used to will be fine. You now need to create an **MSTest** project.

Create a new folder named Sample. Open the **Integrated Terminal** window from the **View** menu or by using the shortcut keys (*Ctrl + `*). From within the Terminal window, type dotnet new mstest and hit *Enter*. Now, you need to restore your packages by typing dotnet restore into the Terminal window and hitting *Enter*.

You should now see a file named UnitTest1.cs within the Sample folder. If you open the file, it should look something like this:

```csharp
using Microsoft.VisualStudio.TestTools.UnitTesting;

namespace Sample
{
  [TestClass]
  public class UnitTest1
  {
    [TestMethod]
    public void TestMethod1()
    {
    }
  }
}
```

Change the first test method to an ItExists test. Do this by changing the name to ItExists and trying to declare an instance to a class that does not yet exist:

```csharp
var sampleClass = new SampleClass();
```

You should see that your sample application will not compile and you will have received the error message, `The type or namespace 'SampleClass' could not be found (are you missing a using directive or an assembly reference?)`.

Now that you have a test failure (remember, failing to compile counts as a failing test in this instance), it's safe to move on to the *Green* step in our *red, green, refactor* cycle. Make the test pass by creating a definition for `SampleClass`. Feel free to create the class in the same file as your unit tests, just to get you started. This can always be extracted and moved to a more appropriate location later:

```
public class SampleClass
{
}
```

Now that you've made the change, run the `test` command `dotnet test` and see the results:

```
Total tests: 1. Passed: 1. Failed: 0. Skipped: 0.
```

Continue exploring VS Code and growing your new class through tests. The C# and .NET examples throughout the rest of the book will be using Visual Studio Community. If you prefer, you may choose to stick with VS Code.

Setting up Visual Studio Community

Most C# and .NET developers will be familiar with Visual Studio. There are a variety of versions available, ranging from free to many thousands of dollars annually. As of this writing, the Enterprise version was the most fully featured version, offering some of the best features for tests and testing. For our purposes, we'll be using Visual Studio Community. This is a free, fully featured development environment that should suit us well.

The Community edition does have some very important caveats. There are limitations to the software license and the use of the Community edition, based on the terms of the license agreement. Please make sure to read the terms before deciding to use Visual Studio Community edition to develop software that you intend to sell. The current terms can be found at https://www.visualstudio.com/license-terms/mlt553321/.

Downloading Visual Studio Community

To get started, download Visual Studio Community (`https://www.visualstudio.com/downloads/`). Feel free to explore and compare the different versions of Visual Studio while you're there:

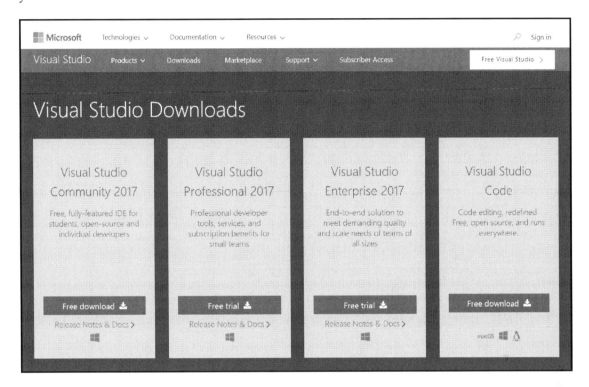

Installing Visual Studio Community

The wizard for installing Visual Studio Community is a little different from the install wizard for VS Code. Of course, to get started, you'll need to read and agree to the license agreement.

At a minimum, you'll want to choose ASP.NET and web development and .NET Core cross-platform development if you plan to follow along with the book. We've also chosen to include ASP.NET MVC 4, .NET Framework 4.6.2 development tools, and .NET Framework 4.7 development tools from the right pane, or from the **Individual components** tab. You might want to explore other components and/or language packs, as well.

Switching to xUnit

MSTest has long shipped with Visual Studio. There are a few other options when it comes to testing frameworks for C# and .NET. Many of these frameworks have feature parity and differ only slightly in their choices of attributes, assertions, and exception handling. Among the top contenders for testing frameworks is xUnit. Many developers actually prefer this to MSTest and would argue that it is more feature-rich and has stronger community support. Arguments aside, we'll be using xUnit for our C# and .NET tests from here on out.

Feel free to stick with MSTest if you prefer. Just know that you'll need to account for the semantic differences (such as *TestMethod* vs *Fact*) and slight differences in functionality.

Code katas

What is a code kata? Code katas are nothing more than repeatable exercises. Generally, these exercises are meant to take no more than 20 minutes to complete. Most code katas are directed at a specific classification of a problem to solve. We'll be utilizing the classic example, FizzBuzz, as a way to get you more comfortable with TDD using xUnit.

FizzBuzz

The rules of FizzBuzz are quite simple. If the number provided is divisible by 3, then you must return `Fizz`. If the number supplied is divisible by 5, then you must return `Buzz`. If the number is divisible by both 3 and 5, then you must return `FizzBuzz`. If it is divisible by neither 3 nor 5, then simply return the number itself.

There are a plethora of options in which to solve the problem. It can be solved in nearly every programming language, in a variety of different ways. What's important here is to practice the techniques of solving the problem simply and effectively.

Let's get started.

Creating the test project

Within Visual Studio Community, create an xUnit test project by choosing **New** | **Project** from the **File** menu or by using the shortcut keys (*Ctrl - Shift - N*). Under **.NET Core,** choose **xUnit Test Project**. Give your project the name `CodeKata` and click on **OK**. You will see a filename `UnitTest1.cs`. This file is fine to get you started. Let's create our first test.

The Given3ThenFizz test

The first test method in the `UnitTest1.cs` file is named `Test1`. Let's change the name of this method to `Given3ThenFizz` and write our first test:

```
[Fact]
public void Given3ThenFizz()
{
  // Arrange
  // Act
  var result = FizzBuzz(3);

  // Assert
  Assert.Equal("Fizz", result);
}
```

Note that the `Fact` attribute and `Assert.Equal` assertion differ only slightly from our previous MSTest example. We're leaving the `Arrange`, `Act`, and `Assert` comments in place, and recommend you do the same. These comments will help you as you get started. They'll also serve to help describe the process to any developers that come behind you in the future.

Now, run the test to see whether it passes by selecting **Run | All Tests** from the **Test** menu, or by using the shortcut keys (*Ctrl + R, A*). You should see a compilation error. Let's resolve the error by creating a `FizzBuzz` method preceding our `test` class. Once you've created the `FizzBuzz` method, rerun your test to see it pass. Remember, based on the third law of TDD, you should only write enough code to make it pass:

```
private object FizzBuzz(int value)
{
  return "Fizz";
}
```

The Given5ThenBuzz test

Our next requirements state that we must return `Buzz` when 5 is supplied. Let's write that test:

```
[Fact]
public void Given5ThenBuzz()
{
  // Arrange
  // Act
  var result = FizzBuzz(5);
```

```
  // Assert
  Assert.Equal("Buzz", result);
}
```

How might we make that test pass? Perhaps a simple ternary operator? Let's take a look at what that might look like:

```
private object FizzBuzz(int value)
{
  return value == 3 ? "Fizz" : "Buzz";
}
```

You might see a problem with our algorithm already. That's OK! We're not done yet. We've only gotten as far as the tests have guided us, and so far we're passing all of our tests. Let's move on to the next most interesting test.

The Given15ThenFizzBuzz test

You might want to write a test method entitled `GivenDivisibleBy3and5ThenFizzBuzz`, but that may be too large of a leap at this point. We know that the first such number divisible by 3 and 5 is 15, so it might make more sense to start with this:

```
[Fact]
public void Given15ThenFizzBuzz()
{
  // Arrange
  // Act
  var result = FizzBuzz(15);

  // Assert
  Assert.Equal("FizzBuzz", result);
}
```

How would you choose to make this test pass? Would you use an *if/else* statement? Perhaps a *switch* statement? We'll leave this one as an exercise for the reader. Feel free to make this test pass in any way that you're comfortable with implementing. Remember to run your tests along the way to ensure you don't introduce a breaking change. If you do experience a test failure, feel free to ignore a test (*Ignore* attribute in MSTest, *Skip* parameter in xUnit), but only one test, while you fix your error(s).

The Given1Then1 test

We've covered `Fizz`. We've covered `Buzz`. And, we've covered `FizzBuzz`. Now we must account for numbers that are divisible by neither 3 nor 5. Remember, in the event that a number is divisible by neither 3 nor 5, we simply return the number supplied. Let's take a look at this test:

```
[Fact]
public void Given1Then1()
{
  // Arrange
  // Act
  var result = FizzBuzz(1);

  // Assert
  Assert.Equal(1, result);
}
```

Theories

This is great! Things are going quite smoothly. Hopefully, you're starting to get the hang of Test-Driven Development. Now, let's look into a slightly more advanced test method using the `Theory` and `InlineData` attributes.

Looking back at our tests, we see that we have a `test` method named `Given15ThenFizzBuzz`. While this is fine, it's a little too specific. Remember, our requirement was that, if the number is divisible by 3 and 5, then we should return `FizzBuzz`. Let's ensure we didn't take too big a leap in logic by writing a new test. This time, we'll supply a number of values, expecting the same results:

```
[Theory]
[InlineData(0)]
[InlineData(15)]
[InlineData(30)]
[InlineData(45)]
public void GivenDivisibleBy3And5ThenFizzBuzz(int number)
{
  // Arrange
  // Act
  var result = FizzBuzz(number);

  // Assert
  Assert.Equal("FizzBuzz", result);
}
```

When you run the test suite, you should now see four new passed test results. If you do experience a failure, the results pane in the **Test Explorer** window should provide a detailed explanation as to which test failed.

Now, do the same thing for `Fizz` and `Buzz` by creating two more test cases using `Theories` and `InlineData`. Go ahead and add `GivenDivisibleBy3ThenFizz`, `GivenDivisibleBy5ThenBuzz`, and `GivenNotDivisibleBy3or5ThenNumber`. Be sure to run your test suite after adding each test and `InlineData` value, fixing any failures along the way.

Solution to the FizzBuzz Problem

What we came up with looks something like this:

```
private object FizzBuzz(int value)
{
  if (value % 15 == 0)
    return "FizzBuzz";

  if (value % 5 == 0)
    return "Buzz";

  if (value % 3 == 0)
    return "Fizz";

  return value;
}
```

Don't worry if you chose to solve the problem a different way. The important thing is that you gained knowledge and understanding during this exercise. Additionally, you now have a comprehensive set of tests and you're comfortable refactoring and/or adding functionality.

What is Speaker Meet?

We're using the *Speaker Meet* application as a case study in Test-Driven Development. Speaker Meet is a website dedicated to connecting technology speakers, user groups, and conferences. Anyone who has helped organize a user group or tech conference knows it's often difficult to find speakers. And as technology speakers, it's often difficult to coordinate speaking engagements outside your immediate area. Speaker Meet helps bring technology speakers and communities together.

At the time of writing, the application is still in development, but it is a terrific platform to explore TDD concepts and principles as they relate to real-world applications. Speaker Meet consists of a RESTful API in .NET with a **Single Page Application** (**SPA**) in JavaScript, utilizing the React library.

Web API project

For our first exercise, we'll be creating a new API endpoint. This new endpoint will return a list of speakers based on a supplied search term. We'll be utilizing this endpoint in our React examples in a later chapter.

Listing Speakers (API)

A list of Speakers will be returned from the database by accessing the back-end API. Before starting on writing the code, a set of requirements must first be established. It's difficult to know where to begin if an agreed upon set of functionality hasn't been defined.

Requirements

Below are the requirements, you might expect to receive from a business analyst or product owner. These are often a good starting point for a broader conversation. If something is not clear, it's best to resolve any ambiguity before you begin.

```
As a conference organizer
  I want to search for available speakers
  So that I may contact them about my conference

Given I am a conference organizer
  And Given a speaker in mind
  When I search for speakers by name
  Then I receive speakers with a matching first name

Given I am a conference organizer
  And Given a speaker in mind
  When I search for speakers by name
  Then I receive speakers with a matching last name
```

Upon speaking with our product owner, we determined that by the requirement of *matching*, what was truly desired was a *starts-with* match. If a conference organizer were to search for the string "Jos," the results for *Josh, Joshua, Joseph*, should be returned by the search routine.

A new test file

We'll start by creating a new test file. Let's name this file
`SpeakerControllerSearchTests.cs`. Now, create the first test, `ItExists`:

```
[Fact]
public void ItExists()
{
  var controller = new SpeakerController();
}
```

To make this compile, you'll need to create a Web API controller called
`SpeakerMeetController`. Add a new ASP.NET Core Web Application project to your
solution. Give your project a name of `SpeakerMeet.API` and choose the Web API template
to get started. Add a reference to this project from your test project and add the appropriate
using statement.

Now, let's ensure that there is a `Search` endpoint available. Let's create another test:

```
[Fact]
public void ItHasSearch()
{
  // Arrange
  var controller = new SpeakerController();

  // Act
  controller.Search("Jos");
}
```

Make this test pass by creating a `Search` method that accepts a string.

Let's confirm that the `Search` action result returns an `OkObjectResult`:

```
[Fact]
public void ItReturnsOkObjectResult()
{
  // Arrange
  var controller = new SpeakerController();

  // Act
  var result = controller.Search("Jos");

  // Assert
  Assert.NotNull(result);
  Assert.IsType<OkObjectResult>(result);
}
```

Note the multiple `Asserts`. While we want to limit our tests to a single `Act`, sometimes it is acceptable, even necessary, to have multiple `Asserts`.

Once the `ItReturnsOkObjectResult` test passes, you should delete the `ItExists` and `ItHasSearch` tests. Remember, we want to finish the *red, green, refactor* cycle and keep our code neat and clean. This includes the test suite, so if you have tests that are no longer valid or add no value, then you should feel free to remove them. You don't want to have to maintain more code than is required. This will help your test suite stay relevant and run nice and fast.

Now, let's test that the result is a collection of speakers:

```
[Fact]
public void ItReturnsCollectionOfSpeakers()
{
  // Arrange
  var controller = new SpeakerController();

  // Act
  var result = controller.Search("Jos") as OkObjectResult;

  // Assert
  Assert.NotNull(result);
  Assert.NotNull(result.Value);
  Assert.IsType<List<Speaker>>(result.Value);
}
```

We're starting to get a little redundant here. Now is a good time to refactor our tests to make them cleaner. Let's extract the creation of the `SpeakerController` and initialize this value in the constructor. Be sure to remove the creation in your tests and use this new instance:

```
private readonly SpeakerController _controller;

public SpeakerControllerSearchTests()
{
  _controller = new SpeakerController();
}
```

Finally, we're ready to start testing the value of the results. Let's write a test entitled `GivenExactMatchThenOneSpeakerInCollection`:

```
[Fact]
public void GivenExactMatchThenOneSpeakerInCollection()
{
  // Arrange
```

```
  // Act
  var result = _controller.Search("Joshua") as OkObjectResult;

  // Assert
  var speakers = ((IEnumerable<Speaker>)result.Value).ToList();
  Assert.Equal(1, speakers.Count);
}
```

To get this test to work, we'll need to hard-code some data. Don't worry, we're building this application slowly. The hard-coded data will be removed at a later point:

```
[Fact]
public void GivenExactMatchThenOneSpeakerInCollection()
{
  // Arrange
  // Act
  var result = _controller.Search("Joshua") as OkObjectResult;

  // Assert
  var speakers = ((IEnumerable<Speaker>)result.Value).ToList();
  Assert.Equal(1, speakers.Count);
  Assert.Equal("Joshua", speakers[0].Name);
}
```

Ensure that our search string is not case-sensitive:

```
[Theory]
[InlineData("Joshua")]
[InlineData("joshua")]
[InlineData("JoShUa")]
public void GivenCaseInsensitveMatchThenSpeakerInCollection (string
searchString)
{
  // Arrange
  // Act
  var result = _controller.Search(searchString) as OkObjectResult;

  // Assert
  var speakers = ((IEnumerable<Speaker>)result.Value).ToList();
  Assert.Equal(1, speakers.Count);
  Assert.Equal("Joshua", speakers[0].Name);
}
```

Next, we need to test to verify that, if the string provided does not match any of our data, then an empty collection is returned:

```
[Fact]
public void GivenNoMatchThenEmptyCollection()
{
  // Arrange
  // Act
  var result = _controller.Search("ZZZ") as OkObjectResult;

  // Assert
  var speakers = ((IEnumerable<Speaker>)result.Value).ToList();
  Assert.Equal(0, speakers.Count);
}
```

And finally, we'll test that any speaker that begins with our search string will be returned:

```
[Fact]
public void Given3MatchThenCollectionWith3Speakers()
{
  // Arrange
  // Act
  var result = _controller.Search("jos") as OkObjectResult;

  // Assert
  var speakers = ((IEnumerable<Speaker>)result.Value).ToList();
  Assert.Equal(3, speakers.Count);
  Assert.True(speakers.Any(s => s.Name == "Josh"));
  Assert.True(speakers.Any(s => s.Name == "Joshua"));
  Assert.True(speakers.Any(s => s.Name == "Joseph"));
}
```

Here's what the code we came up with looks like. Your implementation may vary somewhat:

```
using System;
using System.Collections.Generic;
using System.Linq;
using Microsoft.AspNetCore.Mvc;

namespace SpeakerMeet.Api.Controllers
{
  [Route("api/[controller]")]
  public class SpeakerController : Controller
  {
    [Route("search")]
    public IActionResult Search(string searchString)
    {
```

```
    var hardCodedSpeakers = new List<Speaker>
    {
      new Speaker{Name = "Josh"},
      new Speaker{Name = "Joshua"},
      new Speaker{Name = "Joseph"},
      new Speaker{Name = "Bill"},
    };

    var speakers = hardCodedSpeakers.Where(x =>
x.Name.StartsWith(searchString,
StringComparison.OrdinalIgnoreCase)).ToList();

    return Ok(speakers);
  }
}

public class Speaker
{
  public string Name { get; set; }
}
}
```

Summary

You should now feel quite comfortable with your .NET development environment. The .NET Core SDK should now be installed and your IDE configured. You've had some exposure to unit tests and continuous test runners in Visual Studio and VS Code.

In Chapter 7, *Setting Up the JavaScript Environment*, we'll focus on getting our JavaScript environment set up.

7
Setting Up a JavaScript Environment

In this chapter, we'll explore setting up your JavaScript development environment with examples in pure JavaScript and React.

In this chapter, you will gain an understanding of:

- Installing your IDE
- How to set up your testing framework
- Writing your first tests in JavaScript

Node.js

Node.js, commonly called Node, is practically a requirement for doing modern web application development. In this section, we will discuss what Node is exactly, provide reasons why you need Node, and, finally, talk about where you can get Node installation instructions.

If you are already familiar with these subjects, then feel free to jump to the next section, where we discuss NPM in a similar fashion.

What is Node?

Node was created in late 2009 by Ryan Dahl. Based on Chrome's V8 engine, Node provides a JavaScript runtime built for the purpose of providing evented, non-blocking I/O (input/output) for serving web applications.

At the time, Chrome had created the fastest JavaScript engine available. At the same time, they had decided to open-source the code for it. For these two extremely compelling reasons, Node decided to use the V8 engine.

Ryan Dahl was unhappy with the performance, at the time, of the very popular Apache HTTP server. One of the problems with the way that Apache was handling concurrent connections was that it was creating a new thread for each connection. Task creation and task switching between these threads are both CPU-and memory-intensive. For these reasons, instead of using threads for concurrent connections, Dahl decided to write Node with the intent of using an event loop coupled with a callback paradigm.

Why do we need Node?

To perform TDD in JavaScript for a modern web application, we absolutely need Node. When writing a modern web application, you will very likely be using one of these popular frameworks: ReactJS, Angular, Ember.js, Vue.js, or Polymer. The majority of these applications require a compilation step in Node.

Another reason for using Node is that we want to take advantage of new features in JavaScript. Node doesn't support these features itself, but libraries have been written that will allow you to transpile the newer versions of JavaScript, ECMAScript 2015+, into a version of JavaScript that is supported by your target browsers.

Lastly, we need Node so that we can run our tests. Later, we will discuss how we can also run our tests continuously while we are writing our code. This is known as continuous testing and is a must-have for rapid development.

Installing Node

There are several options for installing Node on your machine. We will cover installing manually and installing from a package management repository.

The benefits of using a package management repository are many. The main reason that you would want to install this way would be the benefit of version management. Node updates versions frequently, and using a package manager can help to notify you of available updates. It can also help install those updates in a simple and efficient manner. We will start with a manual install, followed by installing using a Linux package manager, a Mac OSX package manager, and finally a Windows package manager.

To install Node manually, open your favorite browser and go to `http://nodejs.org`. You should see something similar to the following screenshot. Regardless of your operating system, the Node website will have a download link for both current and **Long Term Support** (**LTS**) versions of Node installation files. For Windows and Mac, the Node website provides installers. For Linux, Node provides binaries and source code. Assuming you are familiar with your operating system, the installation process is fairly straightforward and shouldn't present any issues.

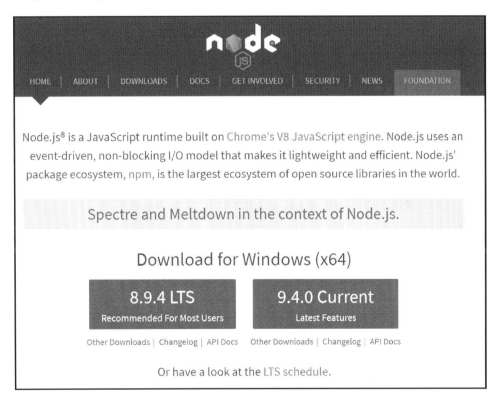

Package managers greatly simplify the installation of many applications. If you are unfamiliar with package managers in general, they are based on the concept of having a repository of applications and tools that are available for installation on the system the package manager is for. Almost every system available has a package manager for it now. Linux has a different package manager for many distributions. Mac uses a system called *Homebrew,* and Windows has a package manager named *Chocolatey.*

Linux

First, we will cover using the Ubuntu package manager, called `apt`, as Ubuntu is one of the most popular Linux systems. If you are using a different distribution, the process should be very similar. The only difference is the name of your package manager. Open a terminal window and enter the following commands to install Node for Ubuntu:

```
$ sudo apt-get update
$ sudo apt-get install nodejs
```

It's that simple; now the latest version of Node is installed and ready for you to begin using. These same commands will update Node when a new version is available.

Mac OSX

Mac doesn't come with a package manager preinstalled. To install Homebrew, you must open a Terminal and execute the following command:

```
ruby -e "$(curl -fsSL
https://raw.githubusercontent.com/Homebrew/install/master/install)"
```

Now that you have Homebrew installed, you also have one more requirement that you must fulfill. You must install Apple's Xcode, which can be found by searching the App Store. Just like any other application on a Mac, once you have found it, just click the Install application button, and Xcode will download and install:

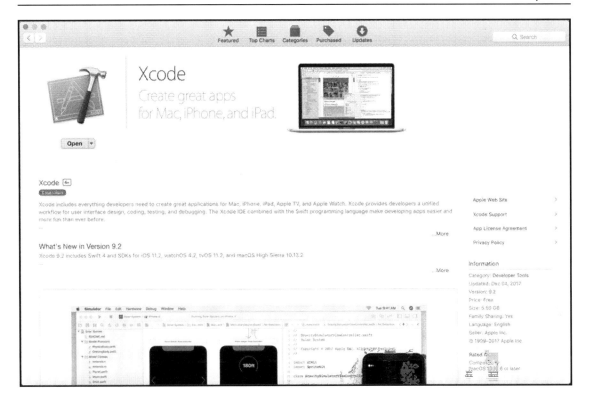

Now that we have both prerequisites for Node installed on the system, installation is extremely simple. From a Terminal window, execute the following command:

```
$ brew install node
```

Updating Node is also just as simple. Occasionally, when you want to update, execute the following command:

```
$ brew update
$ brew upgrade node
```

You now have the latest version of Node installed on your Mac.

Windows

Windows also has a package manager. Just like Mac, the Windows package manager does not come preinstalled. The package manager for Windows is named Chocolatey and can be found at `https://chocolatey.org`:

To install Chocolatey, open a Command Prompt (`cmd.exe`) as administrator and execute the following command:

```
@"%SystemRoot%\System32\WindowsPowerShell\v1.0\powershell.exe" -NoProfile -
ExecutionPolicy Bypass -Command "iex ((New-Object
System.Net.WebClient).DownloadString('https://chocolatey.org/install.ps1'))
" && SET "PATH=%PATH%;%ALLUSERSPROFILE%\chocolatey\bin"
```

After the Chocolatey installation has finished, you may need to restart the command window before you can use it. Restart the Command Prompt as an administrator, and then execute the following commands to install Node on windows using the Chocolatey package manager:

```
C:\>choco install nodejs
C:\>refreshenv
```

Once you've executed the first command, you will be prompted to execute a script. You will need to agree to run the script to install Node.

To upgrade Node using Chocolatey, execute the following command:

```
C:\>choco upgrade nodejs
```

You may need to agree to run the installation script. If prompted, simply hit the *Y* key and press *Enter*. You now have the latest version of Node.

NPM

NPM is a critical piece of the Node environment and community. Without NPM, Node would not have taken off quite like it has. In this section, we will discuss what NPM is, what NPM isn't, why you need NPM for doing Node development, and finally, where you can get NPM and how to install it.

What is NPM?

Initially released in early 2010, **NPM (Node Package Manager)**. NPM was written by Isaac Z. Schlueter, and is now maintained by a team of developers. Although NPM has Node in the acronym, it can also be used to manage packages for the browser.

In the past few years, many package managers were created specifically for browser packages. One of the most prominent is *Bower*. These secondary package managers were created because NPM was perceived as a package manager best suited for, or perhaps only suited for, managing Node packages. This belief has subsided; however, Bower's own website now suggests that it not be used.

Why do we need NPM?

While you do need to install NPM, you don't necessarily have to use it. In late 2016, Facebook released an alternative package manager named *Yarn*, which uses the NPM registry, so all of your favorite packages are available.

There are likely other package management alternatives to NPM as well. These alternative package managers are important because they drive improvements in NPM, but ultimately, they will likely fade and NPM will continue to be the preferred package manager for Node, and for JavaScript in general. If you do decide to use an alternative package manager such as Yarn, you will need to install it using NPM.

Installing NPM?

Good news; you already have NPM installed if you have gone through the process of installing Node. You may occasionally want to upgrade NPM outside Node's release cycle. To attempt an upgrade, simply open your operating system's preferred console or Terminal window and execute the following command:

```
>npm install -g npm
```

NPM is just another executable on your computer. It takes a list of arguments or parameters. In this case, we are asking NPM to install a package. The second argument, -g, tells NPM that we want to install the requested package globally. Lastly, the package we are asking NPM to install is NPM.

A quick introduction to JavaScript IDEs

While you don't need an **IDE (Integrated Development Environment)** per se, you will need a text editor. Why not have a text editor that does a little bit of the heavy lifting for you? There are, essentially, two types of IDEs available for JavaScript development. The first kind is really more of a text editor than anything else, whereas the second kind is a full-blown editor with compiling and source control built in.

While you can work on JavaScript with only a simple text editor and a console/Terminal window, we recommend using something with at least a little more power.

Visual Studio Code

Visual Studio Code, as described in the C# section, is a lightweight editor based on the Electron framework and developed in TypeScript, a language designed by Microsoft to extend JavaScript with static types. TypeScript compiles to JavaScript, so ultimately Visual Studio Code is a JavaScript application.

Why Visual Studio Code?

For working with JavaScript, there are several reasons why you might choose Visual Studio Code or one of the other Electron-based editors. VSCode is lightweight, has an extensive plugin architecture, is integrated with source control, and is very easy to set up and use.

Installing Visual Studio Code

Installing VSCode is extremely simple. If you have already followed along in the C# section, then you likely have VSCode installed already. If not, here are some alternative ways to install it that were not discussed there.

Linux

To install on Linux (again, this is an example for Ubuntu), simply execute the following commands:

```
sudo apt-get update
sudo apt-get install code # or code-insiders
```

Mac

Unfortunately, I don't have a fancy command-line way to install VSCode on a Mac. Instead, go to the Visual Studio Code homepage at `https://code.visualstudio.com` and follow the installation instructions there.

Windows

For Windows, just like with Node, we can install VSCode using Chocolatey. To install using Chocolatey (`https://chocolatey.org/install`), execute the following command in a console window. Remember, you may want to run the console as an administrator:

```
C:\> choco install visualstudiocode
```

Installing the plugins you will need

The two plugins that we would recommend getting are `npm` and `npm-intellisense` because they will aid in the flow and provide hints when you are not 100% sure that you are using the correct package name.

Configuring the testing environment

Visual Studio Code offers built-in test running capabilities. We are not going to choose those options for JavaScript development, however. For the purposes of test driving our application and demonstrating our approach to testing, we think using the available Terminal inside VSCode will be more appropriate and better suited to the flow that will be used.

WebStorm

WebStorm is a full-blown IDE written by JetBrains in Java.

Why WebStorm?

WebStorm basically comes with everything you need to develop a JavaScript-based application. It also supports many of the JavaScript ecosystem alternatives to JavaScript, such as TypeScript, Flow, and React JSX. WebStorm also integrates seamlessly with many code-quality tools such as ESLine, TSLint, and JSHint.

The only downside to WebStorm is that it does cost money. But, when you look at it, a paid product is actually a good thing. The company making the paid product has a good reason to continue maintaining it. JetBrains offers the purchase of WebStorm through a single purchase or through a subscription. We suggest the subscription, as the upfront cost to you is minimized and JetBrains has more motivation to keep you happy this way.

Installing WebStorm

To install WebStorm, we are going to use a newer program created by JetBrains called *The JetBrains Toolbox App*. The Toolbox App is designed to track version updates and provide a common launching point for all JetBrains products. Once installed, it becomes very easy to install any of the JetBrains tools.

Linux

There does not appear to be, at the time of writing, a way to install ToolBox or WebStorm from `apt-get`. So, we will have to do it the hard way. Go to the ToolBox download page at `https://www.jetbrains.com/toolbox/app/` and download the Linux tarball. Then, open a Terminal to your download directory. Once there, execute the following commands:

```
mv jetbrains-toolbox-<version>.tar.gz <application directory
root>/jetbrains-toolbox-<version>.tar.gz
cd <application directory root>
tar -xj jetbrains-toolbox-<version>.tar.gz
chmod -R 777 jetbrains-toolbox-<version>
cd jetbrains-toolbox-<version>
./jetbrains-toolbox
```

Mac

On Mac, we can again use Homebrew for installation. Just execute the following command:

```
brew cask install jetbrains-toolbox
```

Windows

On Windows, we are able to use Chocolatey to install Toolbox. Execute the following command and then launch the app:

```
choco install jetbrainstoolbox
```

Our ultimate goal when installing the Toolbox was to install WebStorm. So, with the Toolbox open, either sign in if you have purchased any JetBrains products or skip the sign in if you just want to try them out. Next, find WebStorm in the products list and click the button to install it. Once the install has finished, you will be able to click a **Launch** button that will replace the **Install** button.

Installing the plugins you will need

We've got good news for plugins with WebStorm. WebStorm offers a great plugin community, with every plugin you could possibly want accessible through a plugin management system built into the application. For the purposes of this book, however, you don't actually need any. So, we are done installing plugins! In fact, if anything, WebStorm has too much functionality built in, and we will be ignoring or even turning off some of it so that we can work the way we want to.

Configuring the testing environment

Just as in Visual Studio Code, for WebStorm we are not going to cover setting up any of the built-in test running capability. WebStorm offers a Terminal display that can be turned on and supports having multiple contexts open at the same time.

Create React App

Now that you have Node and NPM installed and up-to-date, turn your attention to the application you want to test drive. Due to its constantly increasing popularity, we are choosing to explain and demonstrate Test-Driven Development by testing a React application.

According to the React website, React is *A JavaScript library for building user interfaces.* We are going to focus on using it for a front-end browser application, but it can be used to create mobile and desktop applications as well.

React was created and is maintained by Facebook. React was created to solve issues that Facebook had in its own user interface, and it is now taking the internet by storm. Facebook has also created a library called Create React App to quickly get a React application going.

What is Create React App?

Create React App is an NPM package created by Facebook for the purpose of providing a zero-configuration way to create a react application. React requires quite a lot to get started, and it can take days to configure a React application manually. Create React App can reduce that time to under a minute.

Installing the global module

Create React App has a global NPM package that must be installed before you can use the command-line utility to actually create a React application. To install the latest version of the Create React App global script, execute the following command in a console or Terminal window:

```
>npm install -g create-react-app
```

Creating a React application

Once the global module is installed, you will be ready to start using Create React App. Creating a React application is extremely streamlined and simple. On my system, I have a directory \projects that I use to house all my front-end application projects. Open a console/Terminal window to a similarly purposed directory on your machine and execute the following command to create a new React application:

```
\projects>create-react-app <projectName>
```

In our case, the name of our test case is Speaker Meet, so as an example, my command is displayed as follows:

```
\projects>create-react-app speakermeet-spa
```

SpeakerMeet, as mentioned in the C# section, has both a back-end (the RESTful Web API) and a front-end (a React-based **SPA (Single Page Application)**).

Running the Create React App script

When the `create-react-app` script finishes running, a list of available commands is displayed. You want to make sure that everything was successfully created. You can launch the application by executing the following command:

```
>npm start
```

If everything installed correctly, your default browser will open and a new React application will be running.

Mocha and Chai

Create React App supports testing right out of the box. Initially, Create React App uses a testing library named Jest. We want to use Mocha and Chai due to their popularity in the JavaScript community.

Jest

Jest is a testing framework written by Facebook. Just like Create React App, Jest is designed to be a zero-configuration tool. Jest also supports continuous testing and code coverage analysis.

Jest is designed to work within the common **BDD (behavior-driven development)** paradigms, as are many other JavaScript testing frameworks. As such, the testing functions `describe` and `it` can both be used to write your tests.

Mocha

Mocha is another JavaScript testing framework and is the one we would like to use. As for library interaction differences, there doesn't appear to be much different in terms of base interactions. The differences come down to the assertion library and the mocking library.

 Mocking, which will be covered in detail in `Chapter 8`, *What to Know Before Getting Started*, is essentially a way to provide alternative implementations of objects, classes, and functions, specifically to aid the testing process.

Mocha itself doesn't come with an assertion library, so one must be provided. The assertion library is what controls test results and how to verify that your code is executing correctly. Most developers who use Mocha rely on Chai for assertions.

As mentioned previously, another consideration is what mocking library you want to use. For many Mocha users, that library is unquestionably *Sinon*.

We will explain the purpose of any and all parts of Mocha that we use in this book. If you want to know more or want the documentation for quick reference while you are developing, you can go to the Mocha home page at `https://mochajs.org`.

Mocha can be installed into a JavaScript application using the following command:

```
>npm install mocha
```

Chai

Chai is a BDD assertion library. Chai uses a fluent API to allow for extremely flexible assertions. The two most popular ways that Chai is used are through the *should* and *expect* interfaces provided. The way that Chai works, and in fact, the way that every testing frameworks assertion works, is by throwing an exception when the check done by the assertion fails.

For instance, if you had a variable named `foo` with a value 3 and your assertion was `expect(foo).to.equal(5)` when the test ran, that assertion would throw an exception with a message that says `expected 3 to equal 5`.

To install Chai into your project, run the following command:

```
>npm install chai
```

Once you have Chai installed, there is one more step that must be taken to be able to use it within your project. You must include the following import at the top of each test file in your application:

```
import { expect } from 'chai';
```

If you wish to use should assertions, you can either replace `expect` with `should` or add `should` inside the curly braces, separating it from `expect` with a comma.

For more information or to refer to the documentation, the Chai home page is `https://chaijs.com`.

Sinon

We won't be getting into mocking until `Chapter 8`, *What to Know Before Getting Started*, but Sinon is the generally preferred mocking library among Mocha + Chai users. Some testing frameworks, such as Jest and Jasmine, come with their own mocking library features, but Mocha does not, and Sinon provides an excellent mocking experience.

To install Sinon into your project, execute the following command:

```
>npm install sinon
```

Once installed, you will need to import Sinon before you can use it. Use the following import statement to enable the use of Sinon:

```
import sinon from 'sinon';
```

Enzyme

Enzyme is a library designed to aid in the testing of React components.

To install Enzyme into your project, execute the following command:

```
>npm install enzyme react-test-renderer react-dom
```

The extra libraries listed, `react-test-renderer` and `react-dom`, are dependencies of Enzyme that it needs to function correctly.

As with the other testing utilities mentioned in this section, we will get into usage as needed, while we discuss the topics covered in this book. But here is a quick example of a test using Enzyme from the Enzyme documentation at `https://github.com/airbnb/enzyme`:

```
import React from 'react';
import { expect } from 'chai';
import { render } from 'enzyme';
import Foo from './Foo';

describe('<Foo />', () => {
  it('renders three `.foo-bar`s', () => {
    const wrapper = render(<Foo />);

    expect(wrapper.find('.foo-bar').length).to.equal(3);
  });

  it('renders the title', () => {
    const wrapper = render(<Foo title="unique" />);
```

```
        expect(wrapper.text()).to.contain('unique');
});});
```

Ejecting the React app

Unfortunately, this is where we part company with Create React App. In order to use Mocha, we will need to find an alternative way to work with the application. Because of the zero-configuration setup of Create React App, we cannot simply update the testing framework being used, and that is a problem for us.

Thankfully, Create React App gives us an out in the form of ejecting the application. Ejecting the React application will install all the necessary configuration files and utilities into our project and remove Create React App. Once the ejection process is finished, we will have access to all the configuration files and we will have the ability to switch to using Mocha.

To eject Create React App, execute the following command:

```
>npm run eject
```

If you take a look at the `package.json` in the root of the project, you will see that a lot of information and configuration have been added.

 After any major modification to `package.json`, it is a good idea to delete `node_modules` and `package-lock.json` and then re-run `npm install`.

Configuring to use Mocha and Chai

After you have ejected the React app, before you make any further modifications, you should make sure everything still works. Execute the following command before making any further modifications:

```
>npm start
```

Now check that a browser launched and that the application is running correctly. You will have to *Ctrl + C* to exit the running process:

```
>npm run build
```

After this command, check that a build folder was created at the root of your project and that there were no errors displayed in the console:

```
>npm test
```

Even though you are about to change the test configuration, you will be using some of the libraries that were provided by Create React App. You want to make sure that those prerequisites transitioned properly when you ejected. As with `npm start`, you will have to *Ctrl + C* to exit this process.

Assuming all of the commands executed without issues, you can now start the process of switching the test environment over to Mocha. Execute the following command to ensure the installation of the necessary dependencies:

```
>npm install mocha chai sinon enzyme
```

Open `package.json` and update the following lines:

```
"babel": {
  "presets": [
    "react-app"
  ]
},
```

Change the preceding code to:

```
"babel": {
  "presets": [
    "react",
    "es2015"
  ]
},
```

You will also need to install the BabelJS preset for ES2015:

```
>npm install babel-preset-es2015
```

Next, find and delete the `jest` setting in `package.json`. You are now ready to change the `test` script to execute Mocha instead of Jest. Find NPM scripts and update the test script as follows:

```
"test": "node scripts/test.js --env=jsdom"
```

Change the preceding code to:

```
"test": "mocha --require babel-core/register ./scripts/test.js --require
babel-core/register ./src/**/*.spec.js"
```

The change you just made will cause Mocha to execute all of your tests. It will only execute them once, though. You want a way to have your tests running continuously while you work, so you need to add an additional script. Add a comma to the end of the line you just modified and then add the following script just beneath `test`:

```
"test:watch": "npm test -- -w"
```

Now, you need to update the `test.js` file provided when you ejected. Open `<project root>/scripts/test.js` and replace all the code inside with the following:

```
'use strict';

import jsdom from 'jsdom';

global.document = jsdom.jsdom('<html><body></body></html>');
global.window = document.defaultView;
global.navigator = window.navigator;

function noop() {
  return {};
}

// prevent mocha tests from breaking when trying to require a css file
require.extensions['.css'] = noop;
require.extensions['.svg'] = noop;
```

This file just sets up the base environment for your tests to execute inside. Make note of the `noop` function and usage. Currently, you are ignoring the `css` and `svg` extensions that are required by your production code when you are testing. In the course of testing, if you run into issues while requiring a different extension, you might have to come back to this file and add the troublesome extension to the list.

You are almost done; you only have one more modification to make before you are officially switched over to Mocha. Find the file `App.test.js` in your `src` directory, and change its name to `App.spec.js`, then update the contents to the following:

```
import React from 'react';
import ReactDOM from 'react-dom';
import { expect } from 'chai';

import App from './App';
```

```
describe('(Component) App', () => {
  it('renders without crashing', () => {
    const div = document.createElement('div');
    ReactDOM.render(<App />, div);
  });
});
```

All you have really done here is import Chai and add a `describe` block. The rest of this test has remained unchanged and is the default test provided with Create React App.

A quick kata to check our test setup

For this setup test, you are going to do the Palindrome code kata. This code kata can get complex, but you are only going to concern yourself with the most basic form.

The requirements

The requirements for this kata are as follows:

```
Given a string value
 And Given the provided string is not a palindrome
 When checked
 Then return false

Given a string value
 And Given the provided string is a palindrome
 When checked
 Then return true
```

The execution

As you always should, you will begin with a templated test file designed to verify that the unit testing framework is configured correctly:

```
import { expect } from 'chai';

describe('Test Framework', () =>  {
  it('is configured correctly', () => {
    expect(1).to.equal(0);
  }
}
```

We have shown a failing version of this template. Before you begin writing the tests that are actually for the kata, run the `test:watch` NPM script and verify that the test fails. Also, verify that it fails for the right reason. It should fail because *1* was expected but *0* was the actual result. After the test properly fails, change the zero to a one and verify that the test now passes. As long as these two validations work correctly, we will continue and begin working through the code kata.

Starting the kata

The first thing you will do for the kata is write an `ItExists` test. Again, these types of test help to get the ball rolling and prevent writer's block. You will replace the code for checking the framework with the following.

Red phase; write a failing test that expects an `isPalindrome` function to exist:

```
describe('Is Palindrome', () => {
  it('exists', () => {
    expect(isPalindrome).to.exist;
  });
});
```

Verify that this test fails. It's important to see failure before moving on to making the test pass. This will help confirm that your test setup is working properly.

And now the *green phase*; make the test pass. Define an `isPalindrome` function and run the test once more to see it pass.

```
function isPalindrome() {
}
```

For the next test, we want to think of the simplest test case that would produce a result. Again, we are skipping bad data issues. The simplest test case we can think of that would produce a result is a single letter. For the definition of palindrome that you will be using for these tests, a single letter is a palindrome. Add the following test under the previous one:

```
it('a single letter is a palindrome', () => {
  // arrange
  const value = 'a';

  // act
  const result = isPalindrome(value);
```

```
  // assert
  expect(result).to.be.true;
});
```

Now, to make it pass:

```
function isPalindrome() {
  return true;
}
```

Now you have a passing test, but you are always returning true. You want the next test to fail when you write it. So, you should write a test for when the value passed in is not a palindrome. The simplest non-palindrome would be two letters that are not the same:

```
it('two non-matching letters is not a palindrome', () => {
  // arrange
  const value = 'at';

  // act
  const result = isPalindrome(value);

  // assert
  expect(result).to.be.false;
});
```

Now, make it pass:

```
function isPalindrome(value) {
  if(value.length === 1) {
    return true;
  }

  return false;
}
```

Okay, so now you only return true single letters. This opens us up for our next test, flipping back to something that is a palindrome; write a test for two letters that are the same:

```
it('two matching letters are a palindrome', () => {
  // arrange
  const value = 'oo';

  // act
  const result = isPalindrome(value);

  // assert
  expect(result).to.be.true;
});
```

Now, to make it pass:

```
function isPalindrome(value) {
  if (value.length === 1) {
    return true;
  }

  if (value.length === 2 && value[0] === value[1]) {
    return true;
  }

  return false;
}
```

The next test is to have a three-letter word that is a palindrome. Currently, this should fail:

```
it('three letter palindrome', () => {
  // arrange
  const value = 'mom';

  // act
  const result = isPalindrome(value);

  // assert
  expect(result).to.be.true;
});
```

To make this test pass, think about what you have so far. One algorithm for checking a palindrome is to simply start on the outsides and check the two outermost letters. If those two letters are a match, then move in one letter on each side. Repeat this check until you get to the center of the word or phrase. If the center is one letter, then it's a palindrome; otherwise, check if the two center-most characters are a match. Let's try this concept out by using recursion to make the latest test pass:

```
function isPalindrome(value) {
  if (value.length === 1) {
    return true;
  }

  if (value.length === 2 && value[0] === value[1]) {
    return true;
  }
```

```
    if(value[0] === value[value.length -1]) {
      return isPalindrome(value.substring(1, value.length - 1));
    }

    return false;
}
```

We now need to check if a four-letter palindrome will pass:

```
it('four letter palindrome', () => {
  // arrange
  const value = 'abba';

  // act
  const result = isPalindrome(value);

  // assert
  expect(result).to.be.true;
});
```

It passes; excellent! We will end this code kata with two exercises for you. The first exercise is to add a test for "a man a plan a canal panama" and make it pass. The second exercise is to refactor the code for isPalindrome. While this is a small function, it could still do with some tidying up, and potentially some optimizations.

Summary

You should now have Node installed and your JavaScript development environment configured. JavaScript examples throughout the rest of the book will assume your use of WebStorm.

But, before diving right in, Chapter 8, *What to Know Before Getting Started*, will focus on what more you need to know before getting started.

8
What to Know Before Getting Started

You're off to a pretty good start. By now, you should be starting to feel comfortable with the basic concepts behind Test-Driven Development. You know the basic premise behind TDD and how to write a unit test in C# and JavaScript.

In this chapter:

- We'll cover more of the practices behind TDD
- Specific advice will be given on how to avoid pitfalls along the way
- We'll explain the importance of defining and testing boundaries, abstracting away third-party code (including the .NET Framework)
- We'll begin to introduce more advanced concepts, such as spies, mocks, and fakes

First, let's cover some issues you may run into while trying to test an existing application. Hopefully, this will help you avoid problems in your next green-field application.

Untestable code

There are a variety of telltale signs that an application, class, or method will be difficult, or even impossible, to test. Sure, there are ways around some of the following examples but it's usually best to just avoid workarounds and programmatic acrobatics. Simple is usually best, and your future self and/or future maintainers will thank you for keeping things simple.

Dependency Injection

If you're creating instances of external resources within your constructors or inside methods instead of having them passed in, it will be very difficult to write tests to cover these classes and methods. Generally, in today's modern applications, Dependency Injection frameworks are used to create and provide the external dependencies to a class. Many choose to define an *interface* as the contract for the dependency, providing a more flexible method for testing and the coupling to external resources.

Static

You may have a need to access static third-party classes or methods. Instead of accessing static resources directly, it would be better to access these through an *interface*. In the example of `DateTime` in C#, `Now` is a static property, which prevents you from being able to control the `DateTime` value used by the class or method being tested. This makes it more difficult to verify your test cases and ensure your program's logic is behaving correctly, based on specific dates or times.

Singleton

Singletons are the essence of the shared state. In order to ensure your tests run in an isolated environment, it would be best to avoid them. If a *singleton* is required (for example, `Logging`, `Data Context`, and so on), most Dependency Injection frameworks allow for the substitution of a non-singleton class as a single instance, which gives the functionality and flexibility of effectively having a singleton. For production code, this allows you to control the scope of the singleton instance.

Global state

It has long been understood that global state within an application will wreak havoc on a system and cause unexpected behavior that is difficult to trace. Changing the code in one place will possibly have far-reaching side-effects on the rest of your system. For testability, this often means much more effort in setup and slower test execution.

Abstracting third-party software

As your application grows, you'll likely introduce external dependencies. Assuredly, the developers of these systems, applications, and libraries have thoroughly tested their offerings. You should focus your attention on testing your application, not on testing third-party code. Your application should be robust enough to handle edge cases, and you'll want to account for expected and unexpected behavior. You'll want to abstract away the details of the third-party code and test for expected (and unexpected) results.

So, what is *third-party code*? Anything you didn't write. That includes the .NET Framework itself. One way to achieve the abstraction of third-party code is with the use of test doubles.

Test doubles

Test doubles are functions and classes that aid in the testing process by allowing you to either verify functionality or bypass a dependency that would otherwise be difficult to test. Test doubles are used at all levels to isolate the code being tested. Many times, the need for a test double drives the architecture of the code.

The `DateTime` object in C# is an example of when this is the case. `System.DateTime` is part of the .NET Framework, and normally you wouldn't think that you would abstract this in your code. The instinct of most developers is to simply reference it in a *using statement* and then access `DateTime.Now` directly within their code.

 A test that can't be repeated is a bad test.

This is usually difficult to test. If we were to try to test a method using `DateTime.Now`, we would be unable to prevent `DateTime.Now` default functionality. `DateTime.Now` returns the current date and time stored in a `DateTime` object. Not having the ability to manipulate the return of this object causes our tests to be unpredictable and unrepeatable. A test that can't be repeated is a bad test.

Many developers already understand the need for predictability. You may have heard the phrase, *If it can't be reproduced, it's not a bug* or a similar sentiment. This is because, in order to verify that we have fixed a bug, we must be able to predictably repeat the error. This way, once the steps to reproduce it no longer produce the bug, we can confidently say that the bug is fixed. At least we can for that series of steps.

Testing is no different from bug fixing; it follows all the same steps. We just know exactly what caused the bug; the code hasn't been written yet, or the refactoring we just attempted failed.

Creating test doubles can get a little involved at times. For this reason, frameworks to support the creation of these test doubles have been created for nearly every language that has a testing framework. The frameworks are generally referred to as mocking frameworks or libraries. In C#, the predominant framework currently in use is *Moq*, pronounced *mock*. Similarly, in JavaScript, the most referenced mocking library seems to be *Sinon*, pronounced *sign on*.

Mocking frameworks

Mocking frameworks are a great utility to alleviate some of the pressure of testing in a large project. They are especially useful when trying to wrap tests around a legacy system. A legacy system, in this case, is defined as an application that does not already have tests around it. This definition is from Michael Feather's book, *Working Effectively with Legacy Code*.

Use caution while learning Test-Driven Development and using mocking frameworks. Mocking frameworks provide a very attractive alternative to carefully considering your code. It is possible to write a complete set of tests that, in the end, only really test the mocking framework.

Many mocking frameworks are overpowered in this respect. In C#, a classification of mocking frameworks exists that allows you to replace external code. This external code includes `DateTime.Now` and any other class that you don't control. In JavaScript, this is called monkey patching, and every framework allows you to do it.

What's the harm, you ask? One of the benefits of TDD is that it encourages smart architectural choices. When you have the power to override the functionality of the third-party code, you no longer have the need to abstract in order to test.

Why is that a problem? Abstraction of the third-party is necessary if we want to keep the code flexible and if we want to follow the SOLID principles.

The SOLID principles

The SOLID principles are a collection of concepts originally put together by Robert C. Martin, aka "Uncle Bob." Usually advertised as *Object-Oriented Principles*, you should think of them as just plain good architectural choices. The SOLID principles consist of five principles: the Single Responsibility Principle, the Open/Closed principle, the Liskov Substitution principle, the Interface Segregation Principle, and the Dependency Inversion Principle.

The original articles on the SOLID principles are available at `http://butunclebob.com/ArticleS.UncleBob.PrinciplesOfOod`.

The Single Responsibility Principle

In Uncle Bob's article, the **Single Responsibility Principle (SRP)** is defined as, "A class should have only one reason to change."

What does this mean? That is the tough part; there are many approaches to understanding the meaning. One way to look at it is that the class should only support one business user. Another is that, within the application, the class should only be used with a limited or specific scope. Another is that the class should have a limited range of functionality. These are all correct, and yet insufficient. One way to ensure you are following it is to use what we will refer to as the "Rule of Three to Five."

If we're discussing requirements, for example, when a requirement has between three to five acceptance criteria, then it is most likely appropriately sized for its level of detail. Similarly, if we are discussing a method or function, then three to five lines of code is probably appropriately sized.

The Rule of Three to Five is a generic way to know that you are honoring the SRP. The rule states, "Less than three is good. Between three and five is fine. Above five is strongly consider refactoring." It's not quite as elegant as many other laws, principles, and rules, but the rule of three to five is easy to follow. This rule is just a guideline and should not be used as an ultimatum. You should try to apply this rule to just about everything in software development. You have already seen it in action in this book. This rule was used to determine the scope of the requirements in Chapter 5, *Why TDD is Important*, and in all the code samples that have been included so far.

If you use the Rule of Three to Five, it nearly guarantees that you are following SRP, and it keeps your code, file structure, and requirements small and maintainable.

The Open/Closed principle

The Open/Closed principle states, "Software entities (classes, modules, functions, and so on) should be open for extension, but closed for modification." The second of the SOLID principles doesn't sound like it is saying much, but it has a large impact.

There are many ways to honor this principle. You or your development team could put into place a rule that only allows for new development. That is, any existing functionality cannot be updated or changed, only replaced by new methods or classes. When we get to creating dividing lines in the code, you could use those dividing lines to create a place for this functionality swap to take place.

The Open/Closed principle also enables continuous integration and deployment. This is because, if your application never breaks a contract it has with the user, itself, or a third party, then it can always be deployed without fear of causing a production issue.

The Liskov Substitution principle

The Liskov Substitution principle may be difficult to understand at first due to its somewhat complex and mathematical definition. From Barbara Liskov's *Data Abstraction and Hierarchy* [`https://pdfs.semanticscholar.org/36be/babeb72287ad9490e1ebab84e7225ad6a9e5.pdf`], the principle is stated as follows:

> *What is wanted here is something like the following substitution property. If for each object o1 of type S there is an object o2 of type T, such that for all programs P defined in terms of T, the behavior of P is unchanged when o1 is substituted for o2, then S is a subtype of T.*

Uncle Bob has simplified this definition to be, *Functions that use pointers or references to base classes must be able to use objects of derived classes without knowing it.* Looking at this principle, it seems like it would just be inheritance. Except, it's not just inheritance. This principle implies that not only does the object replacing the other have to implement the same interface or contract as the original, it must also adhere to the same expectations as the original.

The classic example of a violation of this principle is the use of a square class in the place of a rectangle class. A typical rectangle class would need to have both length and width properties. In mathematics, a square is just a special type of rectangle. So, many would assume that creating a square class with length and width would be an acceptable swap for the rectangle class.

The problem here is that a square requires that both length and width have the same value. So, when you change either one on the square class, the class will update the other to have the same value. This is a problem because the application using the object doesn't expect this behavior. Therefore, the application must be aware of the possibility of the length or width changing without notice.

A failure to meet the expectations of the application is known as a refused bequest. A refused bequest can cause inconsistent behavior in an application and, at the very least, requires more code to compensate for the mismatch.

The Interface Segregation Principle

The Interface Segregation Principle is about keeping to the contract of interaction presented by your class small. More than small, the contract presented by your class should have a single responsibility.

Sometimes, having a class with a small single responsibility contract is difficult or not desired. In those instances, the class should implement multiple contracts instead of creating a combined contract. We want multiple contracts to reduce the number of far-reaching dependencies.

Every time a base class or interface is modified, the child classes must also be modified. At the very least, the child classes must now be recompiled. By limiting the scope of a contract, we can reduce the impact of changing that contract and improve the overall system architecture.

The Dependency Inversion principle

Inversion of dependencies is important for several reasons, among which are that inverted dependencies increase flexibility, decrease fragility, and help the code to be potentially reused.

Inversion of dependencies allows for a plugin type architecture. By defining a contract of interaction, a module can determine how it wants to interact with dependencies. Then the dependencies depend on that contract.

Because the top-level module has no outgoing dependencies, it can be deployed independently. Deploying a piece of an application independently almost never happens, but having an independently deployable library has the tremendous benefit of not needing to be recompiled when a dependency changes.

In normal development, the dependencies fluctuate a lot more than the higher-level modules. This fluctuation causes the need to recompile. When your application dependencies flow downward, a dependency recompile also triggers a recompile of the dependent library. So, in effect, changing a utility helper class in a tiny, but common library will trigger a recompile of your entire application.

If you are inverting your dependencies, however, a change like this will only trigger a recompile of the utility helper library and the application library. It will not trigger a recompile of every library between.

That does it for the SOLID principles. Please keep them in mind if you choose to use a mocking framework. Make sure you don't allow the mocking framework to trick you into building a rigid, fragile, immobile system.

Timely greeting

Expanding on the classic *Hello World* example, what if you wanted to change your greeting based on the time of day? An example is as follows:

```
As a visitor to the site
 I want to receive a time-appropriate greeting
 So that I may plan the submission of my talks

Given it is before noon
 When greeting is requested
 Then morning message is returned

Given it is afternoon
 When greeting is requested
 Then afternoon message is returned
```

You might think to yourself, this is simple; I can just write a quick method to return the proper message. Of course, you would be right. This is a pretty easy task. You might come up with something like this:

```
public string GetGreeting()
{
  if (DateTime.Now.Hour < 12)
    return "Good morning";

  return "Good afternoon";
}
```

Remember, back in `Chapter 5`, *Why TDD is Important*, we discussed the Three laws of TDD. The all-important first law states that you aren't allowed to write a single line of production code without a failing test.

Fragile tests

"But, this is such a simple method," you might say. What if you encountered a bug? What if you wanted to write some tests for this method after the fact? Would you have to run your test suite at a specific time of day to ensure a passing test? Would you have to alter your tests based on the time of day that you ran them?

False positives and false failures

If we left the code in our *Message* example as-is and wrote a test to cover the method, it might look something like this:

```
[Fact]
public void GivenEvening_ThenAfternoonMessage()
{
    // Arrange
    // Act
    var message = GetGreeting();

    // Assert
    Assert.Equal("Good afternoon", message);
}
```

Can you spot the problem with this test? There's nothing inherently wrong with the test, per se. The problem is that the production code will return a different message, based on the time of day. This means that if you ran the test in the afternoon, it would pass. If you ran the test in the morning, it would fail.

Abstract DateTime

`DateTime` is part of the .NET Framework, and therefore, it should be abstracted away from our system. Typically, we want our system to depend on interfaces, allowing us to substitute implementations at runtime.

Following is an example of ITimeManager:

```
public interface ITimeManager
{
  DateTime Now { get; }
}
```

For testing purposes, you might end up with an implementation of ITimeManager that looks like this:

```
public class TestTimeManager : ITimeManager
{
  public Func<DateTime> CurrentTime = () => DateTime.Now;

  public void SetDateTime(DateTime now)
  {
    CurrentTime = () => now;
  }

  public DateTime Now => CurrentTime();
}
```

This allows us to set the value for Now so that we can supply a known value to our test methods. Now, let's revisit our tests:

```
[Theory]
[InlineData(12)]
[InlineData(13)]
[InlineData(14)]
[InlineData(15)]
[InlineData(16)]
[InlineData(17)]
[InlineData(18)]
[InlineData(19)]
[InlineData(20)]
[InlineData(21)]
[InlineData(22)]
[InlineData(23)]
public void GivenAfternoon_ThenAfternoonMessage(int hour)
{
  // Arrange
  var afternoonTime = new TestTimeManager();
  afternoonTime.SetDateTime(new DateTime(2017, 7, 13, hour, 0, 0));
  var messageUtility = new MessageUtility(afternoonTime);

  // Act
  var message = messageUtility.GetGreeting();
```

```
  // Assert
  Assert.Equal("Good afternoon", message);
}

[Theory]
[InlineData(0)]
[InlineData(1)]
[InlineData(2)]
[InlineData(3)]
[InlineData(4)]
[InlineData(5)]
[InlineData(6)]
[InlineData(7)]
[InlineData(8)]
[InlineData(9)]
[InlineData(10)]
[InlineData(11)]
public void GivenMorning_ThenMorningMessage(int hour)
{
  // Arrange
  var morningTime = new TestTimeManager();
  morningTime.SetDateTime(new DateTime(2017, 7, 13, hour, 0, 0));
  var messageUtility = new MessageUtility(morningTime);

  // Act
  var message = messageUtility.GetGreeting();

  // Assert
  Assert.Equal("Good morning", message);
}
```

Our production code would end up looking something like this:

```
public class MessageUtility
{
  private readonly ITimeManager _timeManager;

  public MessageUtility(ITimeManager timeManager)
  {
    _timeManager = timeManager;
  }

  public string GetMessage()
  {
    if (_timeManager.Now.Hour < 12)
      return "Good morning";

    return "Good afternoon";
```

```
    }
  }
```

Test double types

Test doubles come in many varieties. Those varieties can generally be grouped as dummies, stubs, spies, mocks, and fakes. Coming up, we will discuss the different types and provide examples in C# and in JavaScript for each.

Dummies

Dummies are the simplest form of test double. A dummy has no appreciable functionality. We don't actually expect the dummy class or method to be used in the result of the class or method we are testing.

Dummies are most often used when the class you are testing has a dependency that the method or function you are testing does not use.

You create a dummy by creating a new copy or instance of a class or method and then doing absolutely nothing in the body of the code. Void methods will be empty and methods or functions expecting a return value will either throw when called or return the simplest form of that return value.

Dummy logger

A *Logging* service is a perfect example of something that can be replaced with a dummy. While you are testing specific methods it is unlikely (and not recommended) to also test logging functionality.

Example in C#

The following is an example of a DummyLogger in C#. You'll note that when Log is called nothing happens.

```
enum LogLevel
{
  None = 0,
  Error = 1,
  Warning = 2,
  Success = 3,
  Info = 4
```

```
}

interface ILogger
{
  void Log(LogLevel type, string message);
}

class DummyLogger: ILogger
{
  public void Log(LogLevel type, string message)
  {
    // Do Nothing
  }
}
```

Example in JavaScript

The following is an example of a `DummyLogger` in JavaScript. You'll note that when `info`, `warn`, `error`, and `success` are called nothing happens.

```
export class DummyLogger {
  info(message) {
  }

  warn(message) {
  }

  error(message) {
  }

  success(message) {
  }
}
```

Stubs

Stubs are the next level up from dummies. A Stub test double will provide the same response regardless of the parameters passed into it.

Stubs are used when you want to test different paths of execution in your code. One instance is an error that must be thrown under a particular condition.

Stubs are created by creating a copy or override of the class or method that needs to return the stub value and then setting it to return the needed value. Remember, stubs don't evaluate parameters, so you need to just return the desired value.

Example in C#

The following is an example of a StubSpeakerContactServiceError in C#. You'll note that, when MessageSpeaker is called then a new UnableToContactSpeakerException error is thrown.

```csharp
class StubSpeakerContactServiceError : ISpeakerContactService
{
  public void MessageSpeaker(string message)
  {
    throw new UnableToContactSpeakerException();
  }
}
```

Example in JavaScript

The following is an example of a stubSpeakerReducer in JavaScript. You'll note that regardless of the action passed in, a new *UNABLE_TO_RETRIEVE_SPEAKERS* error is pushed to the error array in the state.

```javascript
import { SpeakerErrors } from './errors';
import { SpeakerFilters } from './actions';

const initialState = {
  speakerFilter: SpeakerActions.SHOW_ALL,
  speakers: [],
  errors: []
};

export function stubSpeakerReducer(state, action) {
  state = state || initialState;
  state.speakerFilter = action.filter || SpeakerFilters.SHOW_ALL;
  state.errors.push(SpeakerErrors.UNABLE_TO_RETRIEVE_SPEAKERS);
  return state;
}
```

Spies

Spies are the next evolution in test doubles. A spy returns a value similar to a stub but has an extremely important and helpful difference. Spies can report back on the information related to the function call.

Spies are most often used when you want to verify that a function was called with specific parameters. This is most useful at third-party boundaries in your application. For instance, it is important to know whether your application is correctly configuring a database connection using the credentials supplied by some configuration service. Also, in some cases, it is difficult to measure the side-effects of the method or function being tested. In those cases, you can use a spy to just make sure you are calling the method or function in the first place.

Spies are created by starting with a stub and adding the functionality to determine whether a function has been called, how many times a function is called, or reporting what values were passed into that function.

Example in C#

The following is an example of a `SpySpeakerContactService` in C#. The `SpySpeakerContactService` allows you to determine if the service has been called and how many times it might have been called.

```csharp
class SpySpeakerContactService : ISpeakerContactService
{
  public bool MessageSpeakerHasBeenCalled { get; private set; }

  public int MessageSpeakerCallCount { get; private set; }

  public void MessageSpeaker(string message)
  {
    MessageSpeakerHasBeenCalled = true;
    MessageSpeakerCallCount++;
  }
}
```

Example in JavaScript

The following is an example of a `spySpeakerReducer` in JavaScript. The `spySpeakerReducer` allows you to determine how many times it might have been called.

```javascript
import { speakerReducer as original_speakerReducer } from './reducers';

export let callCounter = 0;

export function spySpeakerReducer(state, action) {
  callCounter++;
  return original_speakerReducer(state, action);
}
```

Mocks

Mocks are essentially programmable spies. Mocks are useful when you want to use the same test double in multiple tests. Mocks have the ability to return whatever values you set them to return. It is important to note that mocks are still not doing any logic. They return the value that is specified and do not check the parameters passed to the function.

Mocks are used in all the situations where dummies, stubs, and spies are used. Mocks are a heavier implementation of a test double, which is why you may not want to use them all the time. Mocks get less reuse than the previous test doubles because a mock's data must be set for each test, whereas a dummy, stub, or spy has a set return value that does not need to be configured. Setting up the test data that gets returned is often more difficult than simply creating a whole stub or spy class.

Mocks are created by making a copy of a class or method and creating a property that can be set as the return value for a method; then, in the method being mocked, the property value is returned. Once created, before each test, the mock's return value must be set.

Example in C#

The following is an example of a MockDateTimeService in C#. The MockDateTimeService allows you to set the DateTime to be returned by the service in order to reliably test how other parts of the system might behave based on specific DateTime.

```
class MockDateTimeService
{
  public DateTime CurrentDateTime { get; set; } = new DateTime();

  public DateTime UTCNow()
  {
    return CurrentDateTime.ToUniversalTime();
  }
}
```

Example in JavaScript

The following is an example of a MockDateTimeService in JavaScript. Much like the MockDateTimeService in C#, this allows you to set the DateTime to be returned by the service in order to reliably test how other parts of the system might behave based on specific DateTimes.

```
export class MockDateTimeService {
    constructor() {
```

```
      this.currentDateTime = new Date(2000, 0, 1);
    }

  now() {
    return this.currentDateTime;
  }
}
```

Fakes

Fakes are the last and most powerful type of test double. A fake is a class that attempts to behave as if it weren't a test double. While a fake will not connect with a database, it will attempt to behave just like it is connecting to a database. A fake will not use the system clock, but it will attempt to have an internal clock that behaves as close to the system clock as possible.

Fakes either add extra testing functionality or prevent external interference from third-party libraries and systems. Most applications are connected to some data source. A fake repository can be created that uses its own in-memory data source but otherwise behaves just like a normal data connection.

Fakes are created by generating a whole new class or method and then writing enough functionality to be indistinguishable from the production class or method. The only important distinction for a fake versus a production class or method is that the fake does not make external connections and likely has the ability for the tester to control the underlying data set.

Example in C#

The following is an example of a `FakeRepository` and associated *interfaces*. The `FakeRepository` is a fake implementation of a generic repository.

```
public interface IRepository<T>
{
  T Get(Func<T, bool> predicate);
  IQueryable<T> GetAll();
  T Save(T item);
  IRepository<T> Include(Expression<Func<T, object>> path);
}

public interface IIdentity
{
  int Id {get;set;}
}
```

```
public class FakeRepository<T> : IRepository<T> where T : IIdentity
{
  private int _identityCounter = 0;
  public IList<T> DataSet { get; set; } = new List<T>();

  public T Get(Func<T, bool> predicate)
  {
    return GetAll().Where(predicate).FirstOrDefault();
  }

  public IQueryable<T> GetAll()
  {
    return DataSet.AsQueryable();
  }

  public T Save(T item)
  {
    return item.Id == default(int) ? Create(item) : Update(item);
  }

  public IRepository<T> Include(Expression<Func<T, object>> path)
  {
    // Nothing to do here since this function is for EntityFramework
    // We are using Linq to Objects so there is not need for Include
    return this;
  }

  private T Create(T item)
  {
    item.Id = ++_identityCounter;
    DataSet.Add(item);
    return item;
  }

  private T Update(T item)
  {
    var found = Get(x => x.Id == item.Id);

    if(found == null)
    {
      throw new KeyNotFoundException($"Item with Id {item.Id} not
        found!");
    }

    DataSet.Remove(found);
    DataSet.Add(item);

    return item;
```

```
    }
  }
```

Example in JavaScript

The following is an example of a FakeDataContext in JavaScript.

```javascript
export class FakeDataContext {
  _identityCounter = 1;
  _dataSet = [];

  get DataSet() {
    return this._dataSet;
  }

  set DataSet(value) {
    this._dataSet = value;
  }

  get(predicate) {
    if (typeof(predicate) !== 'function') {
      throw new Error('Predicate must be a function');
    }

    const resultSet = this_dataSet.filter(predicate);

    return resultSet.length >= 1 ? {...resultSet[0]} : null;
  }

  getAll() {
    return this._dataSet.map((x) => {
      return {...x};
    });
  }

  save(item) {
    return item.id ? this.update(item) : this.create(item);
  }

  update(item) {
    if (!this._dataSet.some(x => x.id === item.id)) {
      this._dataSet.push({...item});
    } else {
      let itemIndex = this._dataSet.findIndex(x => x.id === item.id);
      this._dataSet[itemIndex] = {...item};
    }

    return {...item};
```

```
      }

    create(item) {
      let newItem = {...item};
      newItem.id = this._identityCounter++;
      this._dataSet.push({...newItem});

      return {...newItem};
    }
  }
```

N-Tiered example

Now, turn your attention back to the API controller in Chapter 6, *Setting Up the .NET Test Environment*. Hard-coded data being returned directly from the controller does not make for a solid foundation on which to build an application. Most modern .NET applications of any size are written in some sort of N-tiered architecture. You'll want to separate your business logic from your presentation, in this instance, the presentation in the API endpoint.

We'll introduce an *interface* for a speaker service in preparation for using Dependency Injection to provide the concrete implementation to the controller, then verify that the proper method in the new service is being called. You'll need to rearrange some tests in order to remove the business logic from the controller.

Presentation layer

To get started, add a new test to verify that the controller accepts an *interface* of ISpeakerService:

```
[Fact]
public void ItAcceptsInterface()
{
  // Arrange
  ISpeakerService testSpeakerService = new TestSpeakerService();

  // Act
  var controller = new SpeakerController(testSpeakerService);

  // Assert
  Assert.NotNull(controller);
}
```

Now, make your test pass by creating a constructor in the SpeakerController to accept the ISpeakerService interface, introducing a field variable and a constructor in your speaker controller class:

```
public SpeakerController(ISpeakerService speakerService)
{
}
```

Your test project should now fail to compile. This is because in our previous example from Chapter 6, *Setting up the .NET Test Environment*, we're defining the controller instance in the constructor of the test class. Modify the constructor to create an instance of TestSpeakerService, which implements the ISpeakerService interface, and pass this to the SpeakerController. Feel free to create the TestSpeakerService in your test class:

```
public SpeakerControllerSearchTests()
{
  var testSpeakerService = new TestSpeakerService();

  _controller = new SpeakerController(testSpeakerService);
}
```

Now, you'll want to verify that the Search method of the SpeakerService is called from the controller. But, how do you do that? One way is to use a mocking framework called *Moq*.

Moq

To add *Moq* to your unit test project, right-click on your test project and choose **Manage NuGet Packages**. Browse for *Moq*, and choose to install the latest stable version. We won't delve too deeply into *Moq*, but we will show how mocking frameworks help facilitate testing the boundaries of your application.

Add a test to verify that the Search method of the SpeakerService is called once from the Search action result of the controller:

```
[Fact]
public void ItCallsSearchServiceOnce()
{
  // Arrange
  // Act
  _controller.Search("jos");

  // Assert
```

```
    _speakerServiceMock.Verify(mock => mock.Search(It.IsAny<string>()),
        Times.Once());
}
```

In order to make the test pass, you will also be required to do a little more setup in the constructor of the test class:

```
private readonly SpeakerController _controller;
private static Mock<ISpeakerService> _speakerServiceMock;

public SpeakerControllerSearchTests()
{
  var speaker = new Speaker
  {
    Name = "test"
  };

  // define the mock
  _speakerServiceMock = new Mock<ISpeakerService>();

  // when search is called, return list of speakers containing speaker
  _speakerServiceMock.Setup(x => x.Search(It.IsAny<string>()))
      .Returns(() => new List<Speaker> { speaker });

  // pass mock object as ISpeakerService
  _controller = new SpeakerController(_speakerServiceMock.Object);
}
```

Be sure to modify the *interface* so that the application will compile:

```
public interface ISpeakerService
{
  IEnumerable<Speaker> Search(string searchString);
}
```

Now, make your test pass by ensuring the Search method of the SpeakerService is called from the Search action result of the controller. If you haven't done so already, create a field variable for _speakerService that is assigned in the constructor by the speakerService parameter:

```
private readonly ISpeakerService _speakerService;

public SpeakerController(ISpeakerService speakerService)
{
  _speakerService = speakerService;
}

[Route("search")]
```

```
public IActionResult Search(string searchString)
{
  var hardCodedSpeakers = new List<Speaker>
  {
    new Speaker{Name = "Josh"},
    new Speaker{Name = "Joshua"},
    new Speaker{Name = "Joseph"},
    new Speaker{Name = "Bill"},
  };

  _speakerService.Search("foo");

  var speakers = hardCodedSpeakers.Where(x =>
                    x.Name.StartsWith(searchString,
                    StringComparison.OrdinalIgnoreCase)).ToList();

  return Ok(speakers);
}
```

Next, add a test to validate that the searchString supplied to the Search action result of the controller is the searchString being passed to the Search method of the SpeakerService:

```
[Fact]
public void GivenSearchStringThenSpeakerServiceSearchCalledWithString(){
  // Arrange
  var searchString = "jos";

  // Act
  _controller.Search(searchString);

  // Assert
  _speakerServiceMock.Verify(mock => mock.Search(searchString),
      Times.Once());
}
```

And make the test pass by supplying searchString to the Search method on the - _speakerService:

```
  _speakerService.Search(searchString);
```

Now, ensure that the results of the `Search` method from the `SpeakerService` are what is being returned by the action result:

```
[Fact]
public void GivenSpeakerServiceThenResultsReturned()
{
  // Arrange
  var searchString = "jos";

  // Act
  var result = _controller.Search(searchString) as OkObjectResult;

  // Assert
  Assert.NotNull(result);
  var speakers = ((IEnumerable<Speaker>)result.Value).ToList();
  Assert.Equal(_speakers, speakers);
}
```

Remember, the results returned by the `Search` method of the `SpeakerService` are being defined by the `Mock`. You'll need to extract a `field` in order to test that the results being returned by the *action result* are the same as those being defined for our `Mock`:

```
private readonly SpeakerController _controller;
private static Mock<ISpeakerService> _speakerServiceMock;
private readonly List<Speaker> _speakers;

public SpeakerControllerSearchTests()
{
  _speakers = new List<Speaker> { new Speaker
  {
    Name = "test"
  } };

  _speakerServiceMock = new Mock<ISpeakerService>();
  _speakerServiceMock.Setup(x => x.Search(It.IsAny<string>()))
                .Returns(() => _speakers);

  _controller = new SpeakerController(_speakerServiceMock.Object);
}
```

There's still the problem of the hard-coded data. Don't forget to remove unnecessary and unneeded code while you're making your test pass. Remember *red, green, refactor*. This applies to your production code as well as your tests.

You may encounter some failing tests once you remove the hard-coded data. For now, skip these tests, as we'll be moving this logic to another part of the application. Now it's time to create a SpeakerService:

```
xUnit
  [Fact(Skip="Reason for skipping")]
MSTest
  [Skip]
```

Business layer

You might want to start thinking about how to organize your tests effectively. As your application grows, and the number of test files increases, you may find it more and more cumbersome to navigate your solution. One answer might be to create individual folders per class under test and a single file per public method within the class folder. This might look something like this:

```
SpeakerService -> Search
```

You don't necessarily need to tackle this now, but it wouldn't hurt to have a plan for the future. Applications tend to grow quite quickly, and before you know it you will have thirteen projects within your solution. You may choose to go ahead and create a Services project with a ServicesTest project at this time, to separate your business layer and associated tests from your presentation layer and its tests. That will be left as an exercise for the reader.

Now, create a new test class for the SpeakerService. Here is where you'll be creating all of your test methods for Search in the SpeakerService:

```
[Fact]
public void ItExists()
{
  var speakerService = new SpeakerService();
}
```

Once you make this test pass, create a few new tests to confirm the Search method exists and that it returns a collection of speakers:

```
[Fact]
public void ItHasSearchMethod()
{
  var speakerService = new SpeakerService();
  speakerService.Search("test");
}
```

Next, test that the SpeakerService implements the ISpeakerService interface:

```
[Fact]
public void ItImplementsISpeakerService()
{
  var speakerService = new SpeakerService();

  Assert.True(speakerService is ISpeakerService);
}
```

Your SpeakerService should now look something like this:

```
public class SpeakerService : ISpeakerService
{
  public IEnumerable<Speaker> Search(string searchString)
  {
    return new List<Speaker>();
  }
}
```

Remember, take slow and methodical steps. You are not allowed to write a line of production code without writing a failing test, and you're not to write more production code than is sufficient to make the tests pass.

Now, begin to move the *skipped* tests from the controller test file to the Speaker Service Search Test file. Start with GivenExactMatchThenOneSpeakerInCollection:

```
[Fact]
public void GivenExactMatchThenOneSpeakerInCollection()
{
  // Arrange
  // Act
  var result = _speakerService.Search("Joshua");

  // Assert
  var speakers = result.ToList();
  Assert.Equal(1, speakers.Count);
  Assert.Equal("Joshua", speakers[0].Name);
}
```

Make this test pass, then move on to GivenCaseInsensitveMatchThenSpeakerInCollection:

```
[Theory]
[InlineData("Joshua")]
[InlineData("joshua")]
```

```
[InlineData("JoShUa")]
public void GivenCaseInsensitveMatchThenSpeakerInCollection(string
searchString)
{
  // Arrange
  // Act
  var result = _speakerService.Search(searchString);

  // Assert
  var speakers = result.ToList();
  Assert.Equal(1, speakers.Count);
  Assert.Equal("Joshua", speakers[0].Name);
}
```

And finally, `GivenNoMatchThenEmptyCollection` and
`Given3MatchThenCollectionWith3Speakers`:

```
[Fact]
public void GivenNoMatchThenEmptyCollection()
{
  // Arrange
  // Act
  var result = _speakerService.Search("ZZZ");
  // Assert
  var speakers = result.ToList();
  Assert.Equal(0, speakers.Count);
}

[Fact]
public void Given3MatchThenCollectionWith3Speakers()
{
  // Arrange
  // Act
  var result = _speakerService.Search("jos");

  // Assert
  var speakers = result.ToList();
  Assert.Equal(3, speakers.Count);
  Assert.True(speakers.Any(s => s.Name == "Josh"));
  Assert.True(speakers.Any(s => s.Name == "Joshua"));
  Assert.True(speakers.Any(s => s.Name == "Joseph"));
}
```

As you get more comfortable with the practice and gain more experience with TDD, you may find it helpful to list the tests which you want to implement. This could be simply jotting them down on a piece of paper, or stubbing out some skipped or ignored tests in your IDE.

If done correctly, your code should look something like this:

```
public class SpeakerService : ISpeakerService
{
  public IEnumerable<Speaker> Search(string searchString)
  {
    var hardCodedSpeakers = new List<Speaker>
    {
      new Speaker{Name = "Josh"},
      new Speaker{Name = "Joshua"},
      new Speaker{Name = "Joseph"},
      new Speaker{Name = "Bill"},
    };

    var speakers = hardCodedSpeakers.Where(x =>
                       x.Name.StartsWith(searchString,
                       StringComparison.OrdinalIgnoreCase)).ToList();

    return speakers;
  }
}
```

We've now moved the hard-coded data out of our controller and into our business layer in the SpeakerService. You may think that a lot of effort was expended simply to move the problem into a new file! While this is true to an extent, this actually puts us in a better place for future development. The "logic", such as it is, has been moved into a class that can be reused by other parts of the application, and by potential new interfaces (think native and/or mobile applications) that would not have access to our original controller.

We'll continue with this example in future chapters. We will *finally* rid ourselves of hard-coded data and implement a data access layer using the Entity framework. All of this can be accomplished with Test-Driven Development.

Summary

In this chapter, we covered some pitfalls that will hinder TDD, such as dependence on third-party libraries, direct instantiation of classes, and fragile tests. We also discussed ways to avoid or work around those issues. We introduced and discussed each of the SOLID principles. We also discussed the different types of test double and when each type is appropriate. Lastly, we gave a short example of an N-tiered application and how it could be tested.

In Chapter 9, *Tabula Rasa – Approaching an Application with TDD in Mind*, we'll explore how to approach and application with a TDD in mind, turning theory into practice, and how better to grow an application through tests.

9

Tabula Rasa – Approaching an Application with TDD in Mind

It might seem a daunting task to develop an entire application with **Test-Driven Development (TDD)**. Until now, all of the examples have been relatively small. The functions and methods have had a tiny, limited scope. How does TDD translate when developing full-fledged applications? Quite well, actually.

Topics discussed in this chapter include:

- Yak shaving
- Big design up front
- YAGNI
- Test small
- Devil's advocate

Where to begin

The best place to begin is at the beginning. Before a developer can start coding, they must know what the goal of the program is. What is the purpose of the application? Without a clear understanding of the problem that they are attempting to solve, it can be difficult to get started. At the very least, it is ill-advised to begin without some kind of plan.

The sooner you start to code, the longer the program will take.

– Roy Carlson, University of Wisconsin

Have you ever started a craft project without any objective in mind? How did you know what it was you were making? Did the project turn out well? If it did, you more than likely picked a direction at some point and set out to achieve a goal. You may have even had to start over or make adjustments along the way in order to complete the project.

Now, imagine starting the same craft project with the desired result defined ahead of time. Perhaps you wanted to make a drawing. Maybe you developed a set of plans. It isn't until a clear understanding is achieved before you start the physical act of beginning the project. In this example, the likelihood of success is much greater. The chance for stumbling blocks along the way are minimized.

Does this mean that all questions need to be asked ahead of time? Should all answers be obtained before you begin? Certainly not. Sometimes just a cursory understanding of a problem is enough to get started. But, the clearer the objectives, the better the likelihood of developing the proper solution.

Yak shaving

In the examples provided in previous chapters, you may have noticed there was a lot of moving around of code that didn't seem to have any immediate benefit. In TDD, especially at the beginning of a project, some work must be done that doesn't seem to make much sense. Tests are written that do nothing more than proving the existence of a class or method. The code is refactored in a way that only pushes hard-coded values into another dependency. This means that more files are created, and you may find yourself writing a significant amount of helper classes. All of these activities are referred to as yak shaving.

Yak shaving has two meanings that pertain to software development. The first and the one to be avoided is writing things that aren't needed as a means of procrastination. The second is the act of doing all the things that must be done to prepare the code. The difference between the two is a fine line. The side of the line you are on is determined by your intent in writing your code. Are you avoiding the code that you should be writing or are you laying the groundwork for efficient and effective software development using TDD?

In our case, as discussed in earlier chapters, we are either laying the groundwork for future tests, or we are implementing a known technique for preventing writer's block in our tests. Sometimes, the process of preparing an application for being tested can take quite a while.

When working in a legacy application, you could spend the better part of a week simply creating factories, adding interfaces to existing classes, writing test doubles, or doing safe refactoring techniques. All of these activities can help to improve testability and ensure a smooth testing experience. It is important to avoid getting carried away with these activities though. We only want to do them as a means of driving the next test forward.

Big design up front

It used to be common practice to have a lengthy, and expensive, **Software Development Life Cycle (SDLC)**. Large teams were assembled. Meetings were scheduled and discussions had, ad nauseam. Requirements were gathered and documents were created which consumed reams of paper that would fill the filing cabinets of each and every team member. A design for the system would often be democratically assembled and a plan laid out for the system.

Once management and/or executive teams were satisfied, development could start. This long and cumbersome process often meant that budgets had already been significantly depleted with the cost of everyone's time in the planning stages. If for some reason, a flaw in the design was discovered during the development cycle, change orders and a slew of meetings would often occur.

Should the requirements change due to a change in markets or other external conditions it could potentially derail an entire program. If the SDLC did not allow for quick adaptation to change and rapid course correction, it would often spell doom for the entire project. Worse, if the change were significant enough it could render the need for the application obsolete.

Unfortunately, developing software in this manner was quite costly and would end in failure more often than success. The cost of change was too great and the resulting disruption was often detrimental to the process. These days software projects are more likely to be developed in some sort of Agile fashion.

A clean slate

So where do we begin a new application with TDD? Starting with TDD in mind is really no different from beginning any software development project. A developer must have some idea as to the goal of the application. The basic requirements should be understood. Just as we grow our application with tests, the requirements should grow with time.

One bite at a time

How do you eat an elephant? One bite at a time.

It is a massive undertaking to try to define and develop a monolithic application all at once. If you were tasked with creating Facebook you might not know where to begin. But, if you break the application down into logical portions such as *Login, User Dashboard,* and *News Feed,* it becomes much more manageable.

Minimum Viable Product

Each definition of work should be broken down into small deliverables. The concept of a **Minimum Viable Product** can apply to all aspects of our code. As the requirements for the monolithic application are broken down into manageable chunks, it might be possible to start coding. If a programming task is small enough to take only a couple of hours to complete, it's quite difficult to deliver something that wildly misses the mark. However, if a change is required, feedback should be given, and adjustments can be made quickly.

Different mindset

As an application is being developed with a view towards TDD, you should take the same approach to small deliverables. Write a little test, write just enough code to make it pass, then refactor. If you're constantly running your test suite, or better yet, you are using a continuous test runner such as NCrunch, your feedback cycles should be quite quick indeed.

 Never leave an ignored test, or ignore more than one test at a time.

If a test begins to fail during the development cycle it should be easy to recover. The code just written must be at fault. Pause the current effort and evaluate. Is the change necessary? Does the failing test need to change? *Skip* (xUnit) or *Ignore* (MSTest) your current test, if needed. Fix the code and resume by un-ignoring your test. Never leave an ignored test, or ignore more than one test at a time. Doing so will only risk the test (or worse, tests) never being completed, fixed, or recovered. An ignored test has no value. If a test is un-ignored at a later date by you or someone else and is now (or still) failing, it may be difficult to determine if the test is valid and indicates a true failure, or invalid and possibly sending you on a wild goose chase. Make sure your tests are valid, accurate, and provide value.

YAGNI – you aren't gonna need it

At times, you might be compelled to write some code because you think you'll need it. It's just a simple method. If you have a table full of data you'll probably need a `GetAll` method and a `GetById` method. A word of caution here: don't write any code until you have a true need for it. The more code that is written, the more code needs to be maintained. If you write code that you think you might need, but never actually use, you've wasted effort. Worse yet, you've introduced code that must be maintained until or unless it is removed.

> Don't write code in anticipation of a future need. This is wasteful and often costly to develop and maintain.

Test small

One of the most important things to consider when doing TDD is the size and scope of your tests. TDD is an exercise in fully understanding the problem you are trying to solve and being able to break the solution up into as many tiny little pieces as possible.

As an example, let us consider something simple: an application to manage a list of items that need to be done. How can we break up the use cases for this application?

First, using what we discussed with yak shaving, we can verify that the application even exists.

```
public class ToDoApplicationTests
{
  [Fact]
  public void TodoListExists()
  {
    var todo = new TodoList();

    Assert.NotNull(todo);
  }
}

internal class TodoList
{
  public TodoList()
  {
  }
}
```

Next, verify that you are able to retrieve a listing of items to be done.

```
[Fact]
public void CanGetTodos()
{
  // Arrange
  var todo = new TodoList();

  // Act
  var result = todo.Items;

  // Assert
  Assert.NotNull(result);
}
```

Devil's advocate

We will continue to demonstrate testing small, but already we have hit our next example. Playing devil's advocate is a useful technique in many circumstances. The way that we play devil's advocate in TDD is by imagining the simplest, and possibly most erroneous, approach to making the test pass. We want to force the test to make the code right instead of writing the code that we believe to be correct. For instance, in this case, the desire is to make the test that was just written pass by adding an *Items* list. But the test doesn't require that at this point. It only requires that Items exists as a property on the class. There is no designation of a type in the test. So, to play devil's advocate, make the test pass by using *Object* as the type and setting the `Items` object to a simple non-null value.

```
internal class TodoList
{
  public object Items { get; } = new object();

  public TodoList()
  {
  }
}
```

Okay, now all the tests pass but that clearly isn't a proper solution. Thinking small steps, we could force the implementation to have a count, surely that will require it to be a list of *Todos*. Add the following to the last test:

```
Assert.Empty();
```

To make that pass, Items must change:

```
public IEnumerable<Object> Items { get; } = new List<Object>();
```

Remember what we discussed about the SOLID principles in Chapter 8, *What to Know Before Getting Started*. We want to use interface segregation and limit ourselves only to the interface we need. We don't need the full IList interfaces capability so we don't need to use it. All that is needed is the ability to iterate over a collection of items. The simplest interface for doing this is IEnumerable.

We still have a problem though: we are using an Object as our enumerable type. We want to use only a specific class. Let's fix that now. Modify the last test one more time to include a type assertion.

```
[Fact]
public void CanGetTodos()
{
  // Arrange
  var todo = new TodoList();

  // Act
  var result = todo.Items;

  // Assert
  Assert.NotNull(result);
  Assert.IsAssignableFrom<IEnumerable<Todo>>(result);
  Assert.Empty();
}
```

Now, update the class, shown as follows:

```
internal class TodoList
{
  public IEnumerable<Todo> Items { get; } = new List<Todo>();

  public TodoList()
  {
  }
}

public class Todo
{
}
```

As you can see, we added what seemed to be a fairly small test and ended up creating a property, assigning a default value, and creating a class. Can you think of any way we could have made this smaller?

Our next test might verify that the Todo items start as empty, but if we think back to the laws of TDD, the first law is to write a failing test. Right now, if we wrote a test that verified Items to be empty we would expect that test to pass. So, what test should we write?

The test we have decided to write next is a test to verify a means to add a Todo item.

```
[Fact]
public void AddTodoExists()
{
  // Arrange
  var todo = new TodoList();
  var item = new Todo();

  // Act
  todo.AddTodo(item);
}

internal class TodoList
{
    public IEnumerable<Todo> Items { get; } = new List<Todo>();

    public TodoList()
    {
    }

    internal void AddTodo(Todo item)
    {
    }
}
```

Up to this point, we have been taking steps that would likely resemble the same steps you would take in normal development, cutting giant swathes of functionality into the code. This is the first test where we stop before we have actually achieved valuable functionality. This is part of taking those small steps though. We could deploy the application right now. It wouldn't be very useful but we do have that option. If we had reached the end of our sprint, the product owner might request that, in order to deploy as soon as possible, we hard code in some Todo items just so something is available in the UI.

Our next test seems to be fairly straightforward. We will verify that we can actually add a
Todo using our new method. There is a catch though because this test is testing
functionality and not general class structure. We suggest having a test class specifically for
this method.

```
public class TodoListAddTests
{
  [Fact]
  public void ItAddsATodoItemToTheTodoList()
  {
    // Arrange
    var todo = new TodoList();
    var item = new Todo();

    // Act
    todo.AddTodo(item);

    // Assert
    Assert.Single(todo.Items);
  }
}

internal class TodoList
{
  private List<Todo> _items = new List<Todo>();

  public IEnumerable<Todo> Items
  {
    get
    {
      return _items;
    }
  }

  public TodoList()
  {
  }

  public void AddTodo(Todo item)
  {
    _items.Add(item);
  }
}
```

Now, that really was a flying leap off a cliff. That one test nearly changed all of our application code. We just completely changed the implementation of `Items`, and we added code to the `AddTodo` method. Is there a way that we could have broken those into two or more steps? We still have a lot to do with this application, and we will cover some of it. But, before we go on, write down the next few tests that you think you would write. Try not to skip this exercise because breaking up functionality into small chunks like this is one of the areas where most developers struggle when learning TDD.

We are going to temporarily pause the forward progress of this sample application because we have already begun to work ourselves into a corner. To prevent getting blocked, we should be testing negative cases first.

Test negative cases first

What does it mean to test negative cases first? In many computer games, especially role-playing games, it is common for the game designers to make it very difficult to win the game if you simply go straight to the boss. Instead, you must make side quests, make wrong turns, and get lost in the story before you can fight the boss. Testing is no different. Before the problem can be solved, we must first handle bad input, prevent exceptions, and resolve conflicts in the business requirements.

In the Todo application, we mistakenly flew through and added an item to the Todo list without verifying that the item was valid. Now, the sprint is over and our user interface developers are mad at us because they do not know what to do with a Todo item that has no details at all. What we should have done is handle the cases where we receive bad data first. Let's rewind and temporarily skip the test we just made.

```
[Fact(Skip="Forgot to test negative cases first")]
public void ItAddsATodoItemToTheTodoList()
```

The test we need to write now should go above the test that was just ignored, but in the same file. Remembering that we need to have small test increments, we can write a test that guards against the simplest bad data, `null`.

```
[Fact]
public void OnNullAnArgumentNullErrorOccurs()
{
  // Arrange
  var todo = new TodoList();
  Todo item = null;

  // Act
  var exception = Record.Exception(() => todo.AddTodo(item));
```

```
  // Assert
  Assert.NotNull(exception);
  Assert.IsType<ArgumentNullException>(exception);
}

public void AddTodo(Todo item)
{
  throw new ArgumentNullException();
}
```

Notice that we have removed the code that was in place for `AddTodo`. We could have left the code in place, but at this point it is clutter and there is currently no test that forces that code to be present. Sometimes, when you ignore a test, it is easier to remove the functionality that test was verifying instead of working around the functionality. There are times when the clutter could restrict your refactoring efforts and could result in worse code. Don't be afraid to delete code for tests that are being skipped, and don't be afraid to delete skipped tests that make their way into source control.

One other issue that we encountered when making this change is that the `AddTodoExists` method defined earlier in the `TodoApplicationTests` class is now failing. This test was a yak shaving test to start with and does not add any real value to the test suite, so just remove it.

Now that we have the null case covered by our method, what is the next thing that could go wrong? Thinking about it, are there any required fields for a Todo? We should probably make sure the Todo has a title or description at least before we add it to the list.

First, before we can verify that the field has been populated, we need to verify that the field exists on the model. Writing model tests might seem a bit like overkill to you, but we find that having these tests helps to better define the application for others coming into it. They also provide a good attachment point for field validation tests later on when your business decides that the description field of a Todo has a maximum length of 255 characters. Let's create a new class for the Todo model tests.

```
public class TodoModelTests
{
  [Fact]
  public void ItHasDescription()
  {
    // Arrange
    var todo = new Todo();

    // Act
    todo.Description = "Test Description";
  }
```

```
  }

  public class Todo
  {
    public string Description { get; set; }
  }
```

As you can see, there is no real assert for this type of test. Simply verifying that we can set the description value without throwing an error will suffice.

Now that we have a description field, we can verify that it is required.

```
  [Fact]
  public void OnNullADescriptionRequiredValidationErrorOccurs()
  {
    // Arrange
    var todo = new TodoList();
    var item = new Todo()
    {
      Description = null
    };

    // Act
    var exception = Record.Exception(() => todo.AddTodo(item));

    // Assert
    Assert.NotNull(exception);
    Assert.IsType(typeof(DescriptionRequiredException), exception);
  }

  internal class TodoList
  {
    ...

    public void AddTodo(Todo item)
    {
      item = item ?? throw new ArgumentNullException();

      item.Description = item.Description ?? throw new
                                      DescriptionRequiredException();
    }
  }
```

We are long overdue for some refactoring and this is a good place to pause our testing efforts and refactor. We would like to move the model validation into the model. Let's create a quick test for a validation method on the Todo model and then move that logic into the Todo class.

```
public class TodoModelValidateTests
{
  [Fact]
  public void ItExists()
  {
    // Arrange
    var todo = new Todo();

    // Act
    todo.Validate();
  }
}

public class Todo
{
  public string Description { get; set; }

  internal void Validate()
  {
  }
}
```

Now, at least for the moment, we want to move our validation logic over from the Todo list into the model. In creating the validation test and moving the logic, we have caused our yak shaving test to fail. The test is failing because, although the required method exists, it is throwing an exception because we have not populated the description of our Todo. We will have to remove this test as it no longer adds value.

```
public class TodoModelValidateTests
{
  [Fact]
  public void OnNullADescriptionRequiredValidationErrorOccurs()
  {
    // Arrange
    var item = new Todo()
    {
      Description = null
    };

    // Act
    var exception = Record.Exception(() => item.Validate());
```

```
      // Assert
      Assert.NotNull(exception);
      Assert.IsType(typeof(DescriptionRequiredException), exception);
   }
}

public class Todo
{
  public string Description { get; set; }

  internal void Validate()
  {
    Description = Description ?? throw new DescriptionRequiredException();
  }
}
```

Finally, the tests we needed to write before we could make the refactoring change we wanted to make are complete. Now we can simply replace the exception logic dealing with model validation in the `TodoList` class with a call to `Validate` on the model.

```
public void AddTodo(Todo item)
{
  item = item ?? throw new ArgumentNullException();

  item.Validate();
}
```

This change should have no effect on our tests or our resulting logic. We are simply relocating the validation code. There are many more validations that could happen. Can you think of a few that might be valuable?

It is now time to add back in our skipped test, with some minor modifications to pass validation.

```
[Fact]
public void ItAddsATodoItemToTheTodoList()
{
  // Arrange
  var todo = new TodoList();
  var item = new Todo
  {
    Description = "Test Description"
  };

  // Act
  todo.AddTodo(item);
```

```
    // Assert
    Assert.Single(todo.Items);
}

public void AddTodo(Todo item)
{
    item = item ?? throw new ArgumentNullException();
    item.Validate();

    _items.Add(item);
}
```

When testing is painful

There may come a time when you may encounter some pain. Perhaps you've forced yourself into a corner with your design. Maybe you're unsure what the next, most interesting test would be. Sure, you didn't mean to, but conceivably you could have taken too great a leap between tests. Whatever the case may be, there may come a time when testing becomes painful.

A spike

If you find that you're stuck or you're debating between options on how to proceed, it might be beneficial to run a spike. A spike is a means with which you can investigate an idea. Give yourself a time limit or some other limiting metric. Once sufficient knowledge or insight has been gained by the exercise, throw away the results. The purpose of the spike is not to walk away with the working code. The goal should be to gain understanding and provide a better idea of a path forward.

Assert first

At times, you may know the next test you want to write without being quite sure how to start. If this happens, start with *Assert* to determine the expected result. With the expectation defined, set out to make the actual value match the expected value. You might want to take this approach more often to assure that you're only writing enough code to make the desired test pass.

Stay organized

Remember, tests are the first consumer of your application. The best and most accurate documentation you can provide is a thorough and well-maintained set of tests. Within your test suite, create folders, nested classes, or utilize features of your test framework to make your tests more readable. Remember, if you do encounter a test failure at a later date, a descriptive test name and proper assertion will go a long way in describing how the result came to be.

Use `Describe` to better organize your JavaScript tests. Nest multiple levels by using more than one `Describe` within your tests.

Breaking down Speaker Meet

The Speaker Meet application started with a simple goal: connecting technology speakers, communities, and conferences. The idea was simple but could evolve into broad complexity. It was decided at an early stage to start small and add features if and when it made sense. New ideas should be able to be implemented and tested with little effort. If an idea turned out to be the wrong direction for the site, the new functionality could easily be removed and abandoned. Start simply and release small features for quick feedback.

Three main sections of the initial site were defined as *Speakers*, *Communities*, and *Conferences*. Each would need to have a listing of all speakers/communities/conferences, provide a way to view details about a selected item, and provide a way to search items based on a predefined set of criteria. This would be the Minimum Viable Product for the initial release.

Speakers

In the beginning, it was decided that speakers would be the initial focus. Speakers would contain a name, email address, technology selections, and location. *Gravatar* would be used to provide an avatar. Future enhancements that were excluded from the Minimum Viable Product include a list of talks, travel distance, and ratings. By focusing on this limited functionality, initial feedback can be collected and future effort can be directed appropriately.

Communities

The secondary focus of the Speaker Meet application revolved around technology communities. Meetups and user groups are typically run by dedicated volunteers that are always looking for new and interesting speakers for their meetings. The main goal of the community section of the website is to define a name, location, meeting day/times, and technology selections of member communities.

Conferences

Technology conferences are the third and final focus of the Speaker Meet site. Conferences have similar requirements to communities, in that they require a name, location, dates, and technology selections. They differ primarily in size, scope, and dates. User groups typically will have one meeting per month where one speaker may present to a small crowd. Conferences typically occur once a year, from one to many days, with many speakers presenting to many more attendees.

Technical requirements

The technologies to be used for this project were decided early on, based on the knowledge and experience of the team. JavaScript and ReactJS were to be utilized for the front-end website. The back-end would utilize C# and WebAPI with .NET Core, Entity Framework, and SQL Server. All would be hosted in Azure. Knowing these technical requirements before coding starts going long way towards defining parts of your system.

Summary

Now, you should have a basic understanding of Yak shaving and how it might help you get started. You've been cautioned about *Big design up front* and creating things that you might not need in anticipation of a time when they might be needed (YAGNI). Be sure to test small, play devil's advocate, and test negative cases.

Testing JavaScript Applications 10

To get started testing in JavaScript, we will need to create a ReactJS application and configure it for testing using the Mocha, Chai, Enzyme, and Sinon libraries.

These steps were discussed in detail in `Chapter 7`, *Setting up the JavaScript Environment*, so here, we will simply walk through the steps and not explain them in detail.

The goals of this chapter are:

- Create the Speaker Meet React application
- Talk through our plan of attack for testing the application:
    - What is our approach?
    - What parts of the app can we even test?
    - What part of the app do we start with?
- Write tests and complete a couple of features for the application:
    - Speaker listing
    - Speaker detail

Once this chapter is finished, you should be capable of unit-testing any React-based application.

Creating a React app

For the application in this book, to maintain compatibility, you will want to use Node.js version 8.5.0, NPM version 5.4.2, and create-react-app version 1.4.0.

Execute the following commands to install and execute the app:

```
>npm install
>npm test
>npm start
```

All three commands should run successfully. After running `npm test`, you will need to exit the test run by hitting <q>. After running `npm start`, you will need to exit the server by hitting *Ctrl + C*.

Ejecting the app

Assuming the previous step went without a hitch, we can proceed to eject the React app. Again, as it has already been explained in detail in Chapter 7, *Setting up the JavaScript Environment*, we will only do a short review here.

There is only a single command to eject the application. After ejection, we will want to rerun the commands in the previous section to ensure that the application still works as expected.

Execute the following command to eject:

```
>npm run eject
```

Configuring Mocha, Chai, Enzyme, and Sinon

Now, we are ready to add the testing facilities that we would like to use for this app. As before, the addition of these utilities has been covered in detail in a previous chapter. So, we will only be providing the commands to execute and the versions of the packages to install.

Execute the following commands to install the libraries we are going to use:

```
>npm install mocha@3.5.3
>npm install chai@4.1.2
>npm install enzyme@2.9.1
>npm install sinon@3.2.1
```

There are also a few other libraries we will be using as part of our Redux workflow:

```
>npm install nock@9.0.1
>npm install react-router-dom@4.2.2
>npm install redux@3.7.2
>npm install redux-mock-store@1.3.0
>npm install redux-thunk@2.2.0
```

Including the version in the install, the command will ensure that you are using the same version of the libraries that we are and will reduce the number of potential issues.

To use the libraries we have just installed, we will also need to install an extra preset for babel:

```
>npm install babel-preset-es2015@6.24.1
```

Update your babel config in `package.json` to remove react-app and include `react` and `es2015`.

```
"babel": {
  "presets": [
    "react",
    "es2015"
  ]
},
```

As described in `Chapter 7`, *Setting up the JavaScript Environment*, delete the test configuration section from `package.json`. Then, update the test script to:

```
"test": "mocha --require ./scripts/test.js --compilers babel-core/register
./src/**/*.spec.js"
```

And add a test watch script:

```
"test:watch": "npm test -- -w"
```

We are now ready to update the test execution file `test.js` in the scripts folder so it's compatible with Mocha. Change all the contents of the file to:

```
'use strict';

import jsdom from 'jsdom';
global.document = jsdom.jsdom('<html><body></body></html>');
global.window = document.defaultView;
global.navigator = window.navigator;

function noop() {
  return {};
```

```
}

// prevent mocha tests from breaking when trying to require a css file
require.extensions['.css'] = noop;
require.extensions['.svg'] = noop;
```

The last step before we can use our new testing libraries is to update the `App.test.js` file to match the conventions used with Mocha and Chai. So, change the filename to `App.spec.js` and update the contents to match the code shown here:

```
import React from 'react';
import ReactDOM from 'react-dom';
import { expect } from 'chai';
import App from './App';
describe('(Component) App', () => {
  it('renders without crashing', () => {
      const div = document.createElement('div');
      ReactDOM.render(<App />, div);
    });
});
```

Now, as before, execute the test script and start the application to make sure nothing broke during our transformation to Mocha.

```
>npm test
>npm run test:watch
>npm start
```

All three of those commands should work. If you have an issue, check all the steps we have just discussed and look to `Chapter 7`, *Setting Up a JavaScript Environment*, for a more detailed explanation.

The plan

Now that our testing config has been updated and is working correctly, we can begin thinking about test-driving our first feature.

In earlier chapters, we discussed where to start testing and decided that if possible an inside-out approach is preferred. To keep with that approach, we want to determine the different parts of our React app so that we can target the purest business logic we can.

Right off the bat, regardless of any other architectural choices, we can identify the React component and a service representing communication with our data source. We are planning to use Redux in this app so that makes up the missing piece and connects our component with our data.

Which one of these is the business logic though? Out of those base options, what would we even test? Let's examine each one a little more closely and see what we could test that would be considered a unit test.

Considering the React component

Generally, we want to avoid unit-testing third-party libraries. So, let's separate the third-party aspects of a React component from the parts that we would potentially unit-test.

The third-party aspects include any inherited features and functionality; this includes to some degree any life cycle methods and the JSX. So, what's left? The answer to this question depends on whether the component in question is a presentational component or a container component.

Presentational components are almost pure HTML and view mechanisms. There is almost no traditionally unit-testable behavior. Certainly, there is no real business logic.

Container components are where the real action happens in a React application. These components can manipulate data and make business decisions that can control the flow of the application. So, let's keep container components in the list of possible places to start our unit-testing efforts.

Looking at Redux testability

Redux is a third-party library, that controls data flow throughout the application and manages quite a bit of the normal data shuffling that we may want to unit test. Because it is third-party though, on the surface there doesn't seem to be too much that we can unit test. Let's take a closer look at the aspects of the Redux data flow to determine if there really is nothing to test or if we still need to unit test parts of Redux.

The store

The Redux store is where all the data lives after it has been acquired by the application. Typically, there is only one store for each application using Redux. The store is almost completely contained within the Redux library and we have very few direct interactions with it. For this reason, there doesn't seem to be much we would or could test for the store and it falls squarely in the realm of third-party code that we must simply trust.

Actions

Actions in Redux represent an event carrying a data packet. The event is usually a command to either retrieve or update data within the data source which should be reflected by the store. Because actions are just a key with some data attached, there doesn't seem to be much to test here.

Reducers

If there is anything to test within the Redux interactions, it is likely in the reducers. Reducers receive the actions and determine what to do, if anything, based on the actions requested and the data provided as part of those actions.

Typically, the reducer is going to simply call the API service once the appropriate service call is determined. It is possible that a reducer might also map the received data into a format that is more appropriate to the service call that must be made.

So, if the reducer is, in all reality, just going to call the service, what would we test for the reducer? Other than ensuring that the appropriate service method is called with the appropriate data there doesn't seem to be much. For completeness, we would want to test those things, but they do not represent the core of our business logic.

In conclusion, it doesn't appear that much is testable in Redux and what is testable doesn't represent the core of our business logic.

Unit-testing an API service

Lastly, let's look at the API service. Normally, the service in a front-end application behaves much like the repository in a back-end application. The service's main function is to abstract data interactions with some data source. Those interactions don't necessarily contain any definable business logic. The real logic, if any, for a service exists on the server and doesn't need to be tested as part of a front-end application. At least it doesn't need to be tested the way you might think it does.

So, if the service doesn't contain any business logic, and Redux doesn't contain much business logic, and the components don't contain much business logic, what do we test and how can it be unit-tested?

The short answer is that we are not off the hook for testing, but we will have to jump through some hoops to do any testing because it is difficult to remove ourselves from integration testing. In a typical front-end application, unlike in C#, there is no clear division between our code and their code. So, we will have to make some concessions and write quite a bit of code to abstract parts of third-party code to allow us to test what we need to be testing.

So, where does this leave us when it comes to a testing direction? Unfortunately, there doesn't seem to be a clear winner. For the purposes of this application, we will work from the data source up so that we have a clear understanding of the data manipulations available to us while we write user interface aspects of the application.

Speaker listing

Following the functionality in our C# backend, we will start by testing a listing of the speakers available. We are not yet ready to connect to the backend and, for any of the tests we will write here as unit tests, we will need to mock the behaviors that the backend would normally present.

For the moment, we are not going to concern ourselves with any kind of authentication. So, the important functionality we will be looking to implement is that when no speakers exist we should let the user know, and when speakers do exist we should list them.

The way that we will produce both situations is through a mock API. As strange as it may seem, most of our business logic will be in the mock API. Because it will be crucial to all of the other tests we will write, we must unit test the mock API as if it were production code.

A mock API service

To begin testing the mock API service, let's create a new services folder and add a `mockSpeakerService.spec.js` file.

Inside that file, we need to import our assertion library, create our initial describe, and write an existence test.

```
import { expect } from 'chai';

describe('Mock Speaker Service', () => {
  it('exits', () => {
    expect(MockSpeakerService).to.exist;
  });
});
```

Start the npm test script with watch. The test we just wrote should fail. To make the test pass, we must create a `MockSpeakerService` object. Let's play devil's advocate a little and create an object in this file, but only enough of an object to make the test pass.

```
let MockSpeakerService = {};
```

This line passes the currently failing test, but clearly isn't what we are after. It does, however, force us to write more robust tests. The next test we can write is one that proves that the `MockSpeakerService` can be constructed. This test should ensure that we have defined the `MockSpeakerService` as a class.

```
it('can be constructed', () => {
  // arrange
  let service = new MockSpeakerService();

  // assert
  expect(service).to.be.an.instanceof(MockSpeakerService);
});
```

This test fails, stating that `MockSpeakerService` is not a constructor. The way to fix this is to change `MockSpeakerService` into a class.

```
class MockSpeakerService {
}
```

Now that we have a class that can be instantiated, the next test we write can start to test actual functionality. So, what functionality are we going to test? Looking at the requirements, we can see that the first scenario involves requesting all the speakers and receiving no speakers. That's a reasonably simple scenario to test. What would we call the function in the `MockSpeakerService` that would get all the speakers? Because we are trying to get all the speakers, a simple name that would not be redundant and fits the repository pattern we discussed in the C# backend is simply `getAll`. Let's create a nested describe and an existence test for a `getAll` class method.

```
describe('Get All', () => {
  it('exists', () => {
    // arrange
    let service = new MockSpeakerService();

    // assert
    expect(service.getAll).to.exist;
  });
});
```

As per usual, this test should fail and it should fail with `expected undefined to exist`. Making this test pass is relatively simple, just add a `getAll` method to the `MockSpeakerService` class.

```
class MockSpeakerService {
  getAll() {
  }
}
```

The next thing we need to decide is the result we should expect when there are no speakers. Looking back at the backend, we should be receiving an empty array when no speakers are present. Looking at the requirements, the system should present a `NO_SPEAKERS_AVAILABLE` message. Should the service be responsible for displaying that message? In this case, the answer is no. The react component should be responsible for displaying the `NO_SPEAKERS_AVAILABLE` message when we get to that portion of the code. For now, we should expect, when no speakers exist, to receive an empty data set.

Because we are extending the context of the test, let's create another describe for that context extension.

```
describe('No Speakers Exist', () => {
  it('returns an empty array', () => {
    // arrange
    let service = new MockSpeakerService();

    // act
```

```
        let promise = service.getAll();
        // assert
        return promise.then((result) => {
          expect(result).to.have.lengthOf(0);
        });
      });
    });
```

Notice the syntax we used for this test. We return the promise and make our assertions inside the then function. This is because we want our test to operate on asynchronous code from our service. The majority of backend operations will need to be asynchronous and one convention for dealing with that asynchronicity is to use promises. Asynchronous tests, that is, tests dealing with promises, in Mocha require that the promise is returned from the test so that Mocha can know to wait for the promise to resolve before closing out the test.

And now, to make the test pass, all we need to do is return a promise that resolves with an empty array from the getAll method. We are going to use a zero delay setTimeout here which will set us up to implement some kind of delay for development purposes later on. The reason we want a delay is so that we can test the operation of the UI in the event of a slow network response.

```
getAll() {
  return new Promise((resolve, reject) => {
    setTimeout(() => {
      resolve(Object.assign([], this._speakers));
    }, 0);
  });
}
```

Now we have the first scenario passing and enough code to warrant a refactoring. We are declaring the service variable in multiple places and we don't have a context that represents a baseline instantiation of that variable. Let's create a describe to wrap all the post instantiation tests and add a beforeEach to initialize a service variable scoped to that describe and available to all the tests within it.

Here are the tests after the refactoring:

```
describe('Mock Speaker Service', () => {
  it('exits', () => {
    expect(MockSpeakerService).to.exist;
  });

  it('can be constructed', () => {
    // arrange
    let service = new MockSpeakerService();
```

```
    // assert
    expect(service).to.be.an.instanceof(MockSpeakerService);
});

describe('After Initialization', () => {
  let service = null;

  beforeEach(() => {
    service = new MockSpeakerService();
  });

  describe('Get All', () => {
    it('exists', () => {
      // assert
      expect(service.getAll).to.exist;
    });

    describe('No Speakers Exist', () => {
      it('returns an empty array', () => {
        // act
        let promise = service.getAll();

        // assert
        return promise.then((result) => {
          expect(result).to.have.lengthOf(0);
        });
      });
    });
  });
});
});
```

The next scenario, the speaker listing, is for when speakers do exist. The first test for this scenario will need to add at least one speaker to the mock API. Let's create a new describe inside GetAll but separate from No Speakers Exist.

```
describe('Speaker Listing', () => {
  it('returns speakers', () => {
    // arrange
    service.create({});

    // act
    let promise = service.getAll();

    // assert
    return promise.then((result) => {
      expect(result).to.have.lengthOf(1);
    });
```

```
    });
  });
```

We have added, as part of the setup for this test, a reference to a `Create` method. This method does not yet exist and our test can't pass without it. So, we need to temporarily ignore this test and write tests for `Create`. We can ignore this test by skipping it.

```
  it.skip('returns speakers', () => {
```

Now, we can write a new describe block inside the `After Initialization` block for `Create`.

```
  describe('Create', () => {
    it('exists', () => {
      expect(service.create).to.exist;
    });
  });
```

And to make the test pass we add the `Create` method to the mock service class.

```
  class MockSpeakerService {
    create() {
    }
  ...
```

We could, from this point, write a few tests to add validation logic to the `Create` method. However, we don't currently have any scenarios that reference a `Create` method on the API. Since this method exists only for testing purposes, we are going to leave it alone with just an exists test. Let's move back to our scenario test.

Now that `Create` exists, we should receive the failure that the test is expecting, which is that we expected a length of 1 but instead we have a length of 0. Remove skip from the test and verify.

To make this test pass, we essentially have to implement the basic logic to create and make a modification to `getAll`.

```
  class MockSpeakerService {
    constructor() {
      this._speakers - [];
    }

    create(speaker) {
      this._speakers.push(speaker);
    }

    getAll() {
```

```
    return new Promise((resolve, reject) => {
      setTimeout(() => {
        resolve(Object.assign([], this._speakers));
      }, 0);
    });
  }
}
```

We can consider the current tests sufficient to move forward and start testing our data flow.

The Get All Speakers action

To begin testing with Redux, there are a few testing entry points we could start with. We could begin by testing actions, reducers, or even interactions with the store. The store tests would be more integration tests and we want to concentrate on unit tests in this chapter. That leaves actions and reducers. Either is a fine place to start, but we will start with actions because they are extremely simple and uncomplicated as a concept for testing.

The action that we need right now is one to request the retrieval of speaker information; in essence, a get all speakers action. As stated earlier, actions can be extremely simple; however, we have an issue in that our get all speakers service call is asynchronous. Actions were not really designed to handle asynchronous calls. For that reason, let's start with something a little bit simpler and we will come back to this problem after we understand how to test a normal action.

Testing a standard action

We will need an action to notify Redux that we have the speakers after they have been loaded. There is no reason why we can't start there. So, let's write a test for the successful retrieval of speakers.

```
import { expect } from 'chai';

describe('Speaker Actions', () => {
  describe('Sync Actions', () => {
    describe('Get Speakers Success', () => {
      it('exists', () => {
        expect(getSpeakersSuccess).to.exist;
      });
    });
  });
});
```

Running this test should fail. To make the test pass, define a function named
`getSpeakersSuccess`.

```
function getSpeakersSuccess() {
  }
```

Because of the simplicity of a typical action, our next test will essentially test the
functionality of the action. We could break this into multiple tests, but all we are really
doing is asserting on the structure of the data returned. Concerning the single assert rule,
we are still only asserting one thing.

```
it('is created with correct data', () => {
  // arrange
  const speakers = [{
    id: 'test-speaker',
    firstName: 'Test',
    lastName: 'Speaker'
  }];

  // act
  const result = getSpeakersSuccess(speakers);

  // assert
  expect(result.type).to.equal(GET_SPEAKERS_SUCCESS);
  expect(result.speakers).to.have.lengthOf(1);
  expect(result.speakers).to.deep.equal(speakers);
});
```

To make this test pass, we need to make significant changes to our current implementation
of the `getSpeakersSuccess` function.

```
const GET_SPEAKERS_SUCCESS = 'GET_SPEAKERS_SUCCESS';

function getSpeakersSuccess(speakers) {
  return { type: GET_SPEAKERS_SUCCESS, speakers: speakers };
}
```

In Redux, actions have an expected format. They must contain a type property and usually
contain some data structure. In the case of `getSpeakersSuccess`, our type is a
constant, `GET_SPEAKERS_SUCCESS`, and the data is an array of speakers passed into the
action. To make them available to the application, let's move the action and the constant
into their own files. We need a `speakerActions` file and an `actionTypes` file,

`src/actions/speakerActions.js`:

```
import * as types from '../reducers/actionTypes';
```

```
export function getSpeakersSuccess(speakers) {
  return { type: types.GET_SPEAKERS_SUCCESS, speakers: speakers };
}
```

`src/reducers/actionTypes.js`:

```
export const GET_SPEAKERS_SUCCESS = 'GET_SPEAKERS_SUCCESS';
```

Add import statements to the test and all the tests should pass. For a typical action, this is the format for testing. The placement of the action types in the reducers folder is for dependency inversion reasons. From a SOLID standpoint, the reducers are defining a contract of interaction, which is represented by the action types. The actions are fulfilling that contract.

Testing a thunk

Because the `getSpeakersSuccess` action is intended to be the resulting action of a successful service call, we need a special kind of action to represent the service call itself. Redux does not inherently support asynchronous actions, as stated before. So, we need some other way to accomplish communication with the backend. Thankfully, Redux does support middleware and much middleware has been designed to add asynchronous capability to Redux. We are going to use `redux-thunk` for simplicity.

To start the next test, we need to first import `redux-thunk` and `redux-mock-store` to our speaker action tests.

```
import thunk from 'redux-thunk';
import configureMockStore from 'redux-mock-store';
```

Then we can test the getting speakers.

```
describe('Async Actions', () => {
  describe('Get Speakers', () => {
    it('exists', () => {
      expect(speakerActions.getSpeakers).to.exist;
    });
  });
});
```

As usual, we start with a test for existence. And, as usual, it is fairly easy to make this test pass. In the speaker actions file, add a definition for the `getSpeakers` function and export it.

```
export function getSpeakers() {
}
```

The next test is slightly more complicated than the tests we have been working on, so we will explain it in rather more detail.

The first thing we will need to do is configure a mock store and add the thunk middleware. We need to do this because to properly test a thunk we will have to pretend that Redux is actually running so that we can dispatch our new action and retrieve the results. So, let's add our mock store configuration to the `Async Actions describe`:

```
const middleware = [thunk];
let mockStore;

beforeEach(() => {
  mockStore = configureMockStore(middleware);
});
```

Now that we have a store available to us, we are ready to begin writing the test.

```
it('creates GET_SPEAKERS_SUCCESS when loading speakers', () => {
  // arrange
  const speaker = {
    id: 'test-speaker',
    firstName: 'Test',
    lastName: 'Speaker'
  };

  const expectedActions = speakerActions.getSpeakersSuccess([speaker]);
  const store = mockStore({
    speakers: []
  });
```

In the arrange, we are configuring a bare minimum speaker. Then, we call the action we previously tested to build the proper data structure. Finally, we define a mock store and its initial state.

```
  // act
  return store.dispatch(speakerActions.getSpeakers()).then(() => {
    const actions = store.getActions();
    // assert
    expect(actions[0].type).to.equal(types.GET_SPEAKERS_SUCCESS);
  });
});
```

Now, when testing asynchronously in Mocha, we can return a promise and Mocha will automatically know that test is asynchronous. Our assertions, for asynchronous tests, go in the resolve or the reject function of the promise. In the case of the get speaker action, we are going to assume a successful server interaction and test the resolved promise.

Because we are not returning anything from our `getSpeakers` action, the `mockStore` throws an error stating that the action may not be an undefined. To move the test forward, we must return something. To move in the direction of using a `thunk`, we need to return a function.

```
export function get.Speakers() {
  return function(dispatch) {
    };
  };
```

Adding the return of a function that does nothing else moves the test failure message forward and now presents us with a failure to read the property `then` of undefined. So, now we need to return a promise from our action. We already have the service endpoint built in the mock API service, so let's call that now.

```
export function getSpeakers() {
  return function(dispatch) {
    return new MockSpeakerService().getAll().then(speakers => {
      dispatch(getSpeakersSuccess(speakers))
    }).catch(err => {
      throw(err);
    });
  };
}
```

Now the test passes and we have written our first test dealing with thunks. As you can see, both the test and the code to pass the test are fairly easy to write.

The Get All Speakers reducer

Now that we have tested the actions related to getting all the speakers, it's time to move on to testing the reducers. As usual, let's begin with an exists test.

```
describe('Speaker Reducers', () => {
  describe('Speakers Reducer', () => {
    it('exists', () => {
      expect(speakersReducer).to.exist;
    });
  });
});
```

To make this test pass, all we need to do is define a function named speakersReducer.

```
function speakersReducer() {
  }
```

Our next test will check the functionality of the reducer.

```
it('Loads Speakers', () => {
   // arrange
   const initialState = [];

   const speaker = {
     id: 'test-speaker',
     firstName: 'Test',
     lastName: 'Speaker'
   };
   const action = actions.getSpeakersSuccess([speaker]);

   // act
   const newState = speakersReducer(initialState, action);

   // assert
   expect(newState).to.have.lengthOf(1);
   expect(newState[0]).to.deep.equal(speaker);
});
```

This test is larger than we normally prefer, so let's walk through it. In the arrange, we configure the initial state and create an action result consisting of an array of a single speaker. When a reducer is called, the previous state of the application and the result of action are passed to it. In this case, we start with an empty array and the modification is the addition of a single speaker.

Next, in the *Act* section of the test, we call the reducer passing in the initialState and the result of our action call. The reducer returns a new state for us to use in the application.

Lastly, in the assert, we expect that the new state consists of a single speaker and that the speaker has the same data as the speaker we created for the action.

To make the test pass we need to handle the action being passed into the reducer.

```
function speakersReducer(state = [], action) {
  switch(action.type) {
    case types.GET_SPEAKERS_SUCCESS:
      return action.speakers;
    default:
      return state;
  }
}
```

Because, in an application using Redux, reducers are called for every action, we need to determine what to do for any action that is not the action we want to handle. The proper response in those cases is to simply return the state with no modification.

For the action type that we do want to handle, in this case, we are returning the actions speakers array. In other reducers, we might combine the initial state with the actions result, but for get speakers success we want to replace the state with the value we receive.

The last step, now that all our tests are passing, is to extract the speaker reducer from the test file and move it to `speakerReducer.js`

The Speaker listing component

Another piece of the application that we can test is the components. There are two types of component in a typical React + Redux application. We have a container and presentational components.

Container components don't typically hold any real HTML in them. The render function for a container component simply references a single presentational component.

Presentational components don't typically have any business logic in them. They receive properties and display those properties.

In our journey from the back-end to the front-end, we have been covering the retrieval and updating of data. Next, let's look at the container component that will use this data.

Our container component is going to be a simple one. Let's start with the typical existence test.

```
import { expect } from 'chai';
import { SpeakersPage } from './SpeakersPage';

describe('Speakers Page', () => {
  it('exists', () => {
```

```
      expect(SpeakersPage).to.exist;
    });
  });
```

Simple and straightforward; now to make it pass.

```
export class SpeakersPage {
  }
```

Next is the render function of the component.

```
import React from 'react';
import Enzyme, { mount, shallow } from 'enzyme';
import Adapter from 'enzyme-adapter-react-16';
import { SpeakersPage } from './SpeakersPage';

describe('Render', () => {
  beforeEach(() => {
    Enzyme.configure({ adapter: new Adapter() });
  });

  it('renders', () => {
    // arrange
    const props = {
      speakers: [{
        id: 'test-speaker',
        firstName:'Test',
        lastName:'Speaker'
      }]
    };

    // act
    const component = shallow(<SpeakersPage { ...props } />);

    // assert
    expect(component.find('SpeakerList')).to.exist;
    expect(component.find('SpeakerList').props().speakers)
      .to.deep.equal(props.speakers);
  });
});
```

This test introduces some new concepts. Starting at the act portion of the test. We are using Enzyme's shallow render. A shallow render will render the React component but not the component's children. In this case, we are expecting that a `SpeakerList` component exists and that this component is rendering it. The Enzyme adapter configuration is shown here, but it can also be moved to `test.js` after the tests pass.

We are also checking the props to make sure we pass the speakers into the presentational component. To make this test pass, we must make modifications to the `SpeakersPage` component, but we must also create a `SpeakerList` component. Let's do that now.

```
export class SpeakersPage extends Component {
  render() {
    return (
      <SpeakerList speakers={this.props.speakers} />
    );
  }
}
```

And then in a new file, we need to add the `SpeakerList`.

```
export const SpeakerList = ({speakers}) => {}
```

You may have noticed that our container component doesn't have any logic. In fact, all it does is render the `SpeakerList` component. If that is all it does, why is it a container component? The reason is that this component is going to be a Redux-connected component. We want to keep the Redux code in our business logic and out of our display components. So, we are treating this as a higher order component and just using it to pass data through to the presentational components. Later, when we get to the speaker detail component you will see a container component with a little business logic.

For now, our `SpeakerList` component looks a little anemic and doesn't really work as part of a React Redux app. Time to test our presentational components.

```
describe('Speaker List', () => {
  it('exists', () => {
    expect(SpeakerList).to.exist;
  });
});
```

Because of the last test, this test will automatically pass. Normally we would not write this test if we followed to progression what we just did. In reality, what we should have done is ignore the previous test, create this test, and then create the `SpeakerList` component. After which, we could have re-enabled the previous test and gotten it to pass.

The next step is to test that a message of no speakers available is rendered when the speakers array is empty.

```
function setup(props) {
  const componentProps = {
    speakers: props.speakers || []
  };

  return shallow(<SpeakerList {...componentProps} />);
}

describe('On Render', () => {
  describe('No Speakers Exist', () => {
    it('renders no speakers message', () => {
      // arrange
      const speakers = [];

      // arrange
      const component = setup({speakers});

      // assert
      expect(component.find('#no-speakers').text())
        .to.equal('No Speakers Available.');
    });
  });
});
```

For this test, we created a helper function to initialize the component with the props that we need. To make the test pass we just need to return a `div` with the correct text.

```
export const SpeakerList = ({speakers}) => {
  return (
    <div>
    <h1>Speakers</h1>
    <div id="no-speakers">No Speakers Available.</div>
    </div>
  );
};
```

While we are only testing for the `no-speakers` div, we can have decoration that we decide not to test. In this case, we want a header on the page. Our tests should pass regardless.

So, now we are ready to test for when speakers do exist.

```
describe('Speakers Exist', () => {
  it('renders a table when speakers exist', () => {
    // arrange
    const speakers = [{
      id: 'test-speaker-1',
      firstName: 'Test',
      lastName: 'Speaker 1'
    }, {
      id: 'test-speaker-2',
      firstName: 'Test',
      lastName: 'Speaker 2'
    }];

    // act
    const component = setup({speakers});

    // assert
    expect(component.find('.speakers')
      .children()).to.have.lengthOf(2);
    expect(component.find('.speakers')
      .childAt(0).type().name).to.equal('SpeakerListRow');
  });
});
```

In this test, we check for two things. We want the correct number of speaker rows to display and we want them to be rendered by a new SpeakerListRow component.

```
export const SpeakerList = ({speakers}) => {
  let contents = <div>Error!</div>;

  if(speakers.length === 0) {
    contents = <div id="no-speakers">No Speakers Available.</div>;
  } else {
    contents = (
      <table className="table">
        <thead>
          <tr>
            <th>Name</th>
            <th></th>
          </tr>
        </thead>
        <tbody className="speakers">
          {
            speakers.map(speaker =>
              <SpeakerListRow key={speaker.id} speaker={speaker} />)
          }
```

```
            </tbody>
          </table>
        );
      }

      return (
        <div>
        <h1>Speakers</h1>
        { contents }
        </div>
      );
    };
```

The component code has changed significantly because of our latest test. We had to add some logic, and we also added a default error case if somehow the content were to make it through without being assigned.

There is one more component to make the code work correctly for this section. We are not going to test that component in this book, though. The component has no logic inside it and is left as an exercise to you to create.

In order to create that component, it would be nice if the application ran. Right now, we have not wired up Redux so the application won't render anything. Let's walk through the configuration we are using for Redux now.

Inside index.js, we need to add a few items to let Redux work. Your index should look similar to this:

```
import React from 'react';
import ReactDOM from 'react-dom';
import {BrowserRouter} from 'react-router-dom';
import {Provider} from 'react-redux';
import registerServiceWorker from './registerServiceWorker';
import configureStore from './store/configureStore';
import { getSpeakers } from './actions/speakerActions';
import 'bootstrap/dist/css/bootstrap.min.css';
import './index.css';
import App from './components/App.js';

const store = configureStore();
store.dispatch(getSpeakers());

ReactDOM.render(
  <Provider store={store}>
    <BrowserRouter>
      <App/>
    </BrowserRouter>
```

```
    </Provider>,
    document.getElementById('root')
);

registerServiceWorker();
```

The two parts that we have added are the Redux store including an initial call to dispatch the load speakers action, and markup to add the Redux provider.

Where your other routes are defined, you will need to add routes for the speaker section. We are placing the Routes in `App.js`.

```
<Route exact path='/speakers/:id' component={SpeakerDetailPage}/>
<Route exact path='/speakers' component={SpeakersPage}/>
```

Lastly, we have to convert our component to a Redux component. Add the following lines to the bottom of your speaker's page component file.

```
import { connect } from 'react-redux';

function mapStateToProps(state) {
    return {
      speakers: state.speakers
    };
}

function mapDispatchToProps(dispatch) {
    return bindActionCreators(speakerActions, dispatch);
}

export default connect(mapStateToProps, mapDispatchToProps)(SpeakersPage);
```

Starting at the bottom of the code sample, the connect function is provided by Redux and will wire up all the Redux functionality into our component. The two functions passed in, `mapStateToProps` and `mapDispatchToProps`, are passed in as a way to populate state and provide actions for our component to execute.

Inside `mapDispatchToProps` we are calling `bindActionCreators`; this is another Redux-provided function and will give us an object containing all the actions. By returning that object directly from `mapDispatchToProps`, we are adding the actions directly to props. We could also create our own object containing an actions property and then assign the result of the `bindActionCreators` to that property.

Anywhere inside the application that references `SpeakersPage` can now be changed to just `SpeakersPage`, which will grab our new default export. Do not make this change in the tests. Inside the tests we still want the named import.

With those things done, we should be able to run the application and navigate to the speakers route. If you have not added a link to the speakers route, now would be a good time so that you don't have to type the route directly in the URL every time.

Once you arrive at the speakers route, you should see that there are no speakers and we receive our message. We need some way to populate the speakers so that we can test the listing. We will cover a way to populate speakers in the next section. For now, in the mock API modify the constructor to contain a couple of speakers. Modifying the service in this way will cause a few tests to break, so after you have visually verified that everything is looking good, be sure to remove or at least comment out the code you added.

Speaker detail

Now that we have our speakers listing nicely, it would be nice to be able to view a bit more information about a specific speaker. Let's look at the tests involved in retrieving and viewing a speakers-detailed information.

Adding to the mock API Service

In the mock API, we need to add a call to get the details for a specific speaker. We can assume that the speaker has an ID field that we can use to gather that information. As usual, let's start our tests with a simple exists check. We will need to add a new describe inside the `After Initialization` describe for getting a speaker by ID.

```
describe('Get Speaker By Id', () => {
    it('exists', () => {
      // assert
      expect(service.getById).to.exist;
    });
  });
```

To make this test pass, we need to add a method to the mock API.

```
getById() {
  }
```

Now, we can write a test to verify the functionality we expect when a matching speaker cannot be found. The functionality we want in this case is for a SPEAKER_NOT_FOUND message to be shown once we get to the user interface. At the mock API level, we could assume that a 404 will be sent from the server. We can respond from the mock API with an error containing the SPEAKER_NOT_FOUND type. This is similar to the way an action would be used.

Let's create another describe for our speaker not found scenario.

```
describe('Speaker Does Not Exist', () => {
  it('SPEAKER NOT FOUND error is generated', () => {
    // act
    const promise = service.getById('fake-speaker');

    // assert
    return promise.catch((error) => {
      expect(error.type).to.equal(errorTypes.SPEAKER_NOT_FOUND);
    });
  });
});
```

You may have noticed that we snuck in errorTypes. The errorTypes are in their own folder, but build exactly like actionTypes.

To make this test pass, we must add a rejected promise to our mock API.

```
getById(id) {
  return new Promise((resolve, reject) => {
    setTimeout(() => {
      reject({ type: errorTypes.SPEAKER_NOT_FOUND });
    }, 0);
  });
}
```

We don't have any tests that enforce a positive result from this method, so we can reject every time for now.

That brings us to our next test. What happens if the speaker is found? Ideally, the speaker and all the speakers details would be delivered back to the caller. Let's write that test now.

```
describe('Speaker Exists', () => {
  it('returns the speaker', () => {
    // arrange
    const speaker = { id: 'test-speaker' };
    service.create(speaker);

    // act
```

```
    let promise = service.getById('test-speaker');

    // assert
    return promise.then((speaker) => {
      expect(speaker).to.not.be.null;
      expect(speaker.id).to.equal('test-speaker');
    });
  });
});
```

To pass this test we will have to add some logic to the production code.

```
getById(id) {
    return new Promise((resolve, reject) => {
      setTimeout(() => {
        let speaker = this._speakers.find(x => x.id === id);
        if(speaker) {
          resolve(Object.assign({}, speaker));
        } else {
          reject({ type: errorTypes.SPEAKER_NOT_FOUND });
        }
      }, 0);
    });
}
```

To make the test pass, we need to first check to see if the speaker exists. If the speaker does exist, we return that speaker. If the speaker does not exist, we reject the promise and provide our error result.

The Get Speaker action

We now have a mock API to call that behaves the way we want it to. Next on our list is creating the actions that will handle the results from our mock API. For the process of getting a speaker, we will need two actions. One of the actions will notify the application about a successful find and provide the found speaker to the reducers. The other action will notify the application about the failure to find the requested speaker.

Let's write a test to confirm its existence. This test should be inside the synchronous tests section of the speaker actions tests. We will also want to create a new describe for the get speaker success action.

```
describe('Find Speaker Success', () => {
    it('exists', () => {
```

```
      expect(speakerActions.getSpeakerSuccess).to.exist;
    });
  });
```

To make this test pass, we just create the action function.

```
export function getSpeakerSuccess() {
}
```

Now we need to verify the return value of the action. Just like our get all speakers success action, the get speaker success action will receive the found speaker and return an object containing a type and the speaker data. Let's write the test for that now.

```
it('is created with correct data', () => {
  // arrange
  const speaker = {
    id: 'test-speaker',
    firstName: 'Test',
    lastName: 'Speaker'
  };

  // act
  const result = speakerActions.getSpeakerSuccess(speaker);

  // assert
  expect(result.type).to.equal(types.GET_SPEAKER_SUCCESS);
  expect(result.speaker).to.deep.equal(speaker);
});
```

This test is fairly straightforward so let's look at the production code to pass it.

```
export function getSpeakerSuccess(speaker) {
  return { type: types.GET_SPEAKER_SUCCESS, speaker: speaker };
}
```

Again, this code is straightforward. Next, let's handle the failure action. We will need to create a new describe for this test as well.

```
describe('Get Speaker Failure', () => {
  it('exists', () => {
    expect(speakerActions.getSpeakerFailure).to.exist;
  });
});
```

Nothing new here, you should be starting to get a feel for the flow by now. Let's keep going and make this test pass.

```
export function getSpeakerFailure() {
  }
```

The data we should be getting back for a failure to retrieve a speaker should be the SPEAKER_NOT_FOUND error type. In our next test, we will receive that error and create the action type from it.

```
it('is created with correct data', () => {
    // arrange
    const error = {
      type: errorTypes.SPEAKER_NOT_FOUND
    };

    // act
    const result = speakerActions.getSpeakerFailure(error);

    // assert
    expect(result.type).to.equal(types.GET_SPEAKER_FAILURE);
    expect(result.error).to.deep.equal(error);
  });
```

Making this test pass is very similar to the implementation for the other synchronous actions.

```
export function getSpeakerFailure(error) {
    return { type: types.GET_SPEAKER_FAILURE, error: error }
  }
```

Looking at the code, there is one important difference. This code doesn't have speaker data. The reason is because this action will need to be handled by a different reducer, an error reducer. We will create the error reducer and error component shortly. But first, we need to create the asynchronous action that will make the call to the mock API.

In testing the asynchronous action to get speakers, we should start with the failure case. In this case, the failure case is GET_SPEAKER_FAILURE. Here is a test to ensure the correct secondary action is triggered.

```
it('creates GET_SPEAKER_FAILURE when speaker is not found', () => {
    // arrange
    const speakerId= 'not-found-speaker';
    const store = mockStore({
      speaker: {}
    });
```

```
// act
return (
  store.dispatch(speakerActions.getSpeaker(speakerId)).then(() => {
    const actions = store.getActions();

    // assert
    console.log(actions);
    expect(actions[0].type).to.equal(types.GET_SPEAKER_FAILURE);
  })
);
});
```

The code to make this test pass is similar to the code we have for getting all the speakers.

```
export function getSpeaker(speakerId) {
  return function(dispatch) {
    return new MockSpeakerService().getById(speakerId).catch(err => {
      dispatch(getSpeakerFailure(err));
    });
  };
}
```

Here, we have called the mock API and we expect it to reject the promise, resulting in the dispatching of the getSpeakerFailure action.

Our next test is the successful retrieval of a specific speaker. We do have a problem though. You may have noticed that we are creating a new MockSpeakerService for each asynchronous action. This is problematic because it prevents us from pre-populating our mock API with values for the test. Later in the development of this application, the back-end will be ready and we will want to point our front-end code to a real back-end. We can't do that as long as we are directly referencing and creating a mock API service.

There are many solutions for the problem that we are facing. We will explore making a factory to decide what back-end to provide for us. A factory will also allow us to treat the mock API as a singleton. Treating the service as a singleton will allow us to prepopulate the service as part of the test setup.

In the services folder, let's create a new set of tests for creating the factory class and functionality.

```
import { expect } from 'chai';
import { ServiceFactory as factory } from './serviceFactory';

describe('Service Factory', () => {
  it('exits', () => {
    expect(factory).to.exist;
  });
```

```
});
```

All we need to make this test pass is a class definition.

```
export class ServiceFactory {
}
```

Now we want a method to create a speaker service. Add a new describe to the factory tests.

```
describe('Create Speaker Service', () => {
  it('exists', () => {
    expect(factory.createSpeakerService).to.exist;
  });
});
```

Notice the way we are using the factory, we are not initializing it. We want the factory to be a class with static methods. Having static functions will give us the singleton ability we want.

```
static createSpeakerService() {
}
```

Next up, we want to ensure that the `createSpeakerService` factory method will provide us with an instance of the mock API.

```
it('returns a speaker service', () => {
  // act
  let result = factory.createSpeakerService();

  // assert
  expect(result).to.be.an.instanceof(MockSpeakerService);
});
```

Making this test pass is easy, just return a new mock speaker service from the factory method.

```
static createSpeakerService() {
  return new MockSpeakerService();
}
```

This isn't a singleton though. So, we still have some more work to do here. Let's write one more test in the factory before we swap out all the service calls in the application for factory calls. To verify that something is a singleton, we have to make sure it is the same throughout the application. We can do that by doing reference comparisons on successive calls. Another option is to create the speaker service, add a speaker to it, create a new speaker service, and try to pull the speaker from the second service. If we have done things correctly, the second option is the most thorough. We will do the first option here, but it would be a good exercise to do the second option on your own.

```
it('returns the same speaker service', () => {
    // act
    let service1 = factory.createSpeakerService();
    let service2 = factory.createSpeakerService();

    // assert
    expect(service1).to.equal(service2);
});
```

To pass the test, we must ensure that the same instance of the speaker service is returned every time.

```
export default class ServiceFactory {
    constructor() {
        this._speakerService = null;
    }

    static createSpeakerService() {
        return this._speakerService = this._speakerService ||
                                      new MockSpeakerService();
    }
}
```

The factory will now return the current value or create a new speaker service if the current value is null.

The next step is to go to each place where we are directly instantiating a mock speaker service and swap it out with a factory call. We will leave that as an exercise for you to do, but know that going forward we will assume that it has been done.

Now that we have the factory swapped out and it is generating a singleton, we can write the next action test. We want to test a successful retrieval of a speaker.

```
it('creates GET_SPEAKER_SUCCESS when speaker is found', () => {
    // arrange
    const speaker = {
        id: 'test-speaker',
```

```
      firstName: 'Test',
      lastName: 'Speaker'
    };
    const store = mockStore({ speaker: {} });
    const expectedActions = [
      speakerActions.getSpeakerSuccess([speaker.id])
    ];
    let service = factory.createSpeakerService();
    service.create(speaker);

    // act
    return store.dispatch(
      speakerActions.getSpeaker('test-speaker')).then(() => {
        const actions = store.getActions();

        // assert
        expect(actions[0].type).to.equal(types.GET_SPEAKER_SUCCESS);
        expect(actions[0].speaker.id).to.equal('test-speaker');
        expect(actions[0].speaker.firstName).to.equal('Test');
        expect(actions[0].speaker.lastName).to.equal('Speaker');
      });
  });
```

There is a lot going on in this test; let's walk through it. First in the arrange, we create a speaker object to be placed in the service, and used for the assertions. Next, still in the arrange, we create and configure the mock store. Lastly, in the arrange, we create the speaker service and we create our test speaker using the service.

Next, in the act, we dispatch a call to get the test speaker. Remember, this call is asynchronous. So, we must subscribe to then.

When the promise is resolved, we store the actions in a variable and assert that the first action has the correct type and payload.

Now to make this test pass we need to make some modifications to the getById method on the service.

```
export function getSpeaker(speakerId) {
   return function(dispatch) {
      return factory.createSpeakerService().getById(speakerId).then(
         speaker => {
           dispatch(getSpeakerSuccess(speaker));
         }).catch(err => {
           dispatch(getSpeakerFailure(err));
         });
   };
}
```

All we have really done here is add a then to handle the resolving of the promise. We now have, for all current intents and purposes, a working speaker service. Let's move on to creating the reducers for handling the get speaker actions.

The Get Speaker reducer

To handle the actions related to getting a speaker, we must create two reducers. The first reducer is extremely similar to the reducer we made for the get speakers actions. The second is going to need to be slightly different and is for handling the error case.

Let's begin with the simplest of the two and create the speaker reducer.

```
describe('Speaker Reducer', () => {
    it('exists', () => {
        expect(speakerReducer).to.exist;
    });
});
```

Our typical existence test is easily passed.

```
export function speakerReducer() {
}
```

The next test ensures that the reducer updates state properly, and will close out the tests needed for this reducer.

```
it('gets a speaker', () => {
    // arrange
    const initialState = { id: '', firstName: '', lastName: '' };
    const speaker = { id: 'test-speaker', firstName: 'Test', lastName:
'Speaker'};
    const action = actions.getSpeakerSuccess(speaker);

    // act
    const newState = speakerReducer(initialState, action);

    // assert
    expect(newState).to.deep.equal(speaker);
});
```

The changes from this test are the inputs to the reducer, and the output of a state. Let's make this test pass by modeling our reducer after the speakers reducer.

```
export function speakerReducer(state = {
    id: '',
    firstName: '',
    lastName: ''
}, action) {
    switch(action.type) {
      case types.GET_SPEAKER_SUCCESS:
        return action.speaker;
      default:
        return state;
    }
}
```

Similar to the speakers reducer, this reducer simply checks the action type for GET_SPEAKER_SUCCESS and, if found, returns the speaker attached to the action as the new state. Otherwise, we just return the state object we received.

Next up, we need an error reducer.

```
describe('Error Reducer', () => {
    it('exists', () => {
      expect(errorReducer).to.exist;
    });
});
```

Passing this test is just as easy as all the other existence tests.

```
import * as types from './actionTypes';
import * as errors from './errorTypes';

export function errorReducer() {
}
```

The error reducer will have some interesting functionality. In the event that an error is received, we want multiple errors to stack up so we won't be replacing the state. Instead, we will be cloning and adding to the state. However, when an action is received that is not an error we will want to clear the errors and allow normal program execution to continue. We will also want to ignore duplicate errors. First, we will handle the error we know about.

```
it('returns error state', () => {
    // arrange
    const initialState = [];
    const error = { type: errorTypes.SPEAKER_NOT_FOUND };
    const action = actions.getSpeakerFailure(error);
```

```
  // act
  const newState = errorReducer(initialState, action);

  // assert
  expect(newState).to.deep.equal([error]);
});
```

Our test is slightly different from the previous reducer test. The main difference is that we are wrapping our expected value in an array. We are doing this to meet the need for having multiple errors potentially stack up and display for the user.

To make this test pass we follow the familiar reducer pattern we have been using.

```
export function errorReducer(state = [], action) {
  switch(action.type) {
    case types.GET_SPEAKER_FAILURE:
      return [...state, action.error];
    default:
      return state;
  }
}
```

For the same reasons as stated previously, notice how we use the rest of the parameter syntax to spread the existing state into a new array, effectively cloning state.

We have two more tests for the error reducer; the first is to ensure duplicate errors are not added. The second test will be to clear the errors when a non-error action is called.

```
it('ignores duplicate errors', () => {
  // arrange
  const error = { type: errorTypes.SPEAKER_NOT_FOUND };
  const initialState = [error];
  const action = actions.getSpeakerFailure(error);

  // act
  const newState = errorReducer(initialState, action);

  // assert
  expect(newState).to.deep.equal([error]);
});
```

In the test, to set the condition of having a prepopulated state, all we had to do was modify the `initialState` parameter.

```
export function errorReducer(state = [], action) {
    switch(action.type) {
      case types.GET_SPEAKER_FAILURE:
        let newState = [...state];

        if(newState.every(x => x.type !== action.error.type)) {
          newState.push(action.error);
        }

        return newState;
      default:
        return state;
    }
}
```

All we must do to make this test pass is to make sure that the error type is not already present in the state array. There are many ways to do this; we have chosen to use the `every` function as a check that none of the existing errors match. It is likely that this method is not extremely performant, but there should only be a couple errors at most so it shouldn't be a performance issue.

The next test is to clear the error state when a non-error is received.

```
it('clears when a non-error action is received', () => {
    // arrange
    const error = { type: errorTypes.SPEAKER_NOT_FOUND };
    const initialState = [error];
    const action = { type: 'ANY_NON_ERROR' };

    // act
    const newState = errorReducer(initialState, action);

    // assert
    expect(newState).to.deep.equal([]);
});
```

Making this test pass is exceedingly simple. All we have to do is replace the default functionality where the existing state is returned.

```
default:
    return [];
```

The Speaker Detail component

We are now ready to create our `SpeakerDetailPage`. There isn't much to this component. It will need to be another container component so that it can use the get speaker action. Because it is a container component, we will not be placing any markup directly into this component. The good news for us is that it means our tests will be short and simple.

To get the tests started, create an existence test.

```
describe('Speaker Detail Page', () => {
    it('exists', () => {
        expect(SpeakerDetailPage).to.exist;
    });
});
```

Create a `SpeakerDetailPage` file and add a component to it.

```
export class SpeakerDetailPage extends Component {
    render() {
        return (<div></div>);
    }
}
```

The next thing we want to test, the only other thing we can test without directly specifying the design, is that the model is received and somehow makes it to the screen. We only need to test one property of the model for now. We will write a test that shows that the first name of the speaker is displayed.

```
describe('Render', () => {
    it('renders', () => {
        // arrange
        const props = {
            match: { params: { id: 'test-speaker' } },
            actions: { getSpeaker: (id) => { return Promise.resolve(); } },
            speaker: { firstName: 'Test' }
        };

        // act
        const component = mount(<SpeakerDetailPage { ...props } />);

        // assert
        expect(component.find('first-name').text()).to.contain('Test');
    });
});
```

If you are paying attention, you might have wondered why the get speaker action is just returning an empty resolved promise. We are not attached to Redux, so kicking off the action doesn't trigger a reducer, which doesn't update the store and doesn't trigger a refresh of the component state. We still want to complete the contract of the component in the test setup though and this component will call that function. We could leave this line out, but we will be adding it back as soon as we wire up Redux.

To make the test pass, we will need to make a couple of simple changes in the SpeakerDetailPage component, and create a whole new component. Following are the changes to this component, but it will be an exercise for you to create the next component. It is only for display and we are testing that it gets populated here so all you have to do is write the presentational component.

```javascript
export class SpeakerDetailPage extends Component {
  constructor(state, context) {
    super(state, context);

    this.state = {
      speaker: Object.assign({}, this.props.speaker)
    };
  }

  render() {
    return (
      <SpeakerDetail speaker={this.state.speaker} />
    );
  }
}
```

The previous code will make the test pass, but now we have to connect the component to Redux. We will be adding a call to the getSpeaker action, binding to the componentWillReceiveProps life cycle event, and mapping props and dispatch using the connect function. Here is the final SpeakerDetailPage component.

```javascript
export class SpeakerDetailPage extends Component {
  constructor(state, context) {
    super(state, context);

    this.state = {
      speaker: Object.assign({}, this.props.speaker)
    };

    this.props.actions.getSpeaker(this.props.match.params.id)
  }

  componentWillReceiveProps(nextProps) {
```

```
      if(this.props.speaker.id !== nextProps.speaker.id) {
        this.setState({ speaker: Object.assign({}, nextProps.speaker) });
      }
    }

    render() {
      return (
        <SpeakerDetail speaker={this.state.speaker} />
      );
    }
  }

  function mapStateToProps(state, ownProps) {
    let speaker = { id: '', firstName: '', lastName: '' }

    return {
      speaker: state.speaker || speaker
    };
  }

  function mapDispatchToProps(dispatch) {
    return {
      actions: bindActionCreators(speakerActions, dispatch)
    }
  }

  export default  connect(
    mapStateToProps,
    mapDispatchToProps
  )(SpeakerDetailPage);
```

Now that everything passes the tests, we have one last thing we need to do before we can properly develop further. Earlier we replaced the mock API with a call to a factory. We did this so that the tests could affect the state of the mock API in the actions. That same modification has made it possible to configure a starting point for our application. In the index.js file, add the following code after the store has been configured; now, when you run the app, you will have speakers available to test the UI with.

```
const speakers = [{
    id: 'clayton-hunt',
    firstName: 'Clayton',
    lastName: 'Hunt'
}, {
    id: 'john-callaway',
    firstName: 'John',
    lastName: 'Callaway'
}];
```

```
let service = factory.createSpeakerService();
speakers.forEach((speaker) => {
  service.create(speaker);
});
```

Summary

That does it for unit-testing a React application, for now. We still don't have an example of testing some kind of input. Try to test and implement a CreateSpeakerPage. What would you need to do from a React standpoint? What would Redux cause you to do? In this chapter, we have attacked the React components as if they were components. For display-only components, which is what these have been, this approach is probably better. However, for a component with some real functionality, you might want to try testing the functionality as a plain old JavaScript class before even attaching it to React. We also left quite a bit of work for you to do in this chapter. Don't be shy about looking at the source related to this chapter if you get lost or need a hint while you are filling in the blanks to complete the code.

11
Exploring Integrations

In this chapter, we'll explore integration-testing the Speaker Meet application. The React front-end application will be tested and configured to hit the real back-end API, and the .NET application will be tested to ensure that it functions properly from controller to database.

In this chapter, we cover:

- Implementing a real API service
- Removing mocked API calls
- End-to-end integration
- Integration tests

Implementing a real API service

The time has come to actually receive data from the server. Our current data model is still not 100% correct, but the groundwork is there. When we receive the correct data structure from the server, we will need to update our views accordingly. We will leave that part as an exercise for you.

In this section, we will look at pulling our mocked API out of the factory that we created and replacing it with a real API. In our existing tests, we will use Sinon to override the default functionality of our Ajax component with the functionality from our mock API.

Lastly, we will need to create an application configuration object to manage the base path for the API to determine the correct path in both dev and prod.

Replacing the mock API with the real API service

To keep things as simple as possible, we will be using the fetch API to get data from the server. We will begin by breaking all the tests that are currently using the mock API. That is because we are going to create a stub class that implements the same interface as the mock API, but it will not be doing anything:

src/services/fetchSpeakerService.js

```
import * as errorTypes from '../reducers/errorTypes';

export default class FetchSpeakerService {
  constructor() { }

  create(speaker) {
    return;
  }

  getAll() {
    return;
  }

  getById(id) {
    return;
  }
}
```

Now, replace the mock service that is created by the factory with the creation of the fetch based service:

```
import FetchSpeakerService from './fetchSpeakerService';

export default class ServiceFactory {
  constructor() {
    this._speakerService = null;
  }

  static createSpeakerService() {
    return this._speakerService =
      this._speakerService || new FetchSpeakerService();
  }
}
```

Thankfully, only four tests are failing because of that change. Looking at the failed tests, three of them are failing because we did not return a promise. One test, however, is failing because we are no longer returning the mock API. We are going to ignore the failing tests caused by missing promises by excluding them temporarily. Then, we will focus on test checking for a specific instance.

The test that is failing is in the service factory tests. We don't actually want the service factory to return a `MockSpeakerService`. We want it to return a `FetchSpeakerService`. Even more accurately, we want any implementation of a `SpeakerService`. Let's create a base class that will behave like an interface or abstract class from C#:

`/src/services/speakerService.js`

```
export default class SpeakerService {
    create(speaker) {
        throw new Error("Not Implemented!")
    }

    getAll() {
        throw new Error("Not Implemented!")
    }

    getById(id) {
        throw new Error("Not Implemented!")
    }
}
```

Now we have an abstract base class, we need to inherit from that base class in both our existing service classes:

```
import SpeakerService from './speakerService';

export default class MockSpeakerService extends SpeakerService {
    constructor() {
        super();

        this._speakers = [];
    }
    ...
```

```
import SpeakerService from './speakerService';

export default class FetchSpeakerService extends SpeakerService {
  constructor() {
    super();
  }
  ...
```

And then we need to modify the factory tests to expect an instance of the base class instead of the derived class:

```
it('returns a speaker service', () => {
  // act
  let result = factory.createSpeakerService();

  // assert
  expect(result).to.be.an.instanceOf(SpeakerService);
});
```

Using Sinon to mock Ajax responses

Now, it is time to tackle the three tests that we have ignored. They are expecting actual responses from our service. Right now, our service is completely empty. Keep in mind, those tests were written to be unit tests and we need to protect them from the changes in the response that the real endpoint will experience over time. For that reason, we are going to, finally, introduce Sinon.

We will use Sinon to return the results from our mock API instead of the real API. This will allow us to continue to use the work we have already put into the mock API.

After we have our existing tests covered, we are going to introduce integration tests by using Sinon to mock the back-end server. Using Sinon in that way will allow us to test-drive our fetch based speaker service.

Fixing existing tests

First things first; we must make our existing tests pass. In the `speakerActions.spec.js` file, find the first test that we skipped and remove the skip. This will cause that test to fail with:

```
Cannot read property 'then' of undefined
```

Back in the `beforeEach` method, where we are creating the speaker service, we need to create a new Sinon stub for a service method. Looking at the test, we can see that the first service call we make is to get all speakers. So, let's start there:

```
beforeEach(() => {
    let service = factory.createSpeakerService();
    let mockService = new MockSpeakerService();

    getAll = sinon.stub(service, "getAll");
    getAll.callsFake(mockService.getAll.bind(mockService));

    mockStore = configureMockStore(middleware);
});
```

Looking at this code, what we have done is to create a new Sinon stub and redirect calls to the service `getAll` method to the `mockService` `getAll` method. Lastly, we bind the `mockService` call to the `mockService` to preserve access to private variables in the `mockService`.

Running the tests again, we get a new error:

```
Attempted to wrap getAll which is already wrapped
```

What this error is telling us is that we have already created a stub for the method we are trying to stub. At first, this error may not make any sense. But, if you look we are doing this in a `beforeEach`. Sinon is a singleton and we are running our mocking commands inside a `beforeEach`, so it already has a `getAll` stub registered by the time the second test is preparing to run. What we must do is remove that registration before we try to register it again. Another way to say this is that we must remove the registration after each test run. Let's add an `afterEach` method and remove the registration there:

```
afterEach(() => {
    getAll.restore();
});
```

That fixes the first failing test that we had, now to fix the other two. The process will be largely the same, so let's get started.

Remove the skip from the next test. The test fails. We are calling the `getSpeaker` action in this test and if we look at the speaker actions, we can see that it uses the `getById` service method. As before we will need to stub this method in the `beforeEach`.

```
getById = sinon.stub(service, "getById");
getById.callsFake(mockService.getById.bind(mockService));
```

As before, we are now getting the already wrapped message:

```
Attempted to wrap getById which is already wrapped
```

We can fix this one the same way we fixed the last one, by removing the stub in the afterEach function.

```
getById.restore();
```

We are back to all passing tests with one skipped. The last test is the exact same process. Here are the full beforeEach and afterEach functions when we are done:

```
beforeEach(() => {
    let service = factory.createSpeakerService();
    let mockService = new MockSpeakerService();

    getAll = sinon.stub(service, "getAll");
    getAll.callsFake(mockService.getAll.bind(mockService));

    getById = sinon.stub(service, "getById");
    getById.callsFake(mockService.getById.bind(mockService));

    create = sinon.stub(service, "create");
    create.callsFake(mockService.create.bind(mockService));

    mockStore = configureMockStore(middleware);
});

afterEach(() => {
  create.restore();
  getAll.restore();
  getById.restore();
});
```

Don't forget to remove the skip from the last test. When all is said and done you should have 42 passing tests and 0 skipped tests.

Mocking the server

Now that we have fixed our existing tests, we are ready to start writing tests for our real service, the fetchSpeakerService. Let's get started by looking at the test we used for our mock service. The tests will largely be the same as we are trying to achieve the same pattern of functionality.

First, we will want to create the test file `fetchSpeakerService.spec.js`. Once the file is created, we can add the standard existence test:

```
describe('Fetch Speaker Service', () => {
    it('exits', () => {
        expect(FetchSpeakerService).to.exist;
    });
});
```

Because we stubbed out the fetch speaker service earlier, this test should just pass after we add the appropriate import.

Following the mock speaker service tests, the next test is a construction and type verification test:

```
it('can be constructed', () => {
    // arrange
    let service = new FetchSpeakerService();

    // assert
    expect(service).to.be.an.instanceof(FetchSpeakerService);
});
```

This test, too, should pass right away, because when we stubbed the fetch service we created it as a class. Continuing to follow the progression of the mock service tests, we have an After Initialization section with a Create section inside it. The only test in the Create section is an exists test for the Create method. Writing this test, it should pass:

```
describe('After Initialization', () => {
    let service = null;

    beforeEach(() => {
        service = new FetchSpeakerService();
    });

    describe('Create', () => {
        it('exists', () => {
            expect(service.create).to.exist;
        });
    });
});
```

Because we are copying the flow from the mock service tests, we have already extracted the service to a `beforeEach` instantiation.

In the next section, our tests will start to get interesting and won't just pass right away. Before we move on, to verify that the tests are doing what they should be doing, it is a good idea to comment out parts of the fetch service and see the appropriate tests pass.

Moving on to the `Get All` section, still inside the `After Initialization` section, we have an existence test checking the `getAll` method:

```
describe('Get All', () => {
    it('exists', () => {
      // assert
      expect(service.getAll).to.exist;
    });
});
```

As with the other tests so far, to fail this test you will have to comment out the `getAll` method in the fetch service to see it fail. Immediately following this test are two more sections: `No Speakers Exist` and `Speaker Listing`. We will add them one at a time starting with `No Speakers Exist`:

```
describe.skip('No Speakers Exist', () => {
    it('returns an empty array', () => {
      // act
      let promise = service.getAll();

      // assert
      return promise.then((result) => {
        expect(result).to.have.lengthOf(0);
      });
    });
});
```

Finally, we have a failing test. The failure is complaining because it doesn't look like we returned a promise. Let's begin the proper implementation of the fetch service and we will use Sinon in the tests to mock the back-end. In the fetch service, add the following:

```
constructor(baseUrl) {
    super();

    this.baseUrl = baseUrl;
}

getAll() {
    return fetch(`${this.baseUrl}/speakers`).then(r => {
```

```
            return r.json();
        });
    }
```

This is a very basic fetch call. We are use the HTTP verb, GET, so there is no reason to call a method on fetch; by default it will use GET.

In our tests, we are now getting a meaningful result. fetch is not defined. This result is because fetch does not exist as part of our testing setup yet. We will need to import a new NPM package to handle fetch calls in testing. The package we want to import is fetch-ponyfill.

```
>npm install fetch-ponyfill
```

After installing the ponyfill library, we must modify our test setup file scripts/test.js:

```
import { JSDOM } from'jsdom';
import Enzyme from 'enzyme';
import Adapter from 'enzyme-adapter-react-16';
import fetchPonyfill from 'fetch-ponyfill';
const { fetch } = fetchPonyfill();

const jsdom = new JSDOM('<!doctype html><html><body></body></html>');
const { window } = jsdom;
window.fetch = window.fetch || fetch;

...

global.window = window;
global.document = window.document;
global.fetch = window.fetch;
```

After those modifications, we must restart our tests for the changes to take effect. We are now getting a test failure telling us that only absolute URLs are supported. We are getting this message because when we instantiate our fetch service we aren't passing a baseURL. For the tests it doesn't matter what the URL is so let's just use localhost:

```
beforeEach(() => {
    service = new FetchSpeakerService('http://localhost');
});
```

After making this change we have moved the error forward and now we are getting a fetch error to the effect that localhost refused a connection. We are now ready to replace the back-end with Sinon. We will start in the `beforeEach` and `afterEach`:

```
let fetch = null;

beforeEach(() => {
  fetch = sinon.stub(global, 'fetch');
  service = new FetchSpeakerService('http://localhost');
});

afterEach(() => {
  fetch.restore();
});
```

In the test, we will need some items from the `fetch-ponyfill` package so let's add the import statements while we are close to the top of the file.

```
import fetchPonyfill from 'fetch-ponyfill';
const {
  Response,
  Headers
} = fetchPonyfill();
```

And now in the test, we need to configure the response from the server:

```
it('returns an empty array', () => {
  // arrange
  fetch.returns(new Promise((resolve, reject) => {
    let response = new Response();
    response.headers = new Headers({
      'Content-Type': 'application/json'
    });
    response.ok = true;
    response.status = 200;
    response.statusText = 'OK';
    response.body = JSON.stringify([]);

    resolve(response);
  }));

  // act
  let promise = service.getAll();

  // assert
  return promise.then((result) => {
```

```
            expect(result).to.have.lengthOf(0);
        });
    });
```

That finishes the `No Speakers Exist` scenario. We will refactor the server response once we have a better idea about what data will be changing.

We are now ready for the speaker listing scenario. As before, we start by copying the test from the mock service tests. Remove the arrange from the mock service test and copy the arrange from our previous test.

After adding the arrange from the no speakers test, we get a message expecting a length of 1 instead of 0. This is an easy fix and for the purposes of this test, we can simply add an empty object to the body array of the response. Here is what the test should look like, once it is passing:

```
describe('Speaker Listing', () => {
    it('returns speakers', () => {
        // arrange
        fetch.returns(new Promise((resolve, reject) => {
            let response = new Response();
            response.headers = new Headers({
                'Content-Type': 'application/json'
            });
            response.ok = true;
            response.status = 200;
            response.statusText = 'OK';
            response.body = JSON.stringify([{}]);

            resolve(response);
        }));

        // act
        let promise = service.getAll();

        // assert
        return promise.then((result) => {
            expect(result).to.have.lengthOf(1);
        });
    });
});
```

Now that we are using basically the same arrange twice, it's time to refactor our tests. The only thing that has really changed is the body. Let's extract an okResponse function to use:

```
function okResponse(body) {
    return new Promise((resolve, reject) => {
        let response = new Response();
        response.headers = new Headers({
          'Content-Type': 'application/json'
        });
        response.ok = true;
        response.status = 200;
        response.statusText = 'OK';
        response.body = JSON.stringify(body);

        resolve(response);
    });
}
```

We have placed this helper function at the top of the After Initialization describe. Now in each test, replace the arrange with a call to the function, passing in the body that is specific to that test.

The get all speakers functionality is now covered by the tests. Let's move on to getting a specific speaker by ID. Copy the tests for getById from the mock service tests and apply a skip to the describes. Now, remove the skip from the outer-most describe. This should enable the existence test, which should pass.

The next test is for when a speaker is not found; removing skip from that test results in a message indicating that we are not returning a promise. Let's go into the body of the getById function and use fetch to get a speaker:

```
getById(id) {
    return fetch(`${this.baseUrl}/speakers/${id}`);
}
```

Adding fetch to our function should have fixed the error but hasn't. Remember we are mocking the response from fetch so if we don't set a response then fetch won't return anything at all. Let's configure the mock response. In this case we are expecting a 404 from the server so let's configure that response:

```
// arrange
 fetch.returns(new Promise((resolve, reject) => {
    let response = new Response();
    response.headers = new Headers({
      'Content-Type': 'application/json'
    });
```

```
        response.ok = false;
        response.status = 404;
        response.statusText = 'NOT FOUND';

        resolve(response);
    }));
```

That makes our test pass, but it's not for the right reason. Let's add a `then` clause to the assertion to prove the false positive:

```
// assert
 return promise}).then(() => {
    throw { type: 'Error not returned' };
}).catch((error) => {
    expect(error.type).to.equal(errorTypes.SPEAKER_NOT_FOUND);
});
```

Now our test will fail with expected `'Error not returned'` to equal `'SPEAKER_NOT_FOUND'`. Why is this? Shouldn't a 404 cause a rejection of the promise? With fetch, the only thing that will cause a rejected promise is a network connection error. For that reason, we didn't reject when we mocked the server response. What we need to do is check for that condition in the service and cause a promise rejection on that side. The easiest way to accomplish this is to wrap the fetch call with a promise of our own. Once wrapped, we can check for the appropriate condition and reject our promise:

```
getById(id) {
    return new Promise((resolve, reject) => {
        fetch(`${this.baseUrl}/speakers/${id}`).then((response) => {
            if (!response.ok) {
                reject({
                    type: errorTypes.SPEAKER_NOT_FOUND
                });
            }
        });
    });
}
```

That should do it for this test. We are now ready for our last test. Before we move on, let's do a quick refactoring of the arrange in this test to shorten the test and have it make a bit more sense to future readers. While we are doing that, we will refactor the existing response function to reduce duplication and enforce some default values:

```
function baseResponse() {
    let response = new Response();
    response.headers = new Headers({
        'Content-Type': 'application/json'
    });
```

```
      response.ok = true;
      response.status = 200;
      response.statusText = 'OK';

      return response;
    }

    function okResponse(body) {
      return new Promise((resolve, reject) => {
        let response = baseResponse();
        response.body = JSON.stringify(body);

        resolve(response);
      });
    }

    function notFoundResponse() {
      return new Promise((resolve, reject) => {
        let response = baseResponse();
        response.ok = false;
        response.status = 404;
        response.statusText = 'NOT FOUND';

        resolve(response);
      })
    }
```

Use the `notFoundResponse` function in the test just like we used the `okResponse` function. Moving on to our last test for the current functionality of the fetch service, remove the skip from the next describe and we will begin looking at the errors generated and make the necessary changes to make the test pass.

This last test is fairly simple after the work we have already done to make mock responses easier. We need the fetch call to return an `ok` response with the speaker as the body:

```
    describe('Speaker Exists', () => {
      it('returns the speaker', () => {
        // arrange
        const speaker = {
          id: 'test-speaker'
        };
        fetch.returns(okResponse(speaker));

        // act
        let promise = service.getById('test-speaker');

        // assert
```

```
        return promise.then((speaker) => {
          expect(speaker).to.not.be.null;
          expect(speaker.id).to.equal('test-speaker');
        });
      });
    });
```

Now, we are getting a timeout error. That is because our service isn't actually handling the case where the speaker exists. Let's add that now:

```
getById(id) {
    return new Promise((resolve, reject) => {
        fetch(`${this.baseUrl}/speakers/${id}`).then((response) => {
            if (response.ok) {
              resolve(response.json());
            } else {
              reject({
                type: errorTypes.SPEAKER_NOT_FOUND
              });
            }
        });
    });
}
```

Now all our tests are passing and we have verified all the expected behavior of the system. There are a few more things we could do and some developers will choose to do them. We will discuss some of them but will not be providing examples.

Application configuration

Now that all the tests are passing there is still some application configuration that must be taken care of before the application can be used.

In the service factory, we must set a base URL for the fetch service to use when the application is running. This can be done many different ways and which way exactly is up to you. The simplest but least flexible way is to just hard-code a string value as the base URL used to construct the service. However, you could get as fancy as having a dynamic class that sets the value based on the applications, running environment. Again this decision is left to you.

End-to-end integration tests

The last subject we will discuss in this chapter is end-to-end integration tests. These tests involve actually calling the server and checking the real responses.

Benefits

So, what are the benefits of testing the actual client-server connection? The most valuable benefit is that you know your application will work in the deployed environment. Sometimes an application will get deployed and not work because a network or database connection was incorrectly configured and that will wreak havoc on a deployment.

Additionally, this will help to verify the system is working properly. A series of smoke tests could be employed after a deployment to ensure the deployment was successful.

Detriments

E2E tests are usually skipped for one of two reasons. The first reason is that they are difficult to write. You have a lot of extra setup to get these tests to run, including a completely different test runner than what you normally use for unit testing. If not a different runner, they at least need to be a separate test run and not included in your normal unit tests.

The second issue is that E2E tests are fragile. Any change to the system and these tests break. They are not commonly run all the time like a unit test is and so the broken code will not be noticed until they are run in the production environment.

For these reasons we generally do not write that many E2E tests, if any at all.

How much end-to-end testing should you do?

If you choose to do end-to-end testing, you will want to do as little as possible. These are the top tier of tests and should be the least numerous type of test in your system. A recommendation is to only write as many tests as you have third-party connections to your application, that is, one test for each back-end server that you must communicate with. Additionally, use the simplest and most basic case which is not anticipated to change.

That completes integration testing from the front-end. There are still some things that can be done. We will leave them as an exercise for you. You might have noticed that the front-end and back-end are not fully in agreement for the model that is being passed back and forth. As an exercise, add or remove and refine the model that is being used by both systems so that they agree on the format.

Another task would be to set the base URL for the fetch service and run both applications locally to verify interconnectability.

Configuring the API project

With the React project now configured to hit the real API, it's time to turn our attention to the .NET solution. In order to verify that everything is wired up correctly, you'll want to write a series of integration tests to ensure that the whole system is working properly.

Integration test project

Create a new xUnit Project called `SpeakerMeet.Api.IntegrationTest` within the existing solution. This will be where the .NET integration tests will be created. You may want to explore separating these out according to your preferences and/or team coding standards, but that can wait. For now, a single integration test project will do.

For our purposes, we'll be testing whether the system functions from API entry all the way to the database, and back. However, it's best to start small test individual integration points and grow from there.

Where to begin?

You could certainly start by creating a test that will call an API endpoint. In order to achieve this, an HTTP Request will need to be made to a controller. The controller will then call into a service within the business layer, which in turn will make a call to the repository, and finally a command is sent to the database. That feels like a lot of moving parts. Perhaps there's a better place to start.

In order to break down the problem into smaller, more manageable pieces, perhaps it's best to start testing closer to the persistence layer of the application.

Verifying the repository calls into the DB context

A good place to start is verifying that the system is fully integrated; let's first test that the repository can access the database. Create a folder within the integration test project called `RepositoryTests` and create a new test file called `GetAll`. This will be where the integration tests for the `GetAll` method of the repository will be created.

You could create a test that verifies that the repository can be created, like so:

```
[Fact]
public void ItExists()
{
  var options = new DbContextOptions<SpeakerMeetContext>();
  var context = new SpeakerMeetContext(options);

  var repository = new Repository.Repository<Speaker>(context);
}
```

However, that's not going to pass. If you run the test you will receive the following error:

```
System.InvalidOperationException: No database provider has been
configured for this DbContext.
```

This is easily fixed by configuring an appropriate provider.

InMemory database

Running tests against a SQL Server is time-consuming, error-prone, and potentially costly. Establishing a connection to a database takes time, and remember, you want your test suite to be lightning-fast. It might also be a problem to rely on data if the database is used by others, whether in a development environment, by quality assurance engineers, and so on. You certainly wouldn't want to run your integration tests against a production database. Additionally, running tests against a database hosted in the cloud (for example, AWS, Azure, and so on) could potentially incur a dollar cost in terms of bandwidth and processing.

Luckily, it's quite trivial to configure a solution that uses Entity Framework to use an `InMemory` database.

First, install a `NuGet` package for the `InMemory` database.

```
Microsoft.EntityFrameworkCore.InMemory
```

Now, modify the test you created before so that the database context is created `InMemory`:

```
[Fact]
public void ItExists()
{
  var options = new DbContextOptionsBuilder<SpeakerMeetContext>()
      .UseInMemoryDatabase("SpeakerMeetInMemory")
      .Options;

  var context = new SpeakerMeetContext(options);

  var repository = new Repository.Repository<Speaker>(context);
}
```

The test should now pass because the context is now being created `InMemory`.

Next, create a test to verify that a collection of Speaker entities is returned when the `GetAll` method is called:

```
[Fact]
public void GivenSpeakersThenQueryableSpeakersReturned()
{
  using (var context = new SpeakerMeetContext(_options))
  {
    // Arrange
    var repository = new Repository.Repository<Speaker>(context);

    // Act
    var speakers = repository.GetAll();

    // Assert
    Assert.NotNull(speakers);
    Assert.IsAssignableFrom<IQueryable<Speaker>>(speakers);
  }
}
```

Now, turn your attention to the `Get` method in the repository. Create a new test method to verify that a null Speaker entity is returned when a speaker with the given ID is not found:

```
[Fact]
public void GivenSpeakerNotFoundThenSpeakerNull()
{
  using (var context = new SpeakerMeetContext(_options))
  {
    // Arrange
    var repository = new Repository.Repository<Speaker>(context);

    // Act
```

```
        var speaker = repository.Get(-1);

        // Assert
        Assert.Null(speaker);
    }
}
```

This should pass right away. Now, create a test to verify that a Speaker entity is returned when a speaker with the supplied ID exists:

```
[Fact]
public void GivenSpeakerFoundThenSpeakerReturned()
{
    using (var context = new SpeakerMeetContext(_options))
    {
        // Arrange
        var repository = new Repository.Repository<Speaker>(context);

        // Act
        var speaker = repository.Get(1);

        // Assert
        Assert.NotNull(speaker);
        Assert.IsAssignableFrom<Speaker>(speaker);
    }
}
```

This test will not pass quite yet. Regardless of whether or not a Speaker with the ID of 1 exists in your development database, the speakers table in the InMemory database is currently empty. Adding data to the InMemory database is quite simple.

Adding speakers to the InMemory database

In order to test that the repository will return specific Speaker entities when querying the database, you first must add Speakers to the database. In order to do this, add a few lines of code to your test file:

```
using (var context = new SpeakerMeetContext(_options))
{
    context.Speakers.Add(new Speaker { Id = 1, Name = "Test"... });
    context.SaveChanges();
}
```

Feel free to add as many speakers as you want, with as much detail as you feel necessary. Your test should now pass. More tests can be created and should continue to be added as the system grows in functionality and complexity. The bulk of the logic should be tested already in the unit tests, but verifying that the system functions as a whole are equally important.

Verify that the service calls the DB through the repository

Moving on to the business layer, you should verify that each service can retrieve data from the `InMemory` database through the repository.

First, create a new folder in the integration test project called `ServiceTests`. Within that folder, create a folder named `SpeakerServiceTests`. This folder is where the tests specific to the `SpeakerService` will be created.

Create a new test file named `GetAll`. Add a test method to verify that the service can be created:

```
[Fact]
public void ItExists()
{
  var options = new DbContextOptionsBuilder<SpeakerMeetContext>()
      .UseInMemoryDatabase("SpeakerMeetInMemory")
      .Options;

  var context = new SpeakerMeetContext(options);

  var repository = new Repository<Speaker>(context);
  var gravatarService = new GravatarService();

  var speakerService = new SpeakerService(repository, gravatarService);
}
```

ContextFixture

There's a lot of setup code here and quite a bit of duplication from our previous tests. Luckily, you can use what's known as a *Test Fixture*.

A Test Fixture is simply some code that is run to configure the system under test. For our purposes, create a *ContextFixture* to set up an `InMemory` database.

Create a new class named `ContextFixture`, which is where all the `InMemory` database creation will happen:

```
public class ContextFixture : IDisposable
{
  public SpeakerMeetContext Context { get; }

  public ContextFixture()
  {
    var options = new DbContextOptionsBuilder<SpeakerMeetContext>()
        .UseInMemoryDatabase("SpeakerMeetContext")
        .Options;

    Context = new SpeakerMeetContext(options);

    if (!Context.Speakers.Any())
    {
      Context.Speakers.Add(new Speaker {Id = 1, Name = "Test"...});
      Context.SaveChanges();
    }
  }

  public void Dispose()
  {
    Context.Dispose();
  }
}
```

Now, modify the test class to use the new `ContextFixture` class:

```
[Collection("Service")]
[Trait("Category", "Integration")]
public class GetAll : IClassFixture<ContextFixture>
{
  private readonly IRepository<Speaker> _repository;
  private readonly IGravatarService _gravatarService;

  public GetAll(ContextFixture fixture)
  {
    _repository = new Repository<Speaker>(fixture.Context);
    _gravatarService = new GravatarService();
  }

  [Fact]
  public void ItExists()
```

```
    {
        var speakerService = new SpeakerService(_repository, _gravatarService);
    }
}
```

That's quite a bit cleaner. Now, create a new test to ensure a collection of SpeakerSummary objects is returned when the GetAll method of the SpeakerService is called:

```
[Fact]
public void ItReturnsCollectionOfSpeakerSummary()
{
    // Arrange
    var speakerService = new SpeakerService(_repository, _gravatarService);

    // Act
    var speakers = speakerService.GetAll();

    // Assert
    Assert.NotNull(speakers);
    Assert.IsAssignableFrom<IEnumerable<SpeakerSummary>>(speakers);
}
```

Next, create a new test class for the Get method of the SpeakerService. The first test should validate that an exception is thrown when a speaker does not exist with the supplied ID:

```
[Fact]
public void GivenSpeakerNotFoundThenSpeakerNotFoundException()
{
    // Arrange
    var speakerService = new SpeakerService(_repository, _gravatarService);

    // Act
    var exception = Record.Exception(() => speakerService.Get(-1));

    // Assert
    Assert.IsAssignableFrom<SpeakerNotFoundException>(exception);
}
```

You can reuse the ContextFixture that you created earlier:

```
[Fact]
public void GivenSpeakerFoundThenSpeakerDetailReturned()
{
    // Arrange
    var speakerService = new SpeakerService(_repository, _gravatarService);
```

```
  // Act
  var speaker = speakerService.Get(1);

  // Assert
  Assert.NotNull(speaker);
  Assert.IsAssignableFrom<SpeakerDetail>(speaker);
}
```

Verify the API calls into the service

Now, turn your attention to the web API controllers. As covered in a previous chapter, you could simply create a new instance of the controller and call the method under test. However, that would not exercise the entire system.

It would be far better to call the method with an HTTP request. Deploying to a web server would be prohibitively time-consuming.

TestServer

ASP.NET Core has the ability to configure a host for testing purposes. Install the `TestServer` from `NuGet`:

`Microsoft.AspNetCore.TestHost`

There's a little setup involved. First, you'll add an instance of the `TestServer`. Create a new `WebHostBuilder` and use the existing `Startup` class of the web API project. This will wire up the Dependency Injection container that was set up previously. Now, configure the services to set up a new `InMemory` database.

Take a look at the test here to see the setup required:

```
[Fact]
public async void ItShouldCallGetSpeakers()
{
  // Arrange
  var server = new TestServer(new WebHostBuilder()
      .UseStartup<Startup>()
      .ConfigureServices(services =>
      {
        services.AddDbContext<SpeakerMeetContext>(o =>
          o.UseInMemoryDatabase("SpeakerMeetInMemory"));
      }));

  var client = server.CreateClient();
```

```
    // Act
    var response = await client.GetAsync("/api/speaker");

    // Assert
    Assert.NotNull(response);
}
```

ServerFixture

In order to move the setup out of the controller tests, again use a test fixture. This time, create a new class named `ServerFixture`. This will be where the setup will live for the controller tests:

```
public class ServerFixture : IDisposable
{
  public TestServer Server { get; }
  public HttpClient Client { get; }

  public ServerFixture()
  {
    Server = new TestServer(new WebHostBuilder()
            .UseStartup<Startup>()
            .ConfigureServices(services =>
            {
              services.AddDbContext<SpeakerMeetContext>(o =>
                o.UseInMemoryDatabase("SpeakerMeetContext"));
            }));

    if (Server.Host.Services.GetService(typeof(SpeakerMeetContext)) is
SpeakerMeetContext context)
    {
      context.Speakers.Add(new Speaker {Id = 1, Name = "Test"...});
      context.SaveChanges();
    }

    Client = Server.CreateClient();
  }

  public void Dispose()
  {
```

```
        Server.Dispose();
        Client.Dispose();
    }
}
```

Now, return to the previous test. Modify the test class to use the `ServerFixture`:

```
[Collection("Controllers")]
[Trait("Category", "Integration")]
public class GetAll : IClassFixture<ServerFixture>
{
  private readonly HttpClient _client;

  public GetAll(ServerFixture fixture)
  {
    _client = fixture.Client;
  }

  [Fact]
  public async void ItShouldCallGetSpeakers()
  {
    // Act
    var response = await _client.GetAsync("/api/speaker");

    Assert.NotNull(response);
  }
}
```

Now, verify that the response returns an OK status code by creating a new test:

```
[Fact]
public async void ItShouldReturnSuccess()
{
  // Act
  var response = await _client.GetAsync("/api/speaker/");
  response.EnsureSuccessStatusCode();

  // Assert
  Assert.Equal(HttpStatusCode.OK, response.StatusCode);
}
```

And finally, ensure that the proper speaker is returned:

```
[Fact]
public async void ItShouldReturnSpeakers()
{
  // Act
  var response = await _client.GetAsync("/api/speaker");
```

```
response.EnsureSuccessStatusCode();

var responseString = await response.Content.ReadAsStringAsync();
var speakers =
JsonConvert.DeserializeObject<List<SpeakerSummary>>(responseString);

// Assert
Assert.Equal(1, speakers[0].Id);
}
```

Remember, you want to make sure your test suite is clean and well maintained. To clean this test up a bit, you might want to consider creating a ReadAsJsonAsync extension. Here's what that might look like:

```
public static class Extensions
{
  public static async Task<T> ReadAsJsonAsync<T>(this HttpContent content)
  {
    var json = await content.ReadAsStringAsync();

    return JsonConvert.DeserializeObject<T>(json);
  }
}
```

And now, modify the test to use the new extension method:

```
[Fact]
public async void ItShouldReturnSpeakers()
{
  // Act
  var response = await _client.GetAsync("/api/speaker");
  response.EnsureSuccessStatusCode();

  var speakers = await
response.Content.ReadAsJsonAsync<List<SpeakerSummary>>();

  // Assert
  Assert.Equal(1, speakers[0].Id);
}
```

That's much better. Now this extension can be used and reused over and over, and its first use has now been documented in the ItShouldReturnSpeakers test.

Now, move on to testing that the single speaker endpoint can be called. Create a test named `ItShouldCallGetSpeaker` and ensure that a response is returned:

```
[Fact]
public async void ItShouldCallGetSpeaker()
{
    // Act
    var response = await _client.GetAsync("/api/speaker/-1");

    Assert.NotNull(response);
}
```

Now, test that the proper response code is returned if a Speaker with the given ID does not exist:

```
[Fact]
public async void ItShouldReturnError()
{
    // Act
    var response = await _client.GetAsync("/api/speaker/-1");

    // Assert
    Assert.Equal(HttpStatusCode.NotFound, response.StatusCode);
}
```

Now validate that `OK` status code is returned when a speaker with the supplied ID exists:

```
[Fact]
public async void ItShouldReturnSuccess()
{
    // Act
    var response = await _client.GetAsync("/api/speaker/1");
    response.EnsureSuccessStatusCode();

    // Assert
    Assert.Equal(HttpStatusCode.OK, response.StatusCode);
}
```

And finally, confirm that the speaker returned is the one that is expected. Note that the `ReadAsJsonAsync` can be used here:

```
[Fact]
public async void ItShouldReturnSpeaker()
{
    // Act
    var response = await _client.GetAsync("/api/speaker/1");
    response.EnsureSuccessStatusCode();
```

```
    var speakerSummary = await
response.Content.ReadAsJsonAsync<SpeakerDetail>();

    // Assert
    Assert.Equal(1, speakerSummary.Id);
}
```

Only the `Get` and `GetAll` methods for speakers have been tested in the preceding pages. Feel free to add tests for the `Search` methods to grow your integration test suite.

Summary

You should now have a firm grasp of integration testing, its benefits, and detriments. The mock API calls have been removed and the real API service has been implemented. Integration tests have been created and now ensure separate parts of the application are working well together.

Change is inevitable, especially in software development. In the next chapter, we'll be discussing how to handle a change in requirements. Whether these changes include new features, resolve defects, or change existing logic, through TDD these can be easily managed.

12
Changes in Requirements

As progress is made on any application, new and different requirements will likely be added. Sometimes these requirements enhance the existing functionality of the application. At other times, these new requirements may conflict with the existing functionalities. When requirements conflict, it's important that issues are resolved so that the proper functionality can be built.

So, what are the changes in requirements you might expect to see? Changes often consist of alterations to a business rule, new features or enhancements, or modifications needed to resolve a bug or defect discovered in the system.

As time goes on, there will often be a need to modify an existing business rule. This may be in response to user feedback, clarification from the business, or a need discovered through use of the system. When the need for change is discovered, then the existing application will need to change. A comprehensive test suite will ensure that the rest of the system still operates as expected once the new changes are implemented. Start by modifying and/or creating new tests to cover the new desired functionality of the system.

There's a common saying in software development that *software is never finished; it is merely abandoned*. That is to say that an application will continue to grow and evolve through new development if it is to continue to be useful. If new features aren't being added, then it is likely that the project has simply been abandoned. If an application is to continue to be of use, then you can expect that new features will need to be implemented. Again, start with the tests and add new tests which will help guide your implementation of any and all new features.

When a bug is discovered and the root cause identified, then a change will need to be made to resolve the issue. In order to prevent this bug from appearing again in the future, a new test, or series of tests, should be written to cover any potential scenarios that would result in the erroneous behavior.

In this chapter, we will gain an understanding of:

- Changing requirements
- A new feature
- Dealing with defects
- Changes to Speaker Meet
- Premature optimization

Hello World

Stepping back to one of our first examples, take a look at the sample *Hello World* application. Remember that, depending on the time of day, a different message is displayed to the user. Before noon, the user is greeted with **Good morning**, and after noon, **Good afternoon** is returned to the user.

A change in requirements

Depending on the time of day, the user is greeted with **Good morning** or **Good afternoon**. To extend the functionality and introduce a new feature, let's address the user with **Good evening** if the time of day is between 6 p.m. and midnight.

Good evening

In order to introduce this new feature, begin with the tests. Modification of an existing test will be needed, as well as adding one or more new tests to cover the change in requirements.

Modify the `Theory` data provided to `GivenAfternoon_ThenAfternoonMessage` so that only noon through 6 p.m. are included for this test. Now, create a new test method, `GivenEvening_ThenEveningMessage`:

```
[Theory]
[InlineData(19)]
[InlineData(20)]
[InlineData(21)]
[InlineData(22)]
[InlineData(23)]
public void GivenEvening_ThenEveningMessage(int hour)
{
  // Arrange
```

```
var eveningTime = new TestTimeManager();
eveningTime.SetDateTime(new DateTime(2017, 7, 13, hour, 0, 0));
var messageUtility = new MessageUtility(eveningTime);

// Act
var message = messageUtility.GetMessage();
// Assert
Assert.Equal("Good evening", message);
}
```

Now make the `Theory` pass by modifying the existing code:

```
public string GetMessage()
{
  if (_timeManager.Now.Hour < 12)
    return "Good morning";
  if (_timeManager.Now.Hour <= 18)
    return "Good afternoon";
  return "Good evening";
}
```

This is a fairly simple example, for sure. The implementation is starting to grow a design with which you may or may not be satisfied. Feel free to experiment with alternative implementations. You should now have sufficient tests that you feel safe to refactor to a pattern with which you're happier. If you break the implementation or discover a bug you may have introduced, add a test for this scenario.

FizzBuzz

Moving on to the FizzBuzz example from Chapter 6, *Setting Up the .NET Test Environment*, extend the classic behavior of this code kata and introduce some new behavior.

A new feature

A new requirement has been added to the classic FizzBuzz kata. The new requirement states that when a number is not divisible by 3 or 5 and is greater than 1, then the message **Number not found** should be returned. This should be easy enough. Start, once again, with the tests, and make the necessary modifications.

Number not found

To get started, a new test method is needed to verify that the **Number not found** message is returned:

```
[Fact]
public void GivenNonDivisibleGreaterThan1ThenNumberNotFound()
{
  // Arrange
  // Act
  var result = FizzBuzz(2);
  // Assert
  Assert.Equal("Number not found", result);
}
```

Now, make the test pass by modifying the existing code:

```
private object FizzBuzz(int value)
{
  if (value % 15 == 0)
    return "FizzBuzz";
  if (value % 5 == 0)
    return "Buzz";
  if (value % 3 == 0)
    return "Fizz";
  if (value == 2)
    return "Number not found";
}
```

This covers the first instance. However, does this satisfy the new requirement? Create a `Theory` set to force the proper solution:

```
[Theory]
[InlineData(2)]
[InlineData(4)]
[InlineData(7)]
[InlineData(8)]
public void GivenNonDivisibleGreaterThan1ThenNumberNotFound(int number)
{
  // Arrange
  // Act
  var result = FizzBuzz(number);
  // Assert
  Assert.Equal("Number not found", result);
}
```

Make the test pass, the right way. Modify the existing code so that the desired results are returned:

```
private object FizzBuzz(int value)
{
  if (value % 15 == 0)
    return "FizzBuzz";
  if (value % 5 == 0)
    return "Buzz";
  if (value % 3 == 0)
    return "Fizz";
  return value -- 1 ? (object)value : "Number not found";
}
```

Note that all the existing tests should continue to pass throughout this exercise. If you find a bug, write a new test to verify the scenario, and correct the code accordingly.

TODO app

The *TODO* app was another one of our early TDD examples. This app is far from complete, and we have received new requirements from the business, asking to add a feature to the application.

The business now wants the ability to complete a task in the TODO list. This feature is *schedule current sprint* and is the next story for us to work on.

Mark complete

For the *Mark complete* story, we have been asked to allow the user to complete any of the tasks in the TODO list. Adding this feature should be much like any other TDD exercise in this book. Before reading our solution to this problem, try to complete this one on your own. After you have passing tests, come back and look at the solution in this book.

Adding tests

In the `ToDoApplicationTests` file, we have added a `yak shaving` test to force us to create the complete method. This test also helps to define the API for the method:

```
[Fact(Skip = "Yak shaving - no longer needed")]
public void CompleteTodoExists()
{
  // Arrange
  var todo = new TodoList();
  var item = new Todo();
  todo.AddTodo(item);
  // Act
  todo.Complete(item);
}
```

This causes us to create a method stub in the `TodoList` class. To get this test to pass, we had to remove the not implemented exception from the generated method. After creating the method, we added a skip to this test, similar to the previous `yak shaving` test in the same file.

Next, we needed to create a `TodoListCompleteTests` file to house the functionality tests for the complete method:

```
public class TodoListCompleteTests
{
  [Fact]
  public void ItRemovesAnItemFromTheList()
  {
    // Arrange
    var todo = new TodoList();
    var item = new Todo();
    todo.AddTodo(item);
    // Act
    todo.Complete(item);
    // Assert
    Assert.Equal(0, todo.Items.Count());
  }
}
```

After writing this first test and implementing the code to make it pass, we were hard-pressed to write another test that would fail. So, we assume that we are done for now.

Production code

The code to make the tests for completing a task is quite simple and only requires a single line method:

```
public void Complete(Todo item)
{
  _items.Remove(item);
}
```

That is all we need. We are now ready for the sprint demo.

But don't remove from the list!

During the sprint demo, our product owner asked what happened to the task when it was completed. We explained that it was removed from this list. This was not good. The product owner was hoping that we could provide metrics on tasks further down the road. She would like for us to track the completion of the task instead of deleting it.

After some discussion with the other developers, we have decided the task will gain a completed attribute and be hidden from the list. To accomplish this, we will have to do a bit of refactoring and add new tests. Again, try to complete this exercise on your own and then look at our solution for comparison.

Adding tests

This change required quite a few new tests. Before we could make new tests, though, we had to first rename our existing completion test to represent the correct functionality. Adding two more tests to the `TodoListCompleteTests` file, we verify both that the item is marked complete and that it is not removed from the TODO list:

```
public class TodoListCompleteTests
{
  [Fact]
  public void ItHidesAnItemFromTheList()
  {
    // Arrange
    var todo = new TodoList();
    var item = new Todo { Description = "Test Todo" };
    todo.AddTodo(item);
    // Act
    todo.Complete(item);
    // Assert
```

```
      Assert.Equal(0, todo.Items.Count());
    }
    [Fact]
    public void ItMarksAnItemComplete()
    {
      // Arrange
      var todo = new TodoList();
      var item = new Todo { Description = "Test Todo" };
      todo.AddTodo(item);
      // Act
      todo.Complete(item);
      // Assert
      Assert.True(item.IsComplete);
    }
    [Fact]
    public void ItShowsCompletedItems()
    {
      // Arrange
      var todo = new TodoList();
      var item = new Todo { Description = "Test Todo" };
      todo.ShowCompleted = true;
      todo.AddTodo(item);
      // Act
      todo.Complete(item);
      // Assert
      Assert.Equal(1, todo.Items.Count());
    }
  }
```

In order to add ShowComplete, we created a yak shaving test in the ToDoApplicationTests file for completeness:

```
[Fact(Skip = "Yak shaving - no longer needed")]
public void ShowCompletedExists()
{
  // Arrange
  var todo = new TodoList();
  // Act
  todo.ShowCompleted = true;
}
```

We also had to add a similar test to the TodoModelTests file:

```
[Fact]
public void ItHasIsComplete()
{
  // Arrange
  var todo = new Todo();
```

```
    // Act
    todo.IsComplete = true;
}
```

Production code

For such a small code base, the changes required by the new tests caused a fairly significant change. First, we added an `IsComplete` property to the `Todo` model:

```
internal class Todo
{
  public bool IsComplete { get; set; }
  public string Description { get; set; }
  internal void Validate()
  {
    Description = Description ?? throw new DescriptionRequiredException();
  }
}
```

The rest of the changes affect the `TodoList` class. A boolean property was added to toggle the visibility of completed items, the `Complete` method was modified to only mark the item as complete, and a `where` clause was added to the items retrieved from the list:

```
internal class TodoList
{
  private readonly List<Todo> _items = new List<Todo>();
  public IEnumerable<Todo> Items => _items.Where(t => !t.IsComplete ||
ShowCompleted);
  public bool ShowCompleted { get; set; }
  public void AddTodo(Todo item)
  {
    item = item ?? throw new ArgumentNullException();
    item.Validate();
    _items.Add(item);
  }
  public void Complete(Todo item)
  {
    item.IsComplete = true;
  }
}
```

Changes to Speaker Meet

Change is inevitable with any application. Requirements change as a result of a new business rule, feature enhancement, discovery and remediation of a defect, and so on. Change is especially certain when test driving an application. Luckily, through the process of TDD, your application should be easily and safely modifiable.

If a system is loosely coupled, then changes to one part of a system should, in theory, have little to no impact on the rest of the system. A comprehensive suite of unit tests should alleviate the fear of making changes.

Unfortunately, the tests are only valid for the scenarios which they define. If sufficient tests aren't written to cover certain scenarios or edge cases, then it is certainly possible that a bug could find its way into production. If the TDD approach is not taken, or worse, tests aren't written at all, then you may discover that it is quite easy for a bug to make it through all of the checks of your code review process and CI/CD build pipeline.

Take a look at the new requirements for the Speaker Meet application.

Changes to the back-end

As the Speaker Meet application progressed, a new requirement was introduced. Speakers had to be *approved* before they were visible in parts of the system. This included the full listing of speakers, returning of speaker detail information, and through search results.

In this scenario, a developer came in to help out with the implementation. This developer was not familiar with TDD and did not write tests to validate his work. The new requirement was implemented and a code review was submitted:

```
public Models.SpeakerDetail Get(int id)
{
  var speaker = _repository.Get(id);

  if (speaker == null || speaker.IsDeleted || speaker.IsActive)
  {
    throw new SpeakerNotFoundException(id);
  }

  var gravatar = _gravatarService.GetGravatar(speaker.EmailAddress);

  return new Models.SpeakerDetail
  {
    Id = speaker.Id,
    Name = speaker.Name,
```

```
    Location = speaker.Location,
    Gravatar = gravatar
  };
}
```

And a change to the class was added:

```
public class Speaker
{
  public int Id { get; set; }

  [Required]
  [StringLength(50)]
  public string Name { get; set; }

  [Required]
  [StringLength(50)]
  public string Location { get; set; }

  [Required]
  [StringLength(255)]
  public string EmailAddress { get; set; }
  public bool IsDeleted { get; set; }
  public bool IsActive { get; set; }
}
```

Can you spot the issue?

The code was reviewed and comments left. However, the comments were misunderstood (or just flatly ignored) and the code was committed, merged, and pushed through the deployment process. A breakdown for sure, but one that happens from time to time.

The CI server ran the test suite. The existing tests passed. The bug was not discovered, as there was no existing scenario that would have caught the error. Since new tests were not created, there was no test failure. The CD process ran and the code made it into production.

So what test can be added to ensure the proper code is implemented? When dealing with bugs, it is often best to simply write the test that verifies the incorrect behavior. In this case, we want an error to be thrown. So, the below test should assert that the correct error is thrown:

```
[Fact]
public void GivenSpeakerIsNotActiveThenSpeakerNotFoundException()
{
  // Arrange
  var expectedSpeaker = SpeakerFactory.Create(_fakeRepository);
  expectedSpeaker.IsActive = false;
```

```
    var service = new SpeakerService(_fakeRepository, _fakeGravatarService);
    // Act
    var exception = Record.Exception(() => service.Get(expectedSpeaker.Id));
    // Assert
    Assert.IsAssignableFrom<SpeakerNotFoundException>(exception);
}
```

Make this new test pass by modifying the service:

```
public Models.SpeakerDetail Get(int id)
{
  var speaker = _repository.Get(id);

  if (speaker == null || speaker.IsDeleted || !speaker.IsActive)
  {
    throw new SpeakerNotFoundException(id);
  }

  var gravatar = _gravatarService.GetGravatar(speaker.EmailAddress);

  return new Models.SpeakerDetail
  {
    Id = speaker.Id,
    Name = speaker.Name,
    Location = speaker.Location,
    Gravatar = gravatar
  };
}
```

However, with this change, a number of existing tests will now break. This is because the default value for the IsActive property is false.

To quickly get these tests to pass, you could do something like:

```
public bool IsActive { get; set; } = true;
```

This could potentially introduce unexpected results, so be sure to create some guard tests to verify correctness.

This explains why this bug wasn't initially caught. The IsActive property was added to the database with a default value of true. The bug wasn't discovered until new speakers were added to the database with a value of false in the IsActive column. Once the incorrect behavior was discovered, the defect was easily identified and remedied.

Changes to the front-end

There is no difference, from a concept or approach perspective, for changes to the front-end. You will need to write the appropriate test to ensure the desired behavior from the application and then write the production code to make the test pass.

As a quick example though, let's add a new feature to the front-end code we have been working on.

Sorted by rating on client side

The feature we are going to add is sorting the speakers by rating. In previous chapters, rating was not discussed or even enforced, so modifications will need to happen to include rating in the model that has been built so far. That is, of course, if you have not already completed the full model as defined by the C# code.

As with earlier examples in this chapter, try to add this behavior yourself and then look at our following solution.

In the `speakerReducer.spec.js` file, we have added a single test for default sorting of speakers by rank. The test can be added to the describe block for the speaker reducer:

```
it('sorts speakers by rank', () => {
  // Arrange
  const initialState = [];
  const speaker1 = { id: 'test-speaker-1', firstName: 'Test 1', lastName:
'Speaker', rank: 1};
  const speaker2 = { id: 'test-speaker-2', firstName: 'Test 2', lastName:
'Speaker', rank: 2};
  const action = actions.getSpeakersSuccess([speaker1, speaker2]);
  // Act
  const newState = speakersReducer(initialState, action);
  // Assert
  expect(newState).to.have.lengthOf(2);
  expect(newState[0]).to.deep.equal(speaker2);
});
```

And the code to make this test pass is in the `speakerReducer.js` file:

```
export function speakersReducer(state = [], action) {
  switch(action.type) {
    case types.GET_SPEAKERS_SUCCESS:
      return action.speakers.sort((a, b) => {
        return b.rank > a.rank;
      });
```

```
    default:
       return state;
  }
}
```

What now?

Moving forward, it should be easy to implement any change necessary. This might include a new feature, a change in requirements, or a discovered defect. That isn't to say that the application is complete or error-free, but you should have some level of confidence that the application behaves in the ways accounted for with the existing test suite.

Premature optimization

For the purpose of clarification, we are defining optimization as anything that obfuscates the code, making it less clear or more difficult to understand, or anything that limits the possibilities further than the test requires. A premature optimization is an optimization that is done for any reason other than specified by a requirement.

Typically, optimizations are done using performance as an excuse. Before these types of modifications of the code are done, a requirement specifying the need for the change should exist.

Even through the practice of Test-Driven Development, it is possible to paint yourself into a corner. Often during refactoring or during the process of designing your next test, it is possible to solve too much of the problem at once or refactor too much.

Always keep in mind that, in TDD, we want to break a problem down into the smallest steps possible. Also, don't go for the solution in the first test if the solution is more than a line or two. At the same time, even for small solutions, if the solution is calculation or algorithm heavy, it should still be broken down, even if the eventual solution is a single line of production code.

 Beware of premature optimizations.

Refactoring, according to Kent Beck, is the process of removing duplication. Remember that while refactoring your tests. By only removing duplication, we can avoid premature optimization via refactoring. It is completely possible, and even attractive at times, to refactor a solution and reduce the code significantly, or even to use a fancy new language feature or Linq expression to make your test pass. These solutions are fine in the long run, but while the tests are still being built, these hidden optimizations can cause you and your tests to become derailed extremely quickly.

Summary

You can now see how a change in requirements, a new feature request, or a defect might require an application to change. Through TDD and a comprehensive suite of unit tests, these changes can be made safely and easily.

In `Chapter 13`, *The Legacy Problem*, we'll discuss how to deal with a legacy application that may not have been written with testing in mind.

The Legacy Problem
13

This chapter is all about legacy code. If you have never had to deal with legacy code, count yourself lucky and know that it is coming. Some of you may be permanently stuck in maintenance development. Your life is legacy code. Whatever the situation, this chapter is all about dealing with legacy code. We want to either prevent legacy code from happening, or fight it back to the depths from which it came.

In this chapter, we discuss:

- What makes code legacy
- The issues that legacy code can create
- How legacy code can inhibit testing
- What we can do to deal with and fight back against the legacy problem

What is legacy code?

Most of you have probably had to work on a dreaded legacy project. Working on that project is no fun; the code is a mess, and you want to find whoever wrote it and find out what they were thinking when they wrote it.

At some point in your career, you have been or will be that person to someone else. We all write code that we will not be proud of later. But why does the code get so bad? When does a project become legacy? Lastly, what can be done to prevent this?

Why does code go bad?

In short, the code goes bad because we are afraid to change it. Why would the code not changing cause it to be bad? You would hope that, when the code was written, it was the best code that the developer was capable of producing at the time. So, that code should have been good, right? This is a complicated answer but assume, for the moment, that the code was something to be proud of when it was originally written. That still begs the question, how did it go bad?

The answer is staring you in the face. The only reason you are seeing this code is because it needs to change. Chances are, you are not the first person that has needed to make a change in this code. So, this is not the code that was written by a developer doing his or her best to write good code. This code was written by many developers. Still, each of those developers should have been doing their best to write good code. So, again, how did this code go bad?

This is where the fear comes in because we are afraid to change the code. When we have to change it, we generally try to change the code as little as possible to get the requested update working. After all, we don't want to force ourselves or QA to do a full regression test because we refactored the whole thing, do we? So, we modify the code; we change the way it is expected to work. But we can't change the structure, and we can't modify the decisions of the developer who originally wrote the code.

Over time, making these small changes and being afraid to modify the structure and architectural decisions of the original developer causes severe code rot. Soon, the code will have massive conditional statements and methods that no longer fit on the page. The class containing the code will grow to tens of methods and the file will be thousands of lines long.

When does a project become a legacy?

This is a question that is answered by many people in many different ways. Generally, an application has become legacy when no one wants to work on it anymore.

In the beginning, applications are built with a small and defined purpose. Over time, the scope and breadth of a system may grow beyond its original intent. When any change to the application causes the developer to work against what the application was designed for, it will cause friction.

As mentioned previously, the application design is not simply changed because of the fear a developer might have that the application will break. So, more and more cruft is added to the system. Okay, so how long does it take for this to happen? When do we stop hacking new modifications into the existing application and just rewrite it?

Honestly, the cruft starts getting added by the original developer as he or she is writing the application for the first time. When you start to work on a new application or even just a new feature in an existing application, you start with a preliminary design in mind. Everyone does this. Some developers whiteboard the design or make complete **UML** (**Unified Modeling Language**) diagrams. Other developers just have an idea in their head to guide decisions. Either way, you have a design you want when you sit down to develop an application.

How long is it before you discover an issue with your design and have to start modifying it? You might get one line of code in before you have to change your design, or you might get 75% of the way through before you discover an issue. This is largely determined by the complexity of the problem you are solving and how detailed your planning was. Regardless of the thoroughness of your planning, you will find an issue and have to start changing your design before the first QA review.

The second you make that change, you are adding cruft, so almost all of the time, you are working in a system that was not designed for the code that is being forced into it. In other words, you will probably be writing legacy code the next time you are at work, even if you are working on a new application.

 Cruft, in software, is any code that is unnecessary or needlessly complex.

What can be done to prevent legacy decay?

There must be something that can be done to prevent this decay, right? The answer is probably predictable, given the topic of this book. But let me answer with a quote from Michael Feathers on the definition of legacy code:

> *To me, legacy code is simply code without tests.*

> *- Michael Feathers, Working Effectively with Legacy Code*

As we discussed in earlier chapters, tests allow you to refactor. The ability to change the structure of the code is precisely what can prevent the rot and decay that is legacy code.

While tests can allow you to prevent legacy code from forming, be aware that they themselves do not prevent the legacy problem. It takes the dedication of every person on the team understanding that building cruft into a system is a negative behavior and must be avoided. If you feel yourself working against the design of the system, then it is your responsibility to refactor the application into a design that works for today's needs and is flexible enough for tomorrow's needs.

Making a system flexible is not as hard as you might think. Following the SOLID principles (discussed in `Chapter 7`, *Setting up a JavaScript Environment*) will help to produce a maintainable and flexible system. Even with a flexible system, it takes discipline and determination to maintain a standard of recognizing and fixing friction in the application.

The process of finding that friction could be considered **PDD (Pain Driven Development)**. This concept means to do the simplest thing to solve your existing problem and actively recognize any friction that arises during future modifications to the application.

PDD can be applied to any system, including the application, your team, and your personal life. Following this strategy, you will become obsessed with removing friction in all things, and can get a little carried away. So, it is important to keep in mind that you might be the only one looking for this friction, and the rest of the world might be ignorant to the pain they are causing themselves. Also, keep in mind that people do not, generally, enjoy having their ignorance pointed out.

Typical issues resulting from legacy code

There is a reason we fear working on legacy code. But, what is it that we fear when working on legacy code? It's not the code itself; the code cannot harm us. Instead, what we fear is hearing that we have introduced a bug. The most dreaded word that a developer can hear. A bug means that we have failed and that we will have to work on the legacy code again.

Exploring the types of issues we might run into while working on legacy code, we find several. Firstly, because we don't know the code, a change to one part might cause unintended side effects in a different part of the application. Another issue is the code could be over-optimized or written by someone who was trying to be clever when they wrote it. Lastly, tight coupling can make updating the code difficult.

Unintended side effects

With all the changes that push an application towards the legacy realm, often the methods or functions in the application will be used in unexpected places, far away from the code that you are changing.

There are two primary violations of the SOLID principles that have led to this issue, and the same two can help you to avoid it going forward. The first is the **OCP** (**Open Closed Principle**), and the second is the **LSP** (**Liskov Substitution Principle**).

Open Closed Principle and legacy code

As discussed previously, the Open Closed Principle states that code should be open for extension yet closed for modification. This principle is designed to prevent the issues with legacy code.

If the modification that has been requested of you is one that will change the behavior of a specific piece of the application, then try to instead clone the method in question and modify the clone. Then the part of the application that needs the change can call the clone instead. This will prevent the change from affecting any parts of the application except the parts you are intending to affect.

Until we know for sure that the code we just avoided is not being used elsewhere in the application, we can't delete it. Eventually, once we are sure that the old code is truly orphaned and not used, we want to clean up and delete the unused method to maintain a code base with just a little less cruft.

On the other hand, if the change is for a bug, then the fix is a little more complicated. You must first determine whether the bug should be fixed everywhere that this code might be used, or whether the bug is relative only to a specific portion of the application. When in doubt, fall back to cloning the method and only affecting intentional parts of the application.

Liskov Substitution Principle and legacy code

How do you determine whether a change should affect the entire application or just a slice? One way is to employ the LSP. Simply put, LSP says that a class should do what it sounds like it does. Any behavior change that would change that should be a different dependency.

That is, any change that changes behavior should probably be a new method or a new class with the appropriate method in it. This will prevent accidental side effects in the rest of the application and keep your code cleaner.

Over-optimization

It has been said that premature optimization is a bad thing. What is optimization, though? Generally, to optimize is to reduce the number of steps from point A to point B. In a computer program, that means to reduce the number of cycles required to compute a result.

An unfortunate side effect of optimizing code is that the code usually becomes much more difficult to read and comprehend. Optimizations tend to obfuscate the code in such a way that the only person who can understand it is the person who wrote it, and after some time, they may not be able to understand it either.

It is a fact that hard to understand code is code that is hard to change. This is the reason why optimizations that happen before they are needed are a bad thing.

So, when is an optimization needed? An optimization is needed when it is clear that the current implementation will not be able to meet the demands on the system within a reasonable timeframe in the future.

What makes a timeframe reasonable depends on the complexity of the needed optimization and the speed of the business. When a business is growing quickly, demand will follow along the same curve.

A slower moving company may require several months of planning and preparation before assigning work to a developer. In this situation, it is reasonable to plan for optimizations several months before they are needed. It is important to monitor the performance of an application so that these needs can be predicted.

Overly clever code

Most developers start writing code because they enjoy it. It is not common to find a developer that came into the field simply because they heard they could make lots of money. Working for a company writing the same boring code all the time can cause developers to want to have some fun once in a while.

When developers get bored, they come up with interesting and often overly complicated solutions that are simply not required. Sometimes, developers will come up with the cleverest solution they can figure out to solve a problem.

The problem with clever solutions is that to fix a problem, you have to be more skilled than the person who fixed it. So, if you write the cleverest code you can write, then you are no longer qualified to debug the code, and you bring your own, and everyone else's, progress to a halt.

Tight coupling to third-party software

Everyone uses some third-party plugin or library. In the software community, it is inevitable that you will have to depend on someone else's code. What you don't know when you use that code is the quality, stability, and ability to meet your future needs.

With that in mind, it is a bad idea to rely directly on the classes and interfaces presented to you by that third-party. Instead, use a hexagonal architecture, also known as ports and adapters. For anyone doing C#, this includes abstracting the .NET framework.

Any code that you and your team did not write should be abstracted to protect your code from the potential external changes. This includes code written at your company but by a different team. If it is outside your control, put it behind an abstraction. The preferred abstraction is one or more interfaces that provide the desired functionality.

Issues that prevent adding tests

Deadlines are tight. The scope is ever changing. We just don't have time to write tests. It's more important to get functionality out the door. We've all been there. Whatever the case may be, sometimes you will find yourself working on a project that was not written with testing in mind.

There never seems to be enough time to do it right, but there's always time to do it over.

So, what are the issues you might face that would prevent you from adding tests to a legacy application?

When a system wasn't written with testing in mind, it can be quite difficult to go back and add tests at a later date. Classes with concrete dependencies and tight coupling make software applications difficult to test. Things such as large classes and functions, Law of Demeter violations, global state, and static methods can also make for a system that can be very difficult to test.

Much like building a house by starting with a shaky foundation, untestable code begets untestable code. Unless pieces of the system can be decoupled from the rest of the application, the untestable trend will likely continue, and often does.

Direct dependence on framework and third-party code

Any time that the *new* operator in C#, for example, is invoked, then a direct dependency is made to that particular class. We want to minimize those dependencies as much as possible.

Remember that even framework dependencies should be avoided, or, at the very least, abstracted as much as possible. Think back to the `DateTime` example, where we were able to supply our own `DateTime` value for testing purposes in the sample application.

Any `using` or `import` statement at the top of a class or file should be carefully considered and avoided if at all possible. Instead, ensure that your code is dependent on an *interface* whose definition is directly under your control. That way, you can minimize the coupling and isolate the functionality within your own classes and methods. This will help you write cleaner, more testable code.

Law of Demeter

The Law of Demeter, in its simplest form, states that, *Each unit should have only limited knowledge about other units: only units "closely" related to the current unit.* Further, *Each unit should only talk to its friends; don't talk to strangers.* Simply put, *Only talk to your immediate friends.*

When a class or function has knowledge of the inner workings of something outside its immediate control, then there is some tight coupling happening there. In order to test a method that has one or more Law of Demeter violations, the amount of setup involved is often fairly substantial. In order to test a method of one class that violates the Law of Demeter, you must set up the other class or method, or provide a reasonable fake implementation in order to test effectively.

Remember, keep your test methods small and nimble so that they run quickly and are easy to understand. If you follow this rule, your production code will likely also be similarly simple and easy to follow. This will pay off in the long run, as it will be easier to maintain in the future.

Work in the constructor

When a new instance of a class is created that has logic in the constructor, it is often very difficult to test that class. If for some reason, you need to set up a test scenario that requires different values or behavior than that which is set up in the constructor, it will be quite difficult to proceed. It would be best to minimize the work done in the constructor and extract helper methods or some other scenario more easily tested and better implemented elsewhere.

Keep in mind that particular patterns may prove to be better alternatives to setting up a specific class or function. You should familiarize yourself with common software patterns and how to best implement them. This will help you grow an application by working to solve similar problems that have been resolved by others before you. By utilizing known software patterns, you can more easily communicate your intent with the code within the system.

The builder pattern, for example, might be employed to construct an object with the proper values set that would otherwise be added to the constructor.

Take the following example of the `Car` class:

```
public Car(string make, string model, int doors)
{
  Make = make;
  Model = model;
  Doors = doors;
}
```

You could easily write a builder class to construct a specific type of car, such as a `ToyotaCamryBuilder` or `FordMustangBuilder`. Creating a new instance of either a Toyota Camry or a Ford Mustang would be quite easy, simple, and clean. Not to mention, it would be quite easy to test.

Global state

Global state is prone to the side effects from parts of the application far away. These side effects will change the results of the code you run. Functional programming has caught on in recent years, as one of the tenants is to reduce side effects, as they can cause unpredictable and undesirable behavior in a system. Instead, you should strive to break down your code into what are known as pure functions. Pure functions take an input and produce an output. For any given input, the output will always be the same.

Static methods

Static methods are not in and of themselves bad, but they do hint at a misplaced responsibility code smell. Static anything tells you that you have put the code in the wrong place. It doesn't share anything in common with the rest of the code in the scope and should probably be removed and put somewhere with its friends.

Large classes and functions

Does class size really matter? What's the problem with having a large method or function? Large classes and functions often scream complexity. Remember the SOLID principles and what each letter in the acronym represents. A large class or method is likely violating one or more of the principles.

We want our classes and functions to be small and have only one reason to change (*Single Responsibility Principle*). A large class is likely hiding logic that can and should be broken into two or more separate and distinct classes. A large method or function likewise often hides two or more methods. Look for ways to keep your methods simple and keep an eye out for possible logical boundaries with which to break out smaller helpers, classes, and utilities.

Classes and functions should be divided and grouped logically. The purpose of a system should be easily understood by the names and groupings of the files associated with the application. The structure of the system should be simple and make sense to those in charge of enhancing and maintaining the application.

Dealing with legacy problems

We have been discussing all the issues with legacy code. Now it is time to tackle solving those issues. The first thing we must do is bring sanity to the targeted legacy code, and then we can begin testing and eventually fix the code and bring it back from death.

Safe refactoring

The term refactoring is often used incorrectly. When refactoring, you are merely changing the structure of the code. If the logic and/or signature of the code in question changes, then this does not qualify as refactoring. This is a change; most likely a breaking change.

> *If I'm changing the structure of the code (refactoring), then I don't ever change its behavior at the same time. If I'm changing the interface by which some logic is invoked, I never change the logic itself at the same time.*

> *– Kent Beck*

A safe refactoring is one that is guaranteed to not accidentally break the code. Other changes that aren't intended to actually change the behavior of the code but could do it accidentally are considered unsafe refactoring. These usually involve changes to the private areas of the code that aren't directly exposed to consumers of your application.

Converting values to variables

One of the first and easiest things that can be done is to extract any hard-coded values to be represented by variables. Having a variable allows for a quicker and more consistent update. It also helps to convey intent.

When creating the variables, make sure the name is descriptive enough for the scope of the variable. Variables with a short scope can have a short name. On the other hand, variables with a long scope must have a longer, more descriptive name. The further a variable is from its usages, the more descriptive it needs to be so that the context it represents isn't lost.

Check the scope of your variables and make sure they do not have a larger scope than is necessary. Also, check for variables that should have a larger scope but are instead passed between private methods instead of being class members.

It is not recommended at this time to update the private and protected methods that depend on variables that could be moved to a class scope. Instead, make note of them and move them around after tests have been added.

Extracting a method

Working with legacy code often involves working with very large methods. A large method is any method that is longer than twenty lines. Preferably, methods are kept as small as possible, even down to just a few lines.

A large method can mean that the code is violating the Single Responsibility Principle. What needs to be done is to find the seams in the method. Seams can be found by commenting the different sections of the method. Once you have commented the sections, you have identified the seams.

Seam

In code, this is the location where two pieces of business logic meet. Normally, you might refer to the location where the private method is called by a public method as a seam in the public method. The code has been stitched together at that location. In this case, there are no private methods, so we are identifying where we want the seams to be.

Each one of those seams is probably a lower order method that can be extracted. In most editors and IDEs, highlight the code you want and use the extract method refactoring provided through either a right-click, context, menu, or via the menu bar.

Extracting a class

Just like methods, sometimes a large method should really be a class. While extracting methods, if you extract three or more methods, then you have probably found a class that needs to be extracted.

Extracting a class is similar to extracting a method and is likely supported by your editor or IDE. Group and highlight the code you want to extract, then use the extract class menu option.

If your editor does not support extracting a class, all is not lost. Instead, highlight and cut all the methods you extracted that should be in the class. Create a new class file and paste those methods into the new class. Lastly, replace the calls to those methods in the original method with the instantiation and calling of the new class and methods.

Abstracting third-party libraries and framework code

Now that we have variables, methods, and classes abstracted, it is time to abstract third-party libraries, framework code, and those classes we just created.

Firstly, let's start with framework details. Things like `DateTime`, `Random`, and `Console` are best hidden behind classes that you design to fit the needs of your application. There are several reasons for this; most importantly, putting these in their own classes will allow for testing. Without abstracting these to a separate class, it is almost impossible to test with things like `DateTime` that change values on their own.

Next up are the third-party libraries. Anywhere the code is calling to create a new class from a third-party, you need to abstract that to a new class specifically for the purpose of utilizing that third-party library. For the moment, replace the call that instantiates the third-party library with a call that instantiates your class.

Lastly, we can now deal with the calls to `new` that are left in the code. Everywhere that the code is calling `new` needs to be replaced with dependency injection. This will allow for testing and make the code cleaner and more flexible in the future.

To create the dependency injection without modifying the signature of the class, we will be using a pattern called poor man's dependency injection, also known as property injection. Below is an example of property injection in C#. The same process can be done in JavaScript with almost no modifications:

```
public class Example
{
  private Injected _value;
  public Injected Value
  {
    get => _value = _value ?? new Injected();
    set => _value = value;
  }
}
```

Using this pattern, it is possible to allow the class to create its dependency lazily, when asked for it. It is also possible to set the dependencies value for tests or other purposes. Although not shown in this quick example of the pattern, it is better to have the property and backing variable be of an interface type. This will make the injection of some other value easier.

Early tests

If an application of any significant size and complexity isn't properly segmented, it can be quite a daunting task to know how and where to begin writing tests. With a little practice in testing legacy systems it will become easier.

The *when* to write tests within a legacy system can easily be answered with, "When it makes sense to." It would be difficult to sell the idea to any business owner that time (and money) should be spent going back to write tests to cover the existing functionality of a legacy system. It makes much more sense to add tests as enhancements are added to the application or when defects are being addressed. As you're working in the code and have immediate context surrounding the functionality that you wish to test, that is the optimal time to begin to test parts of a legacy application.

So, how do you begin to write tests against a legacy system? Isolate small functions that can be easily tested. Extract methods and smaller classes as needed. Ensure that functionality is not being modified, but that code is simply being reorganized in order to facilitate testability.

It may be necessary to change a private method to be protected so that it may be tested. Changing the scope of the method does make it more available and can reduce the effective abstraction, but if the change is required to aid in testing, the trade-off is almost always worth it. You might also consider that private methods made public might better belong to a different utility or helper class, and so can remain public. It depends on the method in question, but there are certainly options available to help you make a legacy system more testable.

Gold standard tests

Gold standard tests, or characterization tests, are those tests that simply define the expected functionality of a method. If you were to add tests to a legacy system, you would likely begin by writing gold standard tests to define the "happy path" through the system. You might run the application to determine what values a given method returns based on a given input, and then write a test to duplicate the results.

Gold standard tests are used because they provide a shortcut. Normally, to test legacy code, you would have to abstract third-party libraries and set up dependency injections of some sort. You may also have to refactor the code significantly just to get to the point where you can test anything. By using a gold standard test, most of this work can, temporarily, be bypassed. The only abstractions needed are screen output, date/time, and random. Just about everything else can be used as is.

This would provide a baseline for a suite of tests and help ensure that expected functionality does not change with future refactoring or modifications. Gold standard tests do not validate correctness; they merely confirm that the system does what the system did.

As a basis, gold standard tests provide a certain level of comfort to guard against any unwanted behavior changes. These likely will not be enough to provide adequate code coverage and should have additional tests added to cover edge cases and alternate paths through the system.

As the test suite grows and the coverage becomes more meaningful and complete, it may prove wise to remove the original gold standard tests. Again, you want your test suite to be able to execute quickly so that it is run always and often. Removing tests that may be superfluous will help minimize the feedback cycles when running your tests. In other words, you will know if you have broken something faster and will be more likely to run the tests if the tests complete faster.

Testing all potential outcomes

It's not necessarily important to test for all possible values for an individual method. As in the example of gold standard tests, you certainly don't want to run the application with all possible values in order to write tests for each of the possibilities. It is far more important to test for every path of execution.

If a method is small enough and its potential outcomes limited in scope, it should be quite trivial to write a handful of tests to cover all potential scenarios. Take the following method as an example:

```
public int GetPercent(int current, int maximum)
{
  if (maximum == 0)
  {
    throw new DivideByZeroException();
  }

  return (int) ((double) current / maximum * 100);
```

}

What are the potential paths through this method? What tests might you write to ensure adequate coverage?

First, you might consider writing a test in the case that the *maximum* input parameter is equal to 0. This should cover the `DivideByZeroException` in this scenario.

Next, you might write a test where the *current* parameter is 0, ensuring that the result of this method is always zero, assuming *maximum* is non-zero.

Finally, you would want to write one or more tests to validate that the algorithm above is indeed calculating the percentage correctly, based on inputs.

At this point, it may be tempting to add tests for things like negative values or to check the rounding that C# is doing, but remember that we are working with legacy code and, as far as the business is concerned, this code is working as is. You don't have a record of the business requirements that spawned this code, so it would be unnecessary, and possibly irresponsible, to test more than what this code is telling you. So, if you believe the code is flawed in that it doesn't cover certain business criteria, or that it could produce incorrect values, discuss these things with your business and make a determination together. Any change to the code would have to be through either a bug or new work.

Moving forward

Once the legacy system has been sufficiently refactored and a comprehensive suite of tests has been added, you may begin to think of the application as non-legacy, current, or a present-day system. It should now be trivial to add new features and squash any newly discovered defects. From this point forward, any new feature requested should be easily added with the confidence that other parts of the system will not be negatively affected.

The legacy application is no longer legacy. With a comprehensive suite of tests, you are now safe to proceed in Test-Driven Development fashion and write tests as every new feature is added. Remember to keep your tests as clean and well-refactored as any part of the production system.

Taking the `GetPercent` example above, how might you modify this in order to return two decimal places? Why, by writing new tests, of course! Start by creating a test to return two decimal places based on the input value.

Your test might look something like this:

```
[Fact]
public void ItReturnsTwoDecimalPlaces()
{
  // Arrange
  // Act
  var result = GetPercent(1, 3);
  // Assert
  Assert.Equal(33.33, result);
}
```

Now, modify the existing method to return only two decimal places. We'll leave this as an exercise for the reader.

Fixing bugs

Fixing bugs in a legacy system is a dangerous endeavor. Remember that any existing behavior may be accounted for in other parts of your system, or by external consumers of your application. By fixing a bug, you may be breaking functionality, albeit wrong, that someone else is depending on. So, a change to the execution results of code should be considered carefully before being done.

Free to do unsafe refactoring

Refactoring is, by definition, modifying the structure of the code without modifying its behavior. Safe refactoring includes variable injection, method extraction, and so on. Unsafe refactoring would affect the architecture of the code, the way the code interacts with the rest of the system, and more. By having a fully tested section of code, you can now modify the architecture and be assured that this section still does what it is supposed to do.

Summary

In this chapter, we discussed how we define legacy code and the issues that legacy code can create. Legacy code can inhibit testing, but now you should know how to fight back against the legacy problem.

In Chapter 14, *Unraveling a Mess*, we'll explore a rather extreme example of the types of things you might encounter in a legacy system. We'll explore safe refactoring and how to best unravel a mess into well structured, testable code.

14
Unraveling a Mess

Not all applications were written with testing in mind. Few were originally developed using TDD. Often, the original developers are long gone, and documentation is incorrect, incomplete, or missing entirely.

In this chapter, we will gain an understanding of:

- Dealing with inherited code
- Characterization tests
- Refactoring with tests

Inheriting code

This chapter is a case study of legacy code that needs (what should be) a minor change. We will quickly find out that the change is not so minor. To begin, let's look at what the legacy application does.

Here is some sample output from a run of this code:

```
Take a guess: AAAA
---+
Take a guess: BBBA
-+-+
Take a guess: CBCA
++
Take a guess: DBDA
++-+
```

```
Take a guess: DBEA
++++
Congratulations you guessed the password in 5 tries.
Press any key to quit.
```

Looking at the interactions, this program doesn't look that bad. In speaking with the business analyst, the application was explained as a game.

The game

This particular game is called *Mastermind* and is a code-breaking puzzle. According to the business analyst, the code consists of the letters A through F and contains four of the letters chosen at random. It is the goal of the player to determine the passcode.

The player is given hints along the way. For a correctly placed letter, the player receives a plus symbol. For a correct letter in the wrong position, the player receives a minus symbol. If the letter is incorrect, the player receives no symbol.

A change is requested

During playtesting, it was determined that players were discovering the passcodes too quickly. As a result, the game wasn't as much fun as it could be. The suggested solution was to make the passcode more complex by allowing more than six letters to be used. It is our job to extend the character range to A through Z.

We can start by looking at the existing code to determine where we might have to make the change. That is where we discover this!

In the file `Program.cs`:

```csharp
class Program
{
  static void Main(string[] args)
  {
    char[] g;
    char[] p = new[] { 'A', 'A', 'A', 'A' };
    int i = 0;
    int j = 0;
    int x = 0;
    int c = 0;
    Random rand = new Random(DateTime.Now.Millisecond);
    if (args.Length > 0 && args[0] != null) p = args[0].ToCharArray();
    else goto randomize_password;
```

```
guess: Console.Write("Take a guess: ");
g = Console.ReadLine().ToArray();
i = i + 1;
if (g.Length != 4) goto wrong_size;
if (g == p) goto success;
x = 0;
c = 0;
check_loop:
if (g[x] > 65 + 26) g[x] = (char)(g[x] - 32);
if (g[x] == p[x]) Console.Write("+", c = c + 1);
else if (p.Contains(g[x])) Console.Write("-");
x = x + 1;
if (x < 4) goto check_loop;
Console.WriteLine();
if (c == 4) goto success;
goto guess;
success: Console.WriteLine("Congratulations you guessed the
password in " + i + " tries.");
goto end;
wrong_size: Console.WriteLine("Password length is 4.");
goto guess;
randomize_password: j = 0;
password_loop: p[j] = (char)(rand.Next(6) + 65);
j = j + 1;
if (j < 4) goto password_loop;
goto guess;
end: Console.WriteLine("Press any key to quit.");
Console.ReadKey();
    }
  }
```

We now have several problems. Firstly, it's not exactly clear where the letters are coming from. Secondly, there is no way this code is tested. Lastly, even if making the change were straight forward, making sure we didn't break something would not be. We have to do a full manual regression test to verify that any of this is working, and trying to verify that all letters, A through Z, are possible may take a very long time.

Life sometimes hands you lemons

While I hope you never receive code this bad, we are going to walk through what is needed to turn even this into readable, maintainable, and fully tested code. The best part, the part you aren't going to believe, is that transforming this code is actually safe and fairly easy.

Getting started

In any code situation like this, the first thing we must do is remove the code in question from the environment where we have no control. In this case, we can't test the code if it is sitting in `Program.main`. So, let's grab the whole thing and put it into a class named `Mastermind`. We will have a single function named `Play` that will run the game. This is considered a safe refactoring, because we are not changing any of the existing code, simply moving it somewhere else.

In the file `Program.cs`:

```
class Program
{
  static void Main(string[] args)
  {
    var game = new Mastermind();
    game.Play(args);
  }
}
```

In the file `Mastermind.cs`:

```
class Mastermind
{
  public void Play(string[] args)
  {
    char[] g;
    char[] p = new[] { 'A', 'A', 'A', 'A' };
    int i = 0;
    int j = 0;
    int x = 0;
    int c = 0;
    Random rand = new Random(DateTime.Now.Millisecond);
    if (args.Length > 0 && args[0] != null) p = args[0].ToCharArray();
    else goto randomize_password;
    guess: Console.Write("Take a guess: ");
    g = Console.ReadLine().ToArray();
    i = i + 1;
    if (g.Length != 4) goto wrong_size;
    if (g == p) goto success;
    x = 0;
    c = 0;
    check_loop:
    if (g[x] > 65 + 26) g[x] = (char)(g[x] - 32);
    if (g[x] == p[x]) Console.Write("+", c = c + 1);
    else if (p.Contains(g[x])) Console.Write("-");
    x = x + 1;
```

```
        if (x < 4) goto check_loop;
        Console.WriteLine();
        if (c == 4) goto success;
        goto guess;
        success: Console.WriteLine("Congratulations you guessed the
        password in " + i + " tries.");
        goto end;
        wrong_size: Console.WriteLine("Password length is 4.");
        goto guess;
        randomize_password: j = 0;
        password_loop: p[j] = (char)(rand.Next(6) + 65);
        j = j + 1;
        if (j < 4) goto password_loop;
        goto guess;
        end: Console.WriteLine("Press any key to quit.");
        Console.ReadKey();
    }
}
```

Running the code again at this point shows that everything still works. The next step is a cosmetic one; let's spread the `Play` method out into sections. This should help us determine what private methods exist inside the large public method.

In the file `Mastermind.cs`:

```
class Mastermind
{
    public void Play(string[] args)
    {
        // Variable Declarations - Global??
        char[] g;
        char[] p = new[] { 'A', 'A', 'A', 'A' };
        int i = 0;
        int j = 0;
        int x = 0;
        int c = 0;
        // Initialize randomness
        Random rand = new Random(DateTime.Now.Millisecond);
        // Determine if a password was passed in?
        if (args.Length > 0 && args[0] != null) p = args[0].ToCharArray();
        else goto randomize_password; // Create a password if one was not
        provided
        // Player move - guess the password
        guess: Console.Write("Take a guess: ");
        g = Console.ReadLine().ToArray();
        i = i + 1;
        if (g.Length != 4) goto wrong_size;
        if (g == p) goto success;
```

```
        x = 0;
        c = 0;
        // Check if the password provided by the player is correct
        check_loop:
        if (g[x] > 65 + 26) g[x] = (char)(g[x] - 32);
        if (g[x] == p[x]) Console.Write("+", c = c + 1);
        else if (p.Contains(g[x])) Console.Write("-");
        x = x + 1;
        if (x < 4) goto check_loop; // Still checking??
        Console.WriteLine();
        if (c == 4) goto success; // Password must have been correct
        goto guess; // No correct, try again
        // Game over you win
        success: Console.WriteLine("Congratulations you guessed the
        password in " + i + " tries.");
        goto end;
        // Password guess was wrong size - Error Message
        wrong_size: Console.WriteLine("Password length is 4.");
        goto guess;
        // Create a random password
        randomize_password: j = 0;
        password_loop: p[j] = (char)(rand.Next(6) + 65);
        j = j + 1;
        if (j < 4) goto password_loop;
        goto guess; // Start the game
        // Game is complete - exit
        end: Console.WriteLine("Press any key to quit.");
        Console.ReadKey();
    }
}
```

We have now used whitespace to split the program into several pieces and added comments explaining what we think each piece is doing. At this point, we are almost ready to begin testing. We have just a couple things in the way, the worst of which is the `Console` class.

Abstracting a third-party class

If we tried to test right now, the application would hit the first `ReadLine` call and the test would time out. Console has the ability to redirect the input and output, but we are not going to use this feature, because it is specific to Console and we want to demonstrate a more generic solution that you can apply anywhere.

What we need is a class that gives us a similar interface to Console. Then we can dependency inject our class for the tests and a thin wrapper for the production code. Let's test drive that interface now.

In the file `InputOutputTests.cs`:

```
public class InputOutputTests
{
  [Fact]
  public void ItExists()
  {
    var inout = new MockInputOutput();
  }
}
```

In the file `ReadLineTests.cs`:

```
public class ReadLineTests
{
  [Fact]
  public void ItCanBeReadFrom()
  {
    var inout = new MockInputOutput();
    inout.InFeed.Enqueue("Test");
    // Act
    var input = inout.ReadLine();
  }

  [Fact]
  public void ProvidedInputCanBeRetrieved()
  {
    // Arrange
    var inout = new MockInputOutput();
    inout.InFeed.Enqueue("Test");

    // Act
    var input = inout.ReadLine();

    // Assert
    Assert.Equal("Test", input);
  }

  [Fact]
  public void ProvidedInputCanBeRetrievedInSuccession()
  {
    // Arrange
    var inout = new MockInputOutput();
    inout.InFeed.Enqueue("Test 1");
```

```
    inout.InFeed.Enqueue("Test 2");

    // Act
    var input1 = inout.ReadLine();
    var input2 = inout.ReadLine();

    // Assert
    Assert.Equal("Test 1", input1);
    Assert.Equal("Test 2", input2);
  }
}
```

In the file `ReadTests.cs`:

```
public class ReadTests
{
  [Fact]
  public void ItCanBeReadFrom()
  {
    var inout = new MockInputOutput();
    inout.InFeed.Enqueue("T");

    // Act
    var input = inout.Read();
  }

  [Fact]
  public void ProvidedInputCanBeRetrieved()
  {
    // Arrange
    var inout = new MockInputOutput();
    inout.InFeed.Enqueue("T");

    // Act
    var input = inout.Read();

    // Assert
    Assert.Equal('T', input);
  }

  [Fact]
  public void ProvidedInputCanBeRetrievedInSuccession()
  {
    // Arrange
    var inout = new MockInputOutput();
    inout.InFeed.Enqueue("T");
    inout.InFeed.Enqueue("E");
```

```
    // Act
    var input1 = inout.Read();
    var input2 = inout.Read();

    // Assert
    Assert.Equal('T', input1);
    Assert.Equal('E', input2);
  }
}
```

In the file `WriteTests.cs`:

```
public class WriteTests
{
  [Fact]
  public void ItCanBeWrittenTo()
  {
    var inout = new MockInputOutput();

    // Act
    inout.Write("Text");
  }

  [Fact]
  public void WrittenTextCanBeRetrieved()
  {
    // Arrange
    var inout = new MockInputOutput();
    inout.Write("Text");

    // Act
    var writtenText = inout.OutFeed;

    // Assert
    Assert.Single(writtenText);
    Assert.Equal("Text", writtenText.First());
  }
}
```

In the file `WriteLineTests.cs`:

```
public class WriteLineTests
{
  [Fact]
  public void ItCanBeWrittenTo()
  {
    var inout = new MockInputOutput();
```

```
      // Act
      inout.WriteLine("Text");
    }

    [Fact]
    public void WrittenTextCanBeRetrieved()
    {
      // Arrange
      var inout = new MockInputOutput();
      inout.WriteLine("Text");

      // Act
      var writtenText = inout.OutFeed;

      // Assert
      Assert.Single(writtenText);
      Assert.Equal("Text" + Environment.NewLine, writtenText.First());
    }
  }
```

In the file `IInputOutput.cs`:

```
public interface IInputOutput
{
  void Write(string text);
  void WriteLine(string text);
  char Read();
  string ReadLine();
}
```

In the file `MockInputOutput.cs`:

```
public class MockInputOutput : IInputOutput
{
  public List<string> OutFeed { get; set; }
  public Queue<string> InFeed { get; set; }

  public MockInputOutput()
  {
    OutFeed = new List<string>();
    InFeed = new Queue<string>();
  }

  public void Write(string text)
  {
    OutFeed.Add(text);
  }
```

```
public void WriteLine(string text)
{
  OutFeed.Add(text + Environment.NewLine);
}

public char Read()
{
  return InFeed.Dequeue().ToCharArray().First();
}

public string ReadLine()
{
  return InFeed.Dequeue();
}
}
```

That handles our mock input and output, but we need to create the production wrapper class for Console, and we need to use `Program.cs` to inject that class into the `Mastermind` class.

Unexpected Input

While replacing calls to Console with calls to our injected class, we found two use cases that we did not plan for. The first use case is fairly involved and has a couple parameters we need to handle:

```
Console.Write("+", c = c + 1);
```

The second use case is more simple and doesn't take any parameters:

```
Console.WriteLine();
```

The second use case is the easiest to deal with, so let us write a quick test for that now.

In the file `WriteLineTests.cs`:

```
[Fact]
public void ItCanWriteABlankLine()
{
  // Arrange
  var inout = new MockInputOutput();

  // Act
  inout.WriteLine();

  // Assert
```

```
        Assert.Single(inout.OutFeed);
        Assert.Equal(Environment.NewLine, inout.OutFeed.First());
    }
```

In the file IInputOutput.cs:

```
    void WriteLine(string text = null);
```

In the file MockInputOutput.cs:

```
    public void WriteLine(string text = null)
    {
        OutFeed.Add((text ?? "") + Environment.NewLine);
    }
```

The next issue is slightly more complicated. If we want to handle it accurately, we will need to do quite a bit of regular expression and string manipulation. However, we don't need it to be "correct"; we only need it to work as expected by the application. In the singular case where this is being used, the value that should be placed into the string being written, isn't. The original developer abused the functionality of Console.Write to reduce the number of lines in the if statement so they could avoid brackets. So, all we need to do for the code to continue to work is allow for the input to take place. A simple interface extension should provide that for us.

In the file IInputOutput.cs:

```
    void Write(string text, params object[] args);
```

In the file MockInputOutput.cs:

```
    public void Write(string text, params object[] args)
    {
        OutFeed.Add(text);
    }
```

Back in the application code, we can finish making our changes. Here is the updated application.

In the file ConsoleInputOutput.cs:

```
    public class ConsoleInputOutput : IInputOutput
    {
        public void Write(string text, params object[] args)
        {
            Console.Write(text, args);
        }
```

```
    public void WriteLine(string text)
    {
      Console.WriteLine(text);
    }

    public char Read()
    {
      return Console.ReadKey().KeyChar;
    }

    public string ReadLine()
    {
      return Console.ReadLine();
    }
  }
```

In the file `Program.cs`:

```
class Program
{
  static void Main(string[] args)
  {
    var inout = new ConsoleInputOutput();
    var game = new Mastermind(inout);
    game.Play(args);
  }
}
```

In the file `Mastermind.cs`:

```
public class Mastermind
{
  private readonly IInputOutput _inout;

  public Mastermind(IInputOutput inout)
  {
    _inout = inout;
  }

  public void Play(string[] args)
  {
    // Variable Declarations - Global??
    char[] g;
    char[] p = new[] { 'A', 'A', 'A', 'A' };
    int i = 0;
    int j = 0;
    int x = 0;
    int c = 0;
```

```csharp
            // Initialize randomness
            Random rand = new Random(DateTime.Now.Millisecond);

            // Determine if a password was passed in?
            if (args.Length > 0 && args[0] != null) p = args[0].ToCharArray();
            else goto randomize_password; // Create a password if one was not
            provided
            // Player move - guess the password
            guess: _inout.Write("Take a guess: ");
            g = _inout.ReadLine().ToArray();
            i = i + 1;
            if (g.Length != 4) goto wrong_size;
            if (g == p) goto success;
            x = 0;
            c = 0;

            // Check if the password provided by the player is correct
            check_loop:
            if (g[x] > 65 + 26) g[x] = (char)(g[x] - 32);
            if (g[x] == p[x]) _inout.Write("+", c = c + 1);
            else if (p.Contains(g[x])) _inout.Write("-");
            x = x + 1;
            if (x < 4) goto check_loop; // Still checking??
            _inout.WriteLine();
            if (c == 4) goto success; // Password must have been correct
            goto guess; // No correct, try again

            // Game over you win
            success: _inout.WriteLine("Congratulations you guessed the password
            in " + i + " tries.");
            goto end;
            // Password guess was wrong size - Error Message
            wrong_size: _inout.WriteLine("Password length is 4.");
            goto guess;

            // Create a random password
            randomize_password: j = 0;
            password_loop: p[j] = (char)(rand.Next(6) + 65);
            j = j + 1;
            if (j < 4) goto password_loop;
            goto guess; // Start the game

            // Game is complete   exit
            end: _inout.WriteLine("Press any key to quit.");
            _inout.Read();
        }
    }
```

A quick test run confirms that the application is working correctly:

```
Take a guess: AAAA
Take a guess: BBBB
Take a guess: CCCC
Take a guess: DDDD
+-++
Take a guess: DEDD
+++
Take a guess: DFDD
++++
Congratulations you guessed the password in 6 tries.

Press any key to quit.
```

Now, we can write a gold standard or characterization test that will verify all the parts of the code are working correctly. The only piece of the code this test will not cover is the random password generation:

```
public class GoldStandardTests
{
  [Fact]
  public void StandardTestRun()
  {
    // Arrange
    var inout = new MockInputOutput();
    var game = new Mastermind(inout);

    // Arrange - Inputs
    inout.InFeed.Enqueue("AAA");
    inout.InFeed.Enqueue("AAAA");
    inout.InFeed.Enqueue("ABBB");
    inout.InFeed.Enqueue("ABCC");
    inout.InFeed.Enqueue("ABCD");
    inout.InFeed.Enqueue("ABCF");
    inout.InFeed.Enqueue("  ");

    // Arrange - Outputs
    var expectedOutputs = new Queue<string>();
    expectedOutputs.Enqueue("Take a guess: ");
    expectedOutputs.Enqueue("Password length is 4." +
     Environment.NewLine);
    expectedOutputs.Enqueue("Take a guess: ");
    expectedOutputs.Enqueue("+");
    expectedOutputs.Enqueue("-");
    expectedOutputs.Enqueue("-");
    expectedOutputs.Enqueue("-");
    expectedOutputs.Enqueue(Environment.NewLine);
```

```
expectedOutputs.Enqueue("Take a guess: ");
expectedOutputs.Enqueue("+");
expectedOutputs.Enqueue("+");
expectedOutputs.Enqueue("-");
expectedOutputs.Enqueue("-");
expectedOutputs.Enqueue(Environment.NewLine);
expectedOutputs.Enqueue("Take a guess: ");
expectedOutputs.Enqueue("+");
expectedOutputs.Enqueue("+");
expectedOutputs.Enqueue("+");
expectedOutputs.Enqueue("-");
expectedOutputs.Enqueue(Environment.NewLine);
expectedOutputs.Enqueue("Take a guess: ");
expectedOutputs.Enqueue("+");
expectedOutputs.Enqueue("+");
expectedOutputs.Enqueue("+");
expectedOutputs.Enqueue(Environment.NewLine);
expectedOutputs.Enqueue("Take a guess: ");
expectedOutputs.Enqueue("+");
expectedOutputs.Enqueue("+");
expectedOutputs.Enqueue("+");
expectedOutputs.Enqueue("+");
expectedOutputs.Enqueue(Environment.NewLine);
expectedOutputs.Enqueue("Congratulations you guessed the password
  in 6 tries." + Environment.NewLine);
expectedOutputs.Enqueue("Press any key to quit." +
  Environment.NewLine);
// Act
game.Play(new[] { "ABCF" });

// Assert
inout.OutFeed.ForEach((text) =>
{
  Assert.Equal(expectedOutputs.Dequeue(), text);
});
  }
}
```

This is an extremely long test, and it has an out of the ordinary structure, but this single test runs through almost all the logic in the application. You may not always be able to do this with a single test, but before beginning any heavy refactoring, these tests must exist.

Making sense of the madness

Now that we have the gold standard test written, we can begin to safely refactor the code. Any changes that we try to make that break the gold standard test will have to be undone and a new approach will have to be taken.

Looking at the `Mastermind` class, all those variables at the top of the `Play` method can be moved out to be class level fields. This will make them available to all the code within the class and help to both figure out what they are for and how often they are used in the app:

```
private char[] g;
private char[] p = new[] { 'A', 'A', 'A', 'A' };
private int i = 0;
private int j = 0;
private int x = 0;
private int c = 0;
```

Next, we will just work our way down the `Play` method, extracting all that we can into tiny private methods. We are only able to do some tiny refactoring before we need to switch gears and start fixing some of the antiquated logic in this application:

```
public class Mastermind
{
    private readonly IInputOutput _inout;
    private char[] g;
    private char[] p = new[] { 'A', 'A', 'A', 'A' };
    private int i = 0;
    private int j = 0;
    private int x = 0;
    private int c = 0;

    public Mastermind(IInputOutput inout)
    {
        _inout = inout;
    }

    public void Play(string[] args)
    {
        // Determine if a password was passed in?
        if (args.Length > 0 && args[0] != null) p = args[0].ToCharArray();
        else CreateRandomPassword(); // Create a password if one was not
        provided
        // Player move - guess the password
        guess:
        _inout.Write("Take a guess: ");
        g = _inout.ReadLine().ToArray();
        i = i + 1;
```

```
if (g.Length != 4) goto wrong_size;
if (g == p) goto success;
x = 0;
c = 0;

// Check if the password provided by the player is correct
check_loop:
if (g[x] > 65 + 26) g[x] = (char)(g[x] - 32);
if (g[x] == p[x]) _inout.Write("+", c = c + 1);
else if (p.Contains(g[x])) _inout.Write("-");
x = x + 1;
if (x < 4) goto check_loop; // Still checking??
_inout.WriteLine();
if (c == 4) goto success; // Password must have been correct
goto guess; // No correct, try again

// Password guess was wrong size - Error Message
wrong_size: _inout.WriteLine("Password length is 4.");
goto guess;

// Game over you win
success: _inout.WriteLine("Congratulations you guessed the password
  in " + i + " tries.");
_inout.WriteLine("Press any key to quit.");
_inout.Read();
}
private void CreateRandomPassword()
{
  // Initialize randomness
  Random rand = new Random(DateTime.Now.Millisecond);

  j = 0;

  password_loop:
  p[j] = (char)(rand.Next(6) + 65);
  j = j + 1;
  if (j < 4) goto password_loop;
}
}
```

We were able to break out a password generation method. We were also able to simplify the structure of the success code. We cannot, however, proceed without addressing the complexity of the chosen looping structures. The developer that wrote this did not use general looping structures, such as while and for loops. We need to fix that in order to better understand and work with this code:

```
public void Play(string[] args)
{
  // Determine if a password was passed in?
  if (args.Length > 0 && args[0] != null) p = args[0].ToCharArray();
  else CreateRandomPassword(); // Create a password if one was not
   provided
  // Player move - guess the password
  while (c != 4)
  {
    _inout.Write("Take a guess: ");
    g = _inout.ReadLine().ToArray();

    i = i + 1;

    if (g.Length != 4)
    {
      // Password guess was wrong size - Error Message
      _inout.WriteLine("Password length is 4.");
    }
    else
    {
      // Check if the password provided by the player is correct
      for (x = 0, c = 0; g.Length == 4 && x < 4; x++)
      {
        if (g[x] > 65 + 26) g[x] = (char)(g[x] - 32);
        if (g[x] == p[x]) _inout.Write("+", c = c + 1);
        else if (p.Contains(g[x])) _inout.Write("-");
      }
      _inout.WriteLine();
    }
  }

  // Game over you win
  _inout.WriteLine("Congratulations you guessed the password in " + i +
  " tries.");
  _inout.WriteLine("Press any key to quit.");
  _inout.Read();
}
```

We now have a structure that we can begin to work with. Let's start by making some sense of these variable names:

```
C ~= Correct Letter Guesses
G ~= Current Guess
P ~= Password
I ~= Tries
X ~= Loop Index / Pointer to Guess Character being checked
J ~= Loop Index / Pointer to Password Character being generated
```

We will want to make updates to the Play method that reflect our determinations for what the variables mean. Following we have replaced the single letter variable names with names that more appropriately represent what the variables are used for:

```csharp
public void Play(string[] args)
{
  // Determine if a password was passed in?
  if (args.Length > 0 && args[0] != null) password =
   args[0].ToCharArray();
  else CreateRandomPassword(); // Create a password if one was not
   provided
  // Player move - guess the password
  while (correctPositions != 4)
  {
    _inout.Write("Take a guess: ");
    guess = _inout.ReadLine().ToArray();

    tries = tries + 1;

    if (guess.Length != 4)
    {
      // Password guess was wrong size - Error Message
      _inout.WriteLine("Password length is 4.");
    }
    else
    {
      // Check if the password provided by the player is correct
      for (x = 0, correctPositions = 0; x < 4; x++)
      {
        if (guess[x] > 65 + 26) guess[x] = (char)(guess[x] - 32);
        if (guess[x] == password[x]) _inout.Write("+", correctPositions
          = correctPositions + 1);
        else if (password.Contains(guess[x])) _inout.Write("-");
      }
      _inout.WriteLine();
    }
  }
}
```

```
    // Game over you win
    _inout.WriteLine("Congratulations you guessed the password in " +
    tries + " tries.");
    _inout.WriteLine("Press any key to quit.");
    _inout.Read();
}
```

Next, it would be nice if we could update the interface now that we understand the application a little better. Two things that we would like to change are the input and the very end of the game. It would be nice if the input was a simple string instead of a character array. The `Play` method could take a string and the program could figure out how to get the password string from the arguments.

Along those same lines, we could reduce the overall number of writes and turn the consecutive plus and minus `Write` commands into a single `WriteLine` command. This would break our gold standard test, but wouldn't actually change the functionality of the code. It would still print the pluses and minuses on a single line.

To convert the guess from a character array to a string, we must first understand what is happening on this line:

```
    if (guess[x] > 65 + 26) guess[x] = (char)(guess[x] - 32);
```

Analyzing the line, we see the numbers 65, 26, and 32. If you are familiar with ASCII codes, then these lines might make sense to you. The number 65 is the starting point of the alphabet characters on the ASCII tables. There are 26 letters in the English alphabet. And, there are 32 values between "a" and "A". So, it is to be assumed that this code is either uppercasing or lowercasing the character at the specified index. We can approximate this in C# using the `String.ToUpper()` method.

While we are doing a small bit of gold standard changes, we should also remove the last two lines of the `Play` method and move them to `Program.cs`, as they are more related to a Console application than anything else.

In the file `Program.cs`:

```
class Program
{
    static void Main(string[] args)
    {
        var inout = new ConsoleInputOutput();
        var game = new Mastermind(inout);
        var password = args.Length > 0 ? args[0] : null;
        game.Play(password);
```

```
            inout.WriteLine("Press any key to quit.");
            inout.Read();
        }
    }
```

In the file `Mastermind.cs`:

```csharp
public class Mastermind
{
    private readonly IInputOutput _inout;
    private string guess;
    private int tries;
    private int correctPositions;

    public Mastermind(IInputOutput inout)
    {
        _inout = inout;
    }

    public void Play(string password = null)
    {
        // Determine if a password was passed in?
        password = password ?? CreateRandomPassword();

        // Player move - guess the password
        while (correctPositions != 4)
        {
            _inout.Write("Take a guess: ");
            guess = _inout.ReadLine();
            tries = tries + 1;

            if (guess.Length != 4)
            {
                // Password guess was wrong size - Error Message
                _inout.WriteLine("Password length is 4.");
            }
            else
            {
                // Check if the password provided by the player is correct
                guess = guess.ToUpper();
                var guessResult = "";

                for (var x = 0; x < 4; x++)
                {
                    if (guess[x] == password[x])
                    {
                        guessResult += "+";
                    }
```

```
        else if (password.Contains(guess[x]))
        {
          guessResult += "-";
        }
      }

      correctPositions = guessResult.Count(c => c == '+');
      _inout.WriteLine(guessResult);
    }
  }

  // Game over you win
  _inout.WriteLine("Congratulations you guessed the password in " +
   tries + " tries.");
}

private string CreateRandomPassword()
{
  // Initialize randomness
  Random rand = new Random(DateTime.Now.Millisecond);
  var password = new [] {'A', 'A', 'A', 'A'};

  var j = 0;

  password_loop:
  password[j] = (char)(rand.Next(6) + 65);
  j = j + 1;

  if (j < 4) goto password_loop;
  return password.ToString();
}
}
```

In the file `GoldStandardTests.cs`:

```
public class GoldStandardTests
{
  [Fact]
  public void StandardTestRun()
  {
    // Arrange
    var inout = new MockInputOutput();
    var game = new Mastermind(inout);

    // Arrange - Inputs
    inout.InFeed.Enqueue("AAA");
    inout.InFeed.Enqueue("AAAA");
    inout.InFeed.Enqueue("ABBB");
```

```csharp
inout.InFeed.Enqueue("ABCC");
inout.InFeed.Enqueue("ABCD");
inout.InFeed.Enqueue("ABCF");
inout.InFeed.Enqueue(" ");

// Arrange - Outputs
var expectedOutputs = new Queue<string>();
expectedOutputs.Enqueue("Take a guess: ");
expectedOutputs.Enqueue("Password length is 4." +
Environment.NewLine);
expectedOutputs.Enqueue("Take a guess: ");
expectedOutputs.Enqueue("+---" + Environment.NewLine);
expectedOutputs.Enqueue("Take a guess: ");
expectedOutputs.Enqueue("++--" + Environment.NewLine);
expectedOutputs.Enqueue("Take a guess: ");
expectedOutputs.Enqueue("+++-" + Environment.NewLine);
expectedOutputs.Enqueue("Take a guess: ");
expectedOutputs.Enqueue("+++" + Environment.NewLine);
expectedOutputs.Enqueue("Take a guess: ");
expectedOutputs.Enqueue("++++" + Environment.NewLine);
expectedOutputs.Enqueue("Congratulations you guessed the password
in 6 tries." + Environment.NewLine);

// Act
game.Play("ABCF");

// Assert
inout.OutFeed.ForEach(text =>
{
   Assert.Equal(expectedOutputs.Dequeue(), text);
});
    }
}
```

Final beautification

Now that everything else is done and the code is working correctly, it is time for the last refactoring before we start our enhancement. We want our methods to be as small as possible. In this case, that means that the `Play` function should have practically no logic outside the main game loop.

In general, if a method has any kind of block in it (for example, if, while, for, and so on), we want that block to be the only thing in the method. Often, there are also guard statements checking input, but that should be it. Let's refactor to follow that convention and see what the code looks like afterwards.

In the file `Mastermind.cs`:

```csharp
public class Mastermind
{
    private readonly IInputOutput _inout;
    private int _tries;

    public Mastermind(IInputOutput inout)
    {
        _inout = inout;
    }

    public void Play(string password = null)
    {
        password = password ?? CreateRandomPassword();
        var correctPositions = 0;

        while (correctPositions != 4)
        {
            correctPositions = GuessPasswordAndCheck(password);
        }

        _inout.WriteLine("Congratulations you guessed the password in " +
        _tries + " tries.");
    }

    private int GuessPasswordAndCheck(string password)
    {
        var guess = Guess();
        return Check(guess, password);
    }

    private int Check(string guess, string password)
    {
        var checkResult = "";

        for (var x = 0; x < 4; x++)
        {
            if (guess[x] == password[x])
            {
                checkResult += "+";
            }
```

```
      else if (password.Contains(guess[x]))
      {
        checkResult += "-";
      }
    }

    _inout.WriteLine(checkResult);
    return checkResult.Count(c => c == '+');
  }

  private string Guess()
  {
    _tries = _tries + 1;
    _inout.Write("Take a guess: ");
    var guess = _inout.ReadLine();

    if (guess.Length == 4)
    {
      return guess.ToUpper();
    }

    // Password guess was wrong size - Error Message
    _inout.WriteLine("Password length is 4.");
    return Guess();
  }

  private string CreateRandomPassword()
  {
    // Initialize randomness
    Random rand = new Random(DateTime.Now.Millisecond);

    var password = new[] { 'A', 'A', 'A', 'A' };

    var j = 0;

    password_loop:
    password[j] = (char)(rand.Next(6) + 65);
    j = j + 1;

    if (j < 4) goto password_loop;

    return password.ToString();
  }
}
```

There are many ways that this code could have been refactored; this is just one. Now that the code is refactored, we are ready to move on and begin working on enhancements.

Ready for enhancements

We are now to a point where the code makes enough sense that we can begin to work on our change requests. We have broken the random password generation portion of the code into its own method, so now we can work on it independently.

One of the first things we need to do is to stop using Random. Random is, by nature, unpredictable and outside of our control. We need a way to feed the number generation to verify that we can get the expected outputs when Random provides specific inputs.

We will extract an interface and mock class similar to what we did for Console. Here is the first round of tests, the mock class, and the interface that were created.

In the file RandomNumberTests.cs:

```
public class RandomNumberTests
{
  private readonly MockRandomGenerator _rand;

  public RandomNumberTests()
  {
    _rand = new MockRandomGenerator();
  }

  [Fact]
  public void ItExists()
  {
    _rand.Number();
  }

  [Fact]
  public void ItReturnsDefaultValue()
  {
    // Act
    var result = _rand.Number();

    // Assert
    Assert.Equal(0, result);
  }

  [Fact]
  public void ItCanReturnPredeterminedNumbers()
  {
    // Arrange
    _rand.SetNumbers(1, 2, 3, 4, 5);

    // Act
```

```
    var a = _rand.Number();
    var b = _rand.Number();
    var c = _rand.Number();
    var d = _rand.Number();
    var e = _rand.Number();

    // Arrange
    Assert.Equal(1, a);
    Assert.Equal(2, b);
    Assert.Equal(3, c);
    Assert.Equal(4, d);
    Assert.Equal(5, e);
}

[Fact]
public void ItCanHaveAMaxRange()
{
    // Arrange
    const int maxRange = 3;
    _rand.SetNumbers(1, 2, 3, 4, 5);

    // Act
    var a = _rand.Number(maxRange);
    var b = _rand.Number(maxRange);
    var c = _rand.Number(maxRange);
    var d = _rand.Number(maxRange);
    var e = _rand.Number(maxRange);

    // Arrange
    Assert.Equal(1, a);
    Assert.Equal(2, b);
    Assert.Equal(3, c);
    Assert.Equal(3, d);
    Assert.Equal(3, e);
}

[Fact]
public void ItCanHaveAMinMaxRange()
{
    // Arrange
    const int minRange = 2;
    const int maxRange = 3;
    _rand.SetNumbers(1, 2, 3, 4, 5);

    // Act
    var a = _rand.Number(minRange, maxRange);
    var b = _rand.Number(minRange, maxRange);
    var c = _rand.Number(minRange, maxRange);
```

```
    var d = _rand.Number(minRange, maxRange);
    var e = _rand.Number(minRange, maxRange);

    // Arrange
    Assert.Equal(2, a);
    Assert.Equal(2, b);
    Assert.Equal(3, c);
    Assert.Equal(3, d);
    Assert.Equal(3, e);
  }
}
```

In the file IRandomGenerator.cs:

```
public interface IRandomGenerator
{
  int Number(int max = 100);
  int Number(int min, int max);
}
```

In the file MockRandomGenerator.cs:

```
public class MockRandomGenerator : IRandomGenerator
{
  private readonly List<int> _numbers;
  private List<int>.Enumerator _numbersEnumerator;

  public MockRandomGenerator(List<int> numbers = null)
  {
    _numbers = numbers ?? new List<int>();
    _numbersEnumerator = _numbers.GetEnumerator();
  }

  public int Number(int min, int max)
  {
    var result = Number(max);

    return result < min ? min : result;
  }

  public int Number(int max = 100)
  {
    _numbersEnumerator.MoveNext();
    var result = _numbersEnumerator.Current;

    return result > max ? max : result;
  }
```

```
public void SetNumbers(params int[] args)
{
  _numbers.AddRange(args);
  _numbersEnumerator = _numbers.GetEnumerator();
}
}
```

Now, to create the production RandomGenerator class and inject it into our application.

In the file RandomGenerator.cs:

```
public class RandomGenerator : IRandomGenerator
{
  private readonly Random _rand;

  public RandomGenerator()
  {
    _rand = new Random();
  }

  public int Number(int max = 100)
  {
    rcturn _rand.Next(0, max);
  }

  public int Number(int min, int max)
  {
    return _rand.Next(min, max);
  }
}
```

In the file Program.cs:

```
class Program
{
  static void Main(string[] args)
  {
    var rand = new RandomGenerator();
    var inout = new ConsoleInputOutput();
    var game = new Mastermind(inout, rand);
    var password = args.Length > 0 ? args[0] : null;
    game.Play(password);

    inout.WriteLine("Press any key to quit.");
    inout.Read();
  }
}
```

In the file `Mastermind.cs`:

```
public class Mastermind
{
  private readonly IInputOutput _inout;
  private readonly IRandomGenerator _random;

  private int _tries;
  public Mastermind(IInputOutput inout, IRandomGenerator random)
  {
    _inout = inout;
    _random = random;
  }

  public void Play(string password = null)
  {
    password = password ?? CreateRandomPassword();
    var correctPositions = 0;

    while (correctPositions != 4)
    {
      correctPositions = GuessPasswordAndCheck(password);
    }

    _inout.WriteLine("Congratulations you guessed the password in " +
    _tries + " tries.");
  }

  private int GuessPasswordAndCheck(string password)
  {
    var guess = Guess();
    return Check(guess, password);
  }

  private int Check(string guess, string password)
  {
    var checkResult = "";

    for (var x = 0; x < 4; x++)
    {
      if (guess[x] == password[x])
      {
        checkResult += "+";
      }
      else if (password.Contains(guess[x]))
      {
        checkResult += "-";
      }
```

```
        }

      _inout.WriteLine(checkResult);
      return checkResult.Count(c => c == '+');
    }

    private string Guess()
    {
      _tries = _tries + 1;

      _inout.Write("Take a guess: ");
      var guess = _inout.ReadLine();

      if (guess.Length == 4)
      {
        return guess.ToUpper();
      }

      // Password guess was wrong size - Error Message
      _inout.WriteLine("Password length is 4.");
      return Guess();
    }

    private string CreateRandomPassword()
    {
      var password = new[] { 'A', 'A', 'A', 'A' };

      var j = 0;

      password_loop:
      password[j] = (char)(_random.Number(6) + 65);
      j = j + 1;

      if (j < 4) goto password_loop;

      return new string(password);
    }
  }
}
```

And lastly, let's modify the gold standard test to use random password generation.

In the file `GoldStandardTests.cs`:

```
public class GoldStandardTests
{
  [Fact]
  public void StandardTestRun()
  {
```

```
    // Arrange
    var inout = new MockInputOutput();
    var rand = new MockRandomGenerator();
    var game = new Mastermind(inout, rand);

    // Arrange - Inputs
    rand.SetNumbers(0, 1, 2, 5);
    inout.InFeed.Enqueue("AAA");
    inout.InFeed.Enqueue("AAAA");
    inout.InFeed.Enqueue("ABBB");
    inout.InFeed.Enqueue("ABCC");
    inout.InFeed.Enqueue("ABCD");
    inout.InFeed.Enqueue("ABCF");
    inout.InFeed.Enqueue(" ");

    // Arrange - Outputs
    var expectedOutputs = new Queue<string>();
    expectedOutputs.Enqueue("Take a guess: ");
    expectedOutputs.Enqueue("Password length is 4." +
    Environment.NewLine);
    expectedOutputs.Enqueue("Take a guess: ");
    expectedOutputs.Enqueue("+---" + Environment.NewLine);
    expectedOutputs.Enqueue("Take a guess: ");
    expectedOutputs.Enqueue("++--" + Environment.NewLine);
    expectedOutputs.Enqueue("Take a guess: ");
    expectedOutputs.Enqueue("+++-" + Environment.NewLine);
    expectedOutputs.Enqueue("Take a guess: ");
    expectedOutputs.Enqueue("+++" + Environment.NewLine);
    expectedOutputs.Enqueue("Take a guess: ");
    expectedOutputs.Enqueue("++++" + Environment.NewLine);
    expectedOutputs.Enqueue("Congratulations you guessed the password
    in 6 tries." + Environment.NewLine);

    // Act
    game.Play();

    // Assert
    inout.OutFeed.ForEach(text =>
    {
      Assert.Equal(expectedOutputs.Dequeue(), text);
    });
  }
}
```

Now we are ready to refactor the password generation method and extend it to provide us with the requested change. First, there is a looping structure that is not core to the language. Let's focus in on the `CreateRandomPassword` method and fix the looping structure:

```
private string CreateRandomPassword()
{
  var password = new[] { 'A', 'A', 'A', 'A' };

  for(var j = 0; j < 4; j++)
  {
    password[j] = (char)(_random.Number(6) + 65);
  }

  return new string(password);
}
```

Next, for fun, let's see if we can generalize and compress this loop, since we have a very similar loop in the `Check` method. While not necessary, this is fun example of reducing duplication of code. Here is what that refactoring looks like:

```
private int Check(string guess, string password)
{
  var checkResult = "";

  Times(4, x => {
    if (guess[x] == password[x])
    {
      checkResult += "+";
    }
    else if (password.Contains(guess[x]))
    {
      checkResult += "-";
    }
  });

  _inout.WriteLine(checkResult);
  return checkResult.Count(c => c == '+');
}

private string CreateRandomPassword()
{
  var password = new[] { 'A', 'A', 'A', 'A' };

  Times(4, x => password[x] = (char)(_random.Number(6) + 65));

  return new string(password);
```

```
    }

    private static void Times(int count, Action<int> act)
    {
        for (var index = 0; index < count; index++)
        {
            act(index);
        }
    }
}
```

Now let's do one more refactoring before we extend the application. Looking at how the characters are generated, it is not very obvious what is going on. Instead, we would like the code to be as straightforward as possible. There is no reason that the random generator class can't just directly return letters, so let's add that functionality.

In the file RandomLetterTests.cs:

```
public class RandomLetterTests
{
    private readonly MockRandomGenerator _rand;

    public RandomLetterTests()
    {
        _rand = new MockRandomGenerator();
    }

    [Fact]
    public void ItExists()
    {
        _rand.Letter();
    }

    [Fact]
    public void ItReturnsDefaultValue()
    {
        // Act
        var result = _rand.Letter();

        // Assert
        Assert.Equal('A', result);
    }

    [Fact]
    public void ItCanReturnPredeterminedLetters()
    {
        // Arrange
        _rand.SetLetters('A', 'B', 'C', 'D', 'E');
```

```
  // Act
  var a = _rand.Letter();
  var b = _rand.Letter();
  var c = _rand.Letter();
  var d = _rand.Letter();
  var e = _rand.Letter();

  // Assert
  Assert.Equal('A', a);
  Assert.Equal('B', b);
  Assert.Equal('C', c);
  Assert.Equal('D', d);
  Assert.Equal('E', e);
}

[Fact]
public void ItCanHaveAMaxRange()
{
  // Arrange
  const char maxRange = 'C';
  _rand.SetLetters('A', 'B', 'C', 'D', 'E');

  // Act
  var a = _rand.Letter(maxRange);
  var b = _rand.Letter(maxRange);
  var c = _rand.Letter(maxRange);
  var d = _rand.Letter(maxRange);
  var e = _rand.Letter(maxRange);

  // Arrange
  Assert.Equal('A', a);
  Assert.Equal('B', b);
  Assert.Equal('C', c);
  Assert.Equal('C', d);
  Assert.Equal('C', e);
}

[Fact]
public void ItCanHaveAMinMaxRange()
{
  // Arrange
  const char minRange = 'B';
  const char maxRange = 'C';
  _rand.SetLetters('A', 'B', 'C', 'D', 'E');

  // Act
  var a = _rand.Letter(minRange, maxRange);
  var b = _rand.Letter(minRange, maxRange);
```

```
        var c = _rand.Letter(minRange, maxRange);
        var d = _rand.Letter(minRange, maxRange);
        var e = _rand.Letter(minRange, maxRange);

        // Arrange
        Assert.Equal('B', a);
        Assert.Equal('B', b);
        Assert.Equal('C', c);
        Assert.Equal('C', d);
        Assert.Equal('C', e);
    }
}
```

In the file MockRandomGenerator.cs:

```
public class MockRandomGenerator : IRandomGenerator
{
    private readonly List<int> _numbers;
    private List<int>.Enumerator _numbersEnumerator;

    private readonly List<char> _letters;
    private List<char>.Enumerator _lettersEnumerator;

    private const char NullChar = '\0';

    public MockRandomGenerator(List<int> numbers = null, List<char>
    letters = null)
    {
        _numbers = numbers ?? new List<int>();
        _numbersEnumerator = _numbers.GetEnumerator();

        _letters = letters ?? new List<char>();
        _lettersEnumerator = _letters.GetEnumerator();
    }

    public int Number(int min, int max)
    {
        var result = Number(max);

        return result < min ? min : result;
    }

    public int Number(int max = 100)
    {
        _numbersEnumerator.MoveNext();
        var result = _numbersEnumerator.Current;

        return result > max ? max : result;
```

```
    }

    public void SetNumbers(params int[] args)
    {
      _numbers.AddRange(args);
      _numbersEnumerator = _numbers.GetEnumerator();
    }

    public int Letter(char min, char max)
    {
      var result = Letter(max);

      return result < min ? min : result;
    }

    public char Letter(char max = 'Z')
    {
      _lettersEnumerator.MoveNext();
      var result = _lettersEnumerator.Current;
      result = result == NullChar ? 'A' : result;

      return result > max ? max : result;
    }

    public void SetLetters(params char[] args)
    {
      _letters.AddRange(args);
      _lettersEnumerator = _letters.GetEnumerator();
    }
  }
```

In the file `IRandomGenerator.cs`:

```
  public interface IRandomGenerator
  {
    int Number(int max = 100);
    int Number(int min, int max);
    char Letter(char max = 'Z');
    char Letter(char min, char max);
  }
```

In the file `RandomGenerator.cs`:

```
  public class RandomGenerator : IRandomGenerator
  {
    private readonly Random _rand;

    public RandomGenerator()
```

```
    {
      _rand = new Random();
    }

    public int Number(int max = 100)
    {
      return Number(0, max);
    }

    public int Number(int min, int max)
    {
      return _rand.Next(min, max);
    }

    public char Letter(char max = 'Z')
    {
      return Letter('A', max);
    }

    public char Letter(char min, char max)
    {
      return (char) _rand.Next(min, max);
    }
  }
```

In the file `Mastermind.cs`:

```
  private string CreateRandomPassword()
  {
    var password = new[] { 'A', 'A', 'A', 'A' };

    Times(4, x => password[x] = _random.Letter('F'));

    return new string(password);
  }
```

In the file `GoldStandardTests.cs`:

```
  // Arrange - Inputs
  rand.SetLetters('A', 'B', 'C', 'F');
```

That is the final refactoring for this exercise. We only have one thing to do, and that is to extend the application to generate passwords using the full range of the English alphabet. Because of the effort we put into testing and refactoring, this is now a trivial matter, and, in fact, only requires the removal of three characters in the `Mastermind` class.

In the file `Mastermind.cs`:

```
private string CreateRandomPassword()
{
  var password = new[] { 'A', 'A', 'A', 'A' };

  Times(4, x => password[x] = _random.Letter());

  return new string(password);
}
```

Now a more complicated password, consisting of the full range of the alphabet, is created. This causes a much more difficult password, and a game with output similar to the following:

```
Take a guess: AAAA
Take a guess: BBBB
Take a guess: CCCC
---+
Take a guess: DDDC
+
Take a guess: EEEC
+
Take a guess: FFFC
+
Take a guess: GGGC
+
Take a guess: HHHC
+
Take a guess: IIIC
+
Take a guess: JJJC
+
Take a guess: KKKC
+
Take a guess: LLLC
+
Take a guess: mmmc
+
Take a guess: nnnc
+
Take a guess: oooc
+--+
Take a guess: oppc
++-+
Take a guess: opqc
+++
Take a guess: oprc
```

```
+++
Take a guess: opsc
+++
Take a guess: optc
+++
Take a guess: opuc
+++
Take a guess: opvc
+++
Take a guess: opwc
++++
Congratulations you guessed the password in 23 tries.

Press any key to quit.
```

Summary

You now have a well-written example, covered by tests. The effort involved can be daunting, but for anything more than a trivial application, it can be well worth the effort.

15
Geometry

This chapter includes geometric problems. Some ask you to calculate values such as π or the area below a curve. Others demonstrate useful techniques such as Monte Carlo algorithms. Finally, some are directly useful if you need to perform geometric operations such as drawing arrowheads or finding intersections between line segments.

Many of these problems have intuitive graphical purposes. In those cases, the solutions may include graphical components that draw the problem and its solution. The graphics code usually isn't necessary to solve the problems, however; it just makes visualizing the solution easier, so I won't describe that code in detail. Download the solutions to see all of the details.

Problems

Use the following problems to test your geometric programming skills. Give each problem a try before you turn to the solutions and download the example programs. If you have trouble with the graphical part, try to implement the non-graphical pieces. Then, you can download the example solutions and replace the key parts of the program with your code.

1. Monte Carlo π

A Monte Carlo algorithm uses randomness to approximate the solution to a problem. Often, using more random samples gives you a more accurate approximated solution or gives a greater probability that the solution is correct.

For this problem, use a Monte Carlo algorithm to approximate π. To do that, generate random points in the square (0 ≤ X, Y ≤ 1) and then see how many fall within a circle centered in that square.

2. Newton's π

Various mathematicians have developed many different ways to approximate π over the years. Sir Isaac Newton devised the following formula to calculate π:

$$\pi = 6 \sum_{n=0}^{\infty} \frac{(2n)!}{2^{4n+1}(n!)^2(2n+1)}$$

Use Newton's method to approximate π. Let the user enter the number of terms to calculate. Display the approximation and its error.

How does this value compare to the fraction 355/113? Do you need to use `checked` blocks to protect the code?

3. Bisection root-finding

Root-finding algorithms find values (y) for which an equation $y = F(x)$ equals zero. For example, the equation $y = x^2 - 4$ has roots at $x = 2$ and $x = -2$ because at those values $y = 0$.

To find roots using binary subdivision, the program starts with an interval, $x_0 \le x \le x_1$, which we suspect contains a root. For the method to work, $F(x_0)$ and $F(x_1)$ must have different signs. In other words, one must be greater than zero and one must be less than zero.

To look for the root, the method picks the middle X value, $x_{new} = (x_0 + x_1) / 2$, and then calculates $F(x_{new})$. If the result is greater than zero, then you know that the root lies between x_{new} and whichever of x_0 and x_1 gives a value less than zero.

Similarly, if the result is less than zero, you know that the root lies between x_{new} and whichever of x0 and x1, whichever gives a value greater than zero.

Now, you update x_0 and x_1 to bound the new interval. You then repeat the process until $F(x_0)$ and $F(x_1)$ are within some maximum allowed error value.

Write a program that uses binary subdivision to find roots for equations. Make the equation a delegate parameter to the main method so you can easily pass the method different equations. Use the program to find the roots for the following equations:

$$y = x^2 - 4$$

$$y = x^3 - x^2 + 3$$

$$y = \frac{(x^4 + 2x^3 - 12x^2 - 2x + 6)}{10}$$

For extra credit, make the program draw the equations and their roots.

4. Newton's method

Binary subdivision uses intervals to quickly converge on an equation's root. Newton's method, which is also called the **Newton-Raphson method**, uses a different technique to converge even more quickly.

The method starts with a value (x). As long as $F(x)$ is not close enough to zero, the method uses the derivative of the function to find the slope $F'(x)$. It then follows the tangent line at that point to the new point x' where the line intersects the X axis. The value x' becomes the method's next guess for the root. The program continues calculating new values until $F(x)$ is close enough to 0.

Finding the point of intersection between the tangent line and the X axis is easier than you might think. If you start with the value x_i, you simply use the following equation to find the next value, x_{i+1}:

$$x_{i+1} = x_i - \frac{F(x_i)}{F'(x_i)}$$

Here, F is the function and F' is its derivative.

Write a program that uses Newton's method to find roots for equations. Make the equation and its derivative delegate parameters to the main method so you can easily pass different equations to the method. Use the program to find the roots for the following equations:

$$y = x^2 - 4$$

$$y = x^3 - x^2 + 3$$

$$y = \frac{(x^4 + 2x^3 - 12x^2 - 2x + 6)}{10}$$

In case you don't remember your calculus, the derivatives of those functions are the following:

$$y' = 2x$$

$$y' = 3x^2 - 2x$$

$$y = \frac{(4x^3 + 6x^2 - 24x - 2)}{10}$$

For extra credit, make the program draw the equations and their roots.

5. Gaussian elimination

Bisection and Newton's method let you find solutions to an equation of the form $F(x) = 0$. **Gaussian elimination** lets you find the solution to a system of linear equations of the following form:

$$A_1 \cdot x_1 + B_1 \cdot x_2 + \cdots + N_1 \cdot x_n = C_1$$
$$A_2 \cdot x_1 + B_2 \cdot x_2 + \cdots + N_2 \cdot x_n = C_2$$
$$\vdots$$
$$A_n \cdot x_1 + B_n \cdot x_2 + \cdots + N_n \cdot x_n = C_n$$

For example, consider the following equations where n is 2:

$$9 \cdot x_1 + 4 \cdot x_2 = 7$$
$$4 \cdot x_1 + 3 \cdot x_2 = 8$$

The solution to these equations includes the values for x_1 and x_2 that make both of the equations true. In this example, you can plug in the values $x_1 = -1$ and $x_2 = 4$ to verify that those values form a solution.

This problem asks you to use Gaussian elimination to solve systems of equations. Unfortunately, you need to know a fair amount of background to use Gaussian elimination.

To perform Gaussian elimination, you first represent the equations as a matrix multiplied by a vector of variables $x_1, x_2, \ldots, x_n$ giving a vector of constants $C_1, C_2, \ldots, C_n$, as shown in the following matrix equation:

$$\begin{vmatrix} A_1 & B_1 & \cdots & N_1 \\ A_2 & B_2 & \cdots & N_2 \\ & & \ddots & \\ A_n & B_n & \cdots & N_n \end{vmatrix} \times \begin{vmatrix} x_1 \\ x_2 \\ \vdots \\ x_n \end{vmatrix} = \begin{vmatrix} C_1 \\ C_2 \\ \vdots \\ C_n \end{vmatrix}$$

Next, you convert this into an **augmented matrix** that holds the original coefficients plus two extra columns, one to hold the C values and one to hold the final solution. Initially, that final column should be initialized to all zeros, as shown in the following matrix:

$$\begin{vmatrix} A_1 & B_1 & \cdots & N_1 & C_1 & 0 \\ A_2 & B_2 & \cdots & N_2 & C_2 & 0 \\ & & \ddots & & & \\ A_n & B_n & \cdots & N_n & C_n & 0 \end{vmatrix}$$

Now you perform row operations to reduce this augmented matrix into an upper triangular form.

In a **row operation**, you can add multiples of one row to another row. For example, if you add $-A_2/A_1$ times the first row to the second row, then the new second row has a 0 in its first position. That row's other positions will depend on the other values in the two rows. For example, the entry in its second column will be $B_2 - A_2/A_1 \times B_1$.

The important thing about row operations is that they do not change the truth of the system of equations. If a set of values $(x_1, x_2, ..., x_n)$ solves the original equations, then those values also solve the equations after you perform row operations.

Start by using row operations on the first row to zero out the first entries in all rows after row zero. Next, use row operations with the second row to zero out the entries in the second column below that row. Continue using the kth row to zero out the entries in column k in the rows that follow until the augmented matrix has an upper triangular form, like the following:

$$\begin{vmatrix} A'_1 & B'_1 & \cdots & N'_1 & C'_1 & 0 \\ 0 & B'_2 & \cdots & N'_2 & C'_2 & 0 \\ & & \ddots & & & \\ 0 & 0 & \cdots & N'_n & C'_n & 0 \end{vmatrix}$$

You may run into a problem when you try to put the augmented matrix into upper triangular form. When you're considering row k, you may find that it has a 0 in column k. In that case, you cannot use that row to zero out column k in the following rows because that would require you to divide by zero.

In that case, simply swap row k with a later row that does not have a 0 in column k. Then you can continue converting the matrix into upper triangular form. If you ever find that all of the remaining rows have 0 in column k, then there is no unique solution to the system of equations.

After the augmented matrix is in upper triangular form, you are ready to pull out the solution. At this point, the augmented array represents the following system equations:

$$A'_1 \cdot x_1 + B'_1 \cdot x_2 + \cdots + N'_1 \cdot x_n = C'_1$$
$$0 \cdot x_1 + B'_2 \cdot x_2 + \cdots + N'_2 \cdot x_n = C'_2$$
$$\vdots$$
$$0 \cdot x_1 + 0 \cdot x_2 + \cdots + N'_n \cdot x_n = C'_n$$

Now, you can easily solve the last equation and get $x_n = C'_n / N'_n$. You can save that value in the final column of the augmented matrix's last row. Then, you can plug the value for x_n into the second-to-last equation to find x_{n-1} and save the result in the second-to-last row's final column.

Next, you plug x_n and x_{n-1} into the third-to-last equation to find x_{n-2}.

You continue using the values that you have found so far to find new values farther up in the augmented matrix until you have found all of the values and saved them in the matrix's final column. This process is called **backsolving**.

Now that you understand how Gaussian elimination works, here's your problem. Write a program similar to the one shown in the following screenshot that allows the user to enter the coefficients for a set of linear equations and then solves them:

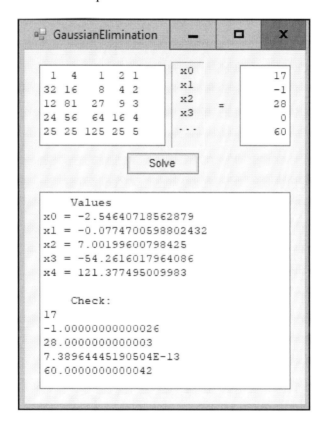

Use the program to solve the following systems of equations:

$$\begin{vmatrix} 1 & -3 & 1 \\ 2 & -8 & 8 \\ -6 & 3 & -15 \end{vmatrix} \times \begin{vmatrix} x_1 \\ x_2 \\ x_3 \end{vmatrix} = \begin{vmatrix} 4 \\ -2 \\ 9 \end{vmatrix}$$

$$\begin{vmatrix} 9 & 3 & 4 \\ 4 & 3 & 4 \\ 1 & 1 & 1 \end{vmatrix} \times \begin{vmatrix} x_1 \\ x_2 \\ x_3 \end{vmatrix} = \begin{vmatrix} 7 \\ 8 \\ 3 \end{vmatrix}$$

$$\begin{vmatrix} 1 & 1 & 1 & 1 & 1 \\ 32 & 16 & 8 & 4 & 2 \\ 243 & 81 & 27 & 9 & 3 \\ 1024 & 256 & 64 & 16 & 4 \\ 3125 & 625 & 125 & 25 & 5 \end{vmatrix} \times \begin{vmatrix} x_1 \\ x_2 \\ x_3 \\ x_4 \\ x_5 \end{vmatrix} = \begin{vmatrix} 1 \\ -1 \\ 8 \\ -56 \\ 569 \end{vmatrix}$$

$$\begin{vmatrix} 2 & -1 & 1 \\ 3 & 2 & -4 \\ -6 & 3 & -3 \end{vmatrix} \times \begin{vmatrix} x_1 \\ x_2 \\ x_3 \end{vmatrix} = \begin{vmatrix} 1 \\ 4 \\ 2 \end{vmatrix}$$

$$\begin{vmatrix} 1 & -1 & 2 \\ 4 & 4 & -2 \\ -2 & 2 & -4 \end{vmatrix} \times \begin{vmatrix} x_1 \\ x_2 \\ x_3 \end{vmatrix} = \begin{vmatrix} -3 \\ 1 \\ 6 \end{vmatrix}$$

6. Monte Carlo integration

Integration is the process of calculating the area inside a region. Typically, this is the area under a curve defined by some function $y = F(x)$. For example, in the following diagram, the goal is to calculate the shaded area under the curve in the domain $-2 \le x \le 1.5$:

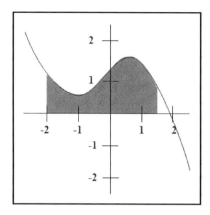

You can use calculus to integrate the area under a curve, at least if you remember your calculus and the function is reasonably well-behaved. If you cannot apply calculus, then you can use **Monte Carlo integration**.

From the name and your experience with Monte Carlo approximation for π, you may be able to guess how this works. Pick a rectangle that includes the area of interest. Then, randomly generate points within the rectangle and see how many lie within the range and between the curve and the X axis. Finally, use the fraction of points in that area to estimate the area beneath the curve.

Write a program that performs Monte Carlo integration. As in the previous examples, pass the function into the method as a parameter so you can easily change it. Use your program to estimate the areas below the following functions within the indicated domains:

Function	Domain
$y = x^2 + 1$	$-1.5 \leq x \leq 1.5$
$y = x^3 - 2x^2 + 2$	$-1 \leq x \leq 2$
$y = \sin(x) + \cos(2x) + 2.5$	$-4 \leq x \leq 3$

If you remember your calculus, make the program calculate the areas exactly and compare the calculated result and the result approximated by Monte Carlo integration.

7. Rectangle rule integration

Monte Carlo integration is relatively simple, but it's also not repeatable. If you perform the same test multiple times with a different selection of random points, you'll get slightly different results.

Another method for estimating an area is to use a **Riemann sum**. (The method is named after the 19th-century German mathematician Bernhard Riemann who made great contributions to integral geometry and other fields.) To calculate a Riemann sum, also known as applying the **rectangle rule**, you divide the area into thin slices and add up the areas of the slices. The following diagram shows an area being approximated by a Riemann sum:

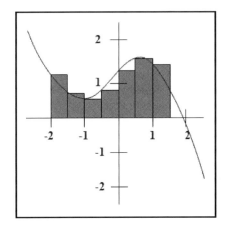

In this example, the height of each rectangle is given by the function's value at the rectangle's left edge, so this is sometimes called the **left Riemann sum**. Other variations use the function's value at the rectangle's right edge (the **right Riemann sum**) or in the rectangle's middle (the **midpoint rule**).

The widths of the rectangles depend on the number of rectangles. Using more, thinner rectangles gives a closer approximation to the actual area.

Write a program that uses the left Riemann sum to approximate the area under a function. Use your program to estimate the areas for the curves described in the preceding problem.

If you remember your calculus, make the program calculate the areas exactly and compare the calculated and estimated results.

8. Trapezoid rule integration

In addition to the left, right, and middle Riemann sum variations, a fourth variation divides an area into trapezoids instead of rectangles, as shown in the following diagram:

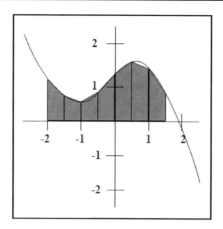

Write a program that uses the trapezoid rule to approximate the area under a curve. Use your program to estimate the areas for the curves described in Problem 25. *Monte Carlo integration.*

9. Arrowheads

Write a program that lets the user click and drag to define a line segment. Add a tail to the segment's starting point and an arrowhead to its ending point, as shown in the following screenshot:

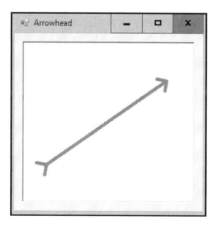

Hint: If *<vx, vy>* is a vector, then *<vy, -vx>* and *<-vy, vx>* are two vectors perpendicular to the original vector.

10. Line-line intersection

Write a program that determines where two lines intersect. Let the user left-click twice to define one line and right-click twice to define another. Be sure that the program can handle horizontal and vertical lines and the case when the lines are parallel.

Hint: Use a parametric definition for the lines as in $p = p_0 + t \times v$ where p_0 is a point on the line, v is a vector pointing in the direction of the line, and t is a real number parameter. If that doesn't make sense to you, then read the solution. You may want to stop after the explanation and try to implement the code yourself before you read the entire solution.

11. Point-line distance

Write a program that determines the closest point and shortest distance between a point and a line. Let the user left-click twice to define the line and right-click once to define the point. Draw the line and point, and a dashed line showing the shortest distance, as shown in the following screenshot:

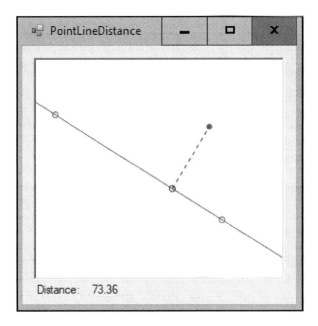

12. Point-segment distance

Write a program that determines the closest point and shortest distance between a point and a line segment. Let the user left-click twice to define the segment and right-click once to define the point. Draw the segment and point, and a dashed line showing the shortest distance, as shown in the following screenshot:

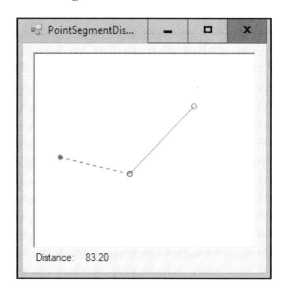

13. Segment-segment distance

Write a program that finds the shortest distance between the two line segments defined by the user. Let the user left- and right-click twice to define the two segments.

14. Circle selection

Write a program that lets the user define a circle by clicking three points.

Hint: The key to solving this problem is to find a circle that passes through the users' three points. There are several approaches that you can take, but the one I use is to note that the perpendicular bisectors of a chord of a circle always pass through the circle's center.

The following diagram shows three points on a circle **A**, **B**, and **C**. The dashed lines show perpendicular bisectors for the segments **AB** and **BC**. The point where the bisectors intersect is the circle's center:

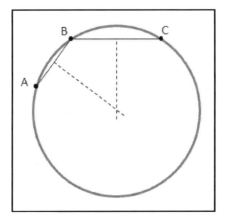

15. Line-circle intersection

Write a program that finds the intersection between a line and a circle. Let the user left-click three times to define the circle and right-click twice to define the line.

16. Circle-circle intersection

Write a program that finds the points where two circles intersect. Let the user left- and right-click three times to define the two circles.

17. Circle-line tangents

Write a program that lets the user click to define a point and a circle. It should then find tangent lines between the two.

(Hint: Look at Solution *35. Circle-circle intersection*)

18. Polygon area

Write a program that lets the user left-click to add points to a polygon. When the user right-clicks, close the polygon and calculate its area.

Hint: Consider the trapezoids defined by the polygon's edges, the X axis, and sides dropped vertically from the polygon's vertices to the X axis.

19. Point in a polygon

Write a program that lets the user right-click to add points to a polygon. When the user right-clicks, finalize the polygon and determine whether the clicked point lies inside the polygon. If the user right-clicks again, determine whether the new point lies within the existing polygon. If the user left-clicks after the polygon has been finalized, start a new polygon.

20. Convexity testing

Write a program that lets the user left-click to add points to a polygon. When the user right-clicks, finalize the polygon and determine whether the polygon is convex.

21. Stars

Write a program that lets the user enter a number of sides and a skip number. It should then draw a regular polygon with the indicated number of sides. It should also draw a star by connecting each of the polygon's vertices to the vertex that is the skip number of steps away around the perimeter of the polygon.

For example, the following screenshot shows the Stars example solution drawing a pentagon and a five-pointed star. The skip number is two, so the program draws the star by connecting each vertex with the point that is two positions away from it around the edge of the polygon:

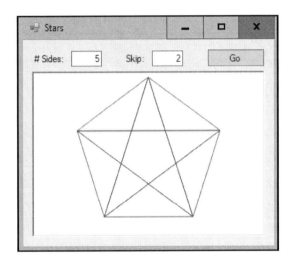

If you experiment with the program, you'll find that some skip numbers produce disconnected stars. In other words, the points on the star are not all joined by a continuous sequence of connected line segments. For example, try a 12-sided polygon with the skip number 8. What is the relationship between the skip number and the number of polygon sides for these disconnected stars?

Solutions

The following sections describe solutions to the preceding problems. You can download the example solutions to see additional details and to experiment with the programs at `https:/ /github.com/PacktPublishing/Improving-your-C-Sharp-Skills/tree/master/ Chapter15`.

1. Monte Carlo π

The following code uses a Monte Carlo algorithm to estimate π:

```
// Use Monte Carlo simulation to estimate pi.
private double MonteCarloPi(long numPoints)
{
    Random rand = new Random();

    // Make a bitmap to show points.
    int wid = pointsPictureBox.ClientSize.Width;
    int hgt = pointsPictureBox.ClientSize.Height;
    Bitmap bm = new Bitmap(wid, hgt);
    using (Graphics gr = Graphics.FromImage(bm))
    {
        gr.Clear(Color.White);
        gr.DrawEllipse(Pens.Black, 0, 0, wid - 1, hgt - 1);
    }

    // Make the random points.
    int numHits = 0;
    for (int i = 0; i < numPoints; i++)
    {
        // Make a random point 0 <= x < 1.
        double x = rand.NextDouble();
        double y = rand.NextDouble();

        // See how far the point is from (0.5, 0.5).
        double dx = x - 0.5;
        double dy = y - 0.5;
        if (dx * dx + dy * dy < 0.25) numHits++;

        // Plots up to 10,000 points.
        if (i < 10000)
        {
            int ix = (int)(wid * x);
            int iy = (int)(hgt * y);
            if (dx * dx + dy * dy < 0.25)
                bm.SetPixel(ix, iy, Color.Gray);
            else
                bm.SetPixel(ix, iy, Color.Black);
        }
    }

    // Display the plotted points.
    pointsPictureBox.Image = bm;
```

```
        // Get the hit fraction.
        double fraction = numHits / (double)numPoints;

        // Estimate pi.
        return 4.0 * fraction;
    }
```

The method starts by creating a `Random` object that it can use to generate random numbers. It then creates a bitmap to fit the program's `PictureBox`, associates a `Graphics` object with it, clears the bitmap, and draws a circle centered in the bitmap.

Next, the code uses a loop to generate the desired number of random points within the square $0 \le X, Y \le 1$. The `NextDouble` method of the `Random` class returns a value between 0 and 1, so generating the point's X and Y coordinates is relatively easy.

The code then determines whether the point lies within the circle that fills the square $0 \le X$, $Y \le 1$. To do that, the method calculates the distance from the random point to the center of the circle *(0.5, 0.5)*. It then determines whether that distance is less than the circle's radius.

Actually, the code doesn't really find the distance between the point and *(0.5, 0.5)*. To do that, it would use the distance formula to find the distance and then use the following equation to determine whether the result is less than the circle's radius 0.5:

$$\sqrt{dx^2 + dy^2} \le 0.5$$

Calculating square roots is relatively slow, however, so the program squares both sides of the equation and uses the following equation instead:

$$dx^2 + dy^2 \le 0.5^2$$

The value 0.5 squared is 0.25, so the program actually tests whether:

$$dx^2 + dy^2 \le 0.25$$

The program then plots the point on the bitmap in either gray or black, depending on whether the point lies within the circle. The code also uses the `numHits` variable to keep track of the number of points that lie within the circle.

After it finishes generating points, the code makes its approximation for π. The square $0 \leq X, Y \leq 1$ has an area of 1.0 and the circle should have the area $\pi \times R^2$ where R is the circle's radius. In this example, R is 0.5, so the fraction of points that fall inside the circle should be the following:

$$fraction = \frac{\pi \times 0.5^2}{1.0} = 0.25\pi$$

If you solve this equation for π, you get the following:

$$\pi = \frac{fraction}{0.25} = 4 \times fraction$$

The code gets the fraction of the points that fell within the circle, multiples that by 4.0, and returns the result as its estimate for π.

The following screenshot shows the `MonteCarloPi` example solution approximating π. After generating 10,000 random points, its approximation for π is off by around 1%. Using more points produces better approximations for π. The result with million points is correct within about 0.1–0.2%, and the result with 100 million points is correct to within around 0.01%:

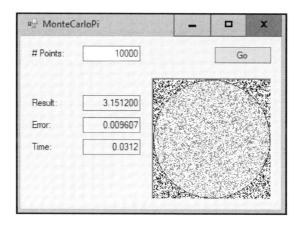

Download the `MonteCarloPi` example solution to see additional details.

2. Newton's π

The following code implements Newton's method for calculating π:

```
// Use Newton's formula to calculate pi.
private double NewtonPi(int numTerms)
{
    double total = 0;
    for (int i = 0; i < numTerms; i++)
    {
        total +=
            Factorial(2 * i) /
            Math.Pow(2, 4 * i + 1) /
            (Factorial(i) * Factorial(i)) /
            (2 * i + 1);
    }

    double result = 6 * total;
    Debug.Assert(!double.IsInfinity(result));
    return result;
}
```

This method simply loops over the desired number of terms, calculates the appropriate term values, and adds them to the result.

To allow the program to work with larger values, it uses the following `Factorial` method:

```
// Return number!
private double Factorial(int number)
{
    double total = 1;
    for (int i = 2; i <= number; i++) total *= i;
    return total;
}
```

This is a normal factorial, except it stores its total in a `double` variable, which can hold larger values than a `long` variable can.

The value *355/113* is approximately 3.1415929, which is remarkably close to π. Newton's method converges very quickly on values close to π, only needing nine terms before it is more accurate than *355/113*.

This method runs into problems when `numTerms` is greater than 86. In that case, the value `Factorial(2 * i)` is too big to fit in a `double` variable. Because the problem occurs in a `double` variable instead of an integer, a `checked` block won't detect the problem.

As is the case with integers, C# doesn't notify you if the value doesn't fit in a `double` variable. Instead, it sets the variable equal to one of the special value, values `double.Infinity` or `double.NegativeInfinity`. The `NewtonPi` method uses a `Debug.Assert` statement to see if this happened.

 The `Debug` class is defined in the `System.Diagnostics` namespace, so the program includes the directive `using System.Diagnostics` to make using that class easier.

The lesson to be learned here is that you should use the `double.IsInfinity` method to check `double` variables for overflow to infinity or negative infinity if that might be an issue.

Some double calculations, such as `total = Math.Sqrt(-1)`, may result in the special value `double.NaN`, which stands for **Not a Number**. You can use the `double.IsNaN` method to check for that situation.

Download the `NewtonPi` example solution to see additional details.

3. Bisection root-finding

Finding roots by using bisection is relatively straightforward, although there are a couple of tricky details. One of the most important is realizing that it's not always obvious what interval to use when looking for a root.

For example, if the function's value at the interval's endpoints, x_0 and x_1, are both positive or both negative, then the interval may contain no roots, one root, or several roots. The following diagram shows three functions. All three start and end with function values greater than zero. The curve on the left has no roots because it does not cross the X axis, the middle curve has a single root where it touches the X axis, and the curve on the right has four roots because it crosses the X axis four times:

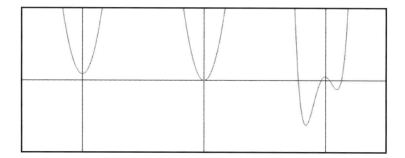

One way to find roots is to manually pick the intervals that the algorithm should examine. That works, but it requires you to know something about the general shape of the function and the locations of its roots.

The approach I took was to allow you to specify a series of intervals. The program then considers each interval, looking for roots.

The following `FindRoots` method starts the process:

```
// Find roots for the equation within the range xmin <= x <= xmax.
private List<double> FindRoots(Func<double, double> F,
    double xmin, double xmax, int numTests,
    double maxError, out List<double> xmins)
{
    xmins = new List<double>();
    List<double> roots = new List<double>();
    double dx = (xmax - xmin) / numTests;
    for (int i = 0; i < numTests; i++)
    {
        double x = xmin + dx * i;
        xmins.Add(x);
        double root = BinarySubdivision(F, x, x + dx, maxError);
        if (!double.IsNaN(root) &&
            !roots.Contains(root, maxError)) roots.Add(root);
    }
    return roots;
}
```

This method's `xmin` and `xmax` parameters define a large range $xmin \leq x \leq xmax$ that should contain all of the roots. The `numTests` parameter indicates the number of intervals into which the program should divide this larger domain to find the roots. The code calculates the size of the intervals and then loops through them, calling the `BinarySubdivision` method described shortly to look for a root in each interval.

If the `BinarySubdivision` method returns a number, the `FindRoots` method calls the `Contains` extension method to determine whether the root is already in the `roots` list. The following code shows the `Contains` method:

```
public static bool Contains(this List<double> values,
    double target, double maxDiff)
{
    foreach (double value in values)
        if (Math.Abs(value - target) <= maxDiff)
            return true;
    return false;
}
```

The problem here is that a list of `double` values might contain two values that should be the same but that are slightly different due to rounding errors. The `Contains` extension method extends `List<double>` objects to determine whether the list contains two values that are very close to each other.

The method simply loops through the list, examining items. It subtracts each item from the target value, takes the absolute value, and determines whether the difference is smaller than the maximum allowed difference. The method returns `true` if the list contains the item and `false` otherwise.

The following code shows the `BinarySubdivision` method, which uses binary subdivision to search an interval for a root:

```
// Search this interval for a root.
private double BinarySubdivision(Func<double, double> F,
    double xmin, double xmax, double maxError)
{
    // Make sure that F(xmin) and F(xmax) have different signs.
    if (Math.Sign(F(xmin)) == Math.Sign(F(xmax)))
        return double.NaN;

    for (;;)
    {
        double x = (xmin + xmax) / 2.0;
        double y = F(x);
        double error = Math.Abs(y);
        if (error < maxError) return x;

        if (Math.Sign(y) == Math.Sign(F(xmin)))
            xmin = x;
        else
            xmax = x;
    }
}
```

This method verifies that the function has values on opposite sides of the *X* axis at the two endpoints `xmin` and `xmax`. If the function's values at both points are either above or below the *X* axis, the method returns `double.NaN` to indicate that it did not find a root.

If the function crosses the *X* axis, the method enters a loop. Each time it goes through the loop, the program calculates the function's y value at the interval's midpoint x. If y is within `maxError` of zero, the code returns x as the function's root.

If y is not close enough to zero, the method compares the sign of the function at this point and at xmin. If the two signs are the same, the method moves xmin to the new position x. If the signs of y and F(xmin) are different, then the method updates xmax to the position x.

Eventually, the interval shrinks until y is close enough to zero and the method returns it.

The following screenshot shows the BisectionSubdivisionRoots example solution:

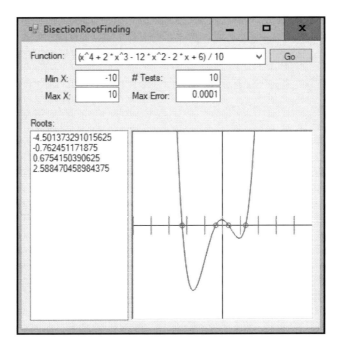

Here the program found the roots for the following equation:

$$F(x) = \frac{x^4 + 2x^3 - 12x^2 - 2x + 6}{10}$$

The short vertical lines crossing the X axis in the screenshot show the intervals that the program used to find the roots. In this example, the program used 10 intervals to find the roots.

Download the BisectionRootFinding example solution to see additional details, such as how the program lets you select a function and how it draws the graph of that function.

4. Newton's method

This program's `FindRoots` method is almost the same as the version used by the preceding solution. The only difference is that the new version calls the following method instead of the `BinarySubdivision` method:

```
// Search this interval for a root.
private double NewtonsMethod(
    Func<double, double> F, Func<double, double> FPrime,
    double x, double maxError, double maxTrials)
{
    for (int trial = 0; trial < maxTrials; trial++)
    {
        x = x - F(x) / FPrime(x);
        double y = F(x);
        double error = Math.Abs(y);
        if (error < maxError) return x;
    }
    return double.NaN;
}
```

Because this method uses a single variable, x, to keep track of its current estimate for the root, it does not need to check that an interval's endpoints lie on opposite sides of the X axis the way the `BinarySubdivision` method does. Instead, it simply enters a loop where it uses the equation in the problem statement to update x. When `F(x)` is close enough to zero, the method returns x.

One place where this method differs from the `BinarySubdivision` method is that it only performs its loop at most `maxTrials` times. Under certain conditions that depend on the function being studied, Newton's method may produce a sequence of repeating or diverging values that don't converge to a root. Limiting the loop prevents the program from being stuck in an infinite loop.

Newton's method converges very quickly, so the example solution sets `maxTrials` to only 1,000. After 1,000 trials, the method has either already found a root or it is probably not converging.

The `NewtonsMethod` example solution looks the same as the `BinarySubdivisionRoots` program shown in the earlier screenshot, so I won't show it here. Download the example to see additional details.

5. Gaussian elimination

The GaussianElimination example solution is fairly complicated, partly because Gaussian elimination is complicated, but also because it must convert user-entered text into an augmented matrix.

The program uses the following code to build the augmented matrix from the user's text. It gets the equations' coefficients from the coefficientsTextBox control. It gets the equations' results (the Cs on the right in the problem description) from the valuesTextBox control:

```
// Load the augmented array.
// Column numCols holds the result values.
// Column numCols + 1 will hold the final values after
// backsolving.
private double[,] LoadArray(out int numRows, out int numCols)
{
    // Build the augmented matrix.
    string[] valueRows = valuesTextBox.Text.Split(
        new string[] { "\r\n" },
        StringSplitOptions.RemoveEmptyEntries);
    string[] coefRows = coefficientsTextBox.Text.Split(
        new string[] { "\r\n" },
        StringSplitOptions.RemoveEmptyEntries);
    string[] oneRow = coefRows[0].Split(
        new string[] { " " }, StringSplitOptions.RemoveEmptyEntries);
    numRows = coefRows.GetUpperBound(0) + 1;
    numCols = oneRow.GetUpperBound(0) + 1;
    double[,] arr = new double[numRows, numCols + 2];
    for (int r = 0; r < numRows; r++)
    {
        oneRow = coefRows[r].Split(
            new char[] { ' ' }, StringSplitOptions.RemoveEmptyEntries);
        for (int c = 0; c < numCols; c++)
        {
            arr[r, c] = double.Parse(oneRow[c]);
        }
        arr[r, numCols] = double.Parse(valueRows[r]);
    }

    return arr;
}
```

This method gets the multiline string of values in `valuesTextBox`, splits the entries delimited by the carriage return/line feed combination, removes any empty entries, and saves the values in the `valueRows` array. It then uses a similar technique to load the rows of coefficients into the `coefRows` array. The method then splits the first row of coefficients delimited by spaces to save that row's coefficients in the `oneRow` array.

The code uses the length of the `coefRows` array to get the number of rows. It uses the length of the `oneRow` array to get the number of columns. Note that the number of columns includes only the equations' coefficients; it does not include the value column or the final result column in the augmented array.

After it knows the numbers of rows and columns, the code creates the `arr` array to hold the augmented matrix. It loops through the values to fill in the array and returns it.

The following `GaussianEliminate` method solves an augmented matrix:

```
// Perform Gaussian elimination.
// Note that arr should be the augmented array.
// Initially the second-to-last column should hold the result values.
// In the end, the final column will hold the final values after
   backsolving.
private void GaussianEliminate(double[,] arr)
{
    const double tiny = 0.00001;

    // Get the number of rows and columns.
    int numRows = arr.GetUpperBound(0) + 1;
    int numCols = arr.GetUpperBound(1) - 1;

    // Start solving.
    for (int r = 0; r < numRows - 1; r++)
    {
        // Zero out all entries in column r after this row.
        // See if this row has a non-zero entry in column r.
        if (Math.Abs(arr[r, r]) < tiny)
        {
            // Too close to zero. Try to swap with a later row.
            for (int r2 = r + 1; r2 < numRows; r2++)
            {
                if (Math.Abs(arr[r2, r]) > tiny)
                {
                    // This row will work. Swap them.
                    for (int c = 0; c <= numCols; c++)
                    {
                        double tmp = arr[r, c];
                        arr[r, c] = arr[r2, c];
```

```
                                arr[r2, c] = tmp;
                            }
                            break;
                        }
                    }
                }

                // If this row has a non-zero entry in column r, use it.
                if (Math.Abs(arr[r, r]) > tiny)
                {
                    // Zero out this column in later rows.
                    for (int r2 = r + 1; r2 < numRows; r2++)
                    {
                        double factor = -arr[r2, r] / arr[r, r];
                        for (int c = r; c <= numCols; c++)
                        {
                            arr[r2, c] = arr[r2, c] + factor * arr[r, c];
                        }
                    }
                }
            }

            // Display the upper-triangular array. (For debugging.)
            PrintArray(arr);

            // See if we have a solution.
            if (arr[numRows - 1, numCols - 1] == 0)
            {
                // We have no solution.
                // If all entries in this row are 0, then there is no solution.
                // Otherwise the solution is not unique.
                for (int c = 0; c <= numCols + 1; c++)
                    if (arr[numRows - 1, c] != 0)
                        throw new Exception("There is no solution");
                throw new Exception("The solution is not unique");
            }

            // We have a solution. Backsolve.
            for (int r = numRows - 1; r >= 0; r--)
            {
                double tmp = arr[r, numCols];
                for (int r2 = r + 1; r2 < numRows; r2++)
                {
                    tmp -= arr[r, r2] * arr[r2, numCols + 1];
                }
                arr[r, numCols + 1] = tmp / arr[r, r];
            }
        }
```

This method first gets the number of rows and columns. Note that the `numColumns` value does not include the augmented matrix's last two columns, which hold the equations' values and the final results.

The method then loops through the rows, using the `r` row to zero out the `r` column values in the following rows. Before it uses the `r` row, the program verifies that it has a non-zero entry in the column `r`. If the row has a zero in that position, the code swaps it with a later row that has a non-zero entry in that column.

 Notice *has a zero in that position* really means *has a small value that could cause overflow when used as a denominator*. It is important to check that floating point numbers are not too small before you divide by them.

After it has finished converting the matrix into upper-triangular form, the code calls the `PrintArray` method to display the array's values in the Console window. That method is straightforward, so I won't include it here. Download the example solution to see the details.

Next, the code checks the final row to see if it has a non-zero entry in its final coefficient column. If that entry is zero, then there is no solution for the original set of equations and the method throws an exception.

If the final row has a non-zero entry for its final coefficient, the method backsolves to find the final solution.

The result is passed back to the calling code through the modified array.

The following code shows how the program uses the `GaussianEliminate` method when you click the program's **Solve** button:

```
// Solve the system of equations.
private void solveButton_Click(object sender, EventArgs e)
{
    // Build the augmented matrix.
    // The values numRows and numCols are the number of rows
    // and columns in the matrix, not the augmented matrix.
    int numRows, numCols;
    double[,] arr = LoadArray(out numRows, out numCols);
    double[,] origArr = LoadArray(out numRows, out numCols);

    // Display the initial arrays.
    PrintArray(arr);
    PrintArray(origArr);
```

```
// Perform Gaussian elimination.
try
{
    GaussianEliminate(arr);
}
catch (Exception ex)
{
    MessageBox.Show(ex.Message);
}

// Display the modified array in the Console window.
PrintArray(arr);

// Display the results on the form.
StringBuilder sb = new StringBuilder();
sb.AppendLine("    Values");
for (int r = 0; r < numRows; r++)
{
    sb.AppendLine("x" + r.ToString() + " = " +
        arr[r, numCols + 1].ToString());
}

// Verify.
sb.AppendLine();
sb.AppendLine("    Check:");
for (int r = 0; r < numRows; r++)
{
    double tmp = 0;
    for (int c = 0; c < numCols; c++)
        tmp += origArr[r, c] * arr[c, numCols + 1];
    sb.AppendLine(tmp.ToString());
}
resultsTextBox.Text = sb.ToString();
}
```

The code first calls the LoadArray method to load the values entered by the user. It calls the method twice to make two copies of the array. It will use one for Gaussian elimination and it will save the other so it can later check the results to verify that the solution works.

The code calls the PrintArray method to display the initial augmented matrix and then calls GaussianEliminate to solve the system of equations.

After the `GaussianEliminate` method returns, the code calls `PrintArray` again to display the finished augmented matrix. It then uses `StringBuilder` to make a string showing the solution.

The method then multiples the original matrix's entries by the solution values to verify that the solution is correct. It adds the results to `StringBuilder` and finally displays the result.

The following table shows the solutions to the systems of equations mentioned in the problem description:

System of Equations	Solution
$\begin{vmatrix} 1 & -3 & 1 \\ 2 & -8 & 8 \\ -6 & 3 & -15 \end{vmatrix} \times \begin{vmatrix} x_1 \\ x_2 \\ x_3 \end{vmatrix} = \begin{vmatrix} 4 \\ -2 \\ 9 \end{vmatrix}$	{3, -1, -2}
$\begin{vmatrix} 9 & 3 & 4 \\ 4 & 3 & 4 \\ 1 & 1 & 1 \end{vmatrix} \times \begin{vmatrix} x_1 \\ x_2 \\ x_3 \end{vmatrix} = \begin{vmatrix} 7 \\ 8 \\ 3 \end{vmatrix}$	{-0.2, 4, -0.8}
$\begin{vmatrix} 1 & 1 & 1 & 1 & 1 \\ 32 & 16 & 8 & 4 & 2 \\ 243 & 81 & 27 & 9 & 3 \\ 1024 & 256 & 64 & 16 & 4 \\ 3125 & 625 & 125 & 25 & 5 \end{vmatrix} \times \begin{vmatrix} x_1 \\ x_2 \\ x_3 \\ x_4 \\ x_5 \end{vmatrix} = \begin{vmatrix} 1 \\ -1 \\ 8 \\ -56 \\ 569 \end{vmatrix}$	{7.87, -82.75, 302.17, -446.75, 220.47}
$\begin{vmatrix} 2 & -1 & 1 \\ 3 & 2 & -4 \\ -6 & 3 & -3 \end{vmatrix} \times \begin{vmatrix} x_1 \\ x_2 \\ x_3 \end{vmatrix} = \begin{vmatrix} 1 \\ 4 \\ 2 \end{vmatrix}$	Has no solution
$\begin{vmatrix} 1 & -1 & 2 \\ 4 & 4 & -2 \\ -2 & 2 & -4 \end{vmatrix} \times \begin{vmatrix} x_1 \\ x_2 \\ x_3 \end{vmatrix} = \begin{vmatrix} -3 \\ 1 \\ 6 \end{vmatrix}$	Has no unique solution

Download the `GaussianElimination` example solution to see additional details.

6. Monte Carlo integration

Monte Carlo integration is actually fairly easy. Most of the example solution's code draws the curve and sample points, lets the user select functions, determines the rectangle where integration should occur, and performs other user interface tasks.

The example solution uses the following method to perform the Monte Carlo integration. The code used by the example solution is heavily interspersed with graphics code, which I have omitted here to save space and to make the integration code easier to understand:

```
// Use Monte Carlo integration to find the area under the curve.
private double MonteCarloIntegrate(Func<double, double> F,
    double xmin, double xmax, double ymin, double ymax, int numPoints)
{
    Random rand = new Random();
    int numHits = 0;

    // Make the random points.
    for (int i = 0; i < numPoints; i++)
    {
        // Make a random point xmin <= x <= xmax, ymin <= y <= ymax.
        double x = rand.NextDouble(xmin, xmax);
        double y = rand.NextDouble(ymin, ymax);

        // See if the point is below the function.
        if ((y >= 0) && (y <= F(x))) numHits++;
    }

    // Get the hit fraction.
    double fraction = numHits / (double)numPoints;

    // Estimate the area.
    return fraction * (xmax - xmin) * (ymax - ymin);
}
```

This code enters a loop to generate the required number of random points within the sample rectangle $xmin \leq x \leq xmax$, $ymin \leq y \leq ymax$. If the point (x, y) lies below the point on the function $(x, F(x))$ and above the X axis, the code increments its hit count.

After it finishes generating the points, the method calculates the fraction of the points that were hits. It then multiplies that fraction by the area of the sample rectangle to estimate the area under the curve.

The following screenshot shows the example solution in action:

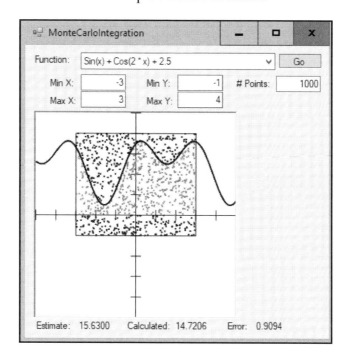

Download the `MonteCarloIntegration` example solution to see additional details, such as how the program lets the user select the function, how the program draws the curve and sample points, and how the code uses calculus to make a calculated value for comparison with the estimated value.

7. Rectangle rule integration

The following equation shows the total area of the rectangles used to approximate the function's area:

$$area = \sum_{i=0}^{N-1} F(x_i)(x_{i+1} - x_i)$$

Here the sum is over *N* slices. The value $F(x_i)$ gives the length of the *i-th* rectangle's left side. The value $(x_{i+1} - x_i)$ is the width of that rectangle.

If all of the rectangles have the same width, dx, then you can factor out that value from each term in the sum to give the following slightly simpler equation:

$$area = dx \sum_{i=0}^{N-1} F(x_i)$$

The following code calculates this sum:

```
// Use the rectangle rule to find the area under the curve.
private double RectangleRuleIntegrate(Func<double, double> F,
    double xmin, double xmax, double ymin, double ymax, int numSlices)
{
    double total = 0;
    double dx = (xmax - xmin) / numSlices;
    double x = xmin;
    for (int i = 0; i < numSlices; i++)
    {
        // Add the height at x.
        total += F(x);
        x += dx;
    }
    return total * dx;
}
```

The code sets dx to the width of the rectangles. It then loops through the rectangles, adding the height of the function at each rectangle's left edge and incrementing the x value by dx to move to the next slice.

After it adds up all of the rectangles' heights, the method multiplies the total by dx and returns the result.

The following screenshot shows the `RectangleRuleIntegration` example solution estimating the area under the same curve shown in the preceding screenshot:

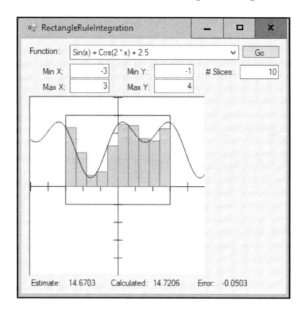

If you look closely at the earlier screenshot, you'll see that Monte Carlo integration used 1,000 random points to estimate the area with an error of roughly 0.9. The new program uses only 10 rectangles to estimate the area with an error of only -0.05.

Download the `RectangleRuleIntegration` example solution to see additional details.

8. Trapezoid rule integration

A **trapezoid** is a quadrilateral (four-sided polygon) that has two parallel sides. The parallel sides are called its **bases** and the other two sides are called its **legs**. The trapezoid's height is the distance between the two bases.

If a trapezoid has a height of *h* and base lengths *b1* and *b2*, then its area is *h* × (*b1* + *b2*) / 2. The following equation gives the sums of the areas used to approximate the area under a function:

$$area = \sum_{i=0}^{N-1} (x_{i+1} - x_i) \frac{F(x_i) + F(x_{i+1})}{2}$$

If we assume that all of the trapezoids have the same height, $dx = (x_{i+1} - x_i)$, then we can factor out the dx and the factor of ½ to get the following:

$$area = \frac{dx}{2} \sum_{i=0}^{N-1} F(x_i) + F(x_{i+1})$$

This is simple, but we can make it even simpler if we notice that most of the x values appear twice in the sum, once as an x_i term and once as an x_{i+1} term. The exceptions are the first (leftmost) and last (rightmost) values, x_0 and x_N, which each appear only once. Using that observation, we can rewrite the equation to get the following version:

$$area = \frac{dx}{2} \left(F(x_0) + F(x_N) + 2 \times \sum_{i=1}^{N-1} F(x_i) \right)$$

Finally, we can rearrange this slightly to get the following:

$$area = dx \left(\frac{F(x_0) + F(x_N)}{2} + \sum_{i=1}^{N-1} F(x_i) \right)$$

The following code calculates this value:

```
// Use the rectangle rule to find the area under the curve.
private double TrapezoidRuleIntegrate(Func<double, double> F,
    double xmin, double xmax, double ymin, double ymax, int numSlices)
{
    double total = 0;
    double dx = (xmax - xmin) / numSlices;
    double x = xmin + dx;
    for (int i = 1; i < numSlices; i++)
    {
        // Add the height at x.
        total += F(x);
        x += dx;
    }
    total = total + (F(xmax) + F(xmin)) / 2;
    return total * dx;
}
```

This code calculates dx and then uses a loop to add up the *x* values, except for the first and last values. After the loop, it adds the first and last values divided by two. Finally, it multiples that sum by dx and returns the result.

9. Arrowheads

This problem is relatively straightforward, but I'm going to describe the solution in some detail because it demonstrates some techniques that will be useful for later problems. This problem has two parts: allowing the user to draw a segment and drawing the segment as an arrow.

The first problem is relatively simple, at least as long as you've seen this sort of thing before. The Arrowhead example solution uses the following code to let the user select the segment:

```
// The segment's endpoint. If they are the same, there's no segment.
private Point StartPoint, EndPoint;

// True while dragging.
private bool Drawing = false;

// Start drawing.
private void arrowPictureBox_MouseDown(object sender, MouseEventArgs e)
{
    Drawing = true;
    StartPoint = e.Location;
    EndPoint = e.Location;
    arrowPictureBox.Refresh();
}

// Continue drawing.
private void arrowPictureBox_MouseMove(object sender, MouseEventArgs e)
{
    if (!Drawing) return;

    EndPoint = e.Location;
    arrowPictureBox.Refresh();
}

// Stop drawing.
private void arrowPictureBox_MouseUp(object sender, MouseEventArgs e)
{
```

```
        if (!Drawing) return;
        Drawing = false;

        EndPoint = e.Location;
        arrowPictureBox.Refresh();
    }
```

The StartPoint and EndPoint fields hold the segment's endpoints. The program needs some way to tell whether the user has made a selection. This program does that by checking whether the two endpoints are the same.

The Drawing field is true while the user is in the process of drawing a segment. When the user presses the mouse button down to start drawing a segment, the MouseDown event handler executes. It sets Drawing to true so the program knows that a draw is in progress. It sets StartPoint and EndPoint to the mouse's current location and refreshes the program's PictureBox control. You'll see shortly how that makes the program draw the arrow.

When the user moves the mouse over the program's PictureBox, the MouseMove event handler executes. If Drawing is false, then the user is moving the mouse with the mouse button up, so no draw is in progress. In that case, the event handler simply exits. However, if Drawing is true, the code updates EndPoint to hold the mouse's new location and refreshes the PictureBox.

When the user releases the mouse button, the MouseUp event handler executes. The program again checks Drawing to see whether a draw is in progress and exits if it is not. It then sets Drawing to false to indicate that the current draw is over. It updates EndPoint and refreshes the program's PictureBox.

When the PictureBox needs to redraw itself, for example when it is refreshed, the following Paint event handler executes:

```
// Draw the arrow.
private void arrowPictureBox_Paint(object sender, PaintEventArgs e)
{
    if (StartPoint == EndPoint) return;

    e.Graphics.Clear(Color.White);
    e.Graphics.SmoothingMode = SmoothingMode.AntiAlias;

    // Make a thick pen.
    using (Pen pen = new Pen(Color.Red, 5))
    {
        pen.LineJoin = LineJoin.Round;
        pen.EndCap = LineCap.Round;
```

```
pen.StartCap = LineCap.Round;

// Draw the segment.
e.Graphics.DrawLine(pen, StartPoint, EndPoint);

// Draw the arrowhead and tail.
DrawArrowPart(e.Graphics, pen, StartPoint, EndPoint, 15,
    false);
DrawArrowPart(e.Graphics, pen, EndPoint, StartPoint, 15, true);
    }
  }
```

If StartPoint and EndPoint are the same, then no segment has been defined, so the method simply returns. Otherwise, if a segment has been defined, the code clears the drawing area and sets the Graphics object's SmoothingMode property to produce smooth lines.

Next, the code creates a thick red pen, setting its properties so line joins and end caps are rounded.

The program then draws a line segment connecting StartPoint and EndPoint. It finishes by calling the DrawArrowPart method described shortly to draw the arrow's head and tail. Before I describe that method, however, I'll explain how it works.

A vector, <*vx, vy*>, represents a direction. For example, the vector <*1, 2*> means you should move one unit to the right in the X direction and two units up in the Y direction—sort of north-northeast.

As I mentioned in the hint, if <*vx, vy*> is a vector, then <*vy, -vx*> and <*-vy, vx*> are two vectors perpendicular to the original vector. The following diagram shows a vector in bold and its two perpendicular vectors created by this method:

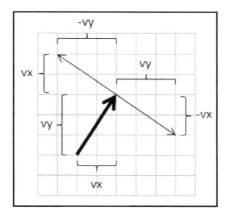

This is all a bit upside down if you remember that Y coordinates increase downward in C#. For now, think of using a normal mathematical coordinate system where Y increases upward. If you add two vectors, the result is a third vector. The result is the same as if you had followed one vector and then the other.

For this problem, you can make an arrowhead or tail by adding a vector parallel to the arrow segment plus a vector perpendicular to it. For example, to create the right side of the arrowhead, you find the right-pointing perpendicular vector shown in the preceding diagram. You add that vector to a vector pointing in the direction opposite that of the line segment to get the dashed vector shown in the following diagram:

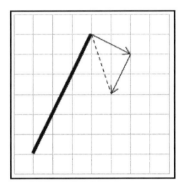

You then add the dashed vector's components to the endpoint of the line segment to get the point at the tip of that side of the arrowhead.

To get the left side of the arrowhead, you repeat the same operations but using the other perpendicular vector on the left side of the original segment.

To create an arrow's tail, you perform similar operations except you reverse the parallel vector's direction.

The final technique that you need to use to make nice arrowheads and tails is scaling a vector. If you multiply a vector's x and y components by a number, you scale its length by that amount. In particular, if you want a vector to have a specific length, L, you can divide it by its current length and then multiply it by L. The result is a vector pointing in the same direction as the original one but with the desired length.

The following code shows how the Arrowhead example solution uses these techniques to add an arrowhead or tail to a line segment:

```
// Draw an arrowhead wedge at point p1.
// If reversed is true, make an arrow tail.
private void DrawArrowPart(Graphics gr, Pen pen, Point p0, Point p1,
```

```
        float sideLength, bool reversed)
{
    // Get a vector along the arrow's length.
    float vx = p1.X - p0.X;
    float vy = p1.Y - p0.Y;

    // If this should be a tail, reverse the vectors.
    if (reversed)
    {
        vx = -vx;
        vy = -vy;
    }

    // Get perpendicular vectors.
    float p0x = vy;
    float p0y = -vx;
    float p1x = -vy;
    float p1y = vx;

    // Get arrowhead/tail vectors.
    float headX0 = p0x - vx;
    float headY0 = p0y - vy;
    float headX1 = p1x - vx;
    float headY1 = p1y - vy;

    // Set the vectors' lengths.
    float length0 = (float)Math.Sqrt(headX0 * headX0 + headY0 *
        headY0);
    headX0 *= sideLength / length0;
    headY0 *= sideLength / length0;
    float length1 = (float)Math.Sqrt(headX1 * headX1 + headY1 *
        headY1);
    headX1 *= sideLength / length1;
    headY1 *= sideLength / length1;

    // Draw it.
    PointF[] points =
    {
        new PointF(p1.X + headX0, p1.Y + headY0),
        p1,
        new PointF(p1.X + headX1, p1.Y + headY1),
    };
    gr.DrawLines(pen, points);
}
```

The method starts by finding a vector <vx, vy> that points along the user's line segment from point p0 to point p1. If the method should draw a tail instead of an arrowhead, the code reverses that vector.

Next, the code finds perpendicular vectors <p0x, p0y> and <p1x, p1y>. (Here, the **p** stands for **perpendicular**.)

The method then adds the parallel and perpendicular vectors as described earlier to make the vectors that give the sides of the arrowhead or tail. It calculates the lengths of those vectors, divides them by their lengths, and multiplies them by the method's sideLength parameter to give them the desired final lengths.

Next, the method adds the vectors to the segment's endpoint to find the locations of the arrowhead/tail's points. It saves the points in an array and uses the array to draw the arrowhead/tail.

These are the main pieces of the program. Download the Arrowhead example solution to see additional details.

The following list shows the key techniques that you should take from this example:

- You can use the MouseDown, MouseMove, and MouseUp event handlers to let the user draw. (You should also consider MouseClick if you only need to let the user select points instead of drawing.)
- If you subtract the components of point *p0* from point *p1*, you get the components for a vector pointing from *p0* to *p1*.
- If *<vx, vy>* is a vector, then *<vy, -vx>* and *<-vy, vx>* are perpendicular to it.
- You can scale a vector by multiplying its components by a number. In particular, you can divide the vector by its length to get a vector of length one. Then, you can multiply it by the desired length if you like.
- If you add a point's coordinates to a vector's components, you get a new point as if you had started at the original point and then moved in the direction and distance given by the vector.

You may find these techniques handy for solving later problems and when facing everyday programming challenges.

10. Line-line intersection

There are several ways you can approach this problem. One approach that doesn't work well is to use slope-intercept equations of the form $y = m \times x + b$ for the lines. The problem with that approach is that it doesn't work for vertical lines. If a line is vertical, then the equation's slope, *m*, is effectively infinite.

The approach that I use defines a line by giving a point $p0$ on the line and a vector v that points in the direction of the line. Then the following equation defines the points on the line:

$$point = p0 + t \times v$$

Here, t is any real number. For example, if $t = 0$, then the point is $p0$.

 This is a **parametric equation**. In a parametric equation, a parameter generates a set of points. In this example, the parameter t generates the points on a line.

If v is the vector between two points, $p0$ and $p1$, then you can use this equation to generate the points along the line segment between those points by setting t to values between 0 and 1.

Note that the preceding vector equation really represents two equations involving X and Y coordinates. If $v = <vx, vy>$, then the vector equation really represents the following two equations:

$$pointx = p0x + t \times vx$$

$$pointy = p0y + t \times vy$$

Now, assume you have two line segments, one defined by points $p00$ and $p01$ and the other defined by points $p10$ and $p11$, so their parametric equations are the following:

$$point = p00 + t0 \times v0$$

$$point = p10 + t1 \times v1$$

When the two lines intersect, their parametric equations give the same point. Setting the two equations equal to each other and considering the equations' x and y components gives us the following two equations with two unknowns $t0$ and $t1$:

$$p00x + t0 \times v0x = p10x + t1 \times v1x$$

$$p00y + t0 \times v0y = p10y + t1 \times v1y$$

You can rearrange these to get the following:

$$p00x + t0 \times v0x - p10x = t1 \times v1x$$

$$p00y + t0 \times v0y - p10y = t1 \times v1y$$

Now, multiply the first equation by *v1y* and the second equation by *–v1x* to get the following:

$$(p00x + t0 \times v0x - p10x)v1y = (t1 \times v1x)v1y$$

$$(p00y + t0 \times v0y - p10y)(-v1x) = (t1 \times v1y)(-v1x)$$

If you add these two equations, the *t1* terms cancel leaving the following:

$$(p00x + t0 \times v0x - p10x)v1y + (p00y + t0 \times v0y - p10y)(-v1x) = 0$$

Grouping the *t0* terms gives the following equation:

$$t0(v0x \times v1y - v0y \times v1x) + v1y(p00x - p10x) - v1x(p00y - p10y) = 0$$

Now, you can solve for *t0*:

$$t0 = \frac{v1y(p00x - p10x) - v1x(p00y - p10y)}{v0y \times v1x - v0x \times v1y}$$

You can solve for *t1* similarly:

$$t1 = \frac{v0y(p10x - p00x) - v0x(p10y - p00y)}{-(v0y \times v1x - v0x \times v1y)}$$

If the denominator is zero, then you cannot calculate *t1* and *t2* because you would need to divide by zero. In that case, the two lines are parallel so they never intersect.

In practice, you don't need to specifically check to see if the denominator is zero. Instead, you can calculate *t0* and use `float.IsInfinity` to see if the result is undefined.

The `LineLineIntesection` example solution uses the following method to determine where two lines intersect:

```
// Find the point of intersection between lines p00-p01 and p10-p11.
private PointF IntersectLines(PointF p00, PointF p01, PointF p10,
    PointF p11)
{
    // Get the segments' parameters.
    float v0x = p01.X - p00.X;
    float v0y = p01.Y - p00.Y;
    float v1x = p11.X - p10.X;
    float v1y = p11.Y - p10.Y;

    // Solve for t0 and t1.
    float denominator = v0y * v1x - v0x * v1y;

    float t0 = (v1y * (p00.X - p10.X) - v1x * (p00.Y - p10.Y))
        / denominator;
    if (float.IsInfinity(t0))
        throw new Exception("The lines are parallel");

    PointF p0 = new PointF(
        p00.X + t0 * v0x,
        p00.Y + t0 * v0y);

    // Check.
    float t1 = (v0y * (p10.X - p00.X) - v0x * (p10.Y - p00.Y))
        / -denominator;
    PointF p1 = new PointF(
        p10.X + t1 * v1x,
        p10.Y + t1 * v1y);
    Debug.Assert(Math.Abs(p0.X - p1.X) < 0.0001);
    Debug.Assert(Math.Abs(p0.Y - p1.Y) < 0.0001);

    return p0;
}
```

This method first calculates the X and Y components of the lines' direction vectors $v0$ and $v1$. It then solves for $t0$. Notice the check that uses the `float.IsInfinity` method to see if the denominator is zero.

The code then uses $t0$ to find the point of intersection. The method doesn't really need to calculate $t1$, but it does so anyway. It uses $t1$ to calculate the point of intersection again and verifies that the two calculations give the same point.

The method finishes by returning the point it calculated.

Download the `LineLineIntersection` example solution to see additional details.

11. Point-line distance

There are several ways that you can attack this problem. I'm going to use a parameterized approach similar to the one used for Problem 29. *Line-line intersection*.

Suppose the point is (*px*, *py*) and the line is given by *p0* + *t* × *v*. Then the distance between the point and a point on the line is given by the following:

$$distance = \sqrt{(p_x - (p_{0x} + t \times v_x))^2 + (p_y - (p_{0y} + t \times v_y))^2}$$

We need to find the value of *t* that minimizes this equation. You can do that with one trick and a little calculus.

The trick is to note that the minimum of this equation has the same X coordinate that minimizes the equation squared. The following shows the squared equation:

$$distance^2 = (p_x - (p_{0x} + t \times v_x))^2 + (p_y - (p_{0y} + t \times v_y))^2$$

Here comes the calculus. To minimize this equation, we take the derivative of the equation with respect to it, set it equal to zero, and solve for *t*. The following code shows the new equation:

$$2(p_x - p_{0x} - t \times v_x)v_x + 2(p_y - p_{0y} - t \times v_y)v_y = 0$$

We can divide both sides by 2 and rearrange a bit to get the following:

$$-t(v_x^2 + v_y^2) + v_x(p_x - p_{0x}) + v_y(p_y - p_{0y}) = 0$$

Now we can solve for *t*:

$$t = \frac{v_x(p_x - p_{0x}) + v_y(p_y - p_{0y})}{v_x^2 + v_y^2}$$

The denominator is zero (and hence the fraction cannot be calculated) only if the vector v has zero length. In that case, the line isn't really a line, so the calculation doesn't make sense.

After you use this equation to solve for t, you can use it to find the point on the line that is closest to the target point p.

Download the `PointLineDistance` example solution to see additional details.

12. Point-segment distance

There are two cases to consider when solving this problem. First, the point on the segment that is closest to the target point might lie on the line segment. In that case, Solution 30 solves this problem.

The second case occurs if the point found by Solution 30 does not lie on the segment but only lies on the line that contains the segment. In that case, the point on the segment that is closest to the point is one of the segment's endpoints.

The following `PointSegmentClosestPoint` method finds the point on a segment that is closest to the target point. It also returns a Boolean through the `isOnSegment` output parameter, indicating whether that point lies on the segment:

```
// Find the point on the line p0-p1 that is closest to point p.
private PointF PointSegmentClosestPoint(PointF p, PointF p0, PointF p1,
    out bool isOnSegment)
{
    float vx = p1.X - p0.X;
    float vy = p1.Y - p0.Y;
    float numerator = vx * (p.X - p0.X) + vy * (p.Y - p0.Y);
    float denominator = vx * vx + vy * vy;
    float t = numerator / denominator;

    // See if the point is on the segment.
    isOnSegment = ((t >= 0) && (t <= 1));
    if (isOnSegment) return new PointF(p0.X + t * vx, p0.Y + t * vy);

    // The point we found is not on the segment.
    // See which end point is closer.
    float dx0 = p.X - p0.X;
    float dy0 = p.Y - p0.Y;
    float dist0squared = dx0 * dx0 + dy0 * dy0;
```

```
        float dx1 = p.X - p1.X;
        float dy1 = p.Y - p1.Y;
        float dist1squared = dx1 * dx1 + dy1 * dy1;

        if (dist0squared <= dist1squared) return p0;
        return p1;
    }
```

This method uses the technique used by Solution 30 to find the point on the segment's line that is closest to the target point. If the parameter *t* lies between 0 and 1, then this point also lies on the segment so the method returns it.

If *t* does not lie between 0 and 1, the method calculates the distances squared between the segment's endpoints and the target point. It then returns whichever endpoint is closer to the target point.

Download the `PointSegmentDistance` example solution to see additional details.

13. Segment-segment distance

If you think about how two segments can be arranged, you'll realize that there are a lot of special cases. The segments could intersect or they could be parallel. If the segments don't intersect and are not parallel, then the closest points could be on the segments' endpoints, in the segments' interiors, or a combination of the two.

Although the problem seems complicated, there are really only two cases that you need to worry about: when the segments intersect and when they don't.

If the segments intersect, then you can use the techniques used by Solution 29, *Line-line intersection*, to find the point of intersection.

If the segments don't intersect, then at least one of the segments' endpoints is the point closest to the other segment. In that case, you can use the method described for the preceding solution, *Point-segment distance*, to find the closest points. Any of the four segment endpoints could be one of the closest points, but you can simply try them all and see which produces the best result.

The last thing you might consider is the special case where the segments are parallel. In that case, multiple endpoints might give the same shortest distance. There may also be pairs of points that give the same shortest distance even though neither of them is an endpoint.

All of these cases give the same shortest distance, however, so it doesn't really matter which one you pick. Unless you have special needs, such as a requirement to find *all* pairs of points that give the shortest distance, then you may as well use the closest points that you find by using the *Point-segment distance* techniques.

The following code shows the `SegmentSegmentClosestPoints` method, which forms the heart of the example solution:

```
// Find the points where the segments p00-p01 and p10-p11 are closest.
private void SegmentSegmentClosestPoints(
    PointF p00, PointF p01, PointF p10, PointF p11,
    out PointF closestPoint0, out PointF closestPoint1,
    out bool isOnSegment0, out bool isOnSegment1)
{
    closestPoint0 = new PointF(-1, -1);
    closestPoint1 = new PointF(-1, -1);
    isOnSegment0 = false;
    isOnSegment1 = false;

    // Look for an intersection.
    PointF intersection = IntersectLines(p00, p01, p10, p11,
        out isOnSegment0, out isOnSegment1);
    if (isOnSegment0 && isOnSegment1)
    {
        closestPoint0 = intersection;
        closestPoint1 = intersection;
        return;
    }

    // See which segment end points are closest to the other segment.
    float testDist, bestDist = float.MaxValue;
    PointF testPoint;
    bool testIsOnSegment;

    // Check p00.
    testPoint = PointSegmentClosestPoint(p00,
        p10, p11, out testIsOnSegment);
    testDist = DistanceSquared(p00, testPoint);
    if (testDist < bestDist)
    {
        closestPoint0 = p00;
        closestPoint1 = testPoint;
        isOnSegment0 = true;
        isOnSegment1 = testIsOnSegment;
        bestDist = testDist;
    }
```

```
// Check p01.
testPoint = PointSegmentClosestPoint(p01,
    p10, p11, out testIsOnSegment);
testDist = DistanceSquared(p01, testPoint);
if (testDist < bestDist)
{
    closestPoint0 = p01;
    closestPoint1 = testPoint;
    isOnSegment0 = true;
    isOnSegment1 = testIsOnSegment;
    bestDist = testDist;
}

// Check p10.
testPoint = PointSegmentClosestPoint(p10,
    p00, p01, out testIsOnSegment);
testDist = DistanceSquared(p10, testPoint);
if (testDist < bestDist)
{
    closestPoint0 = testPoint;
    closestPoint1 = p10;
    isOnSegment0 = testIsOnSegment;
    isOnSegment1 = true;
    bestDist = testDist;
}

// Check p11.
testPoint = PointSegmentClosestPoint(p11,
    p00, p01, out testIsOnSegment);
testDist = DistanceSquared(p11, testPoint);
if (testDist < bestDist)
{
    closestPoint0 = testPoint;
    closestPoint1 = p11;
    isOnSegment0 = testIsOnSegment;
    isOnSegment1 = true;
    bestDist = testDist;
}
}
```

This method uses the IntersectLines method to see whether the segments intersect. That method is similar to the one used in Solution *29. Line-line intersection,* modified to not throw an exception if the lines are parallel. See that solution for more information about the method.

Next, the `SegmentSegmentClosestPoints` method uses the
`PointSegmentClosestPoint` method to see which of the segments' endpoints is closest to
the other segment. That method is similar to the one used in Solution *31. Point-segment
distance,* so you can read more about it there.

That's all there is to this solution. It simply combines methods used by previous solutions to
find the closest points. Download the `SegmentSegmentDistance` example solution and
look at the previous solutions to see additional details.

14. Circle selection

The hint said that the perpendicular bisectors of a chord of a circle pass through the circle's
center. To apply that hint to this problem, find a perpendicular bisector for the segment
connecting two of the points selected by the user. That bisector passes through the circle's
center.

The following `FindBisector` helper method finds a perpendicular bisector for a segment:

```
// Find a bisector for the segment connecting the two points.
private void FindBisector(PointF p0, PointF p1,
    out PointF b0, out PointF b1)
{
    // Find the midpoint.
    b0 = new PointF(
        (p0.X + p1.X) / 2,
        (p0.Y + p1.Y) / 2);

    // Find the p0-p1 direction vector.
    float dx = p1.X - p0.X;
    float dy = p1.Y - p0.Y;

    // Add <dy, -dx> to b0 to get b1.
    b1 = new PointF(
        b0.X + dy,
        b0.Y - dx);
}
```

The method first averages the two points, `p0` and `p1`, to find the point at the center of the
segment. The bisector must pass through that point.

Next, the code finds the <dx, dy> direction vector that points in the direction of the original segment. The two vectors <dy, −dx> and <−dy, dx> are perpendicular to <dx, dy>, one pointing to the left and the other to the right. The code adds <dy, −dx> to the segment's center point to get a new point that lies along the perpendicular bisector.

The following FindCircle method uses the FindBisector helper method to find the circle that passes through three points:

```
// Return a RectangleF that defines a circle
// passing through the three points.
private RectangleF FindCircle(PointF p0, PointF p1, PointF p2)
{
    // Find a bisector for p0-p1.
    PointF b00, b01;
    FindBisector(p0, p1, out b00, out b01);

    // Find a bisector for p1-p2.
    PointF b10, b11;
    FindBisector(p1, p2, out b10, out b11);

    // Find the bisectors' point of intersection.
    bool linesAreParallel;
    PointF center = IntersectLines(b00, b01, b10, b11,
        out linesAreParallel);
    if (linesAreParallel)
    {
        MessageBox.Show("The circle's points are colinear");
        return new RectangleF(-1, -1, -1, -1);
    }

    // Return the circle.
    float radius = Distance(center, p0);
    return new RectangleF(
        center.X - radius, center.Y - radius,
        2 * radius, 2 * radius);
}
```

This method calls the FindBisector helper method to find the chord bisectors. It then calls IntersectLines to see where the bisectors intersect.

The two bisectors will be parallel if the user's three points are co-linear. In that case, there is no circle that includes all three points.

Next, the method uses the `Distance` helper method to find the distance between the center point and one of the user's points. (The `Distance` method simply calculates the distance between two points. It's straightforward so I won't show it here.) That distance gives the radius of the circle.

The method finishes by a `RectangleF` that defines the circle. (You could store the circle's center point and radius instead, but the program's `Paint` event handler uses a `RectangleF` to draw the circle, so it's convenient to represent the circle as `RectangleF`.)

The rest of the program is reasonably straightforward if you use the tools provided by the previous solutions. Download the `CircleSelection` example program to see additional details.

15. Line-circle intersection

Suppose the line is defined by the following parametric equations:

$$x(t) = p_0x + t \times vx$$

$$y(t) = p_0y + t \times vy$$

Here, $p_0 = (p_0x, p_0y)$ is a point on the line and $<vx, vy>$ is a vector pointing in the line's direction. If the second point on the line is $p_1 = (p_1x, p_1y)$, then you can use $<p_1x - p_0x, p_1y - p_0x>$ as the vector.

If the circle is centered at point (cx, cy) and has the radius r, then the following equation defines the circle:

$$(x - cx)^2 + (y - cy)^2 = r^2$$

If we plug the line's parametric equations into the circle's equation, we get the following equation:

$$(p_0x + t \times vx - cx)^2 + (p_0y + t \times vy - cy)^2 = r^2$$

If you multiply this out and group the terms containing t, you get the following rather untidy result:

$$t^2(vx^2 + vy^2) + 2t(vx(p_0x - cx) + vy(p_0y - cy)) + (p_0x - cx)^2 + (p_0y - cy)^2 = r^2$$

This may look messy, but remember that all of the values vx, vy, $p0$, cx, cy, and r are part of the problem statement so we know their values. That means this equation simplifies to the following quadratic:

$$At^2 + Bt + C = 0$$

Here the following is true:

$$A = vx^2 + vy^2$$

$$B = 2(vx(p_0x - cx) + vy(p_0y - cy))$$

$$C = (p_0x - cx)^2 + (p_0y - cy)^2 - r^2$$

Now we can use the quadratic formula to solve for t:

$$t = \frac{-B \pm \sqrt{B^2 - 4AC}}{2A}$$

The value inside the square root is called the equation's **discriminant** because it discriminates among different possible solutions. If the discriminant has a positive, zero, or negative value, the equation has two, one, or zero real solutions respectively. Those correspond to the line cutting through the circle, touching the circle tangentially, or missing the circle entirely.

The following code shows the `FindLineCircleIntersections` method, which finds the points of intersection between a line and a circle:

```
// Find the point of intersection between a circle defined by
// points p0, p1, p2 and the line define by points 10, 11.
private List<PointF> FindLineCircleIntersections(
    PointF c0, PointF c1, PointF c2,
    PointF p0, PointF p1)
{
    // Make a list to hold the points of intersection.
    List<PointF> results = new List<PointF>();
```

```
// Find the circle.
RectangleF circleRect = FindCircle(c0, c1, c2);

// If the points don't define a circle, return the empty results
// list.
if (circleRect.Width < 0) return results;

// Get the circle's center and radius.
float radius = circleRect.Width / 2;
PointF c = new PointF(
    circleRect.X + radius,
    circleRect.Y + radius);

// Find the intersection.
float vx = p1.X - p0.X;
float vy = p1.Y - p0.Y;
float A = vx * vx + vy * vy;
float B = 2 * (vx * (p0.X - c.X) + vy * (p0.Y - c.Y));
float C =
    (p0.X - c.X) * (p0.X - c.X) +
    (p0.Y - c.Y) * (p0.Y - c.Y) -
    radius * radius;

float discriminant = B * B - 4 * A * C;
if (discriminant < 0)
{
    Console.WriteLine("No real solutions");
    return results;
}

if (Math.Abs(discriminant) < 0.0001)
{
    Console.WriteLine("One solution");
    float t = -B / (2 * A);
    results.Add(new PointF(
        p0.X + t * vx,
        p0.Y + t * vy));
}
else
{
    Console.WriteLine("Two solutions");
    float root = (float)Math.Sqrt(discriminant);

    float t0 = (-B + root) / (2 * A);
    results.Add(new PointF(
        p0.X + t0 * vx,
        p0.Y + t0 * vy));
```

```
            float t1 = (-B - root) / (2 * A);
            results.Add(new PointF(
                p0.X + t1 * vx,
                p0.Y + t1 * vy));
    }

    return results;
}
```

The method starts by creating a `results` list to hold any intersections that it finds. It then calls the `FindCircle` method used by the preceding solution to find the circle that the user selected. If the user's points don't define a circle because they are colinear, the method returns the empty results list.

If the `FindCircle` method did find a circle, the code uses its results to find the circle's radius and center.

Next, the method finds the `<vx, vy>` vector pointing from the line's first point to its second. The method uses the values that it has to calculate *A*, *B*, and *C* for use in the quadratic formula.

The code then calculates and checks the quadratic formula's discriminant to see whether we have zero, one, or two solutions. The code calculates the appropriate number of solutions and adds them to the `results` list. The method finishes by returning that list.

The rest of the example solution uses methods defined by previous solutions to perform other tasks, such as finding the circle that the user selected. Download the `LineCircleIntersection` example solution to see additional details.

16. Circle-circle intersection

As is usually the case, you can take several approaches to solve this problem. For example, you could write the equation for one of the circles, solve for *x* and *y*, and plug those values into the equation for the second circle. Then, you would solve the new equation for *x* and *y*.

Unfortunately, as you saw in the preceding solution, the equation for a circle centered at the point *(cx, cy)* is fairly complicated, so solving that equation for *x* and *y* isn't trivial. When you plug those values into the equation for the other circle, things really get complicated.

Instead of using that method, I'm going to use a geometric approach. Take a look at the circles shown in the following diagram. Our goal is to find the points of intersection between the two circles with the centers *C0* and *C1* and radii *R0* and *R1*:

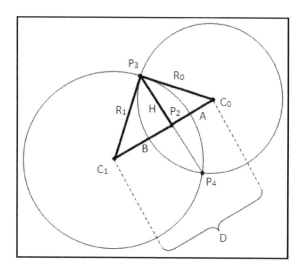

Let *D* be the distance between the circles' centers. There are several possible scenarios:

- If $D > R_0 + R_1$, then the circles are so far apart that they do not intersect
- If $D < | R_0 - R_1 |$, then one circle lies inside the other so, again, the circles do not intersect
- If $D = 0$ *and* $R_0 = R_1$, then the circles are the same
- If $D = R_0 + R_1$, then the circles touch at a single point
- Otherwise, the circles intersect at two points

If you look at the triangle $\Delta C_0 P_2 P_3$, the Pythagorean theorem gives us the equation $H^2 = R_0^2 - A^2$. Similarly, if you look at the triangle $\Delta C_1 P_2 P_3$, the Pythagorean theorem gives us $H^2 = R_1^2 - B^2$. Setting these equations as equal gives the following:

$$R_0^2 - A^2 = R_1^2 - B^2$$

We know that $D = A + B$. If we solve for *A*, that gives us $A = D - B$. If we substitute this value into the preceding equation, we get the following:

$$R_0^2 - (D - B)^2 = R_1^2 - B^2$$

Multiplying this out gives the following:

$$R_0^2 - D^2 + 2BD - B^2 = R_1^2 - B^2$$

If you cancel the $-B^2$ terms on both sides and solve for B, you get the following:

$$B = \frac{R_1^2 - R_0^2 + D^2}{2D}$$

Now, if you go back to the equations given by the Pythagorean theorem and solve for A instead of B, you get the following:

$$A = \frac{R_0^2 - R_1^2 + D^2}{2D}$$

The only difference between these two equations is that the roles of R_0 and R_1 are switched.

We know all of these values, so we can use these equations to find A and B. All that remains is to use those values to find the points of intersection P_3 and P_4.

Let the vector $<vx, vy>$ be the vector between the two circles' centers. Then, the vectors $<vy, -vx>$ and $<-vy, vx>$ are perpendicular to that vector. We can add multiples of those perpendicular vectors to the point P_2 to find the points P_3 and P_4.

To reach the points P_3 and P_4, we need the perpendicular vectors to have the lengths H. We can achieve that by dividing the vectors by their current lengths and then multiplying them by H. We add those vectors to P_2 and we have the points of intersection.

`FindCircleCircleIntersections` uses this method to find the points where two circles intersect:

```
// Find the points of intersection between the circles defined
// by points p00, p01, p02 and p10, p11, p12.
private List<PointF> FindCircleCircleIntersections(
    Point p00, Point p01, Point p02,
    Point p10, Point p11, Point p12)
{
    const float tiny = 0.0001f;

    List<PointF> results = new List<PointF>();

    // Find the two circles, their centers, and their radii.
    Circle0 = FindCircle(p00, p01, p02);
    float R0 = Circle0.Width / 2;
```

```
PointF C0 = new PointF(
    Circle0.X + R0,
    Circle0.Y + R0);

Circle1 = FindCircle(p10, p11, p12);
float R1 = Circle1.Width / 2;
PointF C1 = new PointF(
    Circle1.X + R1,
    Circle1.Y + R1);

// Find the distance between the centers.
double D = Distance(C0, C1);

// See how many solutions there are.
if (D > R0 + R1)
{
    Console.WriteLine(
        "No intersections, the circles are too far apart");
}
else if (D < Math.Abs(R0 - R1))
{
    Console.WriteLine(
        "No intersections, one circle contains the other");
}
else if ((Math.Abs(D) < tiny) && (Math.Abs(R0 - R1) < tiny))
{
    Console.WriteLine(
        "No intersections, the circles are the same");
}
else
{
    // Find A and H.
    double A = (R0 * R0 - R1 * R1 + D * D) / (2 * D);
    double H = Math.Sqrt(R0 * R0 - A * A);

    // Find P2.
    double P2x = C0.X + A * (C1.X - C0.X) / D;
    double P2y = C0.Y + A * (C1.Y - C0.Y) / D;

    // Get the point P3.
    results.Add(new PointF(
        (float)(P2x + H * (C1.Y - C0.Y) / D),
        (float)(P2y - H * (C1.X - C0.X) / D)));

    // See if we a second solution.
    if (Math.Abs(D - (R0 + R1)) >= tiny)
    {
        // Add the second solution with the +/- signs switched.
```

```
                    results.Add(new PointF(
                        (float)(P2x - H * (C1.Y - C0.Y) / D),
                        (float)(P2y + H * (C1.X - C0.X) / D)));
                }

                Console.WriteLine(results.Count.ToString() + " intersections");
            }

            // Return whatever results we found.
            return results;
        }
```

The method starts by using the points that define the circles to find their centers and radii. It then uses the `Distance` helper method to find the distance between the two centers.

The code then uses a sequence of `if` statements to determine the correct number of intersections. If there are any intersections, the code calculates A and H, as described earlier and uses them to find the point P_2.

Next, the code uses P_2 to find the first point of intersection, P_3, and adds it to the `results` list.

The method then checks whether D equals $R_0 + R_1$. If the two valucs are equal, then P_3 is the only point of intersection. If D does not equal $R_0 + R_1$, then the code finds the other point of intersection, P_4 and adds it to the `results` list.

The method finishes by returning any points of intersection that it found.

Download the `CircleCircleintersection` example solution to see additional details.

17. Circle-line tangents

The following diagram shows a circle and point P with their two tangent lines:

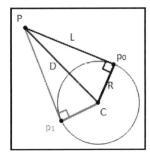

You can calculate the distance between the point P and the circle's center C by using the distance formula. If the point P is at (Px, Py) and the circle's center C is at (Cx, Cy), then the following formula gives the distance between the two points:

$$D = \sqrt{(Cx - Px)^2 + (Cy - Py)^2}$$

A tangent line meets the circle's radius at a 90°. We know D and R, so we can use the Pythagorean theorem to find L:

$$L = \sqrt{D^2 - R^2}$$

At this point, you're basically done. The points p_0 and p_1 are the distance L away from the point P, so they lie on a circle of radius L centered at point P. They also lie on the original circle. Now, you can use the techniques described in Solution 35. *Circle-circle intersection*, to find the points where those two circles intersect, and that gives you the points p_0 and p_1.

The following `FindTangentPoints` method finds the tangent points between a point and a circle:

```
// Find the tangent points for this circle and external point.
private List<PointF> FindLineCircleTangents(PointF center,
    float radius, PointF point)
{
    // Find the distance between center and point.
    float D = Distance(center, point);
    if (D <= radius) return new List<PointF>();

    // Find the distance from point to the tangent points.
    float L = (float)Math.Sqrt(D * D - radius * radius);

    // Find the points of intersection between the original circle
    // and the circle with center point and radius L.
    return FindCircleCircleIntersections(center, radius, point, L);
}
```

This method calculates the distances D and L shown in the preceding diagram. It then calls the `FindCircleCircleIntersections` method to find the intersections of the two circles described earlier.

Note that this version of `FindCircleCircleIntersections` has been modified to take the circles' centers and radii as parameters. Download the `CircleLineTangents` example solution to see the new version of the method and other details.

18. Polygon area

The hint said to consider the trapezoids defined by the polygon's edges, the *X* axis, and sides dropped vertically from the polygon's vertices to the *X* axis. The following diagram shows a polygon with one of those trapezoids shaded:

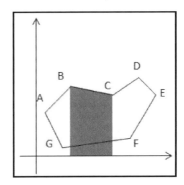

Recall that a trapezoid's bases are its parallel sides. Also recall that a trapezoid with height *h* and base lengths *b1* and *b2* has an area of *h* × *(b1 + b2) / 2*. To calculate a polygon's area, you can simply add the areas of its trapezoids.

You need to understand two non-obvious facts to make this work. First, notice that the shaded trapezoid in the preceding diagram includes an area between the polygon and the *X* axis that obviously should not be included in the polygon's area. To see why this isn't a problem, note that the *X* coordinate of point *F* is greater than the *X* coordinate of point *G*, so when you subtract *Gx – Fx*, you get a negative number. That means the trapezoid that uses the *F-G* segment as its top subtracts some of the area that lies below the polygon.

The trapezoids that use the polygon's top edges add the extra space below the polygon, but then the trapezoids that use the polygon's bottom edges subtract that space out again leaving only the polygon's area.

The second non-obvious fact is that the sum of the trapezoids' areas may be negative depending on the polygon's orientation. In the preceding diagram, the polygon is oriented clockwise so, for example, the *X* coordinate of point *C* is greater than the *X* coordinate of point *B*. That means the top trapezoids such as the shaded one have positive areas.

If the polygon's points were oriented counter-clockwise, then those trapezoids would have negative areas. When you add all of the areas, the final result will be negative. If the result is negative, simply take its absolute value and you'll have the polygon's correct area.

This effect is reversed in C# because *Y* coordinates increase from the top down instead of from the bottom up.

The following `PolygonArea` method uses this technique to calculate a polygon's area:

```
// Calculate the polygon's area.
private float PolygonArea(List<Point> points)
{
    int numPoints = points.Count;
    if (numPoints < 3)
        throw new Exception(
            "The polygon must have at least three vertices");

    // Repeat the first point at the end for convenience.
    points.Add(points[0]);

    // Loop over the polygon's segments.
    float area = 0;
    for (int i = 0; i < numPoints; i++)
    {
        float width = points[i + 1].X - points[i].X;
        area += width * (points[i + 1].Y + points[i].Y) / 2f;
    }

    // Remove the repeated first point.
    points.RemoveAt(numPoints);

    return Math.Abs(area);
}
```

This method first verifies that the polygon has at least three points and throws an exception if it does not.

It then copies the polygon's first point to the end of the polygon's point list to make it easier to loop over the polygon's edges.

Next, the method loops over the polygon's edges and adds the areas of their trapezoids to a total. After it finishes, the method removes the copy of the first point that it added to the point list and returns the total area.

Download the `PolygonArea` example solution to see additional details.

19. Point in a polygon

One way to determine whether a point lies inside a polygon is to add up the angles that it makes with the polygon's vertices. If the test point is *P* and *A* and *B* are two adjacent polygon points, then you look at the angle ∠*APB*.

If you add up all of the angles between the test point and each of the polygon's edges, the result will be either 0, 2π, or –2π. If the total is 2π or –2π, then the point is inside the polygon. If the total is 0, then the point lies outside of the polygon. You can probably convince yourself that this works if you draw a few examples. For example, try placing points inside and outside of a square, draw the angles, and estimate their values.

The idea is straightforward. The hard part is calculating the angles. One way to do that is to use dot products and cross products.

The **dot product** of two vectors, *v0* and *v1*, which is written *v0* • *v1*, equals |*v0*| × |*v1*| *cos(θ)*, where |*v0*| and |*v1*| mean the lengths of the vectors *v0* and *v1*, and θ is the angle between the two vectors.

One nice thing about dot products is that they are easy to calculate. If the vectors have the components *v0* = <*v0x*, *v0y*> and *v1* = <*v1x*, *v1y*>, then their dot product is simply *v0x* * *v1x* + *v0y* * *v1y*. If you calculate a dot product and then divide by the lengths of the two vectors, then the result is the cosine of the angle between the vectors.

Unfortunately, the cosine isn't quite enough to determine the angle because *cos(θ) = cos(-θ)*. Even after you find the cosine, you still don't know which angle to use.

That's where the cross product comes in. The **cross product** of two vectors, *v0* and *v1*, which is written *v0* × *v1*, gives you a new vector that is perpendicular to both *v0* and *v1*. For example, if *v0* and *v1* lie in the plane of your table, then *v0* × *v1* pokes straight up out of (or down into) the table. The length of the new vector is |*v0*| × |*v1*| *sin(θ)*.

If you write the vectors in three dimensions as <*v0x*, *v0y*, *v0z*> and <*v1x*, *v1y*, *v1z*>, then the cross product of the vectors is <*rx*, *ry*, *rz*>, where:

$$rx = v0y \times v1z - v0z \times v1y$$

$$ry = v0z \times v1x - v0x \times v1z$$

$$rz = v0x \times v1y - v0y \times v1x$$

If you assume that the vectors v0 and v1 lie in the *X-Y* plane, then their *Z* coordinates are zero, so the *rx* and *ry* values are also zero. That makes sense because the result of the cross product is a vector that is perpendicular to the plane containing v0 and v1, so it's X and Y components should be zero. Because this vector has only one non-zero component, *rz*, its length is simply *rz = v0x * v1y – v0y * v1x*.

After you calculate the cross product, you simply divide by the lengths of the two original vectors and you know sin(*θ*).

Finally, after you know cos(*θ*) and sin(*θ*), you can use the `arctangent` function to find *θ*.

Now that you know how to find the angle *θ*, it's time to look at some code. The following methods calculate the dot and cross products:

```
// Return the cross product AB x BC.
// Note that |AB x BC| = |AB| * |BC| * Sin(theta).
public static float CrossProductLength(Point A, Point B, Point C)
{
    // Get the vectors' components.
    float ABx = A.X - B.X;
    float ABy = A.Y - B.Y;
    float BCx = C.X - B.X;
    float BCy = C.Y - B.Y;

    // Calculate the Z coordinate of the cross product.
    return (ABx * BCy - ABy * BCx);
}

// Return the dot product AB · BC.
// Note that AB · BC = |AB| * |BC| * Cos(theta).
private static float DotProduct(Point A, Point B, Point C)
{
    // Get the vectors' components.
    float ABx = A.X - B.X;
    float ABy = A.Y - B.Y;
    float BCx = C.X - B.X;
    float BCy = C.Y - B.Y;

    // Calculate the dot product.
    return (ABx * BCx + ABy * BCy);
}
```

These methods take as parameters three points *A*, *B*, and *C*, and calculate *AB* • *BC* and *AB* × *BC*, respectively.

The following `GetAngle` method uses the `DotProduct` and `CrossProduct` methods to find the angle ∠*ABC*:

```
// Return angle ABC between PI and -PI.
// Note that the value is the opposite of what you might
// expect because Y coordinates increase downward.
public static float GetAngle(Point A, Point B, Point C)
{
    // Get the dot product.
    float dotProduct = DotProduct(A, B, C);

    // Get the cross product.
    float crossProduct = CrossProductLength(A, B, C);

    // Calculate the angle.
    return (float)Math.Atan2(crossProduct, dotProduct);
}
```

The method calls the `DotProduct` and `CrossProduct` methods to get the dot and cross products. It then uses the `Math.Atan2` method to find the corresponding angle.

Finally, the following code shows the `PointIsInPolygon` method:

```
// Return true if testPoint lies inside the polygon.
private bool PointIsInPolygon(List<Point> points, Point testPoint)
{
    int numPoints = points.Count;
    if (numPoints < 3)
        throw new Exception(
            "The polygon must have at least three vertices");

    // Repeat the first point at the end for convenience.
    points.Add(points[0]);

    // Loop over the polygon's segments.
    float total = 0;
    for (int i = 0; i < numPoints; i++)
        total += GetAngle(points[i], testPoint, points[i + 1]);

    // Remove the repeated first point.
    points.RemoveAt(numPoints);

    // See if total is +/-2*pi.
    const float tiny = 0.0001f;
    return (Math.Abs(total) > tiny);
}
```

This method first verifies that the polygon contains at least three points and throws an exception if it doesn't. It then adds a copy of the first point to the end of the polygon's point list to make looping through the polygon's edges easier.

Next, the code loops through the polygon's edges. For each edge, it calls the GetAngle method to get the corresponding angle and adds it to the total.

After it has processed all of the edges, the method removes the copy of the first point from the end of the point list. It finishes by returning true if the total angle is not close to 0, which means it is either 2π, or -2π.

Download the PointInPolygon example solution to see additional details.

20. Convexity testing

A **convex polygon** is one where each of its internal angles is less than 180°. Another way to think of it is that you can pass a line through any two adjacent polygon vertices and the line will not cut into the polygon's body.

The GetAngle method described in the preceding solution calculates an angle. Unfortunately, it doesn't return angles greater than 180°. Instead, if an angle is greater than 180°, the method returns 360 minus the angle so the result is always between –180° and 180°.

The method has one other issue that complicates the situation: the sign of the angles depends on the orientation of the points. If *A*, *B*, and *C* are points, then GetAngle(A, B, C) = -GetAngle(C, B, A).

The solution to these problems is to look at the signs of the angles. The GetAngle method returns positive or negative values depending on whether an angle bends to the left or right. If GetAngle returns all positive or all negative values for a polygon's angles, then the polygon is convex. If GetAngle returns some positive values and some negative values, then the polygon is not convex.

The following PolygonIsConvex method returns true if a polygon is convex:

```
// Return true if the polygon is convex.
private bool PolygonIsConvex(List<Point> points)
{
    int numPoints = points.Count;
    if (numPoints < 3)
        throw new Exception(
            "The polygon must have at least three vertices");
```

```
        // Duplicate the first two points.
        points.Add(points[0]);
        points.Add(points[1]);

        // Get the sign of the first angle.
        int sign = Math.Sign(GetAngle(points[0], points[1], points[2]));

        // Loop through the angles.
        bool isConvex = true;
        for (int i = 1; i < numPoints; i++)
        {
            if (Math.Sign(GetAngle(points[i], points[i + 1], points[i +
              2]))
                != sign)
            {
                isConvex = false;
                break;
            }
        }

        // Remove the duplicates that we added.
        points.RemoveAt(numPoints);
        points.RemoveAt(numPoints);

        return isConvex;
    }
```

The method first verifies that the polygon contains at least three points. It then adds copies of the first two points to the end of the point list to make it easier to loop through the polygon's angles.

The code then gets the sign of the first angle and saves it in the sign variable. Next, the code sets the isConvex variable to true and loops through the polygon's remaining angles. If any angle's sign doesn't agree with the value stored in the sign variable, the method sets isConvex to false and breaks out of the loop.

After it finishes the loop, the method removes the duplicate points that it added to the point list and returns the value stored in isConvex.

Download the IsConvex example solution to see additional details.

21. Stars

This is a relatively simple exercise in keeping track of points. To find the polygon's vertices, you can make a `theta` variable loop over angles using sines and cosines to find the vertices.

Because of the way C# calculates angles, and because of the fact that Y coordinates increase downward, `theta` should initially have the value $-\pi/2$ if you want the peak of an odd-sided polygon to be on the top.

When you enter the number of sides and the skip number and click **Go**, the example solution executes the following code:

```
// Get the parameter to draw a new start and refresh.
private void PrepareStar()
{
    NumSides = int.Parse(numSidesTextBox.Text);
    Skip = int.Parse(skipTextBox.Text);
    starPictureBox.Refresh();
}
```

This event handler simply parses the values that you entered and then refreshes the program's `PictureBox` to make it draw using the new parameters. The following code shows how the program draws its polygon and star:

```
// Draw the star.
private void starPictureBox_Paint(object sender, PaintEventArgs e)
{
    e.Graphics.Clear(Color.White);
    e.Graphics.SmoothingMode = SmoothingMode.AntiAlias;

    // Get positioning values.
    PointF center = new PointF(
        starPictureBox.ClientSize.Width / 2f,
        starPictureBox.ClientSize.Height / 2f);
    const float margin = 5;
    float radius = Math.Min(
        starPictureBox.ClientSize.Width / 2f,
        starPictureBox.ClientSize.Height / 2f) - margin;

    // Draw the poylgon.
    double theta = -Math.PI / 2.0;
    double dtheta = 2 * Math.PI / NumSides;
    PointF[] points = new PointF[NumSides];
    for (int i = 0; i < NumSides; i++)
    {
        points[i] = new PointF(
```

```
            (float)(center.X + radius * Math.Cos(theta)),
            (float)(center.Y + radius * Math.Sin(theta)));
        theta += dtheta;
    }
    e.Graphics.DrawPolygon(Pens.Red, points);

    // Draw the star.
    for (int i = 0; i < NumSides; i++)
        e.Graphics.DrawLine(Pens.Blue,
            points[i], points[(i + Skip) % NumSides]);
}
```

This code finds the center of the program's `PictureBox`. It then calculates a radius for the polygon. It sets the radius, which is the distance between the polygon's center and its vertices, to be half of the smaller of the `PictureBox` control's width and height, minus a margin.

Next, the code initializes the `theta` variable to $-\pi/2$. It sets `dtheta` to 2π divided by the polygon's number of sides. The loop can use that value to make `theta` cover 2π values as the program draws the polygon.

The code then loops over the polygon's sides. It uses `theta` to find the next vertex and then increases `theta` by `dtheta`.

After it generates the polygon's vertices, the program simply draws them to display the polygon.

To draw the star, the program loops through the polygon's points and draws a line between each point and the one that comes `Skip` positions later. The code uses the modulus operator `%` to ensure that the points' indices remain within the `points` array.

Download the `Stars` example solution to see additional details. If you experiment with the program, you'll find that it produces a disconnected star if the greatest common divisor of the number of polygon sides and the skip number lies between those values. In other words, if the polygon has P sides and the skip number is S, then the star is disconnected if $1 < GCD(P, S) < P$.

Summary

In this lesson, we covered the various problems to test our geometric programming skills and looked into the various algorithms and methods (programs) to solve these problems. In the next chapter, we will generate random numbers and perform various randomization tasks.

16
Randomization

This chapter deals with generating random numbers and other randomization tasks. Many other applications require random numbers or random selections. You've already seen some, such as the Monte Carlo simulations in Chapter 15, *Geometry*. Some of the solutions described in this chapter make generating and working with random numbers easier.

Problems

Use the following problems to test your skills at working with random numbers and randomization. Give each problem a try before you turn to the solutions and download the example programs.

22. Random doubles

The Random class provides three overloaded versions of its Next method; one that returns a random integer, one that returns an integer between zero and an upper limit, and one that returns an integer between lower and upper limits.

Strangely, the Random class provides only one version of its NextDouble method. That version returns a double value between 0.0 and 1.0.

Add a NextDouble extension method to the Random class to return a random double value between lower and upper bounds.

23. Random items

Add a RandomItem extension method to a generic array to return a randomly selected item from the array. Write a second extension method to do the same for a generic list of items.

24. Randomize items

Write `Randomize` extension methods to randomize the items in a generic array or list.

25. Random groups

Write `ChooseGroup` extension methods that pick a specified number of random items (without duplicates) from a generic array or list without modifying the original array or list.

26. Choose items with probabilities

Write extension methods that choose items from an array or list with given probabilities passed into the method in an array. For example, if the first item's probability is 0.1, then it should be picked roughly 10% of the time.

Write a program to test your methods by performing a large number of trials and displaying the percentage of times the different items were selected.

27. Random passwords

Write an extension method that generates random passwords. Parameters should indicate the minimum and maximum password length, and whether to allow or require lowercase letters, uppercase letters, numbers, special characters, or other, which includes characters entered by the user. Write a program similar to the one shown in the following screenshot to test your method:

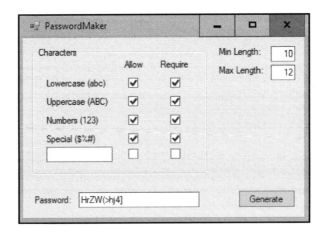

28. Random walks

A random walk is a path consisting of a series of random steps. Build a program that draws random walks similar to the one shown in the following screenshot:

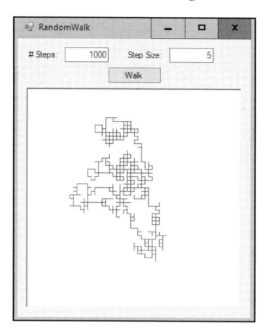

Solutions

You can download the example solutions to see additional details and to experiment with the programs at https://github.com/PacktPublishing/Improving-your-C-Sharp-Skills/tree/master/Chapter16

22. Random doubles

The following NextDouble extension method uses the Random class's existing NextDouble method to generate a double value within a range:

```
public static class RandomExtensions
{
    // A Random objects shared by all extensions.
    private static Random Rand = new Random();
```

```
// Return a double between minValue and maxValue.
public static double NextDouble(this Random rand,
    double minValue, double maxValue)
{
    return minValue + Rand.NextDouble() * (maxValue - minValue);
}
}
```

The RandomExtensions class creates a Random object at the class level. That object is static, so it is available to all extension methods defined in this class.

 If you create a new Random object without passing its constructor a seed value, the class uses the system's time to initialize the new object. If a method creates its own Random object and the main program calls that method many times very quickly, then some of the method calls' Random objects may be initialized with the same system time. That would make them all return the same sequence of *random* numbers, and that wouldn't be very random at all! That's why the RandomExtensions class uses a single static Random object for all of its methods.

The new version of the NextDouble method returns minValue plus a random value times maxValue - minValue. The random value lies between 0.0 and 1.0, so the result lies between minValue and maxValue.

Download the RandomDoubles example solution to see additional details.

23. Random items

The following extension method returns a random object from a generic array:

```
// Return a random object selected from the array.
public static T Random<T>(this T[] values)
{
    return values[Rand.Next(0, values.Length)];
}
```

The method uses the static `Random` object of the `RandomExtensions` class to pick a random index in the array.

The `Random` class's `Next` method returns an integer between an inclusive lower limit and an exclusive upper limit. In other words, the method returns a value, R, where *[lower limit]* ≤ R < *[upper limit]*. In this example, the call to `Next` returns a valid array index between zero and one less than the array's length.

The following code shows a similar method for picking a random item from a generic list:

```
// Return a random object selected from the list.
public static T Random<T>(this List<T> values)
{
    return values[Rand.Next(0, values.Count)];
}
```

Using these methods is easy. The `RandomItems` example solution uses the following two lines to pick random items from its `Animals` array and `Foods` list:

```
arrayItemTextBox.Text = Animals.Random();
listItemTextBox.Text = Foods.Random();
```

Download the `RandomItems` example solution to see additional details.

24. Randomize items

To randomize the items in an array, loop through the items. For each position `i`, pick a random position `j` with `j` ≥ `i` and swap items `i` and `j`.

After you swap an item into position `i`, you don't need to consider moving that item again later. This algorithm puts each item in any given position with an equal probability, at least as long as the random number generator is reasonably random.

The following code shows this algorithm implemented as a generic array extension method:

```
// Randomize the array in place.
public static void Randomize<T>(this T[] values)
{
    int numItems = values.Length;

    // Pick a random item for each position.
    for (int i = 0; i < numItems - 1; i++)
    {
        // Pick a later item to swap into position i.
        int j = Rand.Next(i, numItems);
```

```
        // Swap items i and j.
        T temp = values[i];
        values[i] = values[j];
        values[j] = temp;
    }
}
```

This code simply follows the algorithm. The exact same code also works for a generic list of items. The only difference is that the array method uses the array's Length property to get the number of items while the list version uses the list's Count property.

Using the extension methods is easy. The following code shows how the RandomizeItems example solution randomizes its FirstNames array and LastNames list:

```
FirstNames.Randomize();
LastNames.Randomize();
```

Download the RandomizeItems example solution to see additional details.

25. Random groups

This is slightly more complicated than it might initially appear, largely due to the requirement that we leave the original array or list unmodified. If it weren't for that requirement, you could simply randomize the array or list and then return the required number of items from the randomized values.

That won't work in this case, but it does suggest a simple workaround. Copy the original array or list, randomize the copy, and return the desired number of items. If the items are small, such as integers or references to objects, then that would be reasonable. However, if the items are large, such as large structures, then that would use a lot of memory.

The approach that I use is to make an array of indices. You can then randomize the indices and use them to pick the values to return. The following method demonstrates that approach:

```
// Pick the indicated number of random items.
public static T[] ChooseGroup<T>(this T[] values, int number)
{
    // Make an array holding indices 0, 1, 2, ..., numValues - 1.
    int numItems = values.Length;
    int[] indices = Enumerable.Range(0, numItems).ToArray();

    // Partly randomize the indices array.
    if (number > numItems) number = numItems;
```

```
for (int i = 0; i < number; i++)
{
    // Pick a later item to swap into position i.
    int j = Rand.Next(i, numItems);

    // Swap items i and j.
    int temp = indices[i];
    indices[i] = indices[j];
    indices[j] = temp;
}

// Build the result array.
T[] results = new T[number];
for (int i = 0; i < number; i++) results[i] = values[indices[i]];
return results;
}
```

The method gets the number of items in the array and then uses `Enumerable.Range` to make an array holding the values 0, 1, 2, and so on up to the array's last index.

The method then uses code similar to the code used by Solution 51, *Randomize items,* to randomize the beginning of the array of vertices. You could simply call the index array's `Randomize` extension method, but we don't need to randomize the entire array. This code only randomizes enough indices to return the desired number of items.

Next, the code creates a `results` array. It loops through the desired number of items, uses the corresponding indices to find the randomly selected items, and inserts them into the new array. When it has filled the `results` array, the method returns it.

The code to choose a group of random items from a list is very similar. The main difference is that you need to use the list's `Count` property to determine the number of items in the list.

In the example solution, I also made the list version of the method return a list of items instead of an array of items, mostly to show how you could do that.

Download the `RandomGroups` example solution to see additional details.

26. Choose items with probabilities

The following surprisingly simple method picks items from an array with given probabilities:

```
// Return a random value where the values have the indicated
// probabilities.
// The probabilities must add up to 1.0.
public static T PickWithProbability<T>(this T[] values,
    double[] probabilities)
{
    // Pick a random probability.
    double prob = Rand.NextDouble();

    // Find the selected item.
    for (int i = 0; i < values.Length; i++)
    {
        prob -= probabilities[i];
        if (prob <= 0) return values[i];
    }

    throw new Exception("Probabilities do not add up to 1.0");
}
```

The method uses the `Rand` object's `NextDouble` method to pick a `prob` value between `0.0` and `1.0`. It then loops through the probabilities, subtracting each from `prob`. When `prob` is less than or equal to zero, the method returns the item with the most recently subtracted probability.

Download the `ChooseItemsWithProbabilities` example solution to see additional details.

27. Random passwords

Handling all of this problem's requirements takes some time but is actually fairly easy if you use the randomization tools we've already built in this chapter. The following `RandomPassword` method generates a password:

```
// Make a random password.
private Random Rand = new Random();
private string RandomPassword(
    int minLength, int maxLength,
    bool allowLowercase, bool requireLowercase,
    bool allowUppercase, bool requireUppercase,
    bool allowDigit, bool requireDigit,
```

```
                 bool allowSpecial, bool requireSpecial,
                 bool allowOther, bool requireOther, string other)
{
            const string lowers = "abcdefghijklmnopqrstuvwxyz";
            const string uppers = "ABCDEFGHIJKLMNOPQRSTUVWXYZ";
            const string digits = "0123456789";
            const string specials = @"~!@#$%^&*():;[]{}<>,.?/\|";

            // Make a string containing all allowed characters.
            string allowed = "";
            if (allowLowercase) allowed += lowers;
            if (allowUppercase) allowed += uppers;
            if (allowDigit) allowed += digits;
            if (allowSpecial) allowed += specials
            if (allowOther) allowed += other;

            // Pick the number of characters.
            int passwordLength = Rand.Next(minLength, maxLength + 1);

            // Satisfy the requirements.
            string password = "";
            if (requireLowercase) password += lowers.ToCharArray().Random();
            if (requireUppercase) password += uppers.ToCharArray().Random();
            if (requireDigit) password += digits.ToCharArray().Random();
            if (requireSpecial) password += specials.ToCharArray().Random();
            if (requireOther) password += other.ToCharArray().Random();

            // Add the remaining characters randomly.
            while (password.Length < passwordLength)
                password += allowed.ToCharArray().Random();

            // Randomize so the required characters don't all appear at the
            // front.
            char[] chars = password.ToCharArray();
            chars.Randomize();

            return new string(chars);
}
```

The method begins with some strings that define lowercase letters, uppercase letters, digits, and special characters. It then uses its `allowed` Boolean parameters to build a single string that contains all of the allowed characters.

Next, the method uses the `Rand` object to pick a length for the password between `minLength` and `maxLength`. It then satisfies the character requirements.

If a type of character is required, the code calls the appropriate string's `ToCharArray` method, uses the `Random` extension method to randomly pick a character from the array, and adds it to the password.

After it has picked one character from each of the required character categories, the method picks random characters from the `allowed` string to fill out the password to its desired length.

At this point, the password satisfies the requirements and uses only allowed characters, but one of each of the required characters is at the beginning of the string so the password isn't truly random. In fact, if all of the character types are required, then you know that the password begins with the sequence—lowercase, uppercase, digit, special, and other.

To avoid that kind of pattern, the code converts the password into an array of characters and randomizes the array. It then uses the randomized characters to create a new string and returns that as the password.

Download the `PasswordMaker` example solution to see additional details.

28. Random walks

This problem is relatively straightforward. The example solution uses the following code to generate a random walk:

```
Random Rand = new Random();
Point[] Points = null;

// Generate a random walk.
private void walkButton_Click(object sender, EventArgs e)
{
    // Get parameters.
    int numSteps = int.Parse(numStepsTextBox.Text);
    int stepSize = int.Parse(stepSizeTextBox.Text);

    // Start in the center of the PictureBox.
    int x = walkPictureBox.ClientSize.Width / 2;
    int y = walkPictureBox.ClientSize.Height / 2;

    // Build the points.
    Points = new Point[numSteps];
    for (int i = 0; i < numSteps; i++)
    {
        Points[i] = new Point(x, y);
        switch (Rand.Next(0, 4))
```

```
    {
        case 0: // Up.
            y -= stepSize;
            break;
        case 1: // Right.
            x += stepSize;
            break;
        case 2: // Down.
            y += stepSize;
            break;
        case 3: // Left.
            x -= stepSize;
            break;
    }
}

// Redraw.
walkPictureBox.Refresh();
}
```

The code first creates a form-level `Random` object. It also defines a `Points` array and sets it to `null`.

When you click the **Walk** button, its event handler gets the number of steps and the size of each step that you entered in the text boxes. It positions the point (x, y) in the center of the `PictureBox` and then loops through the desired number of steps.

For each step, the code saves the point (x, y) in the `Points` array. It then uses the `Rand` object to randomly move (x, y) up, down, left, or right for the next point in the walk.

The method finishes by refreshing the `PictureBox`, which makes the following `Paint` event handler execute:

```
// Draw the walk.
private void walkPictureBox_Paint(object sender, PaintEventArgs e)
{
    if (Points == null) return;

    e.Graphics.Clear(walkPictureBox.BackColor);
    e.Graphics.DrawLines(Pens.Blue, Points);
}
```

If the `Points` array has not yet been created, the method simply exits. Otherwise, it clears the `PictureBox` and uses the `Graphics` object's `DrawLines` method to draw lines connecting the points that define the random walk.

Summary

In this chapter, we studied the various method for randomizing items. We saw the methods that can pick a specified number of random items from an array or list without modifying the original array or list. Then we studied the methods to create random passwords. In the next chapter, we will work with files and directories.

17
Files and Directories

This chapter describes problems that work with files and directories. Some merely provide practice on working with files and the filesystem. You may find others to be a welcome addition to your programming toolkit. For example, some examples show how to search for duplicate files, load an image file without locking it, and save JPG images with different levels of compression.

Note that working with files and directories can be particularly dangerous for a program because that are many ways those operations can fail. For example, a directory might not exist, a file might be locked, a program might not have permission to read or write in a particular directory, or a disk drive may be corrupted. The examples in this chapter use `try...catch` blocks to protect themselves from unexpected file and directory errors but, to save space, I have not included that error handling code in the text shown here. To see all of the programs' details, download the example solutions from this book's web page.

Also, note that some example solutions may take a long time to run depending on your system. For example, it may take a while to recursively search an entire 1 TB hard drive for files containing target text.

Problems

Use the following problems to test your skills at working with files and directories. Give each problem a try before you turn to the solutions and download the example programs.

29. Removing blank lines

Write a method that removes the blank lines from a file and returns the number of blank and nonblank lines in the original file. Write a program to test your method.

30. Directory size

Add an extension method to the `DirectoryInfo` class that returns the total size of the directory's files. Give the method an optional parameter indicating whether the method should include subdirectories. Write a program that uses your method to display a directory's size in bytes and file units, as in 24.1 KB.

31. Finding duplicate files

Write a program that searches a directory for duplicate files and displays any duplicates within the same branches of a `TreeView` control, as shown in the following screenshot:

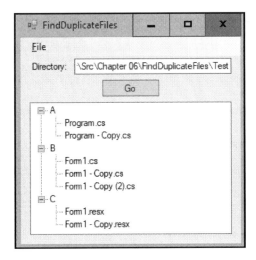

32. Thumbnails

Write a `MakeThumbnail` method that creates a thumbnail bitmap for an image file. Give it `maxWidth` and `maxHeight` parameters to indicate the thumbnail's size.

Use this method to write a program that searches a directory for image files and makes thumbnails for them all, saving the results in a `Thumbnails` subdirectory. Give the thumbnail files the same names as the original files with `thumbnail` added at the end, as in `MyPhoto thumbnail.bmp`.

33. Thumbnail web page

Modify the program you wrote for Problem *67. Thumbnails*, so that it also generates an HTML web page to display the thumbnail images. The page should use relative paths for the thumbnails and images. Clicking a thumbnail on the page should open the original image at full scale.

After it finishes building the thumbnails and web page, the program should display the page in the system's default web browser.

34. Find files

Add an extension method to the `DirectoryInfo` class that searches the directory for files. This method should take an `IEnumerable<string>` parameter, listing patterns that the files should match (such as `*.*` or `*.cs`), optional target text that the files should contain, and a parameter indicating whether the search should include subdirectories.

Write a program to test your method. It should use a `ComboBox` control to allow the user to enter or select a sequence of file-matching patterns separated by semi-colons. Make the program allow the user to enter a multiline target string.

35. Find and Replace

Modify the program you wrote for Problem *69. Find files*, so that it lets the user find and replace strings in files. When the user enters file-matching patterns and a target string and clicks **Find**, the program should display the matching files in a `CheckedListBox` control. If the user checks files and clicks **Replace**, the program should replace the target text with text entered in another text box in the selected files.

This is a dangerous operation because it modifies the selected files. Making the user select specific files for replacement helps prevent the program from modifying files that the user didn't know would be selected.

Because this is a potentially dangerous program, make sure to test it in a directory containing files that you don't mind losing, just in case, until you get the program working correctly.

36. Saving images

Write an extension method for the Image class named SaveImage that saves the image with an appropriate file format. For example, if the method's filename parameter has a .png extension, the method should save the image with the PNG format.

Write a program to test this method.

37. Compressing images

Write an extension method for the Image class named SaveCompressed that saves a JPG image with a specified level of compression. (Hint: Use an ImageCodecInfo object)

To test your method, write a program that lets the user open an image and then use a scrollbar to view the image at different compression levels. When the user changes the compression level, the program should display the compressed image, the compression level, and the compressed file's size. Let the user save the image into a new file at the currently selected compression level.

Solutions

The following sections describe solutions to the preceding problems. You can download the example solutions to see additional details and to experiment with the programs at https:/ /github.com/PacktPublishing/Improving-your-C-Sharp-Skills/tree/master/ Chapter17.

29. Removing blank lines

The following RemoveBlankLines method removes the blank lines from a file:

```
// Remove the empty lines from the indicated file.
private void RemoveBlankLines(string filename, out int numBlankLines,
    out int numNonBlankLines)
{
    // Read the file.
    string[] lines = File.ReadAllLines(filename);
    int totalLines = lines.Length;

    // Remove blank lines.
    List<string> nonblankLines = new List<string>();
```

```
        foreach (string line in lines)
            if (line.Trim().Length > 0)
                nonblankLines.Add(line);

        // Write the processed file.
        numNonBlankLines = nonblankLines.Count;
        numBlankLines = totalLines - numNonBlankLines;
        File.WriteAllLines(filename, nonblankLines.ToArray());
    }
```

This method uses the `File` class's `ReadAllLines` method to read the file's lines into an array of strings. It then creates a list to hold nonblank lines and loops through the array of lines.

The code calls each line's `Trim` method to remove whitespace from the line's ends. If the result is not blank, the code adds the original, non-trimmed line to the nonblank line list.

> The `Trim` method returns a copy of a string with whitespace removed from its ends; it does not modify the original string. That's important in this example so that the trimmed line isn't added to the nonblank lines list.

After it has processed all of the file's lines, the method calculates the number of blank and nonblank lines in the original file and writes the nonblank lines back into the original file.

Download the `RemoveBlankLines` example solution to see additional details.

30. Directory size

The following extension method returns the size of a directory's contents:

```
// Calculate the directory's size.
public static long Size(this DirectoryInfo dirinfo,
    bool includeSubdirs = false)
{
    // Get the files within the directory.
    FileInfo[] fileinfos;
    if (includeSubdirs)
        fileinfos = dirinfo.GetFiles("*", SearchOption.AllDirectories);
    else
        fileinfos = dirinfo.GetFiles("*",
          SearchOption.TopDirectoryOnly);
```

```
        // Add the file sizes.
        long size = 0;
        foreach (FileInfo fileinfo in fileinfos) size += fileinfo.Length;

        return size;
    }
```

This method calls the `DirectoryInfo` object's `GetFiles` method to get information on the files contained within the directory. Depending on the value of its `includeSubdirs` parameter, the method either tells `GetFiles` to consider only files directly contained in the directory or to consider files in the directory's subdirectories.

The method then simply loops through the returned files and adds their sizes. It finishes by returning the total file size.

Download the `DirectorySize` example solution to see additional details.

The program uses the following `ToFileSize` extension method to format value in file units as in 24.1 KB:

```
[DllImport("Shlwapi.dll", CharSet = CharSet.Auto)]
public static extern Int32 StrFormatByteSize(long fileSize,
    [MarshalAs(UnmanagedType.LPTStr)]
    StringBuilder buffer, int bufferSize);

// Use the StrFormatByteSize API function to convert
// a number of bytes into a file size.
public static string ToFileSize(this long fileSize)
{
    StringBuilder sb = new StringBuilder(20);
    StrFormatByteSize(fileSize, sb, 20);
    return sb.ToString();
}
```

This code imports the Windows `StrFormatByteSize` API function. The `ToFileSize` method simply uses that function to format a long value in file units and returns the result.

31. Finding duplicate files

One way to determine whether two files are identical is to compare the files byte-by-byte. The following method uses this approach to determine whether two files are identical:

```
// Return true if the files are identical.
public static bool FilesAreIdentical(FileInfo fileinfo1,
    FileInfo fileinfo2)
{
    byte[] bytes1 = File.ReadAllBytes(fileinfo1.FullName);
    byte[] bytes2 = File.ReadAllBytes(fileinfo2.FullName);
    if (bytes1.Length != bytes2.Length) return false;
    for (int i = 0; i < bytes1.Length; i++)
        if (bytes1[i] != bytes2[i]) return false;
    return true;
}
```

This method uses the `File` class's `ReadAllBytes` method to read the two files into byte arrays. If the arrays have different lengths, then the files are not identical, so the method returns `false`.

If the arrays have the same lengths, then the method loops through the arrays' bytes. If two corresponding bytes are different, the method again returns `false`.

If the method finishes its loop, all of the arrays' bytes are the same, so the method returns `true`.

Unfortunately, this method could be relatively slow, particularly if the files are large or if the directory holds many files. If the directory holds N files, then the program would have to use the method to compare N × (N - 1) pairs of files. For example, if N is 1,000, then the program would have to make 999,000 comparisons. If each of the comparisons is slow, this could take a while.

Fortunately, you can reduce the number of comparisons that you need to make by first comparing the files' sizes. If two files have the same size, they may not be identical, so you still need to compare them byte-by-byte, but if two files have different sizes, then you know for certain that they are different.

That's the approach taken by the example solution. It finds the files in the directory, sorts them by size, finds groups of files with matching sizes, and then examines those groups more closely to see which files are identical.

The following `GetSameSizedFiles` method searches a directory for groups of files that have the same sizes:

```
// Return lists of files with the same sizes.
// If a file is the only one of its size, do not include it.
public static List<List<FileInfo>> GetSameSizedFiles(
    this DirectoryInfo dirinfo)
{
    // Get the directory's files.
    FileInfo[] fileinfos = dirinfo.GetFiles();

    // Get the file sizes.
    long[] filesizes = new long[fileinfos.Length];
    for (int i = 0; i < fileinfos.Length; i++)
        filesizes[i] = fileinfos[i].Length;

    // Sort by file size.
    Array.Sort(filesizes, fileinfos);

    // Find groups of files with the same sizes.
    List<List<FileInfo>> groups = new List<List<FileInfo>>();
    int num = 1;
    while (num < fileinfos.Length)
    {
        if (fileinfos[num].Length != fileinfos[num - 1].Length)
            // No match. Move on to the next size.
            num++;
        else
        {
            // We have a match. Make a list of files with this size.
            List<FileInfo> files = new List<FileInfo>();
            groups.Add(files);
            files.Add(fileinfos[num - 1]);
            long length = fileinfos[num - 1].Length;
            while ((num < fileinfos.Length) &&
                    (fileinfos[num].Length == length))
            {
                files.Add(fileinfos[num++]);
            }
        }
    }
    return groups;
}
```

The method uses the `DirectoryInfo` class's `GetFiles` method to get the directory's files. It then creates an array holding the files' lengths and uses `Array.Sort` to sort the files by their sizes.

Next, the code creates a list of lists of `FileInfo` objects named `groups`. It then loops through the files looking for files that have the same size. Because the files are sorted by their sizes, any files with matching sizes will be adjacent in the `fileinfos` array.

When the code finds two files that have the same size, it creates a list named `files` and adds it to the list of lists named `groups`. It adds the files with the matching size and any other files that have the same size to the `files` list.

When it has finished examining all of the files, the method returns the `groups` list.

After calling the `GetSameSizedFiles` method, the program has lists of files with matching sizes. It still needs to examine files with matching sizes to see which are truly identical. The following `GetIdenticalFiles` method does that:

```
// Return lists of identical files.
public static List<List<FileInfo>> GetIdenticalFiles(
    this DirectoryInfo dirinfo)
{
    // Get lists of files that have the same sizes.
    List<List<FileInfo>> sameSizedFiles = dirinfo.GetSameSizedFiles();

    // Make a list to hold identical file lists.
    List<List<FileInfo>> results = new List<List<FileInfo>>();
    if (sameSizedFiles.Count == 0) return results;

    foreach (List<FileInfo> sizeGroup in sameSizedFiles)
    {
        while (sizeGroup.Count > 1)
        {
            // Make a list for the first file.
            List<FileInfo> identicalGroup = new List<FileInfo>();
            FileInfo fileinfo1 = sizeGroup[0];
            identicalGroup.Add(fileinfo1);
            identicalGroup.RemoveAt(0);

            // See if any other files should be in this group.
            for (int i = sizeGroup.Count - 1; i >= 0; i--)
            {
                if (FilesAreIdentical(fileinfo1, sizeGroup[i]))
                {
                    // The files are identical.
                    // Add the new one to the identical list.
                    identicalGroup.Add(sizeGroup[i]);
                    sizeGroup.RemoveAt(i);
                }
            }
        }
```

```
                    // See if this identical group is empty.
                    if (identicalGroup.Count > 1) results.Add(identicalGroup);
            }
        }

        // Return the identical groups.
        return results;
    }
```

This method calls the `GetSameSizedFiles` method to get the same-sized file lists. It then creates a new list of lists named `results` to hold the final lists of identical files.

Next, the code loops through lists of same-sized files. For each size list, the program enters a loop that continues until that size list is empty.

Inside the loop, the code saves the first item in the `fileinfo1` variable, adds it to a new `identicalGroup` list, and removes it from the size list. The method then loops through the other files in the list and compares them byte-by-byte to the file that it just removed. If a file is identical to the removed file, then the code adds it to the `identicalGroup` list and removes it from the same size list.

After it has finished looking for files that are identical to `fileinfo1`, the code examines the identical file list. If that list contains more than one file, it adds the list to the results. If the list contains only one file, then the method ignores it and it is discarded.

When it finishes examining all of the size lists, the method returns its results.

The final interesting piece in the example solution is the following `ProcessFiles` method:

```
// Process the files.
private void ProcessFiles()
{
    DirectoryInfo dirinfo = new DirectoryInfo(directoryTextBox.Text);
    List<List<FileInfo>> groups = dirinfo.GetIdenticalFiles();

    if (groups.Count == 0)
        filesTreeView.Nodes.Add("No identical files");
    else
    {
        char label = 'A';
        foreach (List<FileInfo> group in groups)
        {
            // Create a branch for this group.
            TreeNode branch =
             filesTreeView.Nodes.Add(label++.ToString());
```

```
            // Add the files.
            foreach (FileInfo fileinfo in group)
            {
                // Display the file's name.
                TreeNode node = branch.Nodes.Add(fileinfo.Name);

                // Save the FileInfo in case we want it later.
                node.Tag = fileinfo;
            }
        }
        filesTreeView.ExpandAll();
    }
}
```

This method creates a `DirectoryInfo` object for the directory entered by the user and then calls that object's `GetIdenticalFiles` extension method. If the result contains no groups of identical files, the program displays a message inside its `TreeView` control.

Otherwise, if there are groups of identical files, the code loops through them. For each group, the method adds a branch to the `TreeView`. It then loops through the `FileInfo` objects in the group and adds their file names to the new branch.

 The code also saves the files' `FileInfo` objects in the new nodes' `Tag` properties in case the program needs them later. For example, you could modify the program to let the user right-click on a branch to delete its file. The program would use the `Tag` property to determine which file should be deleted.

Download the `FindDuplicateFiles` example solution to see additional details.

32. Thumbnails

The following `MakeThumbnail` extension method creates a thumbnail file for an image:

```
// Make a thumbnail for the file with maximum
// dimensions maxWidth x maxHeight.
private Bitmap MakeThumbnail(string filename, int maxWidth,
    int maxHeight)
{
    // Load the image.
    Bitmap bm = LoadImageWithoutLocking(filename);

    // Calculate the scale.
    float xscale = maxWidth / (float)bm.Width;
    float yscale = maxHeight / (float)bm.Height;
```

```
        float scale = Math.Min(xscale, yscale);

        // Make the thumbnail's bitmap.
        int width = (int)Math.Round(bm.Width * scale);
        int height = (int)Math.Round(bm.Height * scale);
        Bitmap thumbnail = new Bitmap(width, height);
        using (Graphics gr = Graphics.FromImage(thumbnail))
        {
            gr.InterpolationMode = InterpolationMode.High;

            Rectangle srcRect = new Rectangle(0, 0, bm.Width, bm.Height);
            Point[] destPoints =
            {
                    new Point(0, 0),
                    new Point(width, 0),
                    new Point(0, height),
                };
            gr.DrawImage(bm, destPoints, srcRect, GraphicsUnit.Pixel);
        }

        return thumbnail;
    }
```

This method first calls the `LoadImageWithoutLocking` method, which is described shortly, to load the image file without locking it. The code then calculates vertical and horizontal scales that it could use to resize the image so that it has the maximum allowed thumbnail width or height. It picks the smaller of the two scales to be the one that it will use so that the resulting thumbnail fits within the allowed bounds and is not stretched out of shape.

Next, the method calculates the image's scaled dimensions and creates a `Bitmap` of that size. It creates an associated `Graphics` object and sets that object's `InterpolationMode` property so that the image is resized smoothly.

The method defines a source rectangle that covers the entire original image. It then creates a destination array of `Point` structures that cover the area of the thumbnail bitmap. Finally, the code calls the `Graphics` object's `DrawImage` method to copy the original image onto the bitmap and returns the result.

Normally, if you load a `Bitmap` object from a file, the program keeps the file locked so that it can use it if necessary to redraw the image. This can be inconvenient if you want to edit or delete the image file while your program is displaying the image.

In this program, this may seem like a non-issue because the `MakeThumbnail` method does not need to redraw the original images. When the method ends, the `Bitmap` objects that it created leave the program so they are destroyed and they unlock their files.

Unfortunately, C# does not necessarily destroy `Bitmap` objects immediately. They may hang around, keeping their files locked, until the garbage collector runs and frees their resources.

One solution is to call the `Bitmap` objects' `Dispose` methods or to place them inside `using` blocks so that the `Dispose` method is called automatically. This example uses a different approach. It uses the following method to open the image files:

```
// Load an image file without locking it.
private Bitmap LoadImageWithoutLocking(string filename)
{
    using (Bitmap bm = new Bitmap(filename))
    {
        return new Bitmap(bm);
    }
}
```

This code opens the image file, placing the `Bitmap` in a `using` block. It then makes a new `Bitmap` from the first bitmap and returns it. The new `Bitmap` contains a copy of the original object's data, but doesn't need the original image file to draw itself.

When the `using` block ends, the original `Bitmap` is disposed, so its resources are freed and its image file is unlocked.

The next major piece in the example is the following `ProcessFiles` method:

```
// Process the files.
private void ProcessFiles()
{
    // Get the input parameters.
    string dirname = directoryTextBox.Text;
    int thumbWidth = int.Parse(widthTextBox.Text);
    int thumbHeight = int.Parse(heightTextBox.Text);

    // Graphic file name patterns.
    string[] patterns = { "*.png", "*.bmp", "*.jpg", "*.jpeg",
        "*.gif" };

    // Make a list of the directory's image files.
    List<string> filenames = new List<string>();
    foreach (string pattern in patterns)
        filenames.AddRange(Directory.GetFiles(dirname, pattern));
```

```
        // Compose the thumbnail directory's name.
        string thumbdir = Path.Combine(dirname, "Thumbnails");

        // Create an empty thumbnail directory.
        EmptyDirectory(thumbdir);
        Directory.CreateDirectory(thumbdir);

        // Process the files.
        foreach (string filename in filenames)
        {
            Bitmap bm = MakeThumbnail(filename, thumbWidth, thumbHeight);
            string thumbname = Path.Combine(thumbdir,
                Path.GetFileNameWithoutExtension(filename)) +
                " thumb.bmp";
            bm.Save(thumbname);
        }
        numCreatedLabel.Text = $"Created {filenames.Count} thumbnails";
    }
```

This code gets the directory name, width, and height entered by the user. It then creates an array holding image file extensions and loops through that array.

For each extension, the method calls the `Directory` class's `GetFiles` method to get files that have the extension and adds the returned file names to the `filenames` list.

Next, the code uses `Path.Combine` to create the name of the thumbnail directory inside the image directory. The code calls the `EmptyDirectory` method, which is described shortly, to remove any files from that directory and then uses the `Directory` class's `CreateDirectory` method to create the directory if it doesn't already exist.

Now, the method loops through the image files, calls `MakeThumbnail` for each, and saves the resulting bitmaps in the thumbnail directory.

The final interesting piece of code in this example is the following `EmptyDirectory` method:

```
        // Delete the files in this directory.
        // Hide errors if the directory doesn't exist.
        private void EmptyDirectory(string dirname)
        {
            DirectoryInfo dirinfo = new DirectoryInfo(dirname);
            if (!dirinfo.Exists) return;

            foreach (FileInfo fileinfo in dirinfo.GetFiles())
        fileinfo.Delete();
        }
```

This method creates a `DirectoryInfo` object for the directory. If the directory exists, the method then loops through the directory's files and deletes them.

Download the `Thumbnails` example solution to see additional details.

33. Thumbnail web page

This solution is similar to the preceding solution. The main differences lie in the `ProcessFiles` method. The following code shows this method with the differences highlighted:

```
// Process the files.
private void ProcessFiles()
{
    // Get the input parameters.
    string dirname = directoryTextBox.Text;
    int thumbWidth = int.Parse(widthTextBox.Text);
    int thumbHeight = int.Parse(heightTextBox.Text);

    // Graphic file name patterns.
    string[] patterns = { "*.png", "*.bmp", "*.jpg", "*.jpeg",
        "*.gif" };

    // Make a list of the directory's image files.
    List<string> filenames = new List<string>();
    foreach (string pattern in patterns)
        filenames.AddRange(Directory.GetFiles(dirname, pattern));

    // Compose the thumbnail directory's name.
    string thumbdir = Path.Combine(dirname, "Thumbnails");

    // Create an empty thumbnail directory.
    EmptyDirectory(thumbdir);
    Directory.CreateDirectory(thumbdir);

    // Start the web page.
    StringBuilder sb = new StringBuilder();
    sb.AppendLine("<html>");
    sb.AppendLine("<body>");

    // Process the files.
    foreach (string filename in filenames)
    {
        // Create the thumbnail.
        Bitmap bm = MakeThumbnail(filename, thumbWidth, thumbHeight);
        string thumbname = Path.Combine(thumbdir,
```

```
                    Path.GetFileNameWithoutExtension(filename)) +
                " thumb.bmp";
            bm.Save(thumbname);

            // Add an entry to the web page.
            FileInfo fileinfo = new FileInfo(filename);
            string bigFilename = Path.Combine("..", fileinfo.Name);
            FileInfo thumbinfo = new FileInfo(thumbname);
            string thumbFilename = thumbinfo.Name;
            sb.AppendLine("  <a href=\"" + bigFilename + "\">" +
                "<img src=\"" + thumbFilename + "\">" +
                "</a>");
        }
        sb.AppendLine("</body>");
        sb.AppendLine("</html>");

        // Write the web page.
        string webFilename = Path.Combine(thumbdir, "Thumbnails.html");
        File.WriteAllText(webFilename, sb.ToString());

        // Display the web page in the system's default browser.
        System.Diagnostics.Process.Start(webFilename);

        numCreatedLabel.Text = $"Created {filenames.Count} thumbnails";
    }
```

The method begins as the previous version did. It then creates a `StringBuilder` to hold the web page and adds `<html>` and `<body>` elements to it.

The code then creates the thumbnails as before. For each thumbnail, it also adds a new line to the web page with the following format:

```
<a href="..\banner.png"><img src="banner thumb.bmp"></a>
```

This is a link to the `banner.png` file in the current directory's parent directory. The link displays the picture in the `banner thumb.bmp` file inside the current directory.

After it processes all of the files, the method adds the closing `</body>` and `</html>` elements and writes the `StringBuilder` contents into the web page file.

The final new piece of the method is the following statement:

```
System.Diagnostics.Process.Start(webFilename);
```

This statement makes the system open the file named `webFilename`. The system opens the file with the default program associated with that type of file. This file's name ends with the .html extension, so the system opens it with its default web browser.

You might prefer to display the new web page within the program in a WebBrowser control. Unfortunately, that control seems to be unable to work with relative image paths such as banner thumb.bmp, so it cannot correctly display this web page. You could modify the code to use absolute paths to the image files, but then the web page would be less useful on an actual website.

Download the ThumbnailWebPage example solution to see additional details.

34. Find files

The following extension method searches a directory for files that match a list of patterns:

```
// Find files that match any of the indicated patterns.
// Do not include duplicates and return the files sorted.
public static FileInfo[] GetFiles(this DirectoryInfo dirinfo,
    IEnumerable<string> patterns,
    SearchOption option = SearchOption.TopDirectoryOnly)
{
    // Find files matching the patterns.
    Dictionary<string, FileInfo> fileDict =
        new Dictionary<string, FileInfo>()

    foreach (string pattern in patterns)
    {
        foreach (FileInfo fileinfo in dirinfo.GetFiles(pattern,
         option))
        {
            if (!fileDict.ContainsKey(fileinfo.FullName))
                fileDict.Add(fileinfo.FullName, fileinfo);
        }
    }

    // Sort and return.
    FileInfo[] fileinfos = fileDict.Values.ToArray();
    string[] filenames = fileDict.Keys.ToArray();
    Array.Sort(filenames, fileinfos);
    return fileinfos;
}
```

The method starts by making a dictionary to hold the files that it finds. Dictionaries are handy for quickly determining whether you have already found something that should be saved only once.

The code then loops through the patterns and calls the `DirectoryInfo` object's `GetFiles` method to find files that match each pattern. It loops through the returned files and adds those that have not already been found to the dictionary. This prevents the method from listing the same file twice case it matches more than one pattern.

After it finishes gathering the files, the code extracts the dictionary's values (the `FileInfo` objects) and keys (the filenames) into arrays. The items in a dictionary are not stored in any particular order, but its `Values` and `Keys` collections do return their contents in the same order, so corresponding items in the arrays go together.

The method sorts the `FileInfo` objects using the filenames as keys and returns the result.

The following method uses the `GetFiles` method to search for files that match patterns and that contain target text:

```
// Find files that match any of the indicated patterns and
// that contain the target string. Do not include duplicates
// and return the files sorted.
public static FileInfo[] FindFiles(this DirectoryInfo dirinfo,
    IEnumerable<string> patterns, string target = "",
    SearchOption option = SearchOption.TopDirectoryOnly)
{
    // Find files matching the patterns.
    FileInfo[] fileinfos = dirinfo.GetFiles(patterns, option);

    // See if we should examine the files' contents.
    if ((target != null) && (target.Length > 0))
    {
        // See which files contain the required contents.
        List<FileInfo> newFiles = new List<FileInfo>();
        foreach (FileInfo fileinfo in fileinfos)
        {
            string text = File.ReadAllText(fileinfo.FullName);
            if (text.Contains(target)) newFiles.Add(fileinfo);
        }
        fileinfos = newFiles.ToArray();
    }

    return fileinfos;
}
```

This method calls the previous `GetFiles` method to get an array of `FileInfo` objects representing files that match the indicated patterns.

Then, if `target` is nonblank, the method loops through the files. For each file, the code uses `File.ReadAllText` to get the file's contents and uses `IndexOf` to see if the text contains the target string. If the file contains `target`, the code adds the file to its result list.

After it has checked every file, the method returns the files that it found.

The only remaining code of any real interest in this program is the following snippet, which converts patterns entered by the user into an array of pattern strings:

```
// Get the patterns.
string patternsString = patternsComboBox.Text;
if (patternsString.Contains(':'))
    patternsString =
        patternsString.Substring(
            patternsString.IndexOf(':') + 1).Trim();
string[] patterns = patternsString.Trim().Split(
    new char[] { ';' }, StringSplitOptions.RemoveEmptyEntries);
for (int i = 0; i < patterns.Length; i++)
    patterns[i] = patterns[i].Trim();
```

This code assumes that the pattern has a format similar to the following:

```
C# Files: *.cs; *.sln; *.resx; *.config
```

If the string contains a colon, the code takes only the characters following it, so it removes the `C# Files:` part of the preceding example. The code then uses the string class's `Split` method to separate the string at the semi-colon characters. It finishes by looping through the patterns and calling their `Trim` methods to remove whitespace from their ends.

The rest of the example solution is relatively straightforward. Download the `FindFiles` example solution to see additional details.

35. Find and Replace

The parts of this program that actually find files and make replacements are relatively straightforward. The following code shows how the example solution searches for files:

```
// Search the directory.
private void findButton_Click(object sender, EventArgs e)
{
    Cursor = Cursors.WaitCursor;
    filesCheckedListBox.DataSource = null;
    Refresh();

    // Get the patterns.
```

```
        string patternsString = patternsComboBox.Text;
        if (patternsString.Contains(':'))
            patternsString =
                patternsString.Substring(
                    patternsString.IndexOf(':') + 1).Trim();

        string[] patterns = patternsString.Trim().Split(
            new char[] { ';' }, StringSplitOptions.RemoveEmptyEntries);

        // Find files matching the patterns and containing the target text.
        DirectoryInfo dirinfo = new DirectoryInfo(directoryTextBox.Text);
        FileInfo[] fileinfos = dirinfo.FindFiles(patterns,
            targetTextBox.Text, SearchOption.AllDirectories);

        // List the files.
        filesCheckedListBox.DataSource = fileinfos;

        Cursor = Cursors.Default;
    }
```

This code separates the user's selected file patterns, as in the preceding solution. Next, it creates a DirectoryInfo object and calls its FindFiles extension method to find matching files. It then simply displays the results in the CheckedListBox named filesCheckedListBox.

The following code shows how the program makes replacements in the files that are checked in the CheckedListBox:

```
        // Replace the target text with the replacement text in
        // the selected files.
        private void replaceButton_Click(object sender, EventArgs e)
        {
            string changeFrom = targetTextBox.Text;
            string changeTo = replaceWithTextBox.Text;
            int numReplacements = 0;
            foreach (FileInfo fileinfo in filesCheckedListBox.CheckedItems)
            {
                MakeReplacement(fileinfo, changeFrom, changeTo);
                numReplacements++;
            }
            MessageBox.Show("Made replacements in " +
                numReplacements.ToString() + " files.");

            // Clear the file list.
            filesCheckedListBox.DataSource = null;
        }
```

This code gets the target and replacement strings. It then loops through the checked files and calls the `MakeReplacement` method, which is described shortly, for each. The code finishes by displaying the number of files that were modified.

The following code shows the `MakeReplacement` method:

```
// Replace changeFrom to changedTo in the file.
private void MakeReplacement(FileInfo fileinfo, string changeFrom,
    string changeTo)
{
    string file = File.ReadAllText(fileinfo.FullName);
    file = file.Replace(changeFrom, changeTo);
    File.WriteAllText(fileinfo.FullName, file);
}
```

This method uses `File.ReadAllText` to read the file's contents. It uses the string class's `Replace` method to make the replacement and then uses `File.WriteAllText` to save the result back into the file.

Download the `FindAndReplace` example solution to see additional details.

36. Saving images

The following extension method saves an image with an appropriate file format:

```
// Save an image in a file with format determined by its extension.
public static void SaveImage(this Image image, string filename)
{
    // Check the extension to see what kind of file this should be.
    string extension = Path.GetExtension(filename);
    switch (extension.ToLower())
    {
        case ".bmp":
            image.Save(filename, ImageFormat.Bmp);
            break;
        case ".exif":
            image.Save(filename, ImageFormat.Exif);
            break;
        case ".gif":
            image.Save(filename, ImageFormat.Gif);
            break;
        case ".jpg":
        case ".jpeg":
            image.Save(filename, ImageFormat.Jpeg);
            break;
```

```
            case ".png":
                image.Save(filename, ImageFormat.Png);
                break;
            case ".tif":
            case ".tiff":
                image.Save(filename, ImageFormat.Tiff);
                break;
            default:
                throw new NotSupportedException(
                    "Unsupported file extension " + extension);
        }
    }
```

This method uses the `Path.GetExtension` method to get the filename's extension. It then uses a `switch` statement to take different actions depending on the extension.

The `switch` statement's `case` blocks call the image's `Save` method, passing it the filename and a parameter, indicating the correct file format for the extension.

The example solution displays an image, text box, and **Save** button. When you enter a filename and click the button, the following code saves the image with the filename that you entered:

```
// Save the image in the appropriate format.
private void saveButton_Click(object sender, EventArgs e)
{
    pictureBox1.Image.SaveImage(filenameTextBox.Text);
    filenameTextBox.Clear();
    filenameTextBox.Focus();
}
```

This code simply calls the `SaveImage` extension method to save the image with the desired filename.

If you open the files in MS Paint or some other image editor, you should be able to see the characteristics of the desired formats. For example, PNG files use lossless compression, JPG files use lossy compression, and GIF files use dithering. You can also use File Explorer to see that some formats are compressed more effectively than others.

This method can be a handy part of your image processing toolkit because it prevents you from saving an image in the wrong format. For example, it prevents you from accidentally saving an image in the `Smiley.bmp` file with the PNG file format.

Download the example solution to see additional details.

37. Compressing images

One of the key pieces of this solution is the following extension method, which saves an image in JPG format with a specified compression level:

```
// Save a JPG file with the indicated compression level.
public static void SaveCompressed(this Image image, string filename,
    int compressionLevel)
{
    // Make an object to hold one encoder parameter.
    EncoderParameters parameters = new EncoderParameters(1);

    // Place the compression level in that parameter.
    parameters.Param[0] = new EncoderParameter(
        System.Drawing.Imaging.Encoder.Quality, compressionLevel);

    // Get the JPG codec.
    ImageCodecInfo codecInfo = GetEncoderInfo("image/jpeg");

    // Create the file, deleting it if it already exists.
    if (File.Exists(filename)) File.Delete(filename);
    image.Save(filename, codecInfo, parameters);
}
```

This method first creates an `EncoderParameters` object to hold a single parameter, which will be used by an image encoder. It sets that parameter's category to `Quality` and sets its value to the desired compression level.

The `Quality` parameter uses a fully qualified namespace because without that there would be ambiguity between `System.Drawing.Imaging.Encoder` and `System.Text.Encoder`.

The `Quality` parameter's value should be between 0 (the most compression) and 100 (the least compression).

Next, the code creates codec information for the `image/jpeg` mime type.

A **codec**, which is short for **coder decoder**, is a program or object that encodes and decodes a stream of data. In this example, it encodes and decodes JPG files.

MIME stands for **Multipurpose Internet Mail Extensions**. As I'm sure you can guess, `image/jpg` is the mime type for image files in the JPG format.

If the file already exists, the method deletes it. It then calls the image's Save method, passing it the ImageCodecInfo object and EncoderParameter to tell it the compression level.

The following code fragment shows how the program uses the SaveCompressed method:

```
// The name of the temporary file.
private static string tempfile = "__temp.jpg";
...
// Process a newly loaded file.
private void ProcessFile(Image image)
{
    if (image == null) return;

    // Save the original image.
    OriginalImage = image;

    // Save the image in a temporary file with
    // the current compression level.
    image.SaveCompressed(tempfile, compressionScrollbar.Value);

    // Reload the file.
    compressedPictureBox.Image = LoadImageWithoutLocking(tempfile);

    // Display the file compression level.
    compressionLabel.Text = compressionScrollbar.Value.ToString();

    // Display the file's size.
    FileInfo fileinfo = new FileInfo(tempfile);
    fileSizeLabel.Text = fileinfo.Length.ToFileSize();
}
```

This method stores the image in the OriginalImage variable so that it can retrieve the original image later. It then calls the SaveCompressed method to save the image in a temporary file at the level of compression selected by the compressionScrollbar control. The code then reloads the image from the file and displays it in the compressedPictureBox control. The result shows the image in its compressed form.

The method finishes by displaying the compressed file's size in a label so that you can see how much space the file occupies.

Download the CompressImages example solution to see additional details.

Summary

In this chapter, we came across various methods used to perform various operations on files and directories such as removing blank lines from a file, calculating the total size of directory files and finding duplicate files in a directory. We created thumbnails files for images and acquainted ourselves with methods to find files in a directory. In the next chapter, we shall have a look at some advanced C# features.

Advanced C# and .NET Features

18

This chapter describes problems that use some of the C# language's more advanced features. Unfortunately, C# has too many capabilities, so we can't cover them all here. The particular features described here include some parts of LINQ, PLINQ, TPL, the `yield` statement, and operator overloading.

 LINQ stands for **Language Integrated Query**, **PLINQ** stands for **Parallel LINQ**, and TPL stands for **Task Parallel Library**.

These techniques provide new ways to simplify program structure and improve performance. Even if you don't use them on a daily basis, it's useful to know how they work so that you can understand other peoples' code when you see these techniques.

Problems

Use the following problems to test your skills at working with advanced C# language features. Give each problem a try before you turn to the solutions and download the example programs.

38. Directory size, LINQ style

Repeat Problem 30. *Directory size*. This time, add a `SizeLINQ` extension method to the `DirectoryInfo` class that uses LINQ to calculate the size of the files inside the directory.

39. Directory size, PLINQ style

Repeat Problem 39. *Directory size, LINQ style*, but this time use PLINQ to add file lengths in parallel. Make the test program perform the same operations using a `foreach` loop, LINQ, and PLINQ, and display the elapsed time for each. Let the user enter a number of times to repeat each operation so that you can get some meaningful times.

 Repeating each operation multiple times limits the time used by disk accesses because the file information should be cached after the first set of calculations.

40. Find files, LINQ style

Repeat Problem 34. *Find files*. This time, give the `DirectoryInfo` class a `FindFilesLINQ` extension method that uses a LINQ query to search for files.

41. Parallel Monte Carlo π

Repeat Problem 1. *Monte Carlo π*, using TPL to perform trials in parallel. Compare the speeds of the parallel and non-parallel methods.

42. Yielding primes

Write a method that uses the `yield` statement to return a specific number of prime numbers. Make the test program display those primes in a `foreach` loop.

43. Yielding Fibonacci numbers

Write a program similar to the one you built for Problem *42. Yielding primes,* but this time make it yield Fibonacci numbers. Make the method yield all of the Fibonacci numbers that it can.

44. Complex numbers

The `System.Numerics` namespace has included the `Complex` structure to represent complex numbers since C# 4.0. Building something similar demonstrates so many useful techniques that it's still worth creating your own version. For this problem, create a `ComplexNumber` structure that has the following features:

- `Re` and `Im` properties that get and set the number's real and imaginary parts
- A `FromPolar` factory method that creates a `ComplexNumber` from a polar coordinate representation
- Static values representing 0, 1, and i
- `ToString` and `Parse` methods that translate a value to and from a string with the format x + yi
- Implementation of the `IEquatable` interface
- An overloaded `Equals` method that determines whether two values are equal with a given precision
- Read-only `Magnitude` and `Angle` properties to get the number's polar coordinate representation
- Operators that convert from a `double` implicitly and to a `double` explicitly
- Arithmetic operators that let you perform addition, subtraction, multiplication, division, and negation with `ComplexNumber` and numeric values

A **factory method** is a method that creates an instance of a class. Usually, it is a static method, so you don't need an instance of the class to invoke it. In this problem, the `FromPolar` method should take the polar coordinates r and θ as parameters and return an appropriate new `ComplexNumber` structure.

If you are unfamiliar with complex numbers or with their polar representation, see `en.wikipedia.org/wiki/Complex_number` or `http://mathworld.wolfram.com/ComplexNumber.html`, or search the web for Complex Numbers.

Hint: Use the following equation to divide two complex numbers:

$$\frac{a + bi}{c + di} = \frac{(ac + bd) + i(bc - ad)}{c^2 + d^2}$$

Write a test program that verifies the `ComplexNumber` class's features.

Solutions

The following sections describe solutions to the preceding problems. You can download the example solutions to see additional details and to experiment with the programs at `https://github.com/PacktPublishing/Improving-your-C-Sharp-Skills/tree/master/Chapter18`.

38. Directory size, LINQ style

Both this solution and Solution *30. Directory size,* use the `DirectoryInfo` class's `GetFiles` method to make an array holding `FileInfo` objects that represent the files contained within the directory. The previous solution then used the following code to add the files' sizes:

```
// Add the file sizes.
long size = 0;
foreach (FileInfo fileinfo in fileinfos) size += fileinfo.Length;
return size;
```

This code loops through `FileInfo` objects and adds their file lengths to the `size` variable.

The new `SizeLINQ` extension method uses the following code to perform the same task:

```
// Add the file sizes.
var sizeQuery =
    from FileInfo fileinfo in fileinfos
    select fileinfo.Length;
return sizeQuery.Sum();
```

This version creates a LINQ query that loops through the `FileInfo` objects and selects their `Length` values. The program then invokes the query's `Sum` LINQ extension method to add the selected length values.

Which version you should use is largely a matter of personal preference. LINQ programs are often slower than other methods because they don't take advantage of any special structure that's available in the data. In this example, however, the time needed to calculate a directory's size is dominated by the time it takes to access the disk, not the time needed to process the results. In one set of tests, the LINQ version of this program took only a little while longer than the non-LINQ version.

What this means is that, in cases like this where LINQ has a negligible performance impact, you should pick whichever approach makes the code easier for you to read and understand.

Download the `DirectorySizeLINQ` example solution to see additional details.

39. Directory size, PLINQ style

Turning a LINQ query into a PLINQ query is usually quite simple. The following code shows the `SizePLINQ` extension method. The difference between this version and the LINQ version is highlighted in bold:

```
// Use PLINQ to calculate the directory's size.
public static long SizePLINQ(this DirectoryInfo dirinfo,
    bool includeSubdirs = false)
{
    // Get the files within the directory.
    FileInfo[] fileinfos;
    if (includeSubdirs)
        fileinfos = dirinfo.GetFiles("*", SearchOption.AllDirectories);
    else
        fileinfos = dirinfo.GetFiles("*",
          SearchOption.TopDirectoryOnly);
```

```
        // Add the file sizes.
        var sizeQuery =
            from FileInfo fileinfo in fileinfos.AsParallel()
            select fileinfo.Length;
        return sizeQuery.Sum();
}
```

The only difference between the PLINQ and LINQ versions is that the PLINQ version adds `.AsParallel()` to the `from` clause. That makes the query system perform loop iterations in parallel.

Unfortunately, the query simply selects the `FileInfo` objects' `Length` values. That is a relatively fast operation, so selecting those values in parallel doesn't save much time. In fact, the extra overhead needed to execute the loop in parallel and then use the `Sum` method to combine the results makes this version of the program slower.

The following screenshot shows a typical run by the example solution. If you look closely, you'll see that the LINQ version runs slightly more slowly than the `foreach` version, and the PLINQ version runs even more slowly:

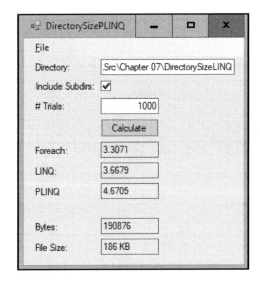

The moral of the story is that PLINQ can hurt performance unless the tasks it performs are naturally parallelizable.

Download the `DirectorySizePLINQ` example solution to see additional details.

40. Find files, LINQ style

Before I describe the new example solution, let's recap how Solution 34. *Find files,* handled this problem. That solution added a `GetFiles` extension method to the `DirectoryInfo` class. The method looped through a list of patterns, calling `GetFiles` for each to find the files matching each pattern. It added the returned files to a dictionary so that it could easily determine whether it had already found a file. After finding the files, the method extracted the dictionary's keys and values, sorted them, and returned the sorted files.

The `FindFiles` extension method called `GetFiles` to find files matching its patterns. It then looped through the files, read each with `File.ReadAllText`, and used the string class's `Contains` method to see if a particular file contained the target text. It added the files containing the target text to a list and, when it had checked every file, returned the list.

The following code shows the LINQ version:

```
// Find files that match any of the indicated patterns and that
// contain the target string.
// Do not include duplicates and return the files sorted.
public static FileInfo[] FindFilesLINQ(this DirectoryInfo dirinfo,
    IEnumerable<string> patterns, string target = "",
    SearchOption option = SearchOption.TopDirectoryOnly)
{
    // Find files that match the patterns.
    var fileQuery =
        from string pattern in patterns
        from FileInfo fileinfo in dirinfo.GetFiles(pattern, option)
        group fileinfo by fileinfo.FullName
        into namegroup
        select namegroup.First();

    // If target isn't blank, select files that contain it.
    if ((target != null) && (target.Length > 0))
        fileQuery =
            from FileInfo fileinfo in fileQuery
            where File.ReadAllText(fileinfo.FullName).Contains(target)
            select fileinfo;

    // Take distinct values, sort, and return as an array.
    return fileQuery.OrderBy(x => x.Name).ToArray();
}
```

This method creates a LINQ query that loops through the file patterns and calls GetFiles to find the files that match each of them. If a file matches more than one pattern, then the result may contain the same file multiple times. To handle this situation, the query groups FileInfo objects by file name. The query finishes by selecting the first FileInfo from each group.

Next, if the target string is nonblank, the code creates a second query that loops through the selected files, uses File.ReadAllText to read each file, and then uses Contains to see if a file contains the target string.

After setting up the query, the method invokes its OrderBy method to sort the results by the files' names. It converts the result into an array and returns it.

Again, the version that you should use depends on your preferences. The LINQ version is undoubtedly shorter than the two methods used by the non-LINQ version, but LINQ queries are fairly complex. You should pick the version that suits you best.

Note that you can also mix LINQ and non-LINQ operations. For example, you could use the first query without the group clause, use C# code to remove duplicate entries, and then feed the result into the final query.

 As was the case in Solution *39. Directory size, PLINQ style*, PLINQ is unlikely to make these queries run faster. The limiting factor will be the speed of the disk accesses, and PLINQ just adds extra overhead, which will slow things down.

Download the FindFilesLINQ example solution to see additional details.

41. Parallel Monte Carlo π

This example solution uses the same approach used by the preceding solution. It uses form-level variables to pass information to the parallel instances of a method. Those instances perform calculations and then use locking to save their results to the form-level variables.

The following code shows the form-level variables:

```
private int NumHits = 0;
private object LockObject = new object();
private int MonteCarloWidth = 0, MonteCarloHeight = 0;
private Bitmap MonteCarloBitmap = null;
private const int PointsPerCall = 10000;
```

The following method starts the parallel execution:

```
// Use Monte Carlo simulation to estimate pi.
private double MonteCarloPi(int numPoints)
{
    // Make a bitmap to show points.
    MonteCarloWidth = pointsPictureBox.ClientSize.Width;
    MonteCarloHeight = pointsPictureBox.ClientSize.Height;
    MonteCarloBitmap = new Bitmap(MonteCarloWidth, MonteCarloWidth);
    using (Graphics gr = Graphics.FromImage(MonteCarloBitmap))
    {
        gr.Clear(Color.White);
        gr.DrawEllipse(Pens.Black, 0, 0,
            MonteCarloWidth - 1, MonteCarloWidth - 1);
    }

    // Make the random points.
    NumHits = 0;
    int numMethods = numPoints / PointsPerCall;
    Parallel.For(0, numMethods, TestPoint);

    // Display the plotted points.
    pointsPictureBox.Image = MonteCarloBitmap;

    // Get the hit fraction.
    double fraction = NumHits / (double)(numMethods * PointsPerCall);

    // Estimate pi.
    return 4.0 * fraction;
}
```

This method creates a bitmap to show some of the test points and saves it in a form-level variable. It then uses `Parallel.For` to launch instances of the `TestPoint` method. After those parallel methods finish, the code calculates the fraction of test points that fell within the circle of radius 1, uses that to calculate an estimate for π, and returns the result.

The following code shows the `TestPoint` method:

```
private void TestPoint(int i)
{
    Random rand = new Random(i * DateTime.Now.Millisecond);
    int myHits = 0;
    for (int pointNum = 0; pointNum < PointsPerCall; pointNum++)
    {
        // Make a random point 0 <= x < 1.
        double x = rand.NextDouble();
        double y = rand.NextDouble();

        // See how far the point is from (0.5, 0.5).
        double dx = x - 0.5;
        double dy = y - 0.5;
        if (dx * dx + dy * dy < 0.25) myHits++;

        if (i == 0)
        {
            int ix = (int)(MonteCarloWidth * x);
            int iy = (int)(MonteCarloHeight * y);
            if (dx * dx + dy * dy < 0.25)
                MonteCarloBitmap.SetPixel(ix, iy, Color.Gray);
            else
                MonteCarloBitmap.SetPixel(ix, iy, Color.Black);
        }
    }

    // Slightly slower.
    //Interlocked.Add(ref NumHits, myHits);

    // Slightly faster.
    lock (LockObject)
    {
        NumHits += myHits;
    }
}
```

This method has a problem that didn't occur in earlier examples. The Random class does not work well when it runs on multiple threads simultaneously. This means the instances of the method cannot share a form-level Random object. Instead, each instance must create its own Random object.

However, the Random class's default constructor uses the system's time to initialize new objects. Because the parallel instances of the method execute very quickly, many of them may use the same system time to initialize their Random objects. When that happens, those instances of the method will generate the same random values, so they will use the same test points. Instead of executing using many different points, the methods use the same points several times.

For example, suppose the program runs 10 instances of the method with 10,000 points each. Instead of using 100,000 points to estimate π, the program basically uses 10,000 points to estimate π 10 times. You still get an estimate, but without the precision that you would get with 100,000 different points.

To solve this dilemma, the program needs to initialize each instance's Random object differently. The example solution does that by multiplying the current time's number of milliseconds by the method instance number and passing that to the Random constructor as a seed value.

Having created a suitable Random object, the method performs its trials and counts the number of generated points that lie within the target circle. Notice that the code stores that count in a local variable. After it has finished counting hits, the method updates the form-level variable NumHits.

The code shows two ways to update NumHits. The first method, which is commented out, uses the System.Threading.Interlocked class's Add method to safely add the myHits value to NumHits. The second method, which seems to be slightly faster, explicitly locks the lock object and updates NumHits.

The following screenshot shows the iterative and parallel versions of this program after using 100 million test points to estimate π. The two programs provide roughly the same accuracy, but the parallel version only takes about 27% as long as the iterative version:

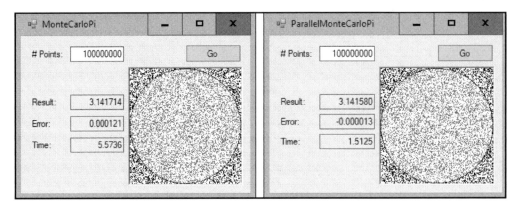

Download the `ParallelMonteCarloPi` example solution to see additional details.

42. Yielding primes

A method can use the `yield` keyword to return a value to the calling code and then resume execution later. The calling code receives the results as an `IEnumerable` and can loop through them as needed.

The following method yields primes:

```
// Yield numPrimes primes.
private IEnumerable<long> Primes(int numPrimes)
{
    // Treat 2 separately.
    yield return 2;
    if (numPrimes == 1) yield break;

    int count = 1;
    for (long i = 3; ; i += 2)
    {
        if (IsPrime(i))
        {
            yield return i;
            if (++count == numPrimes) yield break;
        }
    }
}
```

The method first uses a `yield return` statement to return the first prime, 2. It then loops over odd numbers, looking for other primes.

Inside the loop, the method uses the `IsPrime` method to see if the current value is prime. If the value is prime, the method uses `yield return` to send it to the calling code. Then, if the method has returned the required number of primes, it uses a `yield break` statement to stop yielding values.

The main program uses the following code snippet to display the primes:

```
int numPrimes = int.Parse(numPrimesTextBox.Text);
int i - 1;
foreach (long prime in Primes(numPrimes))
    primesListBox.Items.Add(i++.ToString() + ": " + prime);
```

This code first gets the desired number of values entered by the user. It then uses a `foreach` loop to iterate through the primes returned by `Primes(numPrimes)` and adds them to the form's list box. It uses the count variable `i` to display each prime's position in the primes list, along with its value.

Download the `YieldingPrimes` example solution to see additional details.

43. Yielding Fibonacci numbers

The following method yields Fibonacci numbers:

```
// Yield Fibonacci numbers.
private IEnumerable<long> FibonacciNumbers()
{
    // Treat 0 and 1 separately.
    yield return 0;
    yield return 1;

    // Calculate other values.
    long fiboIMinus2 = 0;
    long fiboIMinus1 = 1;
    long fiboI = 0;
    for (;;)
    {
        try
        {
            fiboI = checked(fiboIMinus2 + fiboIMinus1);
        }
        catch
        {
```

```
            yield break;
        }

        fiboIMinus2 = fiboIMinus1;
        fiboIMinus1 = fiboI;
        yield return fiboI;
    }
}
```

First, the method yields the values 0 and 1. It then enters a loop where it uses previously calculated Fibonacci numbers to calculate the next number. The calculation uses the checked keyword to watch for integer overflow.

If no overflow occurs, the method uses yield return to return the new Fibonacci number. If the operation causes an overflow, the method uses yield break to stop generating values.

The program uses the following code snippet to display Fibonacci numbers:

```
int i = 1;
foreach (long fiboNumber in FibonacciNumbers())
    fiboListBox.Items.Add(i++.ToString() + ": " + fiboNumber);
```

This code simply loops through the values yielded by the FibonacciNumbers method and displays them in the program's list box.

Download the YieldingFibonacciNumbers example solution to see additional details.

44. Complex numbers

The ComplexNumber structure is fairly long, so I'll describe it in pieces.

You could make ComplexNumber either a class or a structure. Many programmers use classes exclusively. This isn't a terrible choice, in part because it frees you from having to deal with the differences between classes and structures.

I've decided to make `ComplexNumber` a structure for a couple of reasons. Microsoft's guidelines generally recommend using a structure if the item meets the following criteria:

- It is relatively small
- It logically represents a primitive type such as a number
- It is immutable, so its value does not change after it has been created
- It will not need to be boxed and unboxed often

 See `docs.microsoft.com/en-us/dotnet/standard/design-guidelines/choosing-between-class-and-struct` for a discussion of this issue.

A `ComplexNumber` clearly meets the first two criteria. The .NET Framework is good at allocating and deallocating small objects, so making the class immutable shouldn't hurt performance.

Finally, if you typically use a `ComplexNumber` for numeric calculations, then you shouldn't need to box and unbox it very often.

Having decided to make this a structure instead of a class, let's look at the structure's requirements. The structure uses the following declaration to indicate that it will implement the `IEquatable` interface:

```
public struct ComplexNumber : IEquatable<ComplexNumber>
```

I'll show you how the structure implements the interface later.

The structure uses the following code to store a number's real and imaginary parts.

```
// Auto-implemented properties.
private double Re { get; }
private double Im { get; }
```

These properties are read-only because they have no `set` accessors. This means that a program cannot change a `ComplexNumber` structure's value after the structure has been created. In fact, even the structure's private code cannot change the properties' values. This makes the structure immutable.

This is a structure, so if you create a `ComplexNumber` without using a constructor, its real and imaginary parts take the default values for the `double` type, which is zero.

The following code shows the structure's explicitly defined constructors:

```
// Constructors.
public ComplexNumber(double re, double im)
{
    Re = re;
    Im = im;
}
public ComplexNumber(double re)
{
    Re = re;
    Im = 0;
}
```

These constructors initialize the number's real and imaginary parts. If you use the second constructor, which omits the imaginary part, the code sets the imaginary part to 0.

All structures always have an implicit, parameterless constructor that takes no parameters and that leaves the properties at their default values. This means that you cannot create your own parameterless constructor for a structure.

Not having a parameterless constructor is okay in this example, but it could be an issue in other cases where you need that constructor to perform more complex actions. For example, suppose you want to make a `Circle` structure that represents a circle drawn on a `PictureBox`. You might want the constructors to give a new `Circle` an ID number. Because you cannot define a parameterless constructor for a structure, you can't do that.

Possibly worse, you cannot prevent the program from creating a new structure without using a constructor. For example, you might want to let the program draw a maximum of 10 circles. Because you can't create a paremeterless constructor, you can't prevent the program from creating as many `Circle` structures as it likes.

Finally, because you can't define a parameterless constructor, you cannot set a breakpoint in it.

If you need a parameterless constructor for any of those reasons, then you need to use a class instead of a structure.

Ideally, we could make another constructor that initializes a number from its polar coordinate representation. Unfortunately, that version would take two `double` values as parameters, so it would have the same signature as the first constructor in the preceding code, and C# would be unable to tell which version you were trying to use.

We cannot create a constructor that uses polar coordinates, but we can create the following factory method instead:

```
// Polar factory method.
public static ComplexNumber FromPolar(double magnitude, double angle)
{
    return new ComplexNumber(
        magnitude * Math.Cos(angle),
        magnitude * Math.Sin(angle));
}
```

A factory method creates a new instance of a structure or class. In general, a factory method can perform a lot of work getting the new object ready. For example, it could load data from a database or network, or perform complex validations on its parameters. This example simply uses the number's polar representation to calculate its real and imaginary parts and then uses them to create a new ComplexNumber.

The following code shows static read-only properties that return ComplexNumber objects representing the special values 0, 1, and i:

```
// Return 0, 1, or i.
private static ComplexNumber ComplexZero = new ComplexNumber();
private static ComplexNumber ComplexOne = new ComplexNumber(1);
private static ComplexNumber ComplexI = new ComplexNumber(0, 1);
public static ComplexNumber Zero
{
    get { return ComplexZero; }
}
public static ComplexNumber One
{
    get { return ComplexOne; }
}
public static ComplexNumber I
{
    get { return ComplexI; }
}
```

These read-only properties return static instances of ComplexNumber structures representing 0, 1, and i. Because the class is immutable, we don't need to worry about the program modifying these values after the properties return them. This means that it's safe to make these values static so that they are shared by any pieces of code that need to use them.

If the values were *not* immutable, then the program could modify these shared values. In that case, the static value, ComplexZero, for example, would no longer represent the number 0 + 0i and that could cause problems in other parts of the program. Therefore, if the items are not immutable, you should not return static values. Instead, you should return new objects for this kind of special value.

The following code shows the structure's ToString method:

```
// Display as in x + yi.
public override string ToString()
{
    return $"{Re} + {Im}i";
}
```

This method simply returns the number's real and imaginary parts in a string with the format x + yi.

When you override the ToString method, other controls can use that method to display a meaningful representation of the object. For example, a ListBox or ComboBox control uses ToString to display the items it contains. Similarly, the Immediate Window, Console window, code editor tooltips, and other Visual Studio features use ToString to display an object's value.

The following code shows the structure's Parse method:

```
// Parse from a string.
public static ComplexNumber Parse(string s)
{
    double re = 0, im = 0;
    if (s.Contains("+"))
    {
        // Real and imaginary parts.
        int pos = s.IndexOf("+");
        string rePart = s.Substring(0, pos - 1);
        re = double.Parse(rePart);

        string imPart =
            s.Substring(pos + 1).ToLower().Replace("i",
            "");
        im = double.Parse(imPart);
    }
    else if (s.ToLower().Contains("i"))
    {
        // Imaginary part only.
        string imPart = s.ToLower().Replace("i", "");
```

```
            im = double.Parse(imPart);
        }
        else
        {
            // Real part only.
            re = double.Parse(s);
        }

        return new ComplexNumber(re, im);
    }
```

The `Parse` method looks for the + character to determine whether the string contains both real and imaginary parts. If the string contains the + character, the method separates the real and imaginary parts, parses them as `double` values, and saves them in the local variables `rePart` and `imPart`.

If the string does not contain +, then it contains either a real part or an imaginary part, but not both. If the string contains an `i`, then it contains an imaginary part. The code removes the `i`, parses the result, and saves it in the `imPart` variable.

If the string contains neither + nor `i`, then it contains only a real part. The code parses the string as a `double` and saves it in the `rePart` variable.

After it has the parsed the number's real and imaginary parts, the method uses them to create a new `ComplexNumber` and returns it.

This simple version of the `Parse` method can only understand the + sign when it is used to separate the real and imaginary parts. It cannot handle more complicated strings such as +1.2E+4 + 5.6E+7 i.

This method also handles negative imaginary parts rather awkwardly, as in 7 + -3i. You can try to improve this method if you like.

The following code shows how the structure implements the `IEquatable` interface and supports other equality tests:

```
    // Equality and IEquatable<ComplexNumber>.
    public bool Equals(ComplexNumber other)
    {
        double dRe = Re - other.Re;
        double dIm = Im - other.Im;
        return (dRe * dRe + dIm * dIm == 0);
    }
    public override bool Equals(object obj)
```

```
    {
        if (!(obj is ComplexNumber)) return false;
        ComplexNumber other = (ComplexNumber)obj;
        return (Re == other.Re) && (Im == other.Im);
    }
    public bool Equals(ComplexNumber other, double precision)
    {
        double dRe = Re - other.Re;
        double dIm = Im - other.Im;
        return (dRe * dRe + dIm * dIm <= precision * precision);
    }
```

The first `Equals` method satisfies the `IEquality` interface. It compares two `ComplexNumber` structures to see if their real and imaginary parts are the same.

The second version overrides the default implementation of `Equals` to perform the same test with a generic `object` instead of a `ComplexNumber`.

As is true with all floating point data types, there may be times when two `ComplexNumber` values should be equal, but they differ slightly due to rounding errors. The final version of the `Equals` method returns `true` if two `ComplexNumber` values are within a certain distance of each other. For example, the `value1.Equals(value2, 0.01)` statement will return `true` if the values are within 0.01 of each other.

Note that this method calculates the distance between two values in the complex plane rather than by simply comparing the values' real and imaginary parts.

The following code show how the structure overloads the `==` and `!=` operators:

```
// Comparison operators.
public static bool operator ==(ComplexNumber c1, ComplexNumber c2)
{
    return c1.Equals(c2);
}
public static bool operator !=(ComplexNumber c1, ComplexNumber c2)
{
    return !(c1 == c2);
}
```

The `==` operator simply invokes the `Equals` method. The `!=` operator invokes `==` and negates the result.

> The == and != operators come as a pair. If you overload one, then you
> must overload the other.

If you override the Equals method (the second version), then Microsoft recommends that you also override the GetHashCode method. That method returns a hash code that objects such as dictionaries can use to quickly determine whether two objects are different. Because hash codes map complicated objects to comparatively simple codes, there will be cases where two different objects may have the same hash code. However, if two objects have different hash codes, then they are definitely not equal.

Being immutable is an advantage when it comes to hash codes because it means that an object's hash code can never change. In turn, this means that you can add a ComplexNumber to a dictionary and you don't need to worry about its values changing and preventing the dictionary from correctly finding it later.

The following code shows the ComplexNumber structure's GetHashCode method:

```
// GetHashCode.
public override int GetHashCode()
{
    return Re.GetHashCode() ^ (Re + Im).GetHashCode();
}
```

This method takes the number's real component and invokes its default GetHashCode method. It then adds the number's real and imaginary parts together and invokes the GetHashCode method for the sum. Finally, it uses the bitwise XOR operator to combine the two hash codes and produce its final result.

The reason GetHashCode doesn't simply calculate the hash codes for the real and imaginary parts and combine them is that the calculation would return the same hash code for the values a + b i and b + a i, and it seems somewhat plausible that an application might use two complex numbers having that relationship. The method shown here maps those values to different hash codes so that objects such as dictionaries can handle them more efficiently.

Of course, there are still many more possible ComplexNumber values than there are hash codes (which must fit in an int), so some collisions are unavoidable, but this change makes those collisions occur randomly. If you use the simpler version of GetHashCode and an application happens to use numbers of the form a + b i and b + a i, then collisions would be guaranteed.

The following read-only property returns a complex number's magnitude, which is also sometimes called its **modulus** or **norm**:

```
// Return the number's magnitude. (Also called its modulus or norm.)
public double Magnitude
{
    get { return Math.Sqrt(Re * Re + Im * Im); }
}
```

This property simply calculates the distance from the value to the origin on the complex plane.

The following read-only property returns the number's angle, which is also sometimes called its **argument** or **phase**:

```
// Return the number's angle. (Also called its argument or phase.)
public double Angle
{
    get { return Math.Atan2(Im, Re); }
}
```

This property uses the `Atan2` method to calculate the arctangent of the number's imaginary part divided by its real part.

> The `Angle` property's result is in radians. If you want the angle in degrees, multiply by 180/`Math.Pi`.

The following conversion operator converts a `double` into a `ComplexNumber`:

```
// Convert the double value re into the ComplexNumber re + 0i.
public static implicit operator ComplexNumber(double re)
{
    return new ComplexNumber(re);
}
```

The real number, R, is the same as the complex number R + 0i, so this operator simply creates and returns the appropriate `ComplexNumber`. Because this operation does not lose any data, this operator is declared `implicit`, so the program can use it without a cast operator. For example, the following statement creates a new `ComplexNumber` with the value 13 + 0i:

```
ComplexNumber f = 13;
```

The following operator converts a `ComplexNumber` into a `double`:

```
// Convert the ComplexNumber into a double by dropping
// the complex part.
public static explicit operator double(ComplexNumber c)
{
    return c.Re;
}
```

This operator drops the number's complex component. Because that causes a loss of data, the method is declared `explicit` to require the code to use a cast operator to perform the conversion. This prevents you from losing data accidentally. For example, the following statement converts the `ComplexNumber` f into the double g:

```
double g = (double)f;
```

Providing arithmetic operators for the `ComplexNumber` structure may seem like a daunting task. You would need to write methods to add, subtract, multiply, divide, and negate `ComplexNumber` values. Then, you would need to write methods showing how to perform those same operations for each of the numeric types `byte`, `sbyte`, `short`, `ushort`, `int`, `uint`, `long`, `ulong`, `float`, and `double`.

To further complicate matters, you would need to specify each method twice, once for the `ComplexNumber` on the left and one for the `ComplexNumber` on the right. For example, you would need methods showing how to calculate `int + ComplexNumber` and `ComplexNumber + int`. Mathematically those values are the same when you work with complex numbers, but C# doesn't know that. In general, operators could give different results when the operands are in different orders, or one of the orders might not be defined for a particular order.

Adding all of the combinations of operations, data types, and left/right orderings gives you more than 100 methods that you might need to write!

Fortunately, C# does something that greatly simplifies this problem. When it performs an arithmetic calculation, the program *promotes* values into the widest data type used by the expression. For example, if you add a `long` and a `double`, the `long` is promoted to a `double`, the two are added, and the result is a `double`.

Because we have already defined an implicit conversion operator that converts from a double to a ComplexNumber, C# will automatically make that conversion if necessary. This means that we only need to provide arithmetic methods to work with ComplexNumber values, and C# will automatically promote other values if necessary to perform the calculations. For example, suppose you add a long and a ComplexNumber. The program will promote the long into a double, then convert the double into a ComplexNumber, and finally perform the addition.

The following code shows the ComplexNumber structure's arithmetic operators:

```
// Arithmetic operators.
public static ComplexNumber operator +(ComplexNumber c1,
    ComplexNumber c2)
{
    return new ComplexNumber(c1.Re + c2.Re, c1.Im + c2.Im);
}
public static ComplexNumber operator -(ComplexNumber c1)
{
    return new ComplexNumber(-c1.Re, -c1.Im);
}
public static ComplexNumber operator -(ComplexNumber c1,
    ComplexNumber c2)
{
    return new ComplexNumber(c1.Re - c2.Re, c1.Im - c2.Im);
}
public static ComplexNumber operator *(ComplexNumber c1,
    ComplexNumber c2)
{
    return new ComplexNumber(
        c1.Re * c2.Re - c1.Im * c2.Im,
        c1.Re * c2.Im + c1.Im * c2.Re);
}
public static ComplexNumber operator /(ComplexNumber c1,
    ComplexNumber c2)
{
    double denominator = c2.Re * c2.Re + c2.Im * c2.Im;
    return new ComplexNumber(
        (c1.Re * c2.Re + c1.Im * c2.Im) / denominator,
        (c1.Im * c2.Re - c1.Re * c2.Im) / denominator);
}
```

These methods are straightforward, so I won't describe them in detail.

The `ComplexNumbers` example solution tests the `ComplexNumber` class. The code is long but straightforward, so I won't describe it in detail here. It tests a number of `ComplexNumber` features, including different constructors, the static `Zero`, `One`, and `I` properties, `ToString`, various arithmetic operations with `ComplexNumber` and integer values, `GetHashCode`, and more.

Download the `ComplexNumbers` example solution to see the results and to see additional details.

Summary

In this chapter, we saw various advanced features of C# such as LINQ, PLINQ, TPL etc. In the next chapter, we will understand the various problems in cryptography.

19
Cryptography

This chapter describes problems in cryptography. The first few problems ask you to use cryptographic systems that were once state-of-the-art but that are now insecure. They are purely for fun and are of historical significance. Later problems use modern, secure techniques, such as the .NET Framework's cryptographic library, to build secure programs.

When studying cryptography, it's useful to know a few basic terms. A **key** is a piece of secret information that you can use to encrypt and decrypt messages. Sometimes, a password is a key. Other times, a password is used to generate a key in a format suitable for use by a particular encryption algorithm. A message that is not encrypted is called **plaintext**. The encrypted version of plaintext is called **ciphertext**.

Traditionally, plaintext and ciphertext are written in five-letter groups of uppercase letters without punctuation or spaces, at least for older encryption systems such as the Caesar substitution and Vigenère ciphers. For example, the message, `This is the secret message`, would be written in plaintext as `THISI STHES ECRET MESSA GE`, and might be encrypted as `WKLVL VWKHV HFUHW PHVVD JH`. An **N-gram** is a sequence of N contiguous pieces of text or speech, so I call these groups *five-grams*. More modern systems encrypt and decrypt streams of bytes that can contain just about anything, including images, documents, and databases. In those systems, it doesn't make much sense to represent messages in five-grams.

Like most of the other topics covered in this book, cryptography is a huge subject, so this chapter covers only a tiny part of it. For more information, consult a book about cryptography, such as Bruce Schneier's excellent book, *Applied Cryptography: Protocols, Algorithms and Source Code in C* (John Wiley & Sons, 2015). You can also search the internet for general information and specific examples. For instance, Wikipedia has an overview at `https://en.wikipedia.org/wiki/Cryptography`, and Khan Academy has a course about cryptography at `https://www.khanacademy.org/computing/computer-science/cryptography`.

Most of the example solutions in this chapter use the .NET Framework's cryptography namespace, so you may want to add the following `using` directive to your code files:

```
using System.Security.Cryptography;
```

Problems

Use the following problems to test your skills at building cryptographic programs. Give each problem a try before you turn to the example solutions for help.

45. Caesar cipher

In a **Caesar cipher**, also called a *Caesar shift*, *Caesar substitution cipher*, or *shift cipher*, you shift the values of the letters in the message by some fixed amount. In the original Caesar cipher, Julius Caesar reportedly used a shift of three to send secret messages to his commanders, so each letter was replaced by the letter that comes three positions later in the alphabet. The letter A was encrypted as D, B was encrypted as E, and so forth. Letters at the end of the alphabet wrap around to the beginning so, for example, X becomes A, Y becomes B, and Z becomes C. In this example, the shift value, 3, was the cipher's key.

Write a program that uses a Caesar cipher to encrypt and decrypt messages. Let the user enter some text and a shift and then click a button to encrypt the message. Let the user then enter a new key and click another button to decrypt the message. Verify that decryption works only when the shift is correct.

To make this easier, write extension methods that encrypt and decrypt strings, strip punctuation and spaces from strings, and break strings into five-grams.

46. Vigenère cipher

The result of a Caesar cipher looks like gibberish, but it's actually quite easy to break a Caesar cipher. Simply try decrypting the message with each of the possible shifts 1 through 26 and look at the results. When the shift is incorrect, the result is still gibberish, but when the shift is correct, the result looks like words, albeit in five-grams without spaces or punctuation.

The Vigenère cipher improves on the Caesar cipher by using multiple interlaced Caesar ciphers. This cipher uses a word as its key. Each letter in the key represents a shift. For example, A represents a shift of 0, B represents a shift of 1, and so forth. The cipher matches letters in the plaintext with letters in the key, repeating the key if necessary. It then uses the key letters' shifts to modify the plaintext letters.

The Vigenère cipher (Vigenère is roughly pronounced *vision-air*) is named after 17th century French cryptographer Blaise de Vigenère. He didn't invent the cipher, but it was misattributed to him and the name stuck.

Write a program similar to the one you wrote for the preceding problem but this time use a Vigenère cipher to encrypt and decrypt messages.

47. Cryptographic pseudorandom numbers

Several of the solutions in earlier chapters used the `Random` class to generate *random* numbers. In fact, those numbers are not really random at all. They use easily predictable algorithms to generate sequences of numbers that are random enough to simulate moving bubbles and random walks, but they are not cryptographically secure. Technically that means an attacker who learns some of the numbers in a sequence of *random* values may be able to predict the values that follow with some success. Even a small advantage at prediction may give an attacker a way to break an encryption system based on the random number generator.

To prevent that from happening, you can use a **Cryptographically Secure Pseudorandom Number Generator (CSPRNG)**, which is also called a **Cryptographic Pseudorandom Number Generator (CPRNG)**.

Note that even these methods are not *truly* random, so they are still called **pseudorandom techniques**.

For this problem, create a method that uses the .NET cryptographic library to generate long integers between inclusive lower and exclusive upper bounds. (Similar to the way the `Random` class's `Next` method generates integers within a range.)

Make the test program generate an indicated number of random values and then display each value's number of occurrences, fraction of occurrences, and error (fraction minus expected fraction of occurrences), as shown in the following screenshot:

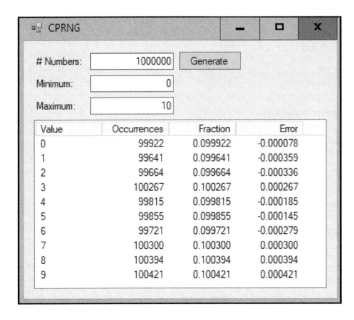

The error values will not be zero, but they should grow smaller when you perform more trials. They should also change relative positions if you click **Generate** repeatedly. For example, if the fraction or error for the value 8 is always greater than the results for the other values, then the values are not uniformly distributed.

48. Find primes

Let the user enter a starting value and the desired probability. Make the program search upward from the starting value until it finds a number that is probably prime to the desired level of probability. Use the program to find the smallest prime larger than 1 trillion.

49. Hash files

In computer programming, **hashing** is the process of converting a larger piece of data, such as a string or file, into a shorter code that you can use to identify it. For example, the following value might be the hash for a large file:

```
F6-72-E5-7E-2E-09-6B-1A-9E-CE-9C-DE-F8-AE-13-98
```

Hashing has several uses. For example, you can use hash codes to identify files in a database, to determine whether two files are different, or to decide whether a file has been modified or corrupted since it was hashed.

For this problem, write a program that uses the MD5 hashing algorithm to find a file's hash code.

50. Steganography

Steganography is the process of hiding data inside a file, image, video, or another piece of data. For example, in **watermarking** you hide a copyright statement inside an image to later show that you own the rights to that file.

Write a program that defines `Bitmap` extension methods to perform steganography. The program should let the user load an image, hide a message in it, and save the result in a new image file. It should also be able to load an image and recover a message hidden inside it.

Hide the data in the low-order bits of the image's pixels. You don't need to encrypt the message for this problem; just hide it.

Use a lossless image format such as BMP or PNG. A lossy format such as GIF or JPG will destroy the message.

51. Encrypt and decrypt strings

Write a program similar to the one shown in the following screenshot to encrypt and decrypt strings:

To do that, write an extension method that encrypts a string and returns a byte array. Write a second method that decrypts a byte array and returns the original string. To make it easier to display the values in a byte array, write extension methods that convert between byte arrays and hexadecimal strings.

To make this easier, write a method that encrypts or decrypts a byte array into another byte array. You may also want to create helper methods: FindKeySize, MakeKeyAndIV, and MakeCryptoTransform.

52. Encrypt and decrypt files

Write a program similar to the one shown in the following screenshot to let the user encrypt or decrypt one file into another file:

Enter the original filename, the name of a file to hold the encrypted results, and a password. When you click **Encrypt**, the program should encrypt the original file and save the result in the encrypted file.

Next, enter a decryption password and the name of a recovery file to hold the decrypted data. When you click **Decrypt**, the program should decrypt the encrypted file and save the result in the recovery file.

Make the program show the original file, the encrypted file (only display the first 1,000 bytes), and the decrypted file in separate tabs as shown in the preceding screenshot.

The program should be able to handle any kind of file. In the screenshot, I used an RTF file containing English, Japanese, and an image. Verify that the program cannot decrypt the encrypted file if the decryption password is wrong by even a tiny-amount.

53. CryptoPad

Write a program that lets the user open a file containing encrypted rich text data, edit it, and save it in the same or another encrypted file.

Do not use the methods from the preceding solution because that would require the program to save unencrypted versions of the file on the computer where an attacker might find them, either while the program is running or later, if the program crashes and does not clean up temporary files correctly.

Solutions

The following sections describe solutions to the preceding problems. You can download the example solutions to see additional details and to experiment with the programs at `https://github.com/PacktPublishing/Improving-your-C-Sharp-Skills/tree/master/Chapter19`.

45. Caesar cipher

This problem is relatively straightforward. Simply loop through the message's letters and shift them by some amount.

The example solution uses the following string extension method to encrypt a string:

```
// Use a Caesar cipher to encrypt the plaintext.
public static string CaesarEncrypt(this string plaintext, int shift)
{
    plaintext = plaintext.StripText();

    // Encrypt.
    char[] chars = new char[plaintext.Length];
    for (int i = 0; i < plaintext.Length; i++)
    {
        int ch = plaintext[i] - 'A';
        ch = (ch + shift + 26) % 26;
        chars[i] = (char)('A' + ch);
    }
    return new string(chars).ToFiveGrams();
}
```

This method calls the `StripText` extension method described shortly to remove any non-letter characters from the string. It then loops through the message's letters, adding the shift to each and storing the results in a `char` array. When it has finished processing the letters, the method converts the `char` array into a string, calls the `ToFiveGrams` extension method (also described shortly), and returns the result.

The following code shows the `StripText` helper extension method:

```
// Convert to uppercase, and remove punctuation and spaces.
public static string StripText(this string text)
{
    text = text.ToUpper();
    text = new string(text.Where(
        ch => (ch >= 'A') && (ch <= 'Z')).ToArray());
    return text;
}
```

This method converts the message into uppercase. It uses a lambda expression to extract the characters between A and Z, and converts those characters into a new string. That removes any non-letter characters from the string. The method then returns the result.

 Unicode didn't exist back in Caesar's day, so this simple code was not intended to handle Unicode characters and this method doesn't even try. Later problems encrypt and decrypt non-letter characters and even more exotic items such as Unicode strings, formatting codes, and images.

The following code shows the `ToFiveGrams` helper method:

```
// Separate the string into five-character pieces.
public static string ToFiveGrams(this string text)
{
    StringBuilder result = new StringBuilder();
    for (int i = 0; i < text.Length; i += 5)
    {
        int length = Math.Min(5, text.Length - i);
        result.Append(" " + text.Substring(i, length));
    }
    result.Remove(0, 1);
    return result.ToString();
}
```

The code first creates a `StringBuilder` to hold the result. It breaks the text into groups of five characters and adds the groups preceded by a space character to the `StringBuilder`. After it has finished processing the text, the code removes the first space character, converts the rest of the `StringBuilder` contents into a string, and returns the result.

After you write the method to encrypt a string, decrypting a string is easy because decrypting a Caesar cipher message is the same as encrypting it with a negative shift. For example, if you encrypt a plaintext message with the shift 4, then you can decrypt it by encrypting the ciphertext with a shift of -4. The `CaesarDecrypt` method shown in the following code does that:

```
// Use a Caesar cipher to decrypt the ciphertext.
public static string CaesarDecrypt(this string ciphertext, int shift)
{
    return ciphertext.CaesarEncrypt(-shift);
}
```

This method simply calls the `CaesarEncrypt` method described earlier to encrypt the ciphertext with a negative shift value.

Download the `CaesarCipher` example solution to see additional details.

46. Vigenère cipher

The Vigenère cipher is only slightly more complicated than the Caesar cipher. The following method encrypts or decrypts a piece of plaintext and returns the resulting ciphertext:

```
// Use a Vigenere cipher to encrypt plaintext.
private static string VigenereEncryptDecrypt(this string plaintext,
    string key, bool decrypt)
{
    key = key.StripText();
    plaintext = plaintext.StripText();

    // Encrypt.
    char[] chars = new char[plaintext.Length];
    for (int i = 0; i < plaintext.Length; i++)
    {
        int shift = key[i % key.Length] - 'A';
        if (decrypt) shift = -shift;
        int ch = plaintext[i] - 'A';
        ch = (ch + shift + 26) % 26;
        chars[i] = (char)('A' + ch);
    }
    return new string(chars).ToFiveGrams();
}
```

This code calls the `StripText` method to remove non-letter characters as in the preceding solution. It then loops through the plaintext's letters.

For each letter, it uses the modulus operator (`%`) to get the matching character in the key word and subtracts the letter A from the key letter to get a shift value. If the method is decrypting, it negates the shift value. It then shifts the plaintext letter just as the preceding solution did. The method converts the ciphertext into five-grams and returns the result.

Download the `CaesarCipher` example solution to see additional details.

47. Cryptographic random numbers

This is much more complicated that you might imagine. (In fact, it's surprising that Microsoft didn't add methods to generate values within a range to its cryptographic random number generator so you wouldn't have to.) To understand why this is hard and to learn how to handle the difficulties, take the following discussion slowly. If you find that you're lost, you may want to start over.

The .NET Framework's RNGCryptoServiceProvider class generates cryptographic random values. It is fairly easy to use but it has a catch—it only generates bytes. If you want some other kinds of data, such as double or int that lies between two bounds, then you need to convert the bytes accordingly.

To make the discussion easier, I'll use the notation [A, B) to mean the range of numbers between A and B, including the A value (the [means include the end value) and not including the B value (the) means exclude the end value). I'll also work through a very simplified example that uses numbers that are much smaller than those typically used by real random number generators.

One simple method for generating numbers within a range is to generate a random number and then take that number mod the number of values that you want to generate. For example, suppose your random number generator creates numbers in the range [0, 9] and you want to pick a value in [0, 7]. Now suppose your random number generator gives you 5. The value $5 \% 8 = 5$, so 5 is the number that you use. I'm using 8 as the modulus because we want one of eight values between 0 and 7 inclusive. Taking the result mod 8 ensures that the result lies between 0 and 7. So far so good.

Next, suppose the generator produces 9. In that case, $9 \% 8 = 2$, so 2 is the number that you would use.

This method is easy to calculate, but it also has a big problem—the resulting values are not evenly distributed. In this example, there's only one way you can generate a 7, namely the generator produces 7. However, there two ways that you can generate the value 0—when the generator produces 0 or 8. That means you're twice as likely to end up with 0 as 7.

The following table shows all of the possible results created by the generator and the final numbers that they produce:

Generated	0	1	2	3	4	5	6	7	8	9
Result	0	1	2	3	4	5	6	7	0	1

You can see in the table that the results 0 and 1 appear twice while the other results appear only once.

Real random number generators produce much larger numbers, so the problem isn't as large. For example, if the random number generator produces values between 0 and 99 and we still map them into the range [0, 7], then there are 13 ways to produce some numbers. For example, you will get a result of 0 if the generator produces 0, 8, 16, 24, 32, 40, 48, 56, 64, 72, 80, 88, or 96. However, there are only 12 ways to get some other values. For example, you get the value 7 if the generator produces one of the values 7, 15, 23, 31, 39, 47, 55, 63, 71, 79, 87, or 95. That's a lot better than producing some values twice as often as others, but it's still a problem, particularly for a CRNG.

The goal of a CRNG is to ensure that an attacker cannot guess the next number in a sequence with even a slightly better than random chance of success.

One way to fix this problem is to discard any values that appear at the end of the range of generated values. To see how that works, let's go back to the example where you need to pick a value in [0, 7] and the generator produces values in [0, 9]. In that case, you simply discard any generated value larger than 7 and try again. You may need to try more than once to pick a number, but you probably won't need more than a few tries.

The following table shows the new results:

Generated	0	1	2	3	4	5	6	7	8	9
Result	0	1	2	3	4	5	6	7	Retry	Retry

The case where the generator produces values in [0, 99] is similar; you just discard any value above 95.

There's one more technique that you need to use to generate values within a range if the lower bound is not zero. In that case, subtract the upper limit from the lower limit to see how many values you need to consider. Pick a random number between zero and the number of values that you need, and add the result to the lower bound.

I know this is confusing, so let's look at an example. Suppose you want to pick a value in [10, 17]. That range includes eight values, so use the previous method to pick a value in the range [0, 7], which also holds eight values. Then add the result to the lower bound 10 to get the final number in the range [10, 17].

The following code shows how the example solution implements this technique to pick a random number in the range [minValue, maxValue). Notice that the range does *not* include the upper limit, maxValue. That makes the method more consistent with the Random class's Next method and makes the math slightly easier:

```
// Generate a cryptographically secure long in [minValue, maxValue).
public static long NextLong(long minValue, long maxValue)
{
    // The biggest value we can create with 16 bytes.
    BigInteger biggest = BigInteger.Pow(2, 8 * 16) - 1;

    // Calculate the number of values in [maxValue, minValue).
    long numValues = maxValue - minValue;

    // The amount of unused space at the end of the biggest range.
    BigInteger numUnused = (biggest + 1) % numValues;

    // The largest usable value.
    BigInteger maxUsable = biggest - numUnused;

    // Generate random BigIntegers until we get one between
    // 0 and maxUsable.
    byte[] bytes = new byte[16];
    for (;;)
    {
        // Get a random BigInteger.
        BigInteger rand = RandomUBigInteger(16);

        // If the value is within the allowed range, use it.
        if (rand <= maxUsable)
            return (long)(minValue + (rand % numValues));
    }
}
```

In order to produce long integer values, the method must use a larger data type than long to perform its calculations. (You can't generate numbers in [0, 7] if the random number generator only produces values in [0, 5].) You might like to use the double data type, but it doesn't have enough resolution to represent all long values. For example, consider the following statement and result from Visual Studio's Immediate Window:

```
(long)(double)1234567890123456789
1234567890123456768
```

The value lost precision when it was stored in a `double`, so when it was turned back into a `long`, the last two digits were modified. Fortunately, the .NET Framework has a data type that can hold very large values and that has perfect integer precision—`BigInteger`.

To use the `BigInteger` data type, give your program a reference to the `System.Numerics` library. You may also want to add the following `using` directive to your code:

```
using System.Numerics;
```

The method sets the `biggest` variable to the largest value that it might generate. This is analogous to the value 9 in the example that generated numbers in [0, 9] and then converted them into the range [0, 7]. This example will use 16-byte values, so those values use 16 * 8 bits. The largest value that you can represent in 16 bytes is $2^{16*8} - 1$ when every bit is 1. (That's big enough to hold any `long` value because the `long` data type also uses 16 bytes.)

Next, the method calculates the number of values in the desired range. For example, if the range is [10, 17), then the number of values is 7.

The code then calculates the number of generated values in the range [0, biggest] that will be *unused*. Those are the values for which the method must try again. Earlier, when we wanted a value in [0, 7], if the random number generator produced 9, we tried again. In that example, `biggest` was 9 (the generator produced values in [0, 9]) and `numValues` was 8 (we wanted numbers in [0, 7]), so `numUnused` would be (9 + 1) % 8 = 2. That means we ignore the two largest values if we generate them. If you look back at the earlier table, you'll see that we retried if we generated the two largest values 8 or 9.

Next, the code uses `numUnused` to calculate the largest value that the method *will* use. For the previous example, `numUnused` is 2 and `biggest` is 9, so the largest usable value is 9 − 2 = 7, which matches the preceding table.

With all that set up, the method is finally ready to pick a number. It creates a `byte` array to hold 16 bytes and then enters an infinite loop.

Inside the loop, the code calls the `RandomUBigInteger` method described shortly to generate a `BigInteger` defined by 16 cryptographically secure random bytes. If the value is less than or equal to the largest usable value, the method adds it to `minValue` and returns the result. If the value is bigger than the largest usable value, the method continues its loop and tries again.

The following code shows the `RandomUBigInteger` method:

```
// A cryptographic pseudorandom number provider.
private static RNGCryptoServiceProvider
    Cprng = new RNGCryptoServiceProvider();

// Return a cryptographically secure random unsigned BigInteger
// with the indicated number of bytes.
private static BigInteger RandomUBigInteger(int numBytes)
{
    // Get the random bytes.
    byte[] bytes = new byte[numBytes];
    Cprng.GetBytes(bytes);

    // Convert the bytes into an unsigned value;
    BigInteger result = 0;
    BigInteger factor = 1;
    for (int i = 0; i < numBytes; i++)
    {
        result += factor * bytes[i];
        factor *= 256;
    }
    return result;
}
```

The code creates a static CPRNG named `Cprng` at the class level so it is available inside all of the class's methods.

The `RandomUBigInteger` method creates an array big enough to hold the desired number of bytes and then calls the `Cprng` object's `GetBytes` method to fill the array with random bytes.

The method then uses the bytes to create a result by multiplying the values of the bytes by powers of 256. This is similar to the way that you calculate the value of a decimal number. For example, the decimal value 1729 is $9 * 10^0 + 2 * 10^1 + 7 * 10^2 + 1 * 10^3$. Similarly the bytes create the value $byte0 * 256^0 + byte1 * 256^1 + byte2 * 256^2 + ... + byteN * 256^N$.

After it finishes processing the bytes, the method returns the resulting `BigInteger`.

That ends the most interesting pieces of the example solution. The rest of the program's code performs such chores as displaying the counts, fractions, and errors. Download the CPRNG example solution to see additional details.

48. Find primes

To find a prime number larger than a given starting number, the program simply considers increasingly large numbers until it finds one that is probably prime. The following `FindNextPrime` method does just that:

```
// Find a prime at least as large a startNumber and with at least the
// given probability of being prime.
// Return the number, probability, and number of tests performed.
public static BigInteger FindNextPrime(this BigInteger startNumber
,
    double desiredProb, out double primeProb, out int numTests)
{
    // Make sure the start number is odd.
    if ((startNumber != 2) && (startNumber % 2 == 0)) startNumber++;

    // Calculate the number of tests we need to run to achieve the
    // desired probability.
    numTests = (int)Math.Log(1.0 / (1.0 - desiredProb), 2) + 1;

    // Test values until we find a prime.
    for (BigInteger p = startNumber; ; p += 2)
    {
        primeProb = p.ProbabilityIsPrime(numTests);
        if (primeProb > 0.1) return p;
    }
}
```

The method first ensures that the number is either 2 or odd. If the number is 2, then it is prime. If the number is even and not 2, the code makes the number odd because no even numbers other than 2 are prime.

Next, the code calculates the number of tests that it must make to ensure the desired probability. The code then enters a loop that begins at `startNumber` and considers increasingly large numbers. It calls `ProbabilityIsPrime` for each number and returns that number if it is probably prime.

The `FindPrimes` example solution shows that the next prime larger than 1 trillion is 1,000,000,000,039. Download the example solution to see additional details.

49. Hash files

Hashing a file is relatively easy in C#. The following `CalculateMD5` method calculates an MD5 hash code for a file:

```
// Return a file's MD5 hash.
public static string CalculateMD5(string filename)
{
    // Make an MD5 hashing object.
    using (MD5 md5 = MD5.Create())
    {
        // Open the file and pass the stream into the MD5 object.
        using (FileStream stream = File.OpenRead(filename))
        {
            byte[] hash = md5.ComputeHash(stream);
            return BitConverter.ToString(hash);
        }
    }
}
```

This method first creates an `MD5` object.

The `MD5` class is one of several .NET Framework classes that represent hashing algorithms. Other hashing classes work with different hashing algorithms such as MD160, SHA1, SHA256, SHA384, SHA512, HMAC, and HMACtripleDES. You can use any of the hashing algorithms as long as you use the same algorithm when you hash a file and later validate its hash code.

The code then opens a stream to the file that you want to hash. It calls the `MD5` object's `ComputeHash` method, passing it the file stream. The result is a byte array. The method finishes by using `BitConverter.ToString` to convert the array into a string with a format similar to `F6-72-E5-7E-2E-09-6B-1A-9E-CE-9C-DE-F8-AE-13-98` and returns that as its result.

Download the `HashFiles` example solution to see additional details.

50. Steganography

Hiding data in an image's least significant bits and then later recovering the data is simple in principle, but it's complicated by the way images store pixel values. A typical 32-bit color image uses 8 bits to store each of a pixel's red, green, blue, and alpha (transparency) color components. We won't use the alpha component because that might cause a noticeable change when parts of the image become slightly transparent. That means we can store three bits of data per pixel.

Unfortunately, data is usually stored in bytes, so a byte of data might start in one pixel and end partway through another pixel.

An alternative storage strategy would be to use three pixels (giving nine bits) to store each 8-bit byte and just ignore the extra unused bit in each group of three pixels. Even that is complicated, however, because a byte might start in one row of pixels and end in the next row.

As long as things are going to be somewhat complicated anyway, I'm going to use every pixel instead of the three-pixels-per-byte strategy.

This isn't really a matter of trying to squeeze every last bit of data out of the image. That may be a concern for some very large messages, but images can store a surprisingly large amount of data. For example, a small 300 × 300 pixel image can hold 300 × 300 × 3 / 8 bytes or roughly 33 KB of data. A larger 1,024 × 1,024 pixel image can hold more than a third of a megabyte of data.

It's actually pretty remarkable how much data you can store in an image without it being obvious. I've written other programs that store the four high-order bits of one image in the four low-order bits of another image and the result still looks good.

The general approach is to write a method that stores one bit of information in one of a pixel's red, green, or blue components. We then write another method that uses the first one to save a byte of data. Next, we write a method that uses the byte method to save an array of bytes. Finally, we write a method that uses the byte array method to store a string or other piece of data. To make it all work, each of the methods must keep track of the row, column, and color component of the pixel that we are using to hold data, so later calls to the methods know where to place future data.

The following code shows the example solution's bit-level method:

```
// The component where a bit should be stored.
private enum RGB { R, G, B }

// Hide a single bit in the image.
// The bit parameter should be true to set the bit, false to clear it.
private static void StegBit(Bitmap bm, bool bit,
    ref int x, ref int y, ref RGB component)
{
    Color color = bm.GetPixel(x, y);
    byte r = color.R;
    byte g = color.G;
    byte b = color.B;
    byte a = color.A;
    if (component == RGB.R)
    {
        if (bit) r |= 0b00000001;
        else r &= 0b11111110;
        color = Color.FromArgb(a, r, g, b);
        bm.SetPixel(x, y, color);
        component = RGB.G;
    }
    else if (component == RGB.G)
    {
        if (bit) g |= 0b00000001;
        else g &= 0b11111110;
        color = Color.FromArgb(a, r, g, b);
        bm.SetPixel(x, y, color);
        component = RGB.B;
    }
    else
    {
        if (bit) b |= 0b00000001;
        else b &= 0b11111110;
        color = Color.FromArgb(a, r, g, b);
        bm.SetPixel(x, y, color);
        component = RGB.R;
        if (++x >= bm.Width)
        {
            // Move to the next row.
            x = 0;
            y++;
        }
    }
}
```

The RGB enumeration indicates a red, green, or blue color component. The `StegBit` method takes as parameters the bitmap where we are storing data, whether the bit should be set or cleared, the pixel's *X* and *Y* location, and the color component to use. Notice that the x, y, and component parameters are passed by reference so the method can update them.

The code first gets the color components of the pixel at position (x, y). It then takes similar actions for each of the possible color components. If the bit should be set, the code uses the OR operator (|) to combine the component's current value with the binary mask 00000001. That sets the least significant bit to 1 and leaves the other bits unchanged.

If the bit should be cleared, the code uses the AND operator (&) to combine the component's current value with the binary mask 11111110. That sets the least significant bit to 0 and leaves the other bits unchanged.

After calculating the new color component, the code updates the pixel's color value. Next, if the code is storing information in the pixel's red or green color component, the code advances the component property to the next color component so the next bit of data will be stored in that component.

If the method is using the blue component, the code increments x to move to the next pixel in the row. If this was the last pixel in the row, the code resets x to 0 and increments y to move to the beginning of the next rows of pixels.

From here, things get easier. The following code shows the example solution's byte-level method:

```
// Hide a byte in the image.
private static void StegByte(Bitmap bm, byte aByte,
    ref int x, ref int y, ref RGB component)
{
    byte mask = 0b00000001;
    for (int i = 0; i < 8; i++)
    {
        bool setBit = (aByte & mask) != 0;
        StegBit(bm, setBit, ref x, ref y, ref component);
        mask <<= 1;
    }
}
```

This method loops through a byte's bits. It uses a mask to figure out whether each bit should be set and calls the earlier `StegBit` method to set or clear the next bit in the image.

The following code shows the example solution's byte array-level method:

```
// Hide an array of bytes in the image.
private static void StegBytes(Bitmap bm, byte[] bytes,
    ref int x, ref int y, ref RGB component)
{
    foreach (byte aByte in bytes)
        StegByte(bm, aByte, ref x, ref y, ref component);
}
```

This method simply loops through the bytes in the array and calls the earlier `StegByte` method to store each byte in the image.

Finally, the following method stores a string in an image:

```
// Return a copy of the bitmap with data embedded in it.
public static Bitmap StegMessage(this Bitmap bm, string message)
{
    // Make sure the image is big enough.
    byte[] messageBytes = Encoding.Unicode.GetBytes(message);
    int numMessageBytes = messageBytes.Length;
    byte[] lengthBytes = BitConverter.GetBytes(numMessageBytes);
    int numLengthBytes = lengthBytes.Length;
    int numMessageBits = 8 * (numMessageBytes + numLengthBytes);
    int numAvailableBits = 3 * bm.Width * bm.Height;
    if (numMessageBits > numAvailableBits)
        throw new IndexOutOfRangeException(
            "The message is too big to fit in the image.\n" +
            $"The message is {numMessageBits} bits long but " +
            $"the image can hold only {numAvailableBits} bits.");

    // Hide the message length.
    Bitmap bmCopy = new Bitmap(bm);
    int x = 0, y = 0;
    RGB component = RGB.R;
    StegBytes(bmCopy, lengthBytes, ref x, ref y, ref component);

    // Hide the message bytes.
    StegBytes(bmCopy, messageBytes, ref x, ref y, ref component);

    // Return the bitmap.
    return bmCopy;
}
```

When we later want to decode the data, we need to know how long the message is so we know how many bits to pull out of the image. This method solves that problem by first storing the length of the message in the data.

The method begins by converting the message string into an array of bytes. The code uses Unicode encoding, so it can store Unicode messages. After converting the string into an array, the code gets the array's length.

Next, the code uses the `BitConverter.GetBytes` method to convert the message's length into an array of bytes. It also gets that arrays' length. The code then calculates the number of bits needed to store the message together with its length, and the number of bits that are available in the image. If there isn't enough storage space, the method throws an exception.

The rest of the method is fairly straightforward. It makes a copy of the bitmap and then uses the `StegBytes` method to store the length of the message in the image. It then uses `StegBytes` again to store the message's bytes and returns the new bitmap.

The example solution's decoding methods undo the steps performed by the encoding methods in reverse order. They're reasonably straightforward if you understand how the encoding methods work, so I won't show them here. You may want to try to write them yourself before you download the example solution.

The example solution includes code to load and save image files. It also includes some code to prevent you from closing the program without saving a newly encoded image. (Because I kept doing that accidentally during testing.)

 This example stores a Unicode message, but the `StegBytes` method just stores an arbitrary array of bytes so it can store just about anything. For example, you could encrypt a message and then store the encrypted version in an image. Then someone else cannot read your message, even if they suspect it is there. Just remember that all data is destroyed if you save the image in a lossy format such as JPG of GIF.

Download the `Steganography` example solution to see additional details.

51. Encrypt and decrypt strings

Before you can use the .NET Framework's cryptography tools to encrypt and decrypt strings (or files, arrays of bytes, or just about anything else), you need to perform some setup. The following method creates an ICryptoTransform object that you can use to encrypt or decrypt data:

```
// Prepare a cryptographic transformation for this password
// and SymmetricAlgorithm.
private static ICryptoTransform MakeCryptoTransform(
    string password, bool doEncryption, SymmetricAlgorithm
cryptoProvider)
{
    // Find a valid key size for this provider.
    int numKeyBits = FindKeySize(cryptoProvider);
    Console.WriteLine($"Key size: {numKeyBits} bits");

    // Get the block size for this provider.
    int blockSizeBits = cryptoProvider.BlockSize;

    // Generate the key and IV.
    byte[] key = null;
    byte[] iv = null;
    byte[] salt = { 0x03, 0x07, 0x11, 0x22, 0xAB, 0xCD, 0x1F,
        0xF1, 0xF1, 0x00, 0xA4, 0x6B, 0xC4, 0x99 };
    MakeKeyAndIV(password, salt, numKeyBits, blockSizeBits,
        out key, out iv);

    // Make the AES encryptor or decryptor.
    ICryptoTransform cryptoTransform;
    if (doEncryption)
        cryptoTransform = cryptoProvider.CreateEncryptor(key, iv);
    else
        cryptoTransform = cryptoProvider.CreateDecryptor(key, iv);
    return cryptoTransform;
}
```

This method takes as parameters a password, a flag indicating whether you want to encrypt or decrypt, and a SymmetricAlgorithm provider object. You'll see how the last one works later when I show you how to use this method.

The code first needs to find an appropriate **key size** for the cryptographic provider that it will use. The key sizes that you can use depend on your version of Windows, and that depends on the country where you bought Windows. For example, the US government may allow Windows to use a 256-bit key in the United States but a shorter, less secure key size in some other countries. The `FindKeySize` method described shortly returns a key size that the algorithm can use.

Next, the program must create a **key** and **initialization vector** (**IV**) to initialize the algorithm. The key is sort of like the password after it has been processed. The IV is an array of bytes that determines the encryption algorithm's initial internal state. The algorithm uses both of those to initialize itself.

The `MakeKeyAndIV` method described shortly creates a key and IV. Most of its parameters are straightforward. The most confusing is the salt.

A **salt** is an array of *random* values that you pick to make it harder for an attacker to build a dictionary of possible passwords. If different programs use different salts, then the attacker cannot use a single dictionary to try to attack them all. You should pick a different salt for your programs. In particular, do not use the one shown here. (Of course, if one program needs to decrypt messages produced by another program, then they need to use the same salt.)

Next, the code calls the cryptographic service provider's `CreateEncryptor` or `CreateDecryptor` method to create the object that will actually encrypt or decrypt messages. Finally, the method returns the resulting transform object.

The following code shows the `FindKeySize` helper method:

```
// Find a valid key size for this algorithm.
private static int FindKeySize(SymmetricAlgorithm algorithm)
{
    for (int i = 1024; i > 1; i--)
    {
        if (algorithm.ValidKeySize(i)) return i;
    }
    throw new InvalidOperationException(
        $"Cannot find a valid key size for
            {algorithm.GetType().Name}.");
}
```

This method loops through possible key sizes starting at 1,024 bits and moving through smaller sizes. It uses the cryptographic provider's `ValidKeySize` method to check each potential key size and returns that size if the method returns `true`.

If the method cannot find a valid key size, it throws an exception.

The following code shows the `MakeKeyandIV` method:

```
// Use a password to make a key and IV.
private static void MakeKeyAndIV(string password, byte[] salt,
    int keySizeBits, int blockSizeBits, out byte[] key, out byte[] iv)
{
    Rfc2898DeriveBytes deriveBytes =
        new Rfc2898DeriveBytes(password, salt, 1000);
    key = deriveBytes.GetBytes(keySizeBits / 8);
    iv = deriveBytes.GetBytes(blockSizeBits / 8);
}
```

This method creates an `Rfc2898DeriveBytes` object. That object is sort of like a CPRNG that initializes itself from a password and salt that you pass into its constructor. The final parameter to the constructor is the number of times that the constructor should run its algorithm (which for this object is the HMACSHA1 algorithm) before generating the key and IV.

Microsoft recommends that you set the iteration count to at least 1,000, at least partly to make the operation take longer. (See the *Remarks* section at `https://docs.microsoft.com/dotnet/api/system.security.cryptography.rfc2898derivebytes.iterationcount`.) If an attacker wants to break your code by trying random passwords, this makes each attempt take longer. Most programs only need to create an `Rfc2898DeriveBytes` object once, so it doesn't hurt you too much to use a large iteration count.

After creating the `Rfc2898DeriveBytes` object, the method calls its `GetBytes` method twice to get the necessary number of bytes for the key and IV.

At this point, you're ready to use the `MakeCryptoTransform` method to encrypt or decrypt strings. The following extension method encrypts or decrypts an array of bytes:

```
// Encrypt or decrypt a byte[].
private static byte[] EncryptDecryptBytes(string password,
    byte[] inputBytes, bool doEncryption)
{
    try
    {
        // Make the encryptor or decryptor.
        ICryptoTransform cryptoTransform = MakeCryptoTransform(
            password, doEncryption, new AesCryptoServiceProvider());

        // Make the output stream.
        using (MemoryStream outputStream = new MemoryStream())
        {
            // Attach a CryptoStream.
            using (CryptoStream cryptoStream = new CryptoStream(
```

```
                    outputStream, cryptoTransform, CryptoStreamMode.Write))
            {
                // Write the bytes into the CryptoStream.
                cryptoStream.Write(inputBytes, 0, inputBytes.Length);
                cryptoStream.FlushFinalBlock();
                return outputStream.ToArray();
            }
        }
    }
    catch (CryptographicException ex)
    {
        // The password is incorrect.
        throw new CryptographicException("Invalid password.", ex);
    }
    catch
    {
        // Re-throw.
        throw;
    }
}
```

This method calls the `MakeCryptoTransform` method to create an `ICryptoTransform` object. That object only works with streams, so the program creates a `MemoryStream` to hold the encrypted output. It then makes a `CryptoStream` associated with the output stream and the `ICryptoTransform` object.

The code then writes the message bytes into the `CryptoStream`. That stream automatically uses the `ICryptoTransform` object to encrypt the message and writes the result into the output stream.

The method then returns the resulting output stream converted into an array of bytes.

Note that the whole method is enclosed in a `try-catch` block. When a cryptographic object fails, it is usually because the program tried to decrypt a message with the wrong password. Unfortunately in that case, the exception usually doesn't tell you that the password was wrong. Instead, it gives you some other cryptic message (no pun intended) that isn't very helpful. This method catches those kinds of exceptions and raises a new one that makes more sense.

Now you can use the `EncryptDecryptBytes` method to encrypt or decrypt strings. The following method encrypts a string:

```
// Encrypt a string into a byte[].
public static byte[] Encrypt(this string plaintext, string password)
{
    byte[] plainbytes = Encoding.Unicode.GetBytes(plaintext);
    return EncryptDecryptBytes(password, plainbytes, true);
}
```

This code converts a Unicode string into a byte array, calls `EncryptDecryptBytes` to encrypt the array, and returns the result.

The following method decrypts a string:

```
// Decrypt a string from a byte[].
public static string Decrypt(this byte[] cipherbytes, string password)
{
    byte[] plainbytes = EncryptDecryptBytes(password, cipherbytes,
        false);
    return Encoding.Unicode.GetString(plainbytes);
}
```

This method calls `EncryptDecryptBytes` to decrypt the encrypted array, converts the resulting bytes into a Unicode string, and returns the result.

Those methods encrypt a string into a byte array and decrypt a byte array into a string. The example solution also displays the encrypted bytes as a string with a format similar to 33-33-93-CB-6E-BE-3F-B4-95-27-EB-2B-C4-... The following method converts a byte array into that kind of string:

```
// Convert a byte[] into hexadecimal values.
public static string BytesToHex(this byte[] bytes)
{
    return BitConverter.ToString(bytes, 0);
}
```

This method simply calls `BitConverter.ToString` to convert the array into a string representation. The last parameter 0 tells the method to start at byte 0 in the array.

Unfortunately, the `BitConverter` class does not have a simple method to convert back from a string representation to a byte array. The following method makes that conversion:

```
// Convert two-digit hexadecimal values into a byte[].
public static byte[] HexToBytes(this string hexString)
{
    // Separate the bytes.
```

```
        char separator = hexString[2];
        string[] hexPairs = hexString.Split(separator);

        // Allocate the array.
        int numBytes = hexPairs.Length;
        byte[] bytes = new byte[numBytes];

        // Parse the pairs.
        for (int i = 0; i < numBytes; i++)
            bytes[i] = Convert.ToByte(hexPairs[i], 16);
        return bytes;
    }
```

This method assumes that the string's third character is a separator such as – or a space. It uses the separator to split the string into pieces, each of which holds two hexadecimal digits that represent a single byte. The code allocates a byte array large enough to hold the bytes and then loops through the values converting the pieces into bytes.

The rest of the example solution uses the methods described earlier to encrypt and decrypt strings. Download the `EncryptDecryptStrings` example solution to see additional details.

52. Encrypt and decrypt files

You could adapt the techniques for encrypting strings from the preceding solution to encrypt files. You would simply use `File.ReadAllBytes` to read a file into a byte array, call the `EncryptDecryptBytes` method to encrypt or decrypt the bytes, and then use `File.WriteAllBytes` to save the results into the output file.

That method would work reasonably well for small files, but holding the file's bytes in memory could be a problem for very large files. Fortunately, there's a better approach.

The encryption methods read and write data through streams. If you use the same setup methods used by the preceding solution, then you can use file streams to easily encrypt and decrypt files. The following code shows the `CryptFile` method that encrypts or decrypts files:

```
    // Encrypt or decrypt a file into another file.
    private static void CryptFile(string password, string inputFilename,
        string outputFilename, bool doEncryption)
    {
        try
        {
            // Make the encryptor or decryptor.
```

```
                    ICryptoTransform cryptoTransform = MakeCryptoTransform(
                        password, doEncryption, new AesCryptoServiceProvider());

                    // Make streams for the input and output files.
                    using (FileStream inputStream = new FileStream(inputFilename,
                        FileMode.Open, FileAccess.Read))
                    {
                        using (FileStream outputStream = new FileStream(
                            outputFilename, FileMode.Create, FileAccess.Write))
                        {
                            // Attach a CryptoStream.
                            using (CryptoStream cryptoStream = new CryptoStream(
                                outputStream, cryptoTransform,
                                CryptoStreamMode.Write))
                            {
                                // Read and write in blocks.
                                const int readingBlockSize = 16 * 1024;
                                byte[] buffer = new byte[readingBlockSize];
                                while (true)
                                {
                                    int numBytesRead = inputStream.Read(
                                        buffer, 0, readingBlockSize);
                                    if (numBytesRead == 0) break;

                                    // Write the bytes into the CryptoStream.
                                    cryptoStream.Write(buffer, 0, numBytesRead);
                                }
                                cryptoStream.FlushFinalBlock();
                            }
                        }
                    }
                }
                catch (CryptographicException ex)
                {
                    // The password is incorrect.
                    throw new CryptographicException("Invalid password.", ex);
                }
                catch
                {
                    // Re-throw.
                    throw;
                }
            }
```

The method encloses all of its code in a try...catch block in case it is trying to decrypt a file with the wrong password. Inside the block, the code uses the MakeCryptoTransform method used by the preceding solution to prepare a cryptographic transform.

Next, the code creates an input file stream to read the input file and an output file stream to write the output file. It then makes a `CryptoStream` object that attaches the cryptographic transform to the output stream.

The method then enters a loop that processes the input file in blocks. Each time through the loop, the code reads a block. If the read returns no bytes, then the program has finished reading the input file so it breaks out of its loop. If the read returns some bytes, the method writes those bytes into the `CryptoStream`, which automatically encrypts or decrypts the bytes and writes the results into the output stream. After the loop ends, the code calls the `CryptoStream` object's `FlushFinalBlock` method to flush any pending data into the output stream.

The following two methods use the `CryptFile` method to encrypt and decrypt files:

```
// Encrypt a file into another file.
public static void EncryptFile(string password,
    string plainFilename, string cipherFilename)
{
    CryptFile(password, plainFilename, cipherFilename, true);
}

// Decrypt a file into another file.
public static void DecryptFile(string password,
    string cipherFilename, string plainFilename)
{
    CryptFile(password, cipherFilename, plainFilename, false);
}
```

These methods simply call `CryptFile`, passing it the appropriate parameters.

The rest of the example solution's code allows you to open a file, encrypt it into a new file, and decrypt an encrypted file. It also displays the original, encrypted, and recovered files. Download the `EncryptDecryptFiles` example solution to see additional details.

53. CryptoPad

This program could use the techniques used by the preceding solution to save data in an encrypted format. When you wanted to load a file, the program would decrypt it into a temporary file, load that file, and then delete the temporary file. When you wanted to save data, the program would write the data into an unencrypted temporary file, encrypt it, and then delete the temporary file.

That method would work, but using unencrypted temporary files is risky. An attacker might be able to grab the temporary file before the program can delete it. Even worse, if the program happens to crash at the wrong moment, the temporary file might not be deleted.

Another, safer approach is to encrypt data directly between the program and the encrypted file so the decrypted file is never stored on the computer's hard drive.

The `CryptoPad` example solution uses a `RichTextBox` to allow you to edit Rich Text. The program is not a full text editor, however, so it does not provide tools that let you indent text, make bulleted and numbered lists, change fonts, and perform other text editing tasks. You can add those tools if you like. The program does, however, allow you to copy and paste formatted code and even images into its `RichTextBox` control, so you can still test it with complex data.

The `RichTextBox` control's `Rtf` property returns the control's contents as a string containing formatting codes. To save its data, the program encrypts that RTF string directly into a file. To load an encrypted file, the program decrypts the file directly into an RTF string and sets the `RichTextBox` control's `Rtf` property to the result.

The following method encrypts string data into a file:

```
// Encrypt a string and save the results in a file.
public static void EncryptIntoFile(this string plaintext,
    string password, string cipherFilename)
{
    try
    {
        // Make the encryptor.
        ICryptoTransform cryptoTransform = MakeCryptoTransform(
            password, true, new AesCryptoServiceProvider());

        // Make streams for the input text and output file.
        byte[] plainbytes = Encoding.Unicode.GetBytes(plaintext);
        using (MemoryStream inputStream = new MemoryStream(plainbytes))
        {
            using (FileStream outputStream = new FileStream(
                cipherFilename, FileMode.Create, FileAccess.Write))
            {
                // Attach a CryptoStream.
                using (CryptoStream cryptoStream = new CryptoStream(
                    outputStream, cryptoTransform,
                    CryptoStreamMode.Write))
                {
                    // Read and write in blocks.
                    const int readingBlockSize = 16 * 1024;
                    byte[] buffer = new byte[readingBlockSize];
```

```
            while (true)
            {
                // Read a block of bytes.
                int numBytesRead = inputStream.Read(
                    buffer, 0, readingBlockSize);
                if (numBytesRead == 0) break;

                // Write the bytes into the CryptoStream.
                cryptoStream.Write(buffer, 0, numBytesRead);
            }
            cryptoStream.FlushFinalBlock();
        }
    }
}
catch (CryptographicException ex)
{
    // The password is incorrect.
    throw new CryptographicException("Invalid password.", ex);
}
catch
{
    // Re-throw.
    throw;
}
}
```

After reading the last few solutions, this code should seem familiar. It uses the
`MakeCryptoTransform` method to make an encryptor, creates an input stream attached to
the string to encrypt, makes an output stream attached to the file, and makes a
`CryptoStream` that connects the encryptor to the output stream. The method reads the
input and writes into the output in blocks. When it has finished processing the input string,
the method flushes the `CryptoStream` and is done.

The following code shows how the program decrypts an encrypted file into an RTF string:

```
// Decrypt a file and return the result in a string.
public static string DecryptFromFile(string password,
    string cipherFilename)
{
    try
    {
        // Make the decryptor.
        ICryptoTransform cryptoTransform = MakeCryptoTransform(
            password, false, new AesCryptoServiceProvider());

        // Make streams for the input file and output MemoryStream.
```

```
    using (FileStream inputStream = new FileStream(cipherFilename,
        FileMode.Open, FileAccess.Read))
    {
        using (MemoryStream outputStream = new MemoryStream())
        {
            // Attach a CryptoStream.
            using (CryptoStream cryptoStream =
                new CryptoStream(outputStream, cryptoTransform,
                    CryptoStreamMode.Write))
            {
                // Read and write in blocks.
                const int readingBlockSize = 16 * 1024;
                byte[] buffer = new byte[readingBlockSize];
                while (true)
                {
                    // Read a block of bytes.
                    int numBytesRead = inputStream.Read(
                        buffer, 0, readingBlockSize);
                    if (numBytesRead == 0) break;

                    // Write the bytes into the CryptoStream.
                    cryptoStream.Write(buffer, 0, numBytesRead);
                }
                cryptoStream.FlushFinalBlock();

                // Return the string.
                byte[] plainbytes = outputStream.ToArray();
                string plaintext =
                    Encoding.Unicode.GetString(plainbytes);
                return plaintext;
            }
        }
    }
}
catch (CryptographicException ex)
{
    // The password is incorrect.
    throw new CryptographicException("Invalid password.", ex);
}
catch
{
    // Re-throw.
    throw;
}
}
```

This code is very similar to the preceding method. The only real difference is that this version converts the output `MemoryStream` into a string and returns it.

The rest of the example solution performs document management tasks such as keeping track of whether the data has been modified so it can warn you if you try to close the program without saving changes. Download the `CryptoPad` example solution to see additional details.

Summary

In this chapter, we learned the various cryptographic methods to encrypt and decrypt messages. We created Hash code of a file using the CalculateMD5 method. We used .NET Framework's cryptography methods to encrypt and decrypt strings. We further improvised the method to encrypt/decrypt files.

Other Books You May Enjoy

If you enjoyed this book, you may be interested in these other books by Packt:

Test-Driven iOS Development with Swift 3
Dr. Dominik Hauser

ISBN: 978-1-78712-907-8

- Implement TDD in Swift application development
- Find bugs before you enter the code using the TDD approach
- Use TDD to build models, view controllers, and views
- Test network code with asynchronous tests and stubs
- Write code that is a joy to read and to maintain
- Develop functional tests to ensure the app works as planned
- Employ continuous integration to make testing and deployment easier

C# 7 and .NET Core 2.0 Blueprints

Dirk Strauss, Jas Rademeyer

ISBN: 978-1-78839-619-6

- How to incorporate Entity Framework Core to build ASP .NET Core MVC applications
- Get hands-on experience with SignalR and NuGet packages
- Working with MongoDB in your ASP.NET Core MVC application
- Get hands-on experience with .NET Core MVC, Middleware, Controllers, Views, Layouts, Routing, and OAuth
- Implementing Azure Functions and learn what Serverless computing means
- See how .NET Core enables cross-platform applications that run on Windows, macOS, and Linux
- Running a .NET Core MVC application with Docker Compose

Leave a review - let other readers know what you think

Please share your thoughts on this book with others by leaving a review on the site that you bought it from. If you purchased the book from Amazon, please leave us an honest review on this book's Amazon page. This is vital so that other potential readers can see and use your unbiased opinion to make purchasing decisions, we can understand what our customers think about our products, and our authors can see your feedback on the title that they have worked with Packt to create. It will only take a few minutes of your time but is valuable to other potential customers, our authors, and Packt. Thank you!

Index

Printed in Great Britain
by Amazon